Jesus the Samaritan

Biblical Interpretation Series

Editors-in-Chief

Paul Anderson (*George Fox University*)
Jennifer L. Koosed (*Albright College, Reading*)

Editorial Board

A.K.M. Adam (*University of Oxford*)
Colleen M. Conway (*Seton Hall University*)
Amy Kalmanofsky (*Jewish Theological Seminary*)
Vernon Robbins (*Emory University*)
Annette Schellenberg (*Universität Wien*)
Johanna Stiebert (*University of Leeds*)
Duane Watson (*Malone University*)
Christine Roy Yoder (*Columbia Theological Seminary*)
Ruben Zimmermann (*Johannes Gutenberg-Universität Mainz*)

VOLUME 170

The titles published in this series are listed at *brill.com/bins*

Jesus the Samaritan

Ethnic Labeling in the Gospel of John

By

Stewart Penwell

BRILL

LEIDEN | BOSTON

Library of Congress Cataloging-in-Publication Data

Names: Penwell, Stewart, 1981– author.
Title: Jesus the Samaritan : ethnic labeling in the Gospel of John /
    by Stewart Penwell.
Description: Leiden ; Boston : Brill, [2019] | Series: Biblical
    interpretation series, ISSN 0928-0731 ; Volume 170 | Includes
    bibliographical references and index.
Identifiers: LCCN 2018061470 (print) | LCCN 2019001451 (ebook) |
    ISBN 9789004390706 (ebook) | ISBN 9789004390690 (hardback : alk. paper)
Subjects: LCSH: Bible. John—Criticism, interpretation, etc. | Ethnicity in
    the Bible. | Ethnicity—Religious aspects—Christianity. |
    Jesus Christ—Person and offices.
Classification: LCC BS2615.6.E815 (ebook) | LCC BS2615.6.E815 P46 2019
    (print) | DDC 226.5/06—dc23
LC record available at https://lccn.loc.gov/2018061470

Typeface for the Latin, Greek, and Cyrillic scripts: "Brill". See and download: brill.com/brill-typeface.

ISSN 0928-0731
ISBN 978-90-04-39069-0 (hardback)
ISBN 978-90-04-39070-6 (e-book)

Copyright 2019 by Koninklijke Brill NV, Leiden, The Netherlands.
Koninklijke Brill NV incorporates the imprints Brill, Brill Hes & De Graaf, Brill Nijhoff, Brill Rodopi,
Brill Sense, Hotei Publishing, mentis Verlag, Verlag Ferdinand Schöningh and Wilhelm Fink Verlag.
All rights reserved. No part of this publication may be reproduced, translated, stored in a retrieval system,
or transmitted in any form or by any means, electronic, mechanical, photocopying, recording or otherwise,
without prior written permission from the publisher.
Authorization to photocopy items for internal or personal use is granted by Koninklijke Brill NV provided
that the appropriate fees are paid directly to The Copyright Clearance Center, 222 Rosewood Drive, Suite 910,
Danvers, MA 01923, USA. Fees are subject to change.

This book is printed on acid-free paper and produced in a sustainable manner.

*Dedicated to my wife Rachel,
my love and life*

In Memory of

Steve Kitterman (1941–2016)
Who taught me how to live and love

Otto Maduro (1945–2013)
Who taught me how to see and understand/Verstehen

Jerry Garcia (1942–1995)
Who taught me how to listen and show kindness

∴

Contents

Acknowledgments XI
Abbreviations XII

Introduction 1
  Key Methodological Terms in the Study 6

1 Surveying Jesus's Ethnic Incarnation 8
  Introduction 8
  1 Jesus the Jew 8
  2 Jesus the Samaritan 14
  3 Conclusion: Jesus's Ethnic Incarnation 17

2 Ethnicity and Labeling 19
  1 Delineation of Terms: "Ethnic" and ἔθνος 20
  2 Theories of Ethnicity 27
      2.1 *Ethnicity and Ethnic Group Defined* 30
      2.2 *Current Competing Ethnicity Theories* 31
      2.3 *"Dear Symbols" of Ethnic Identity* 33
  3 Socialization: Establishing Social Norms 35
      3.1 *Destabilizing Roles/Categories: the Stranger and the Heretic* 37
  4 Labeling: Types and Functions 40
  5 Conclusion 44

3 Naming Narratives 46
  Introduction 46
  1 The Judeans' Narratives: the Label "Judean" in the Texts of the
     Hebrew Bible 48
      1.1 *The Judean Label for "Samaritans" in the Texts of the
           Hebrew Bible* 56
  2 The Samaritan's Narrative: the Label "Israelite" for Self- or
     Group Identification 58
      2.1 *Delos Inscriptions* 58
      2.2 *The Samaritan Pentateuch and Mount Gerizim as
           Identity Indicator* 60
      2.3 *Who Are These "Samaritans" You Speak of?:
           Etymology of a Name* 64

VIII CONTENTS

 2.4 *The Samaritan Labels for the "Judeans": the Categorization of Judeans* 67

 3 Labeling the Samaritans in Josephus 67
  3.1 *Josephus's Three Samaritan Origin Stories* 69
 4 Labeling the Samaritans in the Synoptic Gospels and Acts 81
  4.1 *Gospel of Matthew* 81
  4.2 *Luke-Acts* 83
 5 Conclusion 93

4 Labeling an Ethnic Jesus 95
 Introduction 95
 1 The Father, the Son, and the Children of God 96
  1.1 *Jesus and the Gathering of "His Own"* 101
  1.2 *Broadening Horizons* 104
  1.3 *Children of God* 104
 2 Jesus "the Jew" 105
  2.1 *Setting the Scene: Jacob's Well* 105
  2.2 *Setting the Labeling Context: if You Only Knew* 108
  2.3 *How Jesus the "Jew" Asks for a Drink* 118
  2.4 *Labeling Jesus a "Jew"* 120
 3 Jesus the Samaritan 123
  3.1 *Setting the Scene: Jesus in the Jerusalem Temple* 124
  3.2 *Setting the Labeling Context: You Are Your Father's Children* 125
  3.3 *True Disciples* 128
  3.5 *Labeling Jesus a "Samaritan"* 135
 4 Intra-textual Labeling of an Ethnic Jesus 138
 5 Conclusion 144

5 Ethnic Assessments in the Gospel of John 146
 Introduction 146
 1 Who Are "the Jews" in the Gospel of John? A Retrospective 148
  1.1 *"The Jews" as Judeans* 148
  1.2 *"The Jews" as the Enemies of Jesus* 150
  1.3 *"The Jews" as the Religious Authorities* 151
  1.4 *The Gospel of John's Jewish Occurrences* 152
 2 "Misrecognizing" Jesus in the World 154
 3 Ethnic Assessments in the Gospel of John 155
  3.1 *First Occurrence of "the Jews"—Ethnic Assessments of John the Baptist* 156

CONTENTS

IX

    3.2   *First Occurrence of Belief—the Disciples' Ethnic Assessments of Jesus*   159

    3.3   *"The Jews" as Judeans in Galilee*   161

    3.4   *"The Jews" as the Religious Authorities—Fear and Division of "the Jews"*   165

    3.5   *"The Jews" as the Enemies of Jesus—Jesus and the Bultmannian Jews*   168

    3.6   *Every Jewish Occurrence*   172

4 Implications of John's Employment of the Ethnic Label "Jew(s)"   174

5 Conclusion   176

Conclusion   177

Bibliography   181

Index of Modern Authors   207

Index of Ancient Sources   212

Index of Subjects   222

Acknowledgments

What a long strange trip it's been and I am *grateful* for the opportunity to acknowledge at least a few people who made this study possible. The following is a revised version of my doctoral thesis, accepted by St. Mary's University (Twickenham, London). I am very proud and honored to be the first student and the first graduate from Centre for the Social-Scientific Study of the Bible at St. Mary's University. I am thankful to Philip Esler who, in 2012, initiated this project at St. Mary's University and who shaped the foundation of this study in the social-sciences. This project would not have reached its full potential were it not for my *Doktorvater* Chris Keith who pushed me, often in the manner of an NCAA basketball coach, in order to get me to produce to the very best that I am capable of doing.

I also am grateful for the faculty at Drew Theological School and particularly my Master of Sacred Theology supervisor Virginia Burrus. I have not been in her classroom for over a decade yet she continues to teach and challenge me. I am indebted to Tom Thatcher for instilling in me a love of Johannine Literature. I am honored to be mentioned among your former students. To my entire Bible College faculty who taught me faith with critical analysis and, in this regard, a special appreciation for Daniel J. Dyke. I also want to acknowledge all of my classmates who are smarter than me but pursued the ministry instead of academics. A special thanks to Jim Lloyd and Scott Lloyd the library directors who not only curate an amazing Biblical Studies collection, and offered me employment for 10 years, but who also show great kindness and friendship to everyone they encounter. Finally, I am grateful for my nephew Bram Kitterman whose constant asking "Are you done with your book yet?" helped to keep me going. Thanks, Kid!

March 2019
Corydon, IN

Abbreviations

AB	Anchor Bible Commentary
Acts	Acts of the Apostles
Ag. Ap.	Against Apion
AF	*The Kitāb Al-Tarīkh of Abu 'L-Fath*
ANF	Alexander Roberts and James Donaldson (eds.) *The Ante-Nicene Fathers: Translations of the Writings Of the Fathers down to AD 325.* 10 vols. Grand Rapids: Eerdmans, 1989.
ANET	James Bennett Pritchard (ed.) *Ancient Near Eastern Texts Relating to the Old Testament.* 3d ed. with suppl. Princeton: Princeton University Press, 1969.
Ant.	*Antiquities of the Jews*
ANTC	Abingdon New Testament Commentaries
1 Apol.	*First Apology*
2 Apol	*Second Apology*
ArBib	Michael Maher (ed.), *The Aramaic Bible* (Collegeville, MN: Liturgical Press, 1992)
ASE	*Annali di storia dell'esegesi*
b.	Babylonian Talmud
BAG	*Greek-English Lexicon of the New Testament and Other Early Christian Literature.* (1957/1971)
BAGD	*Greek-English Lexicon of the New Testament and Other Early Christian Literature.* 2d (1979)
BCE	Before Common Era
BCH	*Bulletin de correspondance hellénique*
BDAG	*Greek-English Lexicon of the New Testament and Other Early Christian Literature.* 3d
BDF	*A Greek Grammar of the New Testament and Other Early Christian Literature*
BECNT	The Baker Exegetical Commentary on the New Testament
Beṣa	*Betzah (= Yom Tov)*
BHQ	*Biblia Hebraica Quinta*
BHS	*Biblia Hebraica Stuttgartensia*
Bib	*Biblica*
BibInt	*Biblical Interpretation*
BJRL	Bulletin of the John Rylands University Library of Manchester
BNTC	Black's New Testament Commentaries
c.	circa
CBQ	*Catholic Biblical Quarterly*

ABBREVIATIONS

XIII

1 Chr	1 Chronicles
2 Chr	2 Chronicles
CBR	*Currents in Biblical Research*
CE	Common Era
Cels.	*Contra Celsum*
CHJ	Cambridge History of Judaism
Comm. Jo.	*Commentary on John*
CQ	*Classical Quarterly*
Dan	Daniel
Deut	Deuteronomy
Dial.	*Dialogue with Trypho*
Embassy	*On the Embassy to Gaius*
1 Esd	1 Esdras
Esth	Esther
Exod	Exodus
Exod. Rab.	*Exodus Rabbah*
ExpTim	*Expository Times*
Ezek	Ezekiel
FC	*Fathers of the Church*
Flac.	*Pro Flacco*
Gen	Genesis
Gen. Rab.	*Genesis Rabbah*
HALOT	Köhler, Baumgartner, Stamm (eds.), *The Hebrew and Aramaic Lexicon of the Old Testament*. (Leiden: Brill, 1994)
H-S	Hutchinson and Smith, *Ethnicity* (Oxford: Oxford University Press, 1996)
H-S#1	A common proper name to identify the group;
H-S#2	A myth of common ancestry;
H-S#3	A shared history or shared memories of a common past, events, and their commemoration;
H-S#4	A common culture, embracing such things as customs, language and religion;
H-S#5	A link with a homeland, either through actual occupation or by symbolic attachment to the ancestral land, as with diaspora peoples; and
H-S#6	A sense of communal solidarity.
Hist. eccl.	*Ecclesiastical History*
Hom. Jo.	*Homilies on the Gospel of St. John*
Hos	Hosea
ICC	International Critical Commentary
Isa	Isaiah
JBL	*Journal of Biblical Literature*
Jdt	Judith

Jer	Jeremiah
JETS	*Journal of the Evangelical Theological Society*
Josh	Joshua
JQR	*Jewish Quarterly Review*
JSJ	*Journal for the Study of Judaism in the Persian, Hellenistic, and Roman Periods*
JSNTSup	Journal for the Study of the New Testament: Supplement Series
JTS	*Journal of Theological Studies*
Judg	Judges
J.W.	*Jewish War*
1 Kgs	1 Kings
2 Kgs	2 Kings
L&N	Louw and Nida (eds.), *Greek-English Lexicon of the New Testament: Based on Semantic Domains* (New York: United Bible Societies, 1989)
LCL	Loeb Classical Library
LEH	Lust, Eynikel, Hauspin (eds.), *A Greek-English Lexicon of the Septuagint* (Stuttgart: Deutsche Bibelgesellschaft, 2003)
Lev	Leviticus
Life	*The Life of Flavius Josephus*
Jn	John
Josh	Joshua
LSJ	Liddell, Scott, Jones, McKenzie (eds.), *A Greek-English Lexicon* (Oxford: Oxford University Press, 1996)
LXX	Septuagint
m.	Mishna
1 Macc	1 Maccabees
2 Macc	2 Maccabees
4 Macc	4 Maccabees
Matt	Matthew
MT	Masoretic Text
Naz	*Nazir*
NCBC	New Cambridge Bible Commentary
Neh	Nehemiah
NICNT	New International Commentary on the New Testament
Nid	*Niddah*
NIDNTT	Colin Brown (ed.) *The New International Dictionary of New Testament Theology*. 3 vols. Grand Rapids: Zondervan, 1975.
NIDNTTE	Moisés Silva (ed.) *New International Dictionary of New Testament Theology and Exegesis*. 5 vols. Second edition. Grand Rapids: Zondervan, 2014.
NIDOTTE	Willem Van Gemeren (ed.) *New International Dictionary of Old Testament Theology & Exegesis*. 5 vols. Grand Rapids: Zondervan, 1997.

ABBREVIATIONS

NovT	*Novum Testamentum*
NPNF	Philip Schaff (ed.) *Nicene and Post-Nicene Fathers. First Series.* Peabody, MA: Hendrickson, 1994.
NRSV	New Revised Standard Version
NTApoc	New Testament Apocrypha
NTS	*New Testament Studies*
Num	Numbers
OL	Old Latin
Onom.	*Onomasticon*
OTL	Old Testament Library
Pss. Sol.	Psalms of Solomon
4Q22	4QpaleoExod^m
Qidd	*Qiddushin*
R.Hist.	*Roman History*
RSV	Revised Standard Version
2 Sam	2 Samuel
Sanh.	Sanhedrin
scil.	*scilicet* (namely; to wit)
SEÅ	Svensk Exegetisk Årsbok
Seb	*Shevi'it*
Sir	Sirach/Ecclesiasticus
Somn.	*De Somniis*
Sot.	*Sotah*
SP	Sacra pagina
SP	Samaritan Pentateuch
Spec. Laws	*On the Special Laws*
Str-B	*Kommentar zum Neuen Testament aus Talmud und Midrasch*
Syr^s	Syriac Sinaitic
Syr^c	Syriac Curetonian
t.	*Tosefta*
Ter.	*Terumot*
TDNT	Gerhard Kittel, Geoffrey William Bromiley, Gerhard Friedrich, and Ronald E. Pitkin (eds.) *Theological Dictionary of the New Testament.* 10 vols. Grand Rapids: Eerdmans, 1964.
TDOT	G. Johannes Botterweck and Helmer Ringgren (eds) *Theological Dictionary of the Old Testament.* Rev. ed. Grand Rapids: Eerdmans, 1977.
Tg. Ps.-J	*Targum Pseudo-Jonathan*
TWNT	Gerhard Kittel (ed.) *Theologisches Wörterbuch Zum Neuen Testament.* Stuttgart: Kohlhammer, 1949.

TynBul	*Tyndale Bulletin*
Virt.	*On the Virtues*
WBC	Word Biblical Commentary
WUNT	Wissenschaftliche Untersuchungen zum Neuen Testament
ZAW	*Zeitschrift für die alttestamentliche Wissenschaft*
Zech	Zechariah

Introduction

The Samaritan woman said to him, 'How is it that you, a Jew, ask a drink of me, a woman of Samaria?'[1]

JOHN 4:9

The Jews answered him, 'Are we not right in saying that you are a Samaritan and have a demon?'

JOHN 8:48

∴

This book will argue that the function of ethnic labeling in the Gospel of John is to enable the author of the Gospel of John to assert a trans-ethnic identity for the followers of Jesus. The Gospel of John's trans-ethnic identity is established by Jesus's broadening of traditional Judean ethnic identity into the "children of God, who were born, not of blood or of the will of the flesh or of the will of man, but of God" (John 1:12b–13). The primary examples of ethnic labeling for this book are John 4:9 and 8:48. In John 4:9, the Samaritan woman labels Jesus a "Jew" without explaining how that identification is made. There is only a comment in John 4:9b that the two groups ("Samaritans" and "Jews") do not share things in common with one another. The Samaritan woman's identification of Jesus as a "Jew" is significant here because it is the only place where the narrative identifies Jesus himself as a "Jew" and is one of the few positive portrayals of the "the Jews" in the Gospel of John. They otherwise frequently appear as the antagonists of the story. Later in the narrative, in the midst of a long discourse in John 8, "Jews" label Jesus a "Samaritan" (8:48).

The question that arises from these two passages and the Gospel of John as a whole, and sets the general basis of this book, is: How and why is Jesus identified, or identifiable, with either group of people? This question is particularly important since both groups use such labels in order to place Jesus outside their own group. In light of the history of discourse between "the Jews" and "Samaritans," who both identify themselves as Israelites and the other as not Israelites, it is important to each ethnic group that Jesus is not categorized with their own group identity so that Jesus is not one of "us" but one of "them."

---

1 All scriptural citations are from the NRSV unless indicated otherwise.

Whoever this Jesus of Nazareth is in the Gospel of John, members from "the Jews" and "Samaritans" label him as a member of the other group.

A popular proposal for Jesus's ethnic labeling in the Gospel of John is C. K. Barrett's statement: "The Samaritans call Jesus a Jew [4:9], just as the Jews call him a Samaritan (8:48); in this world [Jesus] is never anything but a stranger."[2] However, it is, strictly speaking, incorrect. Jesus is not labeled a stranger, in the sense of an unknown entity. He is labeled by both groups with a known group identity. This fact raises the question that proceeds from the more general question regarding the portrayal of Jesus himself in these texts and that serves as the primary focus of this book: How does ethnic labeling function in the Gospel of John?

Chapter One offers a history of research on the relationship between John 4:9 and 8:48. It will conclude that the importance of these verses has been overlooked regarding our understanding of the portrayal of the identity of Jesus in the Gospel of John.[3] As we will see, the majority of scholarship on John 4:9 focuses upon the explanatory statement "Jews do not share things in common with Samaritans." This explanatory comment draws attention for two reasons. The first reason is due to a text-critical issue concerning the absence of 4:9b in Codex Sinaiticus and Codex Bezae.[4] The second reason is due to interpretive issues concerning the translation of συγχράομαι as either "share things in common with" or "share vessels with." Notably absent in the discussion of John 4:9 are the implications of the ethnic labeling of Jesus as a "Jew" in the Gospel of John.

Similarly, the scholarship on John 8:48 has focused attention upon whether the two accusations ("a Samaritan" and "have a demon") are in fact two charges (i.e. being a "Samaritan" is to have a demon). Past scholarship has focused on the likelihood that the charge of being a "Samaritan" is synonymous with the charge of demon possession especially because of the connection in later church history of Samaria and demons.[5] Some scholars, however, note the tenuous connection between the charge of being "Samaritan" and demon

---

2 C. K. Barrett, *The Gospel According to St. John: An Introduction with Commentary and Notes on the Greek Text* (Philadelphia: Westminster, 1978), 232.

3 After all, as Craig Koester remarks: "Those who are truly human have some sort of ethnic identity" (Craig Koester, "Aspects of Historicity in John 1–4: A Response" in *John, Jesus and History (Volume 2): Aspects of Historicity in the Fourth Gospel* [eds. Paul Anderson, Felix Just, and Tom Thatcher; Atlanta: Society of Biblical Literature, 2009], 95).

4 The omission of John 4:9b is found in ℵ*, D, ita, b, d, e, j, copfay (Bruce Metzger, *A Textual Commentary on the Greek New Testament* [New York: United Bible Society, 2002], 177).

5 In particular, both Simon Magus (Justin Martyr, *1 Apol.* 26, 56; *2 Apol* 15; *Dial.* 20) and Dositheus (Origen, *Cels.* 1.57; Eusebius, *Hist. eccl.* iv. 22) are cited as equivalence for "Samaritans" and the demonic.

INTRODUCTION

possession and have instead focused on the result of the charge of being a "Samaritan" as meaning to be a "heretic" or an "apostate."[6] This book will largely follow this latter line of enquiry. There are, however, two problems that it will address. The first issue is that the current discussion overlooks *how* the label "Samaritan" means "heretic" or "apostate." The second, and related issue, is that the discussion of John 8:48 overlooks how this charge functions within the context of John 8. Consequently, also overlooked are the implications resulting from the ethnic labeling of Jesus as a "Samaritan" within the Gospel of John as a whole. This chapter will therefore introduce these lacunae in light of the broader history of research on the relationship between John 4:9 and 8:48.

Chapter Two will present a methodology for understanding the Gospel of John's portrayal of the Samaritan woman labeling of Jesus as a "Jew" and "the Jews'" labeling of Jesus as a "Samaritan" and how this labeling socially structures their interaction with one another. Since these labels were ethnic appellations,[7] the social-scientific model of ethnicity will prove useful for considering the Gospel of John. Accordingly, Chapter Two will employ modern ethnicity theory in order to provide a theoretical approach to ancient perceptions of people groups. An important element in ethnicity theory is to identify ethnic groups' cultural features in order to ascertain how cultural features form the basis for the norms of their group, how they are instilled into the individual group members' own identity, and how they are used to identify non-group members.[8]

However, in addition to ethnicity theory, we will also incorporate labeling theory in order to examine the proposal that "the Jews" label Jesus a "Samaritan" to mean that he is a "heretic." Labeling theory was developed as part of the research on social deviance wherein a person's individual deviant behavior does not *make* them a social deviant until they are publicly or

---

6 Rudolf Bultmann, *The Gospel of John: A Commentary* (trans. G. R. Beasley-Murray; Philadelphia: Westminster, 1971), 299 n. 4; Andrew T. Lincoln, *Gospel According to St John* (BNTC 4; Peabody, MA: Hendrickson, 2005), 274.

7 For the "Jews" ('Ιουδαῖοι) as an ancient ἔθνος, see Philip F. Esler, "Judean Ethnic Identity in Josephus' Against Apion," in *A Wandering Galilean: Essays in Honor of Sean Freyne* (ed. Zuleika Rodgers with Margaret Daly-Denton and Anne Fitzpatrick McKinley; Leiden, Boston: Brill, 2009), 73–92; John M. G. Barclay, "Constructing Judean Identity After 70 CE: A Study of Josephus' Against Apion," in *Identity and Interaction in the Ancient Mediterranean: Jews, Christians and Others: Essays in honor of Stephen G. Wilson* (eds. Zeba A. Crook and Philip A. Harland; Sheffield: Sheffield Phoenix Press, 2007), 99–112.

8 Particularly insightful here is Peter Berger's formulation for the processes of socialization in Peter Berger, *The Sacred Canopy: Elements of a Sociological Theory of Religion* (New York: Anchor Books, [1969] 1990), 3–28.

officially labeled a deviant.[9] For example, many individuals break the law but they are not all labeled criminals. Likewise, heresy exists only when people and institutions label it as such. Chapter Two will demonstrate how labels function by structuring interactions between individuals by maintaining or establishing social boundaries.

Chapter Three will return to the questions concerning Samaritan and Jewish identities in the first century CE and, therefore, provide perspective on how "Samaritan" and "Jew" could function as ethnic labels. This chapter examines the history of Judeo-Samaritan relations, drawing upon passages from the texts of the Hebrew Bible, Josephus, the Synoptic Gospels, and the Acts of the Apostles. The specific questions driving this chapter are "What cultural features were made salient by texts for constructing the Samaritan-Israelite identity over against the Judean-Israelite identity?" and "How do the Gospel of Matthew and Luke draw on this discourse for their narrative portrayals of Jesus in their Gospels as well as Luke's accounts of the early evangelists in Acts?" This chapter will provide an appropriate socio-historical background for understanding the appearance of these terms in the Gospel of John by considering how the labels "Jew" and "Samaritan" were used elsewhere. Chapter Three will conclude that the texts of the Hebrew Bible and Josephus established social distance, or boundaries, between themselves ("Jews") and the "Samaritans" by using labels that emphasize the Samaritans' non-Judean ethnicity (particularly Josephus's use of "Cutheans," "Sidonians," "Shechemites," etc.). Nevertheless, even though the texts of the Hebrew Bible and Josephus distance themselves from the "Samaritans," they do not label the "Samaritans" as "gentiles" either. This chapter will conclude further, then, that Jewish authors of the relevant period simultaneously considered the Samaritans not to be Judeans (because they were adherents of the Israelite traditions fostered outside of the geographical area of Judea), but also not to be gentiles (because were still adherents of a Mosaic tradition [albeit fostered in the old northern kingdom of Israel]). Thus, among many Second Temple Jews, Samaritans fell into a liminal zone where their identity could be exploited rhetorically.

After establishing the previous understandings of the ethnic labels "Jew" and "Samaritan," Chapter Four will examine how the Gospel of John participates in the discussion concerning the "Jews'" and "Samaritans'" identities by addressing the questions of the Samaritan woman (4:9) and "the Jews" (8:48) concerning Jesus. Frederick Dale Bruner describes Jesus as "the great Barrier

---

9   Howard S. Becker, *Outsiders: Studies in the Sociology of Deviance* (New York: The Free Press, 1963), 1–18.

INTRODUCTION

Breaker" in John 4.[10] This observation might be correct, but different people reacted differently to the barriers being broken. In this regard, the Gospel of John contrasts the portrayals of the Samaritan woman in John 4 and "the Jews" in John 8. The Samaritan woman's affirmation of Jesus as Messiah leads the Samaritans of Sychar to confess that Jesus "is truly the Savior of the world" (4:42). The interaction of Jesus with the Samaritan woman eclipsed the boundaries established by the label "Jew" and reduced the previously understood social distance between them (cf. John 4:21, 23). In John 8, "the Jews" label Jesus a "Samaritan" in order to distance Jesus from themselves because they are opposed to his broadening of Judean ethnic identity.[11] In particular, Jesus challenges the primacy that "the Jews" placed on Abrahamic descent (8:33, 37) by asserting that that to be "children of Abraham/God" is to do the things of Abraham namely receiving God's messenger (8:39, 42).

Chapter Four also addresses the purpose for the Johannine Jesus's boundary breaking. The Johannine Jesus's dialogues in John 4 and 8 function to establish a trans-ethnic identity for the "children of God" that features elsewhere in the narrative (1:12; 11:52). The function of the ethnic labels in John 4:9 and 8:48 is to structure the social interactions by casting one another into prescribed social roles that prompt appropriate actions. This allows Jesus to appropriate the ethnic appellations "Jew" and "Samaritan" for the purpose of transforming Judean ethnic identity into a trans-ethnic identity—the "children of God." The Gospel of John asserts the trans-ethnic identity "children of God" in the Prologue and defines it as "born, not of blood or of the will of the flesh or of the will of man, but of God" (1:13). John's trans-ethnic identity reduces in importance, for example, both Jerusalem temple worship (John 4) and descent from Abraham (John 8) as necessary criteria for understanding and worshiping their God.[12]

Chapter Five will apply the findings of this book to the vexed issue of the identity of "the Jews" in the Gospel of John. Previous Johannine scholarship explained "the Jews" in terms of "Judeans," Jesus's enemies, or generally as the religious authorities. Based on the main chapters of the book, I will argue that

---

10   Frederick Dale Bruner, *The Gospel of John: A Commentary* (Grand Rapids: Eerdmans, 2012), 246.

11   Rudolf Schnackenburg, *The Gospel According to St. John* (London: Burns & Oates, 1982), 2.207. Craig Keener notes: "Ancients employed such labeling to control marginal voices viewed as a threat, and evidence suggests that opponents raised such charges even during Jesus' public ministry (Mark 3:22)" (*The Gospel of John: A Commentary* [Peabody, MA: Hendrickson, 2003], 1.765).

12   Similar early Christian traditions are found in the synoptic tradition; for example, "Do not begin to say to yourselves, 'We have Abraham as our ancestor'; for I tell you, God is able from these stones to raise up children to Abraham" (Matt 3:9//Luke 3:8).

6 INTRODUCTION

previous scholarship on the identity of "the Jews" has overlooked the significance of the Gospel of John's portrayal of Jesus as a "Jew" who challenges "the Jews'" seemingly static ethnic identity.

The conclusion will summarize the discussion, re-state the main points, and raise future areas of research. In addition, this chapter will address how Jesus's ethnic labeling as a Jew in 4:9 and a Samaritan in 8:48 affects our understanding of how the Gospel of John "is both Jewish and anti-Jewish."[13]

Key Methodological Terms in the Study

This book uses "the Jews" (with quotation marks) as the traditional translation for Ἰουδαῖος/Ἰουδαῖοι in the Gospel of John. Although "the Jews" (with quotation marks) is generally used to denote a particular group or recurring character in the Gospel of John, we use "the Jews" primarily to signify its use as an ethnic label just as with the label "Samaritan." Chapter Three uses "Judeans" as the standard translation for יְהוּדִי in the texts of the Hebrew Bible (e.g. 2 Kgs 16:6; 25:25) and uses the label "Judean" (with quotation marks) to indicate its reference to the ethnic group. Chapter Four and Five will use "Judean" when referring to the cultural traits of the ethnic group. Finally, like Max Weber who said "religion" could only be defined after its examination, we too will address the issue of the identification of "the Jews" in Chapter Five only after determining the purpose of labeling Jesus a "Samaritan" and a "Jew" in Chapter Four.[14]

Regarding the purpose of labeling Jesus, we will use the term "trans-ethnic identity" to describe an identity that binds its members by their faith/belief in Jesus. Although those who believe in Jesus are still recognized as Judeans, Galileans, Samaritans, etc., their belief in Jesus transcends the importance of those distinctions. Those who believe in Jesus, the "children of God" (1:12–13), are united into a "fictive kinship" with God the Father and Jesus the Son. Yet, it is important to note that, although the "Samaritans" proclaim Jesus is "the savior of the world" (4:42), he asserts that "salvation is from the Jews" (4:22) to the Samaritan woman. Therefore, despite the fact that not everyone can be a physical "descendant of Abraham" (8:33), Jesus proclaims that anyone can become "children of Abraham" (8:39) if they receive God's messenger (8:42)

---

13   C. K. Barrett, *The Gospel of John and Judaism* (translated by D. Moody Smith; Philadelphia: Fortress, 1975), 71.

14   See Max Weber, *The Sociology of Religion* (translated by Ephraim Fischoff; Boston, Beacon Press, 1969), 1.

and, in so doing, he gives them power to become "children of God" (1:12–13). In this way, those "who believe in his name" (1:12), do not lose their ethnic group identity by gaining membership in the "children of God." Nor does the base referent for the concept of "children of God" cease being the traditions and history of ancient Israel.

CHAPTER 1

Surveying Jesus's Ethnic Incarnation

And the Word became flesh and lived among us
JOHN 1:14

Those who are truly human have some sort of ethnic identity.[1]

∵

Introduction

This chapter calls attention to the fact that the history of research on John 4:9 and 8:48 does not substantially feature Jesus's ethnic labels and identity. In fact, the connection between the ethnic labeling of John 4:9 and 8:48 is not always even identified and when a connection is made between John 4:9 and 8:48, it is usually a passing note without further implications concerning the reason and purpose for the ethnic labeling of Jesus in the Gospel of John.[2] The following sections will survey the analysis of John 4:9 and 8:48 with particular attention given to proposals concerning Jesus's identification as a "Jew" and as a "Samaritan."

1   Jesus the Jew

Much scholarly analysis of John 4:9 revolves around the explanatory comment in 4:9b, "Jews do not share things in common with Samaritans" (οὐ γὰρ συγχρῶνται Ἰουδαῖοι Σαμαρίταις). One reason the explanatory comment acquires scholarly attention is the issue of whether it is a textual gloss; this is due to its absence in Codex Sinaiticus and Codex Bezae.[3] Blass, Debrunner,

---

1   Koester, "Aspects of Historicity in John 1–4: A Response," 95.
2   Jerome Neyrey, however, does observe a connection between John 4 and 8 in the rhetorical pattern of statement—misunderstanding—clarification (*The Gospel of John*, NCBC [New York: Cambridge University Press, 2007], 78).
3   The omission of John 4:9b are also found in it[a, b, d, e, j] cop[fay] (Metzger, *A Textual Commentary on the Greek New Testament*, 177).

© KONINKLIJKE BRILL NV, LEIDEN, 2019 | DOI:10.1163/9789004390706_003

SURVEYING JESUS'S ETHNIC INCARNATION

and Funk, state twice that John 4:9b "is a spurious addition."[4] However, in his *Textual Commentary*, Bruce Metzger offers an alternative interpretation for the absence of John 4:9b: "The omission, if not accidental, may reflect scribal opinion that the statement is not literally exact and therefore should be deleted."[5] Metzger does not explain why John 4:9b was "not literally exact," and therefore his statement requires further discussion.

Metzger may have in mind that the explanatory comment is "not literally exact" because another focus of scholarly analysis of John 4:9b is the meaning of συγχράομαι. Frederick Danker defines συγχράομαι as, "To associate on friendly terms with, *have dealings with*" (BDAG).[6] David Daube, however, proposes an alternative rendering of συγχράομαι as: "Jews do not use—*scil.* vessels—with Samaritans."[7] In this way, the explanatory comment is "not literally exact" because John 4:9b shows concern for ritual purity whereas John 4:8, where the disciples went into the Samaritan city to buy food, does not evidence concern for purity.[8] Regardless of Metzger's intentions, however, some scholars view Daube's translation as problematic. Rudolf Schnackenburg, for example, finds the absence of the object (i.e. "vessel") significant because it "would seem

---

4 BDF §193.5 and §262, 3. C. K. Barrett and Rudolf Schnackenburg also assert that this section is a gloss or interpolation. See: Barrett, *Gospel According to St. John*, 232; Schnackenburg, *The Gospel according to St. John*, 1.425.

5 Metzger, *Textual*, 177. Joachim Jeremias also supports its authenticity because "The absence of 4:9b from ℵ* D it hardly justifies our assuming that it is a later gloss but might be simply due to a slip in copying" (Joachim Jeremias, "Samaritan," *TDNT* 91).

6 "συγχράομαι," BDAG, 953–954. Walter Bauer defines συγχράομαι as "Verkehr haben, umgehen τινί mit jmdm" (Walter Bauer, *Griechisch-deutsches Wörterbuch zu den Schriften des Neuen Testaments und der übrigen urchristlichen Literatur* (Berlin: Töpelmann, 1937), 1290. Liddell, Scott, and Jones defines συγχράομαι, "make use of, avail oneself of; of commercial dealings; generally, have dealings, associate with, Σαμαρείταις Ev. Jo.4.9" ("συγχράομαι," LSJ, 1668).

7 David Daube, "Jesus and the Samaritan Woman: The Meaning of συγχράομαι," *JBL* 69.2 (1950): 139. Followed by Barrett, *Gospel According to St. John*, 232–33; Raymond E. Brown, *The Gospel According to John* (AB 29; Garden City, NY: Doubleday, 1966), 1.170; D. A. Carson, *The Gospel According to John* (Grand Rapids: Eerdmans, 1991), 218; Francis J. Moloney, *The Gospel of John* (SP 4; Collegeville: Liturgical Press, 1998), 121; Leon Morris, *The Gospel According to John* (NICNT; Grand Rapids: Eerdmans, 1995), 229.

8 For the *Samaritanologists* Reinhard Pummer, "The translation proposed by Daube, 'Jews and Samaritans, it should be noted, do not use vessels in common' is untenable, primarily because the sources on which it is based are late" (Reinhard Pummer, "New Testament and the Samaritans," in *A Companion to Samaritan Studies* [ed. Alan David Crown, Reinhard Pummer, and Abraham Tal, Tübingen: Mohr Siebook, 1993], 170) Similarly, Isaac Kalimi also states: "Daube assumed that the impure rituals of the Samaritans form the background to the text ... This assumption is not acceptable" (*Early Jewish Exegesis and Theological Controversy: Studies in Scriptures in the Shadow of Internal and External Controversies* [Assen, Netherlands: Royal Van Gorcum, 2002], 57 n. 88).

to be indispensible after συγχρῶνται."[9] Another example is Barnabas Lindars who asserts that Daube's translation "fails as an explanation for Gentiles, being a case of expounding *ignotum per ignotius*."[10] In other words, the reader is required to infer the object ("vessel") of the sentence that is supposed to explain that the ritual purity of sharing "vessels" between "Samaritans" and "the Jews" is what prompted the Samaritan woman's question to Jesus. More recently J. Ramsey Michaels suggests that since "the reader was probably not expected to understand all the particulars of ritual purity (it is mentioned only generally and vaguely in 2:6 and 3:25) ... the translation, 'have nothing to do with,' or 'have no dealings with,' is preferable."[11] Nonetheless, Reinhard Pummer is ultimately correct that "in the last analysis, it is not that important to know the precise meaning of [συγχράομαι]. The phrase shows in either case that Jews and Samaritans had differences."[12]

In fact, these differences and the relationship between Jews and Samaritans have been recorded since the time of John Chrysostom, who noted the general antipathy between the two groups in order to account for the Samaritan woman's reaction to Jesus's request for a drink. Chrysostom states:

> And when things were in this state, the Jews having returned, ever after entertained a jealous feeling towards them as strangers and enemies, and called them from the name of the mountain, "Samaritans." From this cause also there was no little rivalry between them. The Samaritans did not use all the Scriptures, but received the writings of Moses only, and made but little account of those of the Prophets. Yet they were eager to thrust themselves into the noble Jewish stock, and prided themselves upon Abraham, and called him their forefather, as being of Chaldea; and

---

9 Schnackenburg, *The Gospel according to St. John*, 1:425 n. 18. Also see Ernst Haenchen, *John: A Commentary on the Gospel of John*, ed. Ulrich Busse, trans. Robert Walter Funk, 2 vols., Hermeneia (Philadelphia: Fortress, 1984), 1.240.

10 Barnabas Lindars, *The Gospel of John* (NCBC; Grand Rapids: Eerdmans, 1972), 181. David R. Hall astutely notes that "[Daube] objects to the translation 'have dealings with' mainly on the grounds that there is no parallel in Greek literature, while admitting that there is also no parallel for the construction he advocates" ("Meaning of συγχράομαι in John 4:9," *ExpTim* 83.2 [1971]: 56). Furthermore, in response to Daube's rendering of συγχράομαι, Louw and Nida state that "such an interpretation, however, is based upon etymological arguments for which there seems to be no certain justification in general Greek usage" ("συγχράομαι," L&N 34.1).

11 J. Ramsey Michaels, *The Gospel of John*, NICNT (Grand Rapids: Eerdmans, 2010), 240.

12 Reinhard Pummer, *The Samaritans in Flavius Josephus* (Tübingen: Mohr Siebeck, 2009), 35.

SURVEYING JESUS'S ETHNIC INCARNATION

Jacob also they called their father, as being his descendant. But the Jews abominated them as well as all (other nations).[13]

Johannine scholars often add to Chrysostom's summation with citations from the Hebrew Bible, Josephus, and rabbinic tradition. The history of Judeo-Samaritan relations is of great importance for our understanding of the interaction between Jesus and the Samaritan woman in John 4 and will be the focus of Chapter Three. However, what has not been substantially dealt with is the significance of the woman's ethnic identification of Jesus as a "Jew" and how this identification might relate to the theme of Jesus's origins in the Gospel of John or to the question of the identity of "the Jews." As we will discuss in detail in Chapter Three, noting the roots of Judeo-Samaritan relations is not enough to interpret the full implications of Jesus's ethnic labeling in the Gospel of John. There also needs to be an explanatory framework to unpack the significance of the ethnic labels. This is especially true in light of the fact that John 4:9 is the only occurrence in the Gospel of John where Jesus is explicitly labeled a "Jew."[14] The explicit identification in 4:9, as the Samaritan woman's surprise indicates, is due only to the fact that Jesus does what Jews normally do not do.[15] (The same is also true for 8:48 where Jesus does and says things that Jews do not typically do and say, and so he is identified as a Samaritan.)

Nonetheless, some scholars have hypothesized about how the Samaritan woman was able to identify Jesus as a Jew, especially since John 4:9 is "the only passage in the Gospel where Jesus is explicitly called a Jew."[16] Chrysostom suggests that she knew he was a Jew "from His dress, perhaps, and from His dialect."[17] In 1866, Frédéric Louis Godet referenced the hypothesis of Rudolf

---

13   John Chrysostom, *Hom. Jo.* 31.107 (*NPNF* 14.165).

14   There are two other occasions in the Gospel of John where Jesus' Judean ethnicity is evoked. In John 18:35, Pilate infers that Jesus is a Jew because "Your [i.e. Jesus'] own nation (ἔθνος) and the chief priests have handed you over to me." The second occasion is the programmatic statement in John 1:11: "[Jesus] came to what was his own, and his own people did not accept him."

15   In this regards, Jo-Ann A. Brant comments: "[the Samaritan woman's] question delivers an insult by marking the two boundaries of gender and ethnicity that Jesus has breached. Jesus is a Jew, but not a good one by the Jews' standards" (*John: Paideia Commentaries on the New Testament* [Grand Rapids: Baker Academic, 2011], 84). Indeed, as Marie-Joseph Lagrange words it, "How comes it that He, a Jew, is so different from His proud and contemptuous countrymen that He deigns to ask for water from a Samaritan woman? (*The Gospel of Jesus Christ* [trans. Members of the English Dominican Province; Westminster, MD: Newman Press, 1958], 1.112).

16   Lincoln, *Gospel According to St John*, 172.

17   John Chrysostom, *Hom. Jo.* 31.107 (*NPNF* 14.167). J. H. Bernard and Michaels are receptive to Chrysostom's suggestion here. See: J. H. Bernard, *A Critical and Exegetical Commentary on*

12   CHAPTER 1

Stier, who "observed that in some words which Jesus had just spoken the letter ש occurred, which, according to Judges 12:6, distinguished the two pronun-
ciations, the Jewish (*sch*), and the Samaritan (*s*)."[18] Although the text does not
state how the Samaritan woman was able to identify Jesus as a Jew, perhaps
the most plausible way that the Samaritan woman knew Jesus was a Jew (or
the main indicia that Jesus was a "Jew") was because he was a festival pilgrim.[19]
The Samaritan woman's identification of Jesus as festival pilgrim is later confirmed when she raises the issue of where to worship, "on this mountain" or "in
Jerusalem" (John 4:20–22).

Even Rudolf Bultmann concedes the fact that "Jesus is a Ἰουδαῖος, even
though he is a Galilean, because he belongs to the Jewish national (*Volks*) and
cultic community (*Kultusgemeinschaft*)."[20] This concession is short lived because ultimately, for Bultmann, the Johannine Jesus disassociates himself from
"the Jews" and Judaism.[21] In Bultmann's paradigm, "the Jews" fulfill a symbolic
role in John's narrative as the representatives of unbelief and the enemies of
Jesus, even though there are several passages where Jesus interacts with "the
Jews" without any sign of hostility (e.g., John 7:11; 8:31; 10:19; 11:19, 31, 33, 36;
12:9, 11).[22] Nevertheless, as recently as 2009, "there seems to be a consensus on
Bultmann's description of the 'sense' of οἱ Ἰουδαῖοι."[23]

Perhaps as a result of Bultmann's influence, John 4:9 is routinely marginal-
ized in the history of research on "the Jews" in John, precisely because it runs
counter to the predominant interpretation of the term "the Jews" in John. The

---

      the Gospel According to St. John (ICC 29; Edinburgh: T&T Clark, 1928), 1.137; Michaels, *The
      Gospel of John*, 239 n. 33.

18   Frédéric Louis Godet, *Commentary on John's Gospel* (trans. and ed. Timothy Dwight;
      Grand Rapids: Kregel, 1978), 422.

19   Wilhelm Lütgert, "Die Juden im Johannesevangelium," in *Neutestamentliche Studeien für
      Georg Henrici* (Leipzig: J. C. Heinrich, 1914), 152. Lütgert further asserts that what charac-
      terized the Jews was not their language or appearance ("die Sprache oder das Gesicht")
      but their religion.

20   Bultmann, *The Gospel of John*, 178–179n.7. For Bultmann's general comments on 'the Jews'
      in John see Bultmann, *The Gospel of John*, 87.

21   See, for example, Bultmann, *The Gospel of John*, 189–190 n.6 where he refers to Walter
      Grundmann's *Jesus der Galiläer und das Judentum* (Leipzig: Georg Wigand, 1940), 229ff.
      It was, after all, the goal of Grundmann's book "to demonstrate that Jesus was most defi-
      nitely not a Jew" (Susannah Heschel, *The Aryan Jesus: Christian Theologians and the Bible
      in Nazi Germany* [Princeton: Princeton University Press, 2008], 152).

22   Walter Gutbrod, "Ἰουδαῖος, Ἰσραήλ, Ἑβραῖος," *TDNT* 3.378.

23   Cornelis Bennema, "The Identity and Composition of *hoi Ioudaioi* in the Gospel of John,"
      TynBul 60 (2009): 240. Although Bennema adds in a footnote "Yet, *contra* Bultmann,
      οἱ Ἰουδαῖοι are not homogeneous in their response to Jesus" (Bennema, "The Identity and
      Composition of *hoi Ioudaioi* in the Gospel of John," 240 n. 9).

SURVEYING JESUS'S ETHNIC INCARNATION

problem, however, is that built into Bultmann's paradigm is his a priori conclusion: "Oἱ Ἰουδαῖοι does not relate to the empirical state of the Jewish people, but to its very nature."[24] John Ashton affirms and explains this statement: "To its nature, yes, or rather essence (*Wesen*), since the essential role of the Jews in the Fourth Gospel is to represent and symbolize human obduracy and incomprehension when confronted with the revelation of Jesus."[25] However, in response to Ashton's approval and proliferation of Bultmann's paradigm, Daniel Boyarin correctly identifies "this typically Bultmannian attempt to enhance the anti-Judaism of the New Testament at every turn."[26] Consequently, *if the Samaritan woman's identification of Jesus as a "Jew" does nothing else, it should indicate that the ethnic label "Jew" cannot simply be the name of the enemies of Jesus in the Gospel of John.*[27] Rather, it indicates that there are multiple uses of "Jew(s)" in John's Gospel.[28]

If it is the case that, at least this instance in John 4:9, "Jew" is an ethnic term, does the Samaritan woman use "Jew" disparagingly, as is customarily suggested? Theodore of Mopsuestia (c. 350–428 CE) viewed the Samaritan woman's

---

24   Bultmann, *The Gospel of John*, 87.

25   John Ashton, *Understanding the Fourth Gospel* (Oxford: Oxford University Press, 1993), 135. To this Ashton adds: "That the role of the Jews is as Bultmann describes it is surely beyond serious dispute."

26   Daniel Boyarin, "The Ioudaioi in John and the Prehistory of 'Judaism,'" in *Pauline Conversations in Context: Essays in Honor of Calvin J. Roetzel* (ed. J. C. Anderson et al.; JSNTSup 221; Sheffield: SAP, 2002), 223 n.24. Ashton, in his second edition of *Understanding* [2007], removes Bultmann's assertion about the role of "the Jews" in John and further acknowledges that "Daniel Boyarin is right to rebuke me for this" (*Understanding the Fourth Gospel* [Oxford: Oxford University Press, 2007], 69n.18).

27   Contra Walter Bauer, who in his famed *Griechisch-Deutsches Wörterbuch*, ascribes a single definition of the Ἰουδαῖοι in John: "für Johannes sind die Juden feinde Jesu schlechthin" (Walter Bauer, "Ἰουδαῖοι," *Griechisch-Deutsches Wörterbuch zu den Schriften des Neuen Testaments und der übrigen urchristlichen Literatur* [Giessen: Alfred Töpelmann, 1928], 591). Incidentally, this definition did not change in the second edition in BAG (1957/1971) nor BAGD (1979) but only in its third edition BDAG (1999) where Frederick W. Danker appropriately expands the definition in order to better account for the multiple usages of Ἰουδαῖος in John.

28   Urban C. Von Wahlde divides occurrences of Ἰουδαῖος/Ἰουδαῖοι into separate categories. "Twenty-three times the term is used to refer to the Jews as a nation, to their customs or feasts: 2:6, 13; 3:1, 25; 4:9 (twice), 22; 5:1; 6:4; 7:2; 11:55; 18:20, 33, 35, 39; 19:3, 19, 20, 21 (three times), 40, 42. Nine occurrences refer to the common people with no connotation of hostility toward Jesus; this is a neutral sense such as 'inhabitants of Judea': 10:19; 11:19, 31, 33, 36, 45, 54; 19:9, 11. One instance refers to the land of Judea: 3:22. Thirty-eight instances refer to 'religious authorities' with the connotation of hostility toward Jesus: 1:19; 2:18, 20; 5:10, 15, 16, 18; 6:41, 52; 7:1, 11, 13, 15, 35; 8:22, 31,48, 52, 57; 9:18, 22 (twice); 10:24, 31, 33; 11:8; 13:33; 18:12, 14, 31, 36, 38; 19:7, 12, 14, 31, 38; 20:19" (Urban C. von Wahlde, "The Terms for Religious Authorities in the Fourth Gospel: A Key to Literary-Strata?," *JBL* 98.2 [1979]: 233).

14   CHAPTER 1

response to Jesus as virtuous: "because she wanted to warn him not to trans-
gress the rules of the law."[29] Modern critical scholars, however, are less positive of the Samaritan woman's response. J. H. Bernard, for example, describes
the Samaritan woman's response as "her little gibe—half-jest, half-earnest—
recalling to Jesus the old feud between Jews and Samaritans."[30] Raymond
Brown also suggests that the Samaritan woman "mocks Jesus for being so in
need that he does not observe the proprieties."[31] On the other hand, Bultmann
correctly notes, "The view that the question is an unfriendly rejection of Jesus'
request has no basis in the text."[32] As we will see in Chapter Four, the Samaritan
woman's use of the ethnic label "Jew" for Jesus, although informed by the an-
tipathic relations between Jews and Samaritans, was an acknowledgment of
their difference rather than a slur against Jesus.

2   Jesus the Samaritan

Although it might not be an ethnic *slur* in the above case, the label "Jew" is
nevertheless ethnic, and leads us to another clear instance where ethnic
language is used, though this time the ethnic term and the party using it are
reversed. In John 8:48, the Jews ask Jesus, "Are we not right in saying that you
are a Samaritan and have a demon?" Jesus replies in 8:49a, "I do not have a
demon." There are two main lines of thought concerning the accusation of the
Jews. The majority of past scholarship has concluded that the two accusations
are in fact the same, and "the answer in v. 49 refers to the whole question as a
pars pro toto."[33] In this way, to call Jesus a Samaritan is in fact to imply that he
also has a demon. Overall, connecting Samaritan and demonic possession is
the mainstay of comments on John 8:48. For some scholars, such as Michaels,

29   Theodore of Mopsuestia, *Commentary on the Gospel of John* (trans. and ed. Marco Conti
      and Joel C. Elowsky; Downers Grove, IL: InterVarsity Press, 2010), 40–41. Similarly, Lindars
      also suspects: "Out of courtesy [the Samaritan woman] gives [Jesus] the opportunity to
      weigh up whether to insist on his request or to avoid possible subsequent embarrassment
      on account of ceremonial defilement" (*The Gospel of John*, 180).
30   Bernard, *The Gospel According to St. John*, 1.137.
31   Brown, *Gospel According to John*, 177.
32   Bultmann, *The Gospel of John*, 178–179n.7.
33   K. Haacker, "Samaritan, Samaria," *NIDNTT*. For example, Graham Twelftree asserts: "The
      two-part accusation that follow ('you are a Samaritan and have a demon') amounts to one
      and the same thing for Jesus gives a simple catch-all response: 'I do not have a demon'
      (John 8:49)" (Graham H. Twelftree, "In the Name of Jesus: A Conversation with Critics,"
      Journal of Pentecostal Theology 17.2 [2008]: 163).

SURVEYING JESUS'S ETHNIC INCARNATION   15

the connection is touted as an "explicit link."[34] Similarly, Beasley-Murray states, "It is clear that the charges of being a Samaritan and of being possessed were linked."[35] Beasley-Murray observes that this certainty is based on at least one of the following factors: the Samaritans were viewed as heretics,[36] they were linked with magic,[37] or their association with Dositheus and Simon Magus.[38] Not everyone, however, is so certain about the link between "Samaritans" and "demon-possession"; such as, Barrett and Moloney, who use "maybe" and "could" to describe the link.[39] Also, according to Augustine, John 8:48 is a two-part accusation, not one: "Of these two charges cast at Him, He denied the one, but not the other."[40] Some modern commentators also doubt whether "Samaritan" and "having a demon" should be regarded as synonymous or "as if the two were in apposition."[41]

---

34   Michaels, *The Gospel of John*, 523.

35   George Raymond Beasley-Murray, *John* (2d ed.; WBC 36; Waco, TX: Word, 1999), 136.

36   For example, according to Josephus: "the Samaritans, whose chief city at that time was Shechem, which lay beside Mount Gerizim and was inhabited by apostates from the Jewish nation" (*Ant.* 11.340 [Marcus, LCL]).

37   In regards to magic, Beasley-Murray references *b. Sotah 22a* which states: "It has been reported, If one has learnt Scripture and Mishnah but did not attend upon Rabbinical scholars, R. Eleazar says he is an *Am Ha'arets*; R. Samuel b. Nahmani says he is a boor; R. Jannai says he is a Samaritan; R. Aha b. Jacob says he is a magician." Kalimi notes that, according to the minor Talmudic tractate *Kuttim*, "Samaritans are not welcome into the Israelite community unless 'they recant [their belief in] Mount Gerizim and accept [the holiness of] Jerusalem, and the resurrection of the dead'" (*Early Jewish Exegesis and Theological Controversy*, 57–58).

38   For Simon Magus see Justin Martyr, *1 Apol.* 26, 56; *2 Apol* 15; *Dial.* 20. For Dositheus see Origen, *Cels.* 1.57; Eusebius, *Hist. eccl.* iv. 22. Lindars, however, cautions that references to Simon Magus and Dositheus are "too obscure and anachronistic to be altogether certain, and we must be content to admit that the precise reference is unknown to us" (*The Gospel of John*, 331–332).

39   Barrett, *Gospel According to St. John*, 350 and Moloney, *The Gospel of John*, 286.

40   Augustine, *Homilies on Gospel of John* 43.2 (NPNF 7.307). Augustine, however, did *not* believe Jesus was actually a Samaritan but rather interpreted "Samaritan" as "keeper" because "[Jesus] knew that He was our keeper." John Calvin notes, "Augustine flies to allegory, and says that Christ did not refuse to be called a *Samaritan*, because he is a true guardian of his flock" (John Calvin, *Calvin's Commentaries: John* [Edinburgh: Calvin Translation Society, 1845], 355). Calvin, however, is wrong. Augustine did not employ allegory in his comments on John 8:48 but rather, as we will see in Chapter Three, Augustine was aware of the Samaritan etymological tradition that the name "Samaritan" derives from שמרים "keepers" opposed to שַׁמְרִינִים "Samarian/Samaritans."

41   Gerard S. Sloyan, *John* (Interpretation; Atlanta: John Knox, 1988), 104. See also Godet, *Commentary on John's Gospel*, 678. D. A. Carson comments that the link between the two charges of being a Samaritan and demonic possession are uncertain (*Gospel According to John*, 355).

16   CHAPTER 1

Nonetheless, Bultmann is probably correct that "Σαμαρίτης εἶ σὺ perhaps means no more than the accusation made against the *Am Ha'arets*, 'He is a Samaritan', i.e. as it were, a heretic."[42] Bultmann is most likely correct due to the fact that when Jesus is called a Samaritan he was presenting heretical (i.e. unacceptable) opinions. Namely, that Jesus challenges the claim of the Jews to be the children of Abraham (cf. John 8:39), which, as we will see in Chapter Three, was a point of contention with their Samaritan neighbors.[43] Other scholars suggest that labeling Jesus a Samaritan meant that he was "an outsider to the covenant, an apostate from Israel."[44] Yet, as James Dunn observes, "The fact that at various times [Samaritans] called themselves 'Judeans/ Jews' (*Ant.* 11.340), 'Hebrews' (*Ant.* 11.344) and 'Israelites' (in an inscription [150–50 BCE] from Delos) is a further reminder of how careful we have to be in our own use of such descriptive titles."[45] Prior scholarly assessment overlooks how, and in what ways, an ethnic designation *means* "heretic" (Bultmann) or "apostate" (Lincoln). Also absent is a clear understanding of what the term "Samaritan" as heretic or apostate means in the context of John 8. How does accusing Jesus of being a Samaritan inform our understanding of the ethnic identity of Jesus in John? One of the issues that will be raised in the next chapter is what it meant to act like a Jew or a Samaritan in terms of social norms and mores, deviance, and the role of labeling in social contexts.

There is also the matter of ethnic labeling and whether "the Jews" here are casting an ethnic dispersion upon Jesus. As with the interpretation of the term "Jew" in reference to Jesus in John 4:9, it is typically stated that "the Jews'"

---

42   Bultmann, *The Gospel of John*, 299 n. 4. Bultmann here refers to Strack's and Billerbeck's
        Kommentar zum Neuen Testament aus Talmud und Midrasch, citing *b. Sota 22a*, where
        Samaritan and magician appear to be related categories (Str-B 2:524–525). However,
        Schnackenburg notes that the term "'Samaritan'–nowhere attested in Jewish writing as
        an insult—means, when used by the Jews, something like 'heretic'" (Schnackenburg, *The
        Gospel according to St. John*, 2.218). Also see Lindars, *The Gospel of John*, 331.

43   According to John Bowman, "It was as if He were acting the Samaritan in expressing such
        opinions" ("Samaritan Studies," *BJRL* 40 [1958]: 307–308).

44   Lincoln, *Gospel According to St John*, 274. Edwyn Clement Hoskyns and Francis Noel
        Davey notes that the charge means that "[Jesus] is by birth a stranger to the congregation
        of Israel" (*The Fourth Gospel* [London: Faber & Faber, 1947], 345). Andreas J. Köstenberger
        also comments: "Jesus, like the Samaritans, called into question the legitimacy of the
        Jews' worship; hence his opponents' countercharge that it is he who is a 'Samaritan,'
        that is, a Jewish apostate" (Andreas J. Köstenberger, *John* [BECNT 4; Grand Rapids: Baker
        Academic, 2004], 268).

45   James D. G. Dunn, *Christianity in the Making: Jesus Remembered* (Grand Rapids: Eerdmans,
        2003), 279. Consequently, we must be cautious in asserting what it means to be and act
        "more like a Samaritan than like a true Jew" (Köstenberger, *John*, 268 n. 85).

accusation that Jesus is a "Samaritan" in John 8:48 is an ethnic slur.[46] Against this conventional reading is the fact that there is "no evidence that Σαμαρίτης was used simply as a term of abuse."[47] Although, it must also be noted, "nowhere else do these two terms, Σαμαρίτης and δαιμόνιον, occur together" either.[48] The least one can say is that in the instance of John 8:48 the label "Samaritan," in conjunction with the charge of "having a demon," is some sort of a slur. Nonetheless, since there is no evidence that "Samaritan" (or "Jew" for that matter) was ever used as a term of abuse, or as synonymous with demonic possession outside of the text of John, then we must reevaluate the ethnic identifications of Jesus within the Gospel of John; namely, how, why and to what affect Jesus is labeled a "Jew" or "Samaritan."

3   Conclusion: Jesus's Ethnic Incarnation

Scholars who have previously made the connection between John 4:9 and 8:48 often comment similarly to Barrett, who said, "In this world [Jesus] is never anything but a stranger."[49] This assertion, and others like it, is sometimes the full extent of the discussion of Jesus's ethnic identity in the Gospel of John (especially involving 4:9 and 8:48). The one possible exception is Craig Keener, who comments: "John's theology of incarnation includes Jesus' particularity as a 'Jew' (4:9) from Nazareth (1:45) … But what seems most significant is that Jesus is called Jew only by *non-Jews*—the Samaritan woman (4:9) and Pilate

---

46   For example, Walter Bauer states, "die 'Samariter' im Munde der Juden zum Schimpfwort macht" (*Das Johannesevangelium*, 130). Matthew Black offers a more cautious statement, "As the usage in the Fourth Gospel shows (cf. Jn 8:48), the word 'Samaritan' had become practically equivalent in meaning to 'schismatic' or 'heretic', and appears to have passed almost as a term of abuse" (Matthew Black, *The Scrolls and Christian Origins: Studies in the Jewish Background of the New Testament* [Chico, CA: Scholars Press, 1983], 70).

47   Bultmann, *The Gospel of John*, 299 n. 4. Barrett notes: "There is no evidence that 'Samaritan' was a regular term of abuse for heretics" (Barrett, *Gospel According to St. John*, 350). And Schnackenburg adds that Samaritan is "nowhere attested in Jewish writing as an insult" (Schnackenburg, *The Gospel according to St. John*, 2.218). Schnackenburg here is also cited by Urban C. Von Wahlde, *The Gospel and Letters of John* [Grand Rapids: Eerdmans, 2010], 2.402.

48   Pummer, *The Samaritans in Flavius Josephus*, 36.

49   Barrett, *Gospel According to St. John*, 232. Jesus is described as "a stranger to the congregation of Israel" (Hoskyns and Davey, *The Fourth Gospel*, 345), as "alien" by Carson (*Gospel According to John*, 218), as "otherworldly" by Köstenberger (*John*, 149 n. 28), as an "outsider and stranger" by Michaels (*The Gospel of John*, 240), and as a "stranger" by D. Moody Smith, *John* (ANTC; Nashville: Abingdon, 1999), 112.

(18:35)—as if 'his own' would not own up to him (1:11)."[50] However, while Jesus is only called a "Jew" by a non-Jew, what is absent in this discussion is that Jesus is also called a non-Jew by "the Jews"! Accordingly, if the Johannine Jesus is in some sense a non-Jew, heretic, or social deviant, then what were the social implications of this ethnic labeling? What was the role and affect of deviancy in society? The following chapter presents a methodology for understanding theses social issues.

---

50   Keener, *The Gospel of John*, 1.218; original emphasis.

CHAPTER 2

Ethnicity and Labeling

A theory of ethnicity is a framework for understanding interactions between groups of people, specifically how they identify themselves and categorize others.[1] Since the study of ethnicity is a field in its own right, accompanied by a vast research literature, this chapter examines aspects of ethnicity theory that are appropriate for our understanding of how ethnic labels function in the Gospel of John.

We begin with defining terms and call attention to how the Greek word ἔθνος was used in the ancient world and how the term "ethnic" is defined in the social-sciences. The distinction between ancient ἔθνος and the modern term "ethnic" then leads to a discussion of the idea of race, wherein we will conclude that it is a fundamentally inappropriate method for understanding the ancient world. As part of this discussion, we contextualize ethnicity theory within the broader scope of the social-sciences. In so doing, we are in a better position to understand the two competing ethnicity theories: primordialism and instrumentalism. The central issue concerns how we understand ethnic groups' cultural features.

We will highlight six cultural features that can be present, depending on the context, and indicate identification with an ethnic group. These cultural features are embedded in individuals as the result of socialization. During the socialization process, individuals learn their group identification as well as the social categorization of non-members. Since the social world is hardly one of stasis, we will look at two examples of destabilization: the stranger and the heretic. The stranger is the presence of an outsider within the group whereas the heretic is an insider who is a dissenting voice within the group itself. These two destabilizing roles will be particularly insightful in Chapter Three (concerning the history of Judeo-Samaritan relations) and Chapter Four (concerning whether labeling Jesus as a Samaritan equates to labeling him a heretic).

After establishing how ethnic groups signal their group identification by cultural features, we will turn to social categorization and labeling. Here we distinguish between "interactional" and "institutional" labeling. Interactional labeling occurs during everyday social interactions when we assign labels or

---

1 We follow Richard Jenkins who distinguishes between "*self-* or *group identification* (internally-oriented) and the *categorization* of others (externally-oriented)" ("Categorization: Identity, Social Process and Epistemology," *Current Sociology* 48.3 [2000]: 8; emphasis original).

© KONINKLIJKE BRILL NV, LEIDEN, 2019 | DOI:10.1163/9789004390706_004

categories to people. Institutional labeling occurs as a reaction to people who deviate from established practices (i.e. "the way things are done"); such a person is labeled a deviant to mark them off as an outsider.

1 Delineation of Terms: "Ethnic" and ἔθνος

It is important to begin with a discussion acknowledging the relationship between the researcher and the research subject, particularly the distinction between an etic (outsider or social-scientific) perspective and an emic (insider or indigenous) perspective provided by our primary sources.[2] John H. Elliott explains that our sources' emic account(s) "describe *what* and *how* the natives thought but not *why* ... [while etic models] seek to explain *why* the native thought and behaved so and not otherwise."[3] Therefore, as we engage in our textual sources we must bear in mind the distinction between what they thought was so and our interpretive model that explains *why* they thought it was so. Due to their etymological relationship, there may be some confusion between the etic social-scientific model of "ethnicity" and the emic term ἔθνος.[4] However, while the English word and social-scientific concept of ethnicity shares commonalities with the Greek ἔθνος, they are not exactly the same concept. For this reason, we must demarcate the boundaries of the emic term ἔθνος and etic term "ethnic." To be clear, the following is a modern social-scientific or etic framework of ethnicity, which aids the interpretation of the ancient emic understanding of ethnic groups (or ἔθνος/ἔθνοι). Although this will be discussed further below, this application of modern ethnic theories to

---

2   Craig Calhoun explains: "The term *emic* describes an insider's perspective on cultural practices or forms; it refers to the self-description or reflexivity possible within any culture, as well as to the conformity of such description to the categories, values, and terms of the culture. The term *etic*, in contrast, describes an account of practices or forms based on external criteria—the perspective of an outsider" (Craig Calhoun, "emic and etic," in *Dictionary of the Social Sciences* [Oxford: Oxford University Press, 2002], 142).

3   John H. Elliott, *What Is Social-Scientific Criticism?* (Minneapolis: Fortress Press, 1993), 39; emphasis original. For the employment of the etic/emic distinction see: Mason, "Jews, Judeans, Judaizing, Judaism," 457–512; especially 458–459.

4   For example, David Miller explains: "The cognate relationship between 'ethnicity' and the Greek word *ethnos* can also be confusing because it is not always clear whether scholars are discussing ancient ethnicity as defined by a modern etic framework, or an ancient emic understanding of *ethnos* and related terms and concepts" (David Miller, "The Meaning of *Ioudaios* and its Relationship to Other Group Labels in Ancient 'Judaism,'" *CBR* 9.1 [2010]: 122).

ETHNICITY AND LABELING

the ancient world is justified because there is a convergence of ethnographic data for both ancient and modern ethnic groups.

"Ethnicity" and "ethnic" derive from the Greek ἐθνικός ("national; foreign, gentile"), which derives from the older term ἔθνος ("nation; people").[5] We begin with the Greek ἔθνος and its derivative ἐθνικός and then turn to how ἔθνος/ἐθνικός informs the meaning of the English "ethnic/ethnicity."

According to LSJ, Homer is the first to use the term ἔθνος in the extant Greek literature.[6] Homer used it to describe any sort of collective, and the term probably derives from ἔθος—meaning "a usual or customary manner of behavior, *habit*; long-established usage or practice common to a group, *custom*."[7] After the time of Homer, ἔθνος came to signify "*a nation, people*."[8] Karl Schmidt submits that ἔθνος, compared to other Greek words denoting "people" (specifically, φυλή, λαός, γλῶσσα), "is the most general and therefore the weakest of these terms, having simply an ethnographical sense and denoting the natural cohesion of a people in general."[9] However, the fact that ἔθνος encompasses a broader scope of meaning does not necessarily make it the weakest term for describing a people group. Rather, ἔθνος is an umbrella term that encapsulates the varying aspects of "the natural cohesion of a people."[10] For example, Steve Mason observes,

---

5   "ἐθνικός and ἔθνος," LSJ, 480.

6   "ἔθνος," LSJ, 480.

7   "ἔθος," BDAG, 277. LSJ define ἔθνος, as "a number of people living together, company, body of men, band of comrades; host of men; of particular tribes; of animals, swarms, flocks, etc" ("ἔθνος," 480). Karl Ludwig Schmidt explains: "This word [ἔθνος], which is common in Greek, from the very first, probably comes from ἔθος, and means 'mass' or 'host' or multitude' bound by the same manners, customs, or other distinctive features" (Karl Ludwig Schmidt, "ἔθνος, ἐθνικός," *TDNT* 2.369). Hans Bietenhard also notes that "ἔθνος, derived from ἔθος, custom, habit, means a group which is held together by customs, a clan; then, crowd, company, people" ("People, Nation, Gentiles, Crowd, City," *NIDNTT*).

8   "ἔθνος," LSJ, 480. The Greek word traditionally rendered "race" is γένος (i.e. a "race, of beings" ("γένος," III. LSJ, 344). Two of the subdivisions of γένος include a "clan, house, family, Herodotus 1.125, etc. ("γένος," III.b. LSJ, 344); or a "tribe, as a subdivision of ἔθνος, Herodotus 1.56, 101" ("γένος," III.c. LSJ, 344). C. P. Jones has noted that "syntactically, Herodotus uses ἔθνος very differently from γένος.... An ἔθνος is such a group viewed as a geographical, political or cultural entity, often in relation to the time of the narrative context: γένος is such a group viewed as united by birth, and often in relation to some point previous to the narrative time ("ἔθνος and γένος in Herodotus," CQ 16.0 [1996]: 317)

9   Schmidt, *TDNT* 2.369. According to Schmidt, synonyms of ἔθνος "are → φυλή (people as a national unity of common descent), → λαός (people as a political unity with a common history and constitution) and → γλῶσσα (people as a linguistic unity)."

10   Schmidt, *TDNT* 2.369.

Each ἔθνος had its distinctive nature or character (φύσις, ἦθος), expressed in unique ancestral traditions (τὰ πάτρια), which typically reflected a shared (if fictive) ancestry (συγγενεία); each had its charter stories (μῦθοι), customs, norms, conventions, mores, laws (νόμοι, ἔθη, νόμιμα), and political arrangements or constitution (πολιτεία).[11]

In fact, as we will discuss later, modern theories of ethnicity assert that ethnic groups use these cultural features to identify and distinguish themselves from other groups.

Nonetheless, it is also important to note that "the [Persian] invasion acted as a catalyst for the 'invention of the barbarians'—that is, the creation of a derogatory and stereotypical 'other'."[12] Accordingly, after the Persian War of 480–479 BCE, a secondary meaning of ἔθνος developed into (τὰ) ἔθνη, meaning the *"foreign, barbarous nations."*[13] It is this particular sense of ἔθνος that the Septuagint (c. 285–150 BCE) translators use for the Hebrew גּוֹיִם ("non-Jews, Gentiles"); similarly, this is also the sense of (τὰ) ἔθνη in the New Testament.[14] It was during the Hellenistic period (c. 323 BCE with the death of Alexander the Great to 31 BCE with Octavian's victory at Actium) that the word ἐθνικός appears and is used to mean "1. *national* (Polybius 30.13.6; Diodorus Siculus 18.13; Strabo 2.3.1), or 2. *foreign, gentile* (Gospel of Matthew 5:47; Epistle of Galatians 2:14)."[15] In these New Testament texts, Frederick Danker observes

---

11   Mason, "Jews, Judeans, Judaizing, Judaism," 484.

12   Jonathan M. Hall, *Ethnic Identity in Greek Antiquity* (Cambridge: Cambridge University Press, 2000), 44. During the Classical era in Greece (500–336 BCE), βάρβαρος/βάρβαροι [initially] meant "all non-Greek-speaking peoples, then specially of the Medes and Persians" ("βάρβαρος," LSJ, 306) linguistic focus. Hall also insightfully notes: "What has changed between the Archaic and the Classical periods is the *mechanism* of Greek self-definition.... By establishing a stereotypical, generalized image of the exotic, slavish and unintelligible barbarian, Greek identity could be defined 'from without', through opposition with this image of alterity. To find the language, culture or rituals of the barbarian desperately alien was immediately to define oneself as Greek. The construction of a sharp symbolic boundary between Greek and barbarian should theoretically no longer leave any doubt as to the Greekness of those on its inside" (Hall, *Ethnic Identity in Greek Antiquity*, 47; emphasis original).

13   "ἔθνος," LSJ, 480.

14   In the Septuagint ἔθνος is the "stereotypical rendition of גּוֹי; *nation, people*; *non-Jews, Gentiles; the Jewish nation (spoken of by Gentiles)*" (Bernard A. Taylor ed., "ἔθνος," *Analytical Lexicon to the Septuagint* [Peabody, MA: Hendrickson, 2009], 158). In the New Testament ἔθνος is used for "1. a body of persons united by kinship, culture, and common traditions, *nation, people*; 2. people groups foreign to a specific people group; a. *the nations, gentiles, unbelievers*; b. *non-Israelite Christians, gentiles* ("ἔθνος," BDAG, 276–277).

15   "ἐθνικός," LSJ, 480.

ETHNICITY AND LABELING

that ἐθνικός is used "with focus on morality or belief, *unbelieving, worldly, polytheistic*."[16] In the early Christian literature, the focus is on the secondary meaning of ἐθνικός as foreign or gentile. Overall, a good emic definition of ἔθνος is: "A group viewed as a geographical, political or cultural entity."[17]

As we move forward to what is meant by the English "ethnic/ethnicity," it is important to note that in the writings of later Latin Church Fathers, and particularly in translating the Latin Vulgate, the Latin *gentes* was used "like ἔθνος, opposed to Jews and Christians, *pagan nations, heathen, gentiles*."[18] Since "it was Church Latin that dominated literacy in Europe throughout the middle ages ... [with] the Reformation, and the English vernacular rendering of the Bible, it was a 'gentile', not 'ethnic', that the term appeared."[19] Accordingly, the earliest recorded usages (c. 1470–1480 CE) of the English word "ethnic" meant "not a Christian or a Jew," that is, "a Gentile, heathen, pagan."[20]

It was not until the 1850s that the term "ethnic" came to mean "pertaining to race; peculiar to a race or nation; ethnological."[21] Prior to the 1850s, there was a preexisting "discourse built around the idea of 'race', for which 'ethnos' would have been no more than a redundant synonym."[22] Nevertheless, there was a concerted effort by some scholars to alter that discourse by insisting on

---

16   "ἐθνικός," BDAG, 276.

17   Christopher P. Jones, "ἔθνος and γένος in Herodotus," *CQ* 46.2 (1996): 317.

18   Charlton T. Lewis and Charles Short, "gens, gentis," II.2.c. in *A Latin Dictionary* (Oxford: Oxford University Press, 1879). The *Oxford Latin Dictionary* (2012) does not include definitions from 200 CE onwards and so does not include shifts in definitions in ecclesiastical Latin. See John Henderson, "A1-Zythum: Domimina nustio illumea, or out with the OLD (1931–82)" in *Classical Dictionaries Past, Present and Future* (Christopher Stray ed.; London: Duckworth, 2010), 139–76. The *Pocket Oxford Latin Dictionary: Latin-English, however, does include the shift of gens from* "clan; tribe; family; race; nation" in the classical era to *gentiles*, meaning "pagans, heathens," in the Late/Medieval Latin era (James Morwood ed. "gens, gentis" in *The Pocket Oxford Latin Dictionary* [Oxford: Oxford University Press, 1994]).

      Furthermore, while it is commonly assumed that Jerome translated the entire Latin Vulgate "the only justification for calling it 'Jerome's Vulgate' (as we often do) is that there is more of his work in it than there is of anyone else's" (Robert Weber, "Preface to the First Edition," in *Biblia Sacra: Iuxta Vulgatam Versionem* [Stuttgart: Deutsche Bibelgesellschaft, 1994], xxix). For example, according to Robert Weber, while Jerome certainly translated most of the Hebrew Bible, all books of the New Testament have an Old-Latin base that was later revised and even then Jerome is believed to have only revised the Gospels.

19   Elizabeth Tonkin, Maryon McDonald, and Malcolm Chapman, "Introduction—History and Social Anthropology," in *History and Ethnicity* (London and New York: Rutledge, 1989), 13.

20   Oxford English Dictionary, "Ethnic." See A. adj. 1. and B. noun 1.

21   Oxford English Dictionary, "Ethnic." See A. adj. 2a.

22   Tonkin, McDonald, Chapman, "Introduction," 14.

using the term "ethnic groups" opposed to "races" during this period between the 1850s and 1950s. The final impetus for this transition came in the tragedy of World War II. After 1945, the term "ethnic group" meant "a group of people differentiated from the rest of the community by racial origins or cultural background, and usually claiming or enjoying official recognition of their group identity."[23]

1.1 *Ethnicity and Race*

In the previous section we saw that the history of the English word "ethnic," from the mid-nineteenth century, was intimately bound with the concept of "race." To be sure, then, the correlation between "ethnic" and "race" is a modern phenomenon rather than an ancient one. The reason for this is that the concept of "race" is a relatively recent one. For example, the term "race" was first used in the seventeenth century to describe a collectivity, but from the eighteenth century on the term "race" meant "a grouping or classification of people based on what are presumed to be biological differences typically evident as differences in physical appearance due to such features as skin color."[24]

According to Ashley Montagu, in his well known *Man's Most Dangerous Myth*, a major impetus for the conception of "race"—as the classification of people based upon their physical characteristics—was to justify the rapid expansion of the African slave trade in the eighteenth century. In the following passage, Montagu insightfully notes the shift from social differences to a biological difference:

> For the slaveholders the strategic elaboration of erroneous notions which had long been held presented no great difficulty. In order to bolster their self-appointed rights the superior caste did not have far to seek for reasons that serve to justify its conduct. They deliberately maintained illiteracy and the alleged spiritual benightedness of the slaves supplied abundant material for elaboration on the theme of their essential inferiority. Their different physical appearance provided a convenient peg upon which to hang the argument that this represented the external sign

---

23   Oxford English Dictionary, "Ethnic." See A. adj. b. and B. noun 3.

24   Peter Kivisto and Paul R. Croll, *Race and Ethnicity: The Basics* (London and New York: Routledge, 2012), 162. The social-anthropologist Audrey Smedley has also studied the development of the concept of "race" and, in sum, demonstrates that "Race as a mechanism of social stratification and as a form of human identity is a recent concept in human history. Historical records show that neither the idea nor ideologies associated with race existed before the seventeenth century" ("'Race' and the Construction of Human Identity," in *American Anthropologist* 100.3 [1998]: 690).

ETHNICITY AND LABELING

of more profound ineradicable mental and moral inferiorities. It was an easily grasped mode of reasoning, and in this way the obvious difference in their social status, in caste status, was equated with their obviously different physical appearance, which, in turn, was taken to indicate a fundamental biological difference. Thus was a culturally produced difference in social status converted into a difference in biological status. What had once been a social difference was now transformed into a biological difference which served, it was expected, to justify and maintain the social difference.[25]

Before race became a "peg upon which to hang"[26] support for slavery, however, the earliest classificatory scheme of race was monogenesis—meaning that the physical variation between human populations was "representing variants within a single human species."[27] In the monogenesis model, physical differences arose due to environmental factors (i.e. "tribes living in unfavorable conditions developed in response to their station darker and coarser skin"), thereby establishing a causal relationship between physical appearance and civilization.[28] In the late eighteenth and early nineteenth century, however, polygenism—the idea that there were not several "races" of humankind but that they were, in fact, separate human "species"—displaced the environmentalism of the monogenesis model.[29] Now that humanity was thought to be different species, it was possible to further classify and essentially rank these different human species from superior to inferior. Unfortunately, Charles Darwin's *On the Origin of Species by Means of Natural Selection* (1859) aided this particular approach of ranking. It is unfortunate because Darwin "himself was never comfortable applying the theory to cultural or social traits in human populations."[30] Nevertheless, Darwin's theory of "natural selection" was interpreted by the so-called "social Darwinists" as "the survival of the fittest" with the progress of superior races/species. This view reached its zenith

---

25 Ashley Montagu, *Man's Most Dangerous Myth: the Fallacy of Race 6th Edition* (Walnut Creek, CA: Altamira Press, 1997), 76.

26 Montagu, *Man's Most Dangerous Myth*, 76.

27 Audrey Smedley, "Race, Concept of," in *The Oxford Companion to United States History* (ed. Paul S. Boyer; Oxford: Oxford University Press, 2001), 641.

28 Hanah Franziska Augstein, *Race: The Origin of an Idea, 1760–1850* (Bristol, England; Thoemmes Press, 1996), xiii.

29 Augstein, *Race*, xiv

30 Paul Finkelman and Matthew Wilhelm Kapell, "Race, Theories of," in *Encyclopedia of African American History, 1619–1895* (ed. Paul Finkelman; Oxford: Oxford University Press, 2006). Finkelman and Kapell further note that Darwin's conclusion in *The Descent of Man* (1871) was that "all people are related" (i.e. monogenism).

with the rise of Nazi Germany in the 1930s as evidenced by Hans Puvogel, who in 1936 wrote, "Der Wert des Einzelnen für die Gemeinschaft bemißt sich nach seiner rassischen Persönlichkeit. Nur ein rassisch wertvoller Mensch hat innerhalb der Gemeinschaft eine Daseinsberechtigung. Ein wegen seiner Minderwertigkeit für die Gesamtheit nutzloser, ja schädlicher Mensch ist dagegen auszuscheiden."[31]

Even before the rise of Nazi Germany in the 1930s, however, there was a concerted effort to counter the tides of the "social Darwinism" of "race science." For example, at the Berlin sociologists' congress of 1912, Max Weber denounced race theory as a "crime against science."[32] In 1935, Julian Huxley and A. C. Haddon argued, "The term *race* as applied to human groups should be dropped from the vocabulary of science" and replaced by "the term (*ethnic*) *group* or *people* employed for all general purposes."[33] However, Huxley and Haddon had not convinced everyone of their view, even within Great Britain. R. Ruggles Gates, a polygenist who reviewed *We Europeans*, suggests:

> Anthropologists will not all agree with the points of view expressed ... [because] the authors make the conventional assumption that all living peoples belong to one species ... [and] the reviewer has expressed that at present somewhat heretical view that living man represents three or more species.[34]

---

31 Hans Puvogel, *Die leitende Grundgedanken bei der Entmannung gefährlicher Sittlichkeitsverbrecher* (PhD. diss., University of Göttingen, 1937), 34. Montagu both cites and translates Puvogel's statement: "An individual's worth in the community is measured by his racial personality. Only a racially valuable person has a right to exist within the community. Someone who is useless for the community because of his inferiority, or even harmful to it, is to be eliminated" (*Myth*, 53).

32 Joachim Radkau, *Max Weber: A Biography* (trans. Patrick Camiller; Cambridge: Polity Press, 2009), 340; citing Max Weber, *Gesammelte Aufsätze zur Soziologie und Sozialpolitik* (ed. Marianne Weber; Tübingen: Mohr, 1924), 489.

33 Julian Huxley and A. C. Haddon, *We Europeans: A Survey of "Racial" Problems* (London: Jonathan Cape, 1935), 107 and 108; emphasis original. One reviewer of *We Europeans*, reflecting the political urgency created by the rise of Nazi Germany and its effects upon sociology/anthropology, concludes that "this book is one to be read and pondered by serious thinkers who are not moved by scaremongering and who value scientific truth and its necessary companion, freedom of conscience" (H. J. Fleure, "*We Europeans: A Survey of "Racial" Problems* by Julian S. Huxley; A. C. Haddon," in *Geographical Review* 26.4 [1936]: 704).

34 R. Ruggles Gates, "*We Europeans: A Survey of Racial Problems* by Julian S. Huxley and A. C. Haddon" in *Man: Royal Anthropological Institute of Great Britain and Ireland* 36 (1936): 161 and 162. Gates adds that man's "adaptations and numerous physical differences ... would entitle them to specific rank in any other group of mammals" (Gates, "We Europeans," 162). Gates was a Professor of Botany at King's College, London.

Nevertheless, as Gates himself admits, his views fall outside of the majority opinion and, on the whole, it appears Huxley and Haddon's *We Europeans* was a well-received addition in the transition from "race" to "ethnic groups."

The concept of ethnicity is an appropriate etic model for analyzing ancient and modern groups of people who belong together because they share a common cultural milieu. The concept of race, however, is decidedly an inappropriate etic model because "the project was always designed to advance the arguments on behalf of the existence of racial hierarchies as permanent, biologically rooted features of human diversity."[35] However, this is not to say that in our sources there is not ethnocentrism or xenophobia. Philip Esler comments, "The Greeks and the Romans were certainly ethnocentric; they did dislike other peoples, including Judeans and one another, but they did not do so on 'racial' grounds."[36] Accordingly, in the exegesis of the Gospel of John, we apply an ethnicity model that is explicitly concerned with how groups of people understand, participate, and interact with one another.[37]

2   Theories of Ethnicity

As we move forward to theories of ethnicity, it is important first to contextualize that discussion within the broader field of the social-sciences. Within

---

35   Kivisto and Croll, *Race and Ethnicity*, 7. Even the *American Heritage Dictionary*, in their definition of "race," notes: "Most biologists and anthropologists do not recognize race as a biologically valid classification, in part because there is more genetic variation within groups than between them" ("race," in *The American Heritage Dictionary of the English Language, Fifth Edition* [Boston: Houghton Mifflin Harcourt Publishing Company, 2013]). Also see: Audrey Smedley and Brian D. Smedley, "Race as Biology Is Fiction, Racism as a Social Problem Is Real: Anthropological and Historical Perspectives on the Social Construction of Race," *American Psychologist* 60.1 (2005): 16–26.

36   Philip Esler, *Conflict and Identity in Romans: The Social Setting of Paul's Letter* (Minneapolis: Fortress, 2003), 52. Esler adds in a footnote: "Note the view of Sherwin-White ...: 'Though Greeks and Latins refer to the Jews as an ἔθνος or a nation or a genus, i.e. a folk or a tribe, there is not genuinely racial or racist connotation. The distinction is political, social and religious, national rather than genetic'" [Adrian Nicholas Sherwin-White, *Roman Society and Roman Law in the New Testament* (Oxford: Clarendon Press, 1967), 99] (Esler, *Conflict and Identity in Romans*, 374 n. 70).

37   For more on the influence of "race theory" in biblical scholarship see: Shawn Kelley, *Racializing Jesus: Race, Ideology and the Formation of Modern Biblical Scholarship* (London and New York: Routledge, 2002). David Miller also notes the complicity of K. G. Kuhn and Walter Gutbrod whose article on "'Ιουδαῖος, 'Ισραήλ,'Εβραῖος," in *TWNT* 3.356–394 (*TDNT* 3.356–391) "was influenced by the racially-charged ideology of Nazi Germany" (David Miller, "Ethnicity Comes of Age: An Overview of Twentieth-Century Terms for Ioudaios," *CBR* 10.2 [2012]: 297).

the social sciences there are primarily two methodological starting points of analysis: (1) the objectivist approach and (2) the subjectivist approach.[38] The objectivist approach methodologically privileges the macro-level of analysis in a "top-down" approach, in which society coerces individuals into objective role categories and, consequently, into particular social relations. Emile Durkheim, one of the fathers of both sociology and anthropology, encapsulates this view in the following statement:

> Society requires us to make ourselves its servants, forgetful of our own interests. And it subjects us to all sorts of restraints, privations, and sacrifices without which social life would be impossible. And so, at every instant, we must submit to rules of action and thought that we have neither made nor wanted and that sometimes are contrary to our inclinations and to our most basic instincts.[39]

In this way, individuals are societal automatons who are coerced into prescribed norms/values and roles.[40] Individuals are passive actors who are acted upon and coerced by society.

On the other hand, the subjectivist approach methodologically privileges the micro-level of analysis in a "bottom-up" fashion, which focuses on individual(s) as active agents who create and construct the social world they inhabit. The subjectivist premise is that the social categories that individuals think objectively exist in the social world are in fact the reification of ideas and concepts that individuals subjectively and collectively believe to exist. This concept, in fact, is the key aspect of another founder of sociology: Max Weber. Throughout his *Economy and Society*, as Peter Berger notes, Weber stresses that social theory must dehypostatize the social categories that "the man in the street ... [thinks of] as entities existing in and of themselves, detached

---

38   For example, the two major sections in the now classic *The Social Construction of Reality* are "Society as Objective Reality" and "Society as Subjective Reality" (Peter Berger and Thomas Luckmann, *The Social Construction of Reality: A Treatise in the Sociology of Knowledge* (Garden City, NY: Anchor Books, [1966] 1989).

39   Emile Durkheim, *The Elementary Forms of Religious Life* (trans. and introduction by Karen E. Fields; New York: The Free Press, 1995), 209.

40   Another example from Durkheim: "When I fulfill my obligations as brother, husband, or citizen, when I execute my contracts, I perform duties which are defined, externally to myself and my acts, in law and in custom. Even if they conform to my own sentiments and I feel their reality subjectively, such reality is still objective, for I did not create them; I merely inherited them through my education" (Emile Durkheim, *The Rules of Sociological Method* [Glencoe, IL: Free Press, 1950], 1).

ETHNICITY AND LABELING

from human activity and production."[41] One such social hypostatization that is reified is ethnic groups. In an often-cited passage concerning ethnic groups, Weber seeks to explain how and why this reification exists:

> The belief in group affinity, regardless of whether it has any objective foundation, can have important consequences especially for the formation of a political community. We shall call 'ethnic groups' [*ethnische Gruppen*] those human groups that entertain a subjective belief in their common descent because of similarities of physical type or of customs or both, or because of memories of colonization and migration; this belief must be important for the propagation of group formation; conversely, it does not matter whether or not an objective blood relationship exists. Ethnic membership (*Gemeinsamkeit*) differs from the kinship group precisely by being a presumed identity, not a group with concrete social action, like the latter. In our sense, ethnic membership does not constitute a group; it only facilitates group formation of any kind, particularly in the political sphere. On the other hand, it is primarily the political community, no matter how artificially organized, that inspires the belief in common ethnicity.[42]

In this passage, Weber emphasizes that an important factor for ethnic group formation is the constituents' subjective belief(s) about their group because the differences they think objectively exist (e.g. on Durkheim's macro-level) are in fact the reification and "objectivation"[43] of the group.

For Weber, then, common ancestry is not a necessary condition for an ethnic group's formation and propagation. Rather, it is the group's *belief* in their common ancestry that is necessary. Richard Jenkins, explaining Weber's position, notes that the belief in common ancestry (i.e. that these individuals do in fact belong to one another) "is likely to be a *consequence* of collective political action rather than its *cause*; people come to see themselves as *belonging together*—coming from a common background—as a consequence of *acting*

---

41   Berger, *The Sacred Canopy*, 8.

42   Weber, *Economy and Society*, 1.389. Weber defines "political community" as "a community whose social action is aimed at subordinating to orderly domination by the participants a territory' and the conduct of the masses within it, through readiness to resort to physical force" (so, for example, empires, nations, and states) (2.901).

43   "Objectivation" is the term Berger uses to describe the "reality that confronts its original producers as a facticity external to and other than themselves" (Berger, *The Sacred Canopy*, 4).

together."[44] Weber thus locates ethnicity in collective action and this act of collective externalization engenders the subjective belief that the individuals in an ethnic group belong together in communal solidarity.[45]

2.1 *Ethnicity and Ethnic Group Defined*

Weber's definition of ethnic groups will now be taken into consideration as we define the terms and ideas of ethnicity and ethnic group for this book. First, ethnicity is a framework for understanding the classification(s), affiliation(s), and/or cultural traits of ethnic groups. Ethnicity, then, is the explanans (that which does the explaining) while ethnic groups are the explanandum (that which is to be explained).[46] Second, ethnic groups are a collectivity of individuals who consider themselves, and are considered by others, to be one, and typically differentiate one another by their cultural traits. From an etic perspective, ethnic groups are not inherently kinship based (i.e. based on common descent). However, from the emic perspective, shared ancestry is often the *sine qua non* of their group. The "sense of imputed common ancestry and origins" among members of an ethnic group stems from their attachments (i.e. social ties and bonds) to one another and which is reinforced via shared/common cultural beliefs and practices.[47]

---

44 Richard Jenkins, *Rethinking Ethnicity: Second Edition* (Los Angeles: Sage Publications, 2008), 10; original emphasis. Durkheim, in fact, describes this phenomenon of communal solidarity via customs and rituals as "collective effervescence"; defined as "created by the fact of assembling and temporarily living a collective life that transports individuals beyond themselves ... they come to experience themselves as sharing one and the same essence" (Durkheim, *Elementary*, xli).

45 Concerning Max Weber's section on ethnic groups, Michael Banton adds: "There is no point zero at which group formation starts. Groups exist before an individual is born; he or she is socialized into beliefs about their nature"; therefore "beliefs strengthen structures; structures reinforce beliefs" ("Max Weber on 'ethnic communities': a critique," *Nations and Nationalism* 13:1 [2007]: 26).

46 In sociology, the terms "explanans" and "explanandum" are defined as "that which needs to be explained (explanandum) and that which contains the explanation (explanans)—either as a cause, antecedent events, or necessary condition" (John Scott and Gordon Marshall, eds. "explanandum and explanans," in *Oxford Dictionary of Sociology* [Oxford: Oxford University Press, 2009]), 205.

47 Anthony D. Smith, *The Ethnic Origins of Nations* (Oxford: Basil Blackwell, 1986), 24. Smith adds: "A myth of descent attempts to provide an answer to questions of similarity and belonging: Why are we all alike? Why are we one community? Because we came from the same place, at a definite period of time and are descended from the self-same ancestor, we necessarily belong to together and share the same feelings and tastes? This 'explanation' brings together the twin elements of the Greek term ἔθνος, the ideas of living together and being alike in culture, but adds the secondary meaning of the term, namely,

ETHNICITY AND LABELING

2.2 *Current Competing Ethnicity Theories*

In more recent studies of ethnicity, there are also two primary methodological approaches, which are, in many ways, counterparts to the objectivist/subjectivist approaches: (1) the primordialist and (2) the instrumentalist. The primordialist approach to understanding ethnic groups corresponds to the objectivist analysis in that it understands individuals as the result or product of their social world while the instrumentalist approach views individuals as actors who use the "givens" of their social world instrumentally (i.e. as a means to an end). The primordialist and instrumentalist approaches are typically thought of as antinomies but, as we will see, the two should not be sealed off from one another.

Clifford Geertz is credited as the main progenitor of the primordialist approach, particularly his 1963 article about the role of "primordial attachments" in the formation of new nation-states from recently decolonized colonies.[48] The term "attachment" in this discussion means the ties or bonds that hold groups, and even large-scale society, together. Geertz himself defines "primordial attachment" as an attachment "that stems from the 'givens'—or, more precisely, as culture is inevitably involved in such matters, the assumed 'givens'—of social existence."[49] Geertz's examples of these assumed givens of primordial attachments are assumed blood ties, race, language, region, religion, and custom.[50] These attachments are the assumed givens of immediate contiguity and so "are seen [by the individual] to have an ineffable, and at times overpowering, coerciveness in and of themselves."[51] Here again, we see the objectivist approach of Durkheim wherein individuals are coerced

---

      a sense of tribal belonging through common family ties, rather than any sense of genetic and blood ties."

48   Clifford Geertz, "The Integrative Revolution: Primordial Sentiments and Civil Politics in the New States," in *The Interpretation of Cultures: Selected Essays by Clifford Geertz* (New York: Basic Books, 1973), 258. However, it must absolutely be noted that this identification of Geertz as the progenitor of primordialism is a complete misnomer. Rather, Geertz presents an *emic* (insider or indigenous) perspective in which the primordial bonds of blood, language, custom, etc. are *seen* by the individuals to be natural givens of their existence. That is, Geertz is not asserting the objective reality of these bonds but rather that the people groups he studies assert their objective reality. The prime example of this misreading of Geertz is Jack Eller and Reed Coughlan, "The Poverty of Primordialism: the Demystification of Ethnic Attachments," in *Ethnic and Racial Studies* 16.2 (1993): 183–202. For a corrective of Eller and Coughlan see Steven Grosby, "The Verdict of History: the Inexpugnable Th of Primordiality a response to Eller and Coughlan," in *Ethnic and Racial Studies* 17.2 (1994): 164–171.

49   Geertz, "The Integrative Revolution," 259.

50   Geertz, "The Integrative Revolution," 261–263.

51   Geertz, "The Integrative Revolution," 259.

into social categories and obliged to adhere to rules of actions and thoughts. However, contra Durkheim (who was concerned to uncover the laws governing societies), Geertz espouses "that man is an animal suspended in webs of significance he himself has spun."[52] In this way, primordial attachments are the representations (sign-symbols or signifiers) of individual-actors' subjective disposition (the thing being signified) that are forged by their experience of the world and this is why they "seem" to appear as givens in their natural state of social existence.

The origin of the instrumentalist approach is Fredrick Barth, who gave "primary emphasis to the fact that ethnic groups are categories of ascription and identification by the actors themselves, and thus have the characteristic of organizing interaction between people."[53] In true subjectivist manner, the instrumentalist approach prioritizes the role of the individual's action and choices while reducing the importance and influence of social structures (such as social bonds or attachments). Consequently, the presumed givens of an ethnic group's cultural traits are not objective differences between groups. Rather, an ethnic group's cultural traits only exist to the extent that the individual actors themselves regard it as significant to *use* them for indicia of sameness or difference during social interactions.

Barth observes two particular uses of ethnic groups' cultural traits. The first use of cultural traits is the "overt signals or signs—the diacritical features that people look for and exhibit to show identity, often such features as dress, language, house-form, or general style of life."[54] The second use of cultural traits is the "basic value orientations: the standards of morality and excellence by which performance is judged ... implies a claim to be judged, and to judge oneself, by those standards that are relevant to that identity."[55] Therefore, for

---

52   Clifford Geertz, "Thick Description: Toward an Interpretive Theory of Culture," in *The Interpretation of Cultures: Selected Essays by Clifford Geertz* (New York: Basic Books, 1973), 5. Geertz adds: "The concept of culture I espouse ... is essentially a semiotic one.... I take culture to be those webs, and the analysis of it to be therefore not an experimental science in search of law but an interpretive one in search of meaning."

53   Barth, "Introduction," 10. (It should be noted that Barth was a student of Everett C. Hughes at the University of Chicago in what came to be called the Chicago School of Sociology; known particularly by its leading member Robert Ezra Park, who will be discussed later, who established the Chicago School of Sociology's niche in urban sociology and especially the study of race and immigration).

54   Barth, "Introduction," 14.

55   Barth, "Introduction," 14. Barth adds: "The identification of another person as a fellow member of an ethnic group implies a sharing of criteria for evaluation and judgment. It thus entails the assumption that the two are fundamentally 'playing the same game'" (Barth, "Introduction," 15).

ETHNICITY AND LABELING

Barth, individuals use their ethnic group's cultural traits instrumentally during interactions in order to indicate whether a person is a member of that ethnic group or a non-member or outsider.[56]

Perhaps the most well known example of using cultural features as indicia is found in the origin of the English word "Shibboleth," meaning a distinctive use of language or custom. In Judges 12:6, Jephthah used the word שִׁבֹּלֶת ("Shibboleth") as a password so as to distinguish his Gileadites from the Ephraimites who "could not pronounce it right" and said סִבֹּלֶת ("Sibboleth"). According to the narrative, Jephthah was able to utilize a linguistic indicium for the purpose of interaction; namely, to identify who was who during their civil war. Similarly, in the Gospel of Matthew, Peter is identified as a follower of Jesus because of his Galilean accent (Matt 26:73). These people were able to recognize and identify people on the basis of cultural (in this case, linguistic) indicia of their ethnic identity.

2.3 *"Dear Symbols" of Ethnic Identity*

With Weber, we understand that ethnic groups are based upon a "subjective belief" that they are a group and with Barth we add that cultural traits may be used as signals for or emblems of identity construction. Similar to both of these approaches is Everett C. Hughes who, in his study on ethnic relations, contends:

> To be sure, the living of a common life and the facing of common problems—conditions that lead to the growth of an ethnic group, nationality, and even race—will almost certainly encourage the development of a peculiar language, at least of peculiar turns of expression and meaning, and of some unique customs and institutions. Some of these peculiar traits will become the dear symbols of the group's distinction from others; their value for group solidarity may exceed their measurable degree of uniqueness. The essential fact remains, however, that the cultural traits are attributes of the group, and not that the group is the synthesis of its traits.[57]

Bearing this in mind, we can ask what some cultural traits are that "become the dear symbols of the group's distinction from others."[58] John Hutchinson and

---

56 In other words, an ethnic group's cultural traits are *not immutable*, but rather, as Jenkins explains, "ethnicity is situationally defined, produced and reproduced in the course of interactions" (*Rethinking Ethnicity*, 54).

57 Hughes, "The Study of Ethnic Relations," 92.

58 Hughes, "The Study of Ethnic Relations," 92.

Anthony Smith provide a list of six diagnostic characteristics around which ethnic identity is formed:

1) a common proper name to identify the group;
2) a myth of common ancestry;
3) a shared history or shared memories of a common past, including heroes, events and their commemoration;
4) a common culture, embracing such things as customs, language and religion;
5) a link with a homeland, either through actual occupation or by symbolic attachment to the ancestral land, as with diaspora peoples; and
6) a sense of communal solidarity.[59]

These features largely cohere with the ethnic features found in ancient sources and, for this reason, applying this ethnic theory anachronistically to the Gospel of John is warranted. Genesis 10:31, for example, after listing the descendants of Shem, states: "These are the descendants of Shem, by their families, their languages, their lands, and their nations." Herodotus 8.144.2 includes another example, in which the Athenians appeal to the Spartans in the face of the Persian invasion. The basis of the Athenian appeal "is the matter of Greekness—that is, our common blood, common tongue, common cult places and sacrifices, and similar customs; it would not be right for the Athenians to betray all this."[60] In this passage, Herodotus lists four of the six cultural features listed by Hutchinson and Smith above.[61] Clearly, then, we have a convergence of ethnographic and cultural traits when discussing both ancient and modern ethnic groups. Nonetheless, returning briefly to Hughes, it is important to emphasize:

> An ethnic group is not one because of the degree of measurable or observable difference from other groups: it is an ethnic group, on the contrary, because the people in it and the people out of it know that it is one; because the *ins* and the *outs* talk, feel, and act as if it were a separate group. This is possible only if there are ways of telling who belongs to the

---

59 John Hutchinson and Anthony Smith, eds., "Introduction," in *Ethnicity* (Oxford: Oxford University Press, 1996), 6–7.

60 Jonathan M. Hall, "Ethnicity," in *The Oxford Encyclopedia of Ancient Greece and Rome* (Oxford: Oxford University Press, 2010), 1.112. A. D. Godley translates this passage in LCL: "the kinship of all Greeks in blood and speech, and the shrines of gods and the sacrifices that we have in common, and the likeness of our way of life, to all which it would ill beseem Athenians to be false."

61 Namely, a common proper name to identify the groups; a claim to common ancestry; a common culture, embracing customs, language, and religions: and a sense of communal solidarity. See also Esler, *Conflict and Identity in Romans*, 56.

ETHNICITY AND LABELING   35

group and who does not, and if a person learns early, deeply, and usually irrevocably to what group he belongs.[62]

The process of learning group identification (what group they belong to) and social categorization (what group others belong to) is known as socialization to which we now turn our attention.

3 Socialization: Establishing Social Norms

As we just saw from Hughes, an ethnic group exists "because the *ins* and the *outs* talk, feel, and act as if it were a separate group."[63] It should not be over-looked that to "talk, feel, and act" occurs during interaction(s) with one an-other. Here we can see the influence of Robert Ezra Park—Hughes' advisor at the University of Chicago—who first addressed the idea of social interac-tions in 1926. Park, who had clearly read Durkheim, argued, "Everyone is always and everywhere, more or less consciously, playing a role ... It is in these roles that we know each other; it is in these roles that we know ourselves."[64] In this passage, Park does not deny Durkheim's premise that individuals are coerced into societal roles (e.g. husband, brother, citizen etc.). However, Park devel-ops Durkheim's premise further by drawing the macro-level of analysis down to the micro-level where individuals, whether consciously or not, are active participants within their identified roles as well as then using these roles to categorize others.

Although Durkheim is his starting point, individuals in Park's analysis are far from coerced societal automatons that are simply fulfilling their social con-tracts. Instead, on the micro-level, individuals are engaged actors who utilize the categories of prescribed roles as part of their everyday interactions. Park later began to observe the relationship between an individual's prescribed roles, which are pre-existent in a society at-large, and the use of these catego-ries for understanding their everyday interactions. In particular, Park notes:

---

62   Hughes, "The Study of Ethnic Relations," 91; original emphasis.
63   Hughes, "The Study of Ethnic Relations," 91; original emphasis.
64   Robert Ezra Park, "Behind Our Masks" in *Race and Culture* (ed. Everett C. Hughes; Glencoe, IL: Free Press, 1950), 249. Park's later influence is illustrated by the fact that this passage is specifically quoted in the highly influential *The Presentation of Self in Everyday Life* by Erving Goffman (London: The Penguin Press, 1959), 19. (Goffman was a student of Everett C. Hughes who was, in fact, a student of Park at the University of Chicago).

According to the rules of Aristotelian logic—which is the logic of common sense—we may be said to know a thing when we are able to classify it. We have not always recognized that the thinking of the ordinary man proceeds, if less consciously, still substantially, in the same manner.[65]

From this supposition, Park concludes, "Every individual we meet inevitably finds a place in our minds in some category *already* defined."[66]

However, where and how do individuals obtain the knowledge and existence of these identities/categories? The answer is the process of socialization in which individuals internalize the preexisting social structure from the macro-level into their subjective mental structures. Through this process of socialization, individuals are instilled with the categories in which to find their own identity as well as how to categorize the identity of others. Along these lines, Peter Berger describes an individual's social existence in terms of a three step dialectical process of externalization, objectivation, and internalization. Berger explains:

> Externalization is the ongoing outpouring of human being into the world, both in the physical and the mental activity of men. Objectivation is the attainment by the product of this activity (again both physical and mental) of a reality that confronts its original producers as a facticity external to and other than themselves. Internalization is the reappropriation by men of this same reality, transforming it once again from structures of the objective world into structures of the subjective consciousness.[67]

All of this is to say, we have been socialized into particular "structured structures" prescribed by the macro-level social structure of society; especially in our initial and formative socialization (i.e. childhood). This socialization, in turn, functions as the "structuring structures" or "habitus" which is an individual's internal disposition that "tends to reproduce those actions, perceptions, and attitudes consistent with the conditions under which it was produced."[68]

---

65   Robert Ezra Park, "The Bases for Race Prejudice," in *Race and Culture* (ed. Everett C. Hughes; Glencoe, IL: Free Press, 1950), 232.

66   Park, "The Bases for Race Prejudice," 232; added emphasis.

67   Berger, *The Sacred Canopy*, 4.

68   David Swartz, *Culture & Power: The Sociology of Pierre Bourdieu* (Chicago: The University of Chicago Press, 1997), 103. In other words, "categories of understanding are collective representations, and the underlying mental schemata are patterned after the social structure of the group" (Pierre Bourdieu and Loïc J. D. Wacquant, *An Invitation to Reflexive Sociology* [Chicago: University of Chicago Press, 1992], 12).

ETHNICITY AND LABELING

So the way in which individuals learn to identify themselves and categorize others is determined by the way in which they have been initially and formatively socialized. In this way, "habitus calls us to think of action as engendered and regulated by fundamental dispositions that are internalized primarily through early socialization."[69] However, given that an individual's habitus typically reproduces the conditions under which it was initially internalized, how can groups and society be at anything but at constant stasis?

3.1   Destabilizing Roles/Categories: the Stranger and the Heretic

Although the process of socialization remains fairly stable, glitches do occur. An important example is the introduction of the unknown, such as the stranger or heretic. As just noted, individuals are socialized into particular social contexts (via externalization, objectivation, and internalization) in which the world makes sense. This sensibility, however, is threatened by separation from it; that is, being subjected to another or different external-objective structure or surrounding than the ones internalized and objectified in the formative socialization (e.g. culture shock). One way this sensibility, or "givenness," of the social world is threatened is confrontation with "the stranger."

The concept of the stranger derives from the sociologist Georg Simmel. For Simmel, the stranger is not a person "who comes today and goes tomorrow, but rather the person who comes today and stays tomorrow."[70] In other words, the "stranger" refers to the role of an outsider within the group, not an outsider who remains extrinsic to the group. Given that this person is the product of a different socialization, the stranger's position within their new "group is determined, essentially, by the fact that he has not belonged to it from the beginning, that he imports qualities into it, which do not and cannot stem from the group itself."[71] For this reason, Simmel concludes, "the stranger, like the poor and like sundry 'inner enemies,' is an element of the group itself. His position as a full-fledged member involves both being outside it and confronting it."[72]

---

69   Swartz, *Culture & Power*, 104. For Bourdieu, "The word *disposition* seems particularly suited to express what is covered by the concept of habitus (defined as a system of dispositions). It expresses first the *result of an organizing action*, with a meaning close to that of words such as structure; it also designates a *way of being*, a *habitual state* (especially of the body) and, in particular, a *predisposition, tendency, propensity*, or *inclination*" (Pierre Bourdieu, *Outline of a Theory of Practice* [trans. Richard Nice; Cambridge: Cambridge University Press, 1977], 214; original emphasis).

70   Georg Simmel, *The Sociology of Georg Simmel* (trans. and ed. Kurt H. Wolff; New York: The Free Press, 1950), 402. In the Hebrew Bible this phenomena is known as "sojourning."

71   Simmel, *Sociology*, 402.

72   Simmel, *Sociology*, 402–403. In his *The Souls of Black Folk*, W. E. B. DuBois describes an experience similar to that of the "stranger," which he terms "Double Consciousness" and

Upon settling into their new group they are nonetheless "treated as alien by the autochthones who thus shield their way of life from irritation."[73]

In his *The Functions of Social Conflict*, Lewis Coser presents a series of propositions concerning the various functions of social conflict. Concerning in-group conflict, Coser proposes that "the closer the relationship, the more intense the conflict."[74] The reason for this is that the outsider can be ignored or dismissed for misunderstanding the norms and mores of the in-group; this, however, is not possible with the enemy from within such as the heretic. The reason for this is that the heretic is an "insidious danger ... [who] claims to uphold the group's values and interests only proposing different means to this end or variant interpretations of the official creed."[75] Coser turns to what is today called the sociology of heresy. In Coser's analyses, the role of the heretic is one who makes known a "choice" (in which he references the etymology of heresy from αἵρεσις). Coser asserts that the heretic, in making a choice known, "proposes alternatives where the group wants no alternative to exist."[76] Nonetheless, once alternative ideas are made known, the group is thrown into confusion because the givenness of former boundaries are now questioned and reconsidered. A key role of the heretic is therefore to challenge established institutions of orthodoxy by "bring[ing] into the conscious awareness of the contenders and of the community at large, norms and rules that were dormant before the particular conflict."[77] A brief consideration of texts from the Hebrew Bible demonstrates the relevance of this sociological research for understanding the world of ancient Judaism and early Christianity.

---

illustrates with African-American culture: "The Negro is a sort of seventh son, born with a veil, and gifted with second-sight in this American world, a world which yield him no true self-consciousness, but only let him see himself through the revelation of the other world. It is a peculiar sensation, this double-consciousness, this sense of always looking at one's self through the eyes of others" (W. E. B. DuBois, *The Souls of Black Folk* [Rockville, MD: Arc Manor, 2008], 12).

73   Jan A. Fuhse, "Embedding the Stranger: Ethnic Categories and Cultural Differences in Social Networks," *Journal of Intercultural Studies* 33.6 (2012): 652.

74   Lewis Coser, *The Functions of Social Conflict* (New York: The Free Press, 1956), 67.

75   Coser, *The Functions of Social Conflict*, 70.

76   Coser, *The Functions of Social Conflict*, 70.

77   Coser, *The Functions of Social Conflict*, 127. Berger explains this phenomenon as follows: "One may say, then, that the facticity of the social world or of any part of it suffices for self-legitimation as long as there is no challenge. When a challenge appears, in whatever form, the facticity can no longer be taken for granted. The validity of the social order must then be explicated, both for the sake of the challengers and of those meeting the challenge" (Berger, *The Sacred Canopy*, 31).

3.2 Destabilizing Role-Category: the Prophet in the Hebrew Bible

In the texts of the Hebrew Bible, there is a long history of understanding norms and deviancy concerning group identification (whether they are called "Hebrews," "Israelites," or "Judeans") and social categorization. By "norms" we mean social expectations or, as Barth commented earlier, the "basic value orientations: the standards of morality and excellence by which performance is judged."[78] As we previously discussed, a role of the stranger and the heretic is to question and confront the givens of their social group. Within each ethnic group, there are norms followed by its members (legitimated by an authoritative institution as well as the keepers of those institutions) and there are deviant ways to be a member (also determined by an authoritative institution and the keepers of those institutions e.g. kingship, the temple/priests, or tradition-scripture).

In the texts of the Hebrew Bible, the prophets often served the destabilizing role of the heretic. Thus, as Walter Brueggemann explains: *"The task of prophetic ministry is to nurture, nourish, and evoke a consciousness and perception alternative to the consciousness and perception of the dominant culture around us."*[79] The role of the prophet was to confront the status quo of the institutions (i.e. kings and priests) in order to bring into conscious awareness competing possibilities for group identification as the people of Israel. This role, however, was often met with hostility because the prophet, as the heretic, "proposes alternatives where the group [as administered by established institutions] wants no alternative to exist."[80]

The best example of this phenomenon in the texts of the Hebrew Bible is the prophet Jeremiah, who confronted kings, priests, and even other prophets (e.g. Jer 14:14–16) and suffered the threat of death for his pronouncements against the established institutions. According to Jer 26:8, after Jeremiah prophesied in the temple in Jerusalem, "the priests and the prophets and all the people laid hold of [Jeremiah], saying, 'You shall die!'" The stated reason for their attack on Jeremiah was "because he has prophesied against this city" (26:11). Jeremiah

---

78   Barth, "Introduction," 14.

79   Walter Brueggemann, *The Prophetic Imagination*, 2d ed. (Minneapolis: Fortress, 2001), 3; original emphasis. For Brueggemann, the central task of the Prophet in the texts of the Hebrew Bible was "to generate, evoke, and articulate alternative images of reality, images that counter what hegemonic power and knowledge have declared to be impossible. This counter imagination (sub version) of reality thereby deabsolutizes and destabilizes what 'the world' regards as given, and invites the hearers of the text to recharacterize what is given or taken as real" (Walter Brueggemann, *Theology of the Old Testament: Testimony, Dispute, Advocacy* [Minneapolis: Fortress, 1997], 68).

80   Coser, *The Functions of Social Conflict*, 70.

spoke out against the expectations of the institution—the temple priests and prophets—that "the God of Israel" would break "the yoke of the king of Babylon" (Jer 28:3) and return "all the exiles from Judah who went to Babylon" (Jer 28:4) in the near future (cf. Jer 6:13–14; 8:9–11). In Chapter 38, Jeremiah advocates surrender to the Babylonians (38:2) because "this city shall surely be handed over to the army of the king of Babylon and be taken" (Jer 38:3). For this message, Jeremiah is again threatened with death but ultimately imprisoned in a cistern (Jer 38:4–6). In the narrative, Jeremiah was deemed a deviant and suffered the consequences for violating the basic value orientations of the Judeans established by the institutions of the kingship and temple-priests.

Another example of a prophet who spoke against the establishment is Amos. Amos prophesied against priests in the sanctuaries of northern Israel and the king in the house of Jeroboam (Amos 7:9). Afterwards Amaziah, the priest of Bethel, confronts and identifies Amos as a prophet for hire from southern Judah (7:12). He then banned Amos from Bethel because "it is the king's sanctuary, and it is a temple of the kingdom" (7:13).

The prophetic ministry was not rejected by kings and priests only. In Isaiah 30:10, the people (עַם) tell the seers not to see and the prophets not to say what is right but "speak to us smooth things, prophesy illusions." Here in Isaiah 30:10, the people (עַם) are so thoroughly socialized into the givenness of established institutions that they "misrecognize" the rightness of the current state of affairs and are unable to conceive of another possible reality.[81] In the prophetic traditions, those explicating alternative possibilities against the established institutions and their keepers are thereby deemed deviants.

4   Labeling: Types and Functions

All of the previous discussion now comes to a head as we construct a model from which we may understand the labeling of Jesus by the Samaritan woman and "the Jews." We should, at the outset, distinguish between "interactional" and "institutional" labeling. Individuals use interactional labeling in their everyday dealings with people. Robert Ezra Park observes:

---

81   "Misrecognition" is a term Pierre Bourdieu uses for "the form of forgetting that social agents are caught up in and produced by. When we feel comfortable within our roles within the social world, they seem to us like second nature and we forget how we have actually been produced as particular kinds of people" (Jen Webb, Tony Schirato, and Geoff Danaher, *Understanding Bourdieu* [London: Sage Publications, 2002], *xiv*).

ETHNICITY AND LABELING

Every individual we meet inevitably finds a place in our minds in some category already defined. He is either a friend, a neighbor, a mere acquaintance, or, as we often say, a complete stranger. The category into which he falls determines, more or less automatically, and with very little conscious reflection on our part, the attitude we assume toward each individual figure in the changing scene of our daily experiences.[82]

As we have already noted, these categories are the result of socialization and the continual reproduction of our habitus (i.e. structurally structured dispositions). One aspect of the socialization process alluded to earlier is learning what group one belongs to and another aspect is learning to identify other people(s). Richard Jenkins distinguishes between "two ideal-typical modes of identification: *self-* or *group identification* (internally-oriented) and the *categorization* of others (externally-oriented)."[83] The relationship between these two modes of identification is "utterly interdependent" because "the process of defining 'us' demands that 'they' should be contrasted with 'us'."[84] The result of this defining process is that a group's "traits will become the dear symbols of the group's distinction from others."[85] An ethnic group's cultural traits are "the assumed 'givens' of social existence"[86] while at the same time ethnic identification/categorization are "situationally defined, produced and reproduced in the course of interactions."[87] Interactional labeling occurs in the course of our everyday dealings with one another as we assert our group identification and assess the social categorization of others—which then determines the attitude we assume toward them. Accordingly, ethnic labels structure interactions through the "misrecognized" social boundaries that are signaled by the ethnic group's cultural traits.

---

82   Park, "The Bases for Race Prejudice," 232.
83   Jenkins, "Categorization," 8; emphasis original.
84   Jenkins, "Categorization," 9. Jenkins elsewhere states: "The process of defining 'us' demands that 'they' should be split off from, or contrasted with, 'us'; group identification is likely to proceed, at least in part, through categorizing others, whether positively or negatively" (Jenkins, *Rethinking Ethnicity*, 59).
85   Hughes, "The Study of Ethnic Relations," 92.
86   Geertz, "The Integrative Revolution," 259.
87   Jenkins, *Rethinking Ethnicity*, 54. Situations, after all, are not always *sui generius* and, in fact, "situations are often standardized and identities easy to define" (Joel M. Charon, *Symbolic Interactionism: An Introduction, an Interpretation, an Integration 6th Edition* [Upper Saddle River, NJ: Prentice Hall, 1998], 163). Therefore, the standardization of situational interactions are a part of an individual's "assumed 'givens' of social existence" (Geertz, "The Integrative Revolution," 259).

Institutional labeling follows the initial development of labeling theory that emerged within the sociology of deviance. A leading proponent of labeling theory is Howard S. Becker who, in his now classic study *Outsiders*, asserts:

> *Social groups create deviance by making the rules whose infraction constitutes deviance*, and by applying those rules to particular people and labeling them as outsiders. From this point of view, deviance is *not* a quality of the act the person commits, but rather a consequence of the application by others of rules and sanctions to an "offender." The deviant is one to whom that label has successfully been applied; deviant behavior is behavior that people so label.[88]

Becker's premise is that deviancy arises more so from the observer's reactions to the offender than from the deviant act itself. Becker's example is clarifying here:

> Rules tend to be applied more to some persons than others. Studies of juvenile delinquency make the point clearly. Boys from middle-class areas do not get as far in the legal process when they are apprehended as do boys from slum areas. The middle-class boy is less likely, when picked up by the police, to be taken to the station; less likely when taken to the station to be booked; and it is extremely unlikely that he will be convicted and sentenced. This variation occurs even though the original infraction of the rule is the same in the two cases.[89]

Becker shrewdly shifts the focus from the act itself to the role of the labelers and particularly raises the issue "of whose definition of the situation *counts* (put crudely, power). Identification by others has *consequences*. It is the capacity to generate those consequences and make them stick which matters."[90] Consequently, institutional labeling is done by authorized representatives of the social group. (Institutions are defined as: "Patterns of social practice identifying persons that have become established over time as the 'way things are done.'"[91]) In Becker's example above, the police are the authorized

---

88 Becker, *Outsiders*, 9; original emphasis.

89 Becker, *Outsiders*, 12–13. In a succinct comment, Bruce Malina and Jerome Neyrey state: "deviance lies in the eyes of the beholders, not the metaphysical nature of things" (Malina and Neyrey, "Conflict in Luke-Acts," 100).

90 Richard Jenkins, *Social Identity* (3d Edition; London and New York: Routledge, 2008), 43.

91 Jenkins, *Rethinking Ethnicity*, 63. Jenkins's definition of institutions is analogous to Weber's ideal typology of "traditional authority," or "traditional domination," that rests

ETHNICITY AND LABELING   43

representatives of a legal institution who are tasked with the enforcement of laws accepted by its citizens. Therefore, when a person is institutionally labeled negatively (e.g. deviant, criminal, heretic, etc.), they are deemed to be out of place for not "uphold[ing] the group's values and interests."[92]

Concerning ethnic groups it is important to bear in mind that they, like all social groups, are not monolithic entities but are subject to divisions and factions.[93] In his *Introduction to Ethnic Conflict*, Milton Esman states: "Though we speak of ethnic communities—Palestinians and Israelis, Sinhalese and Tamils, Flemings and Walloons—as collectivities, what we really refer to are those who at a particular point in time represent and act in the name of their ethnic community."[94] When factions do arise, they present a choice, like the heretic who offers an alternative vision against the established institutions. Factions within ethnic groups "compete for influence and support among members of their community, for the right to control its institutions and collective resources, to speak authoritatively on its behalf, and to represent it to outsiders."[95] In response to a factionalist challenge, institutional agents may turn to labeling which "serves as a social distancing device, underscoring differences and thus dividing social categories into polarities."[96]

"on an established belief in the sanctity of immemorial traditions and the legitimacy of those exercising authority under them" (Weber, *Economy and Society*, 1.215). In *A Fiddler on the Roof*, Perchik illustrates a person who challenges the givenness of cultural practices. At the wedding of Motel and Tzeitel, Perchik wants to dance with a girl but the wedding guests exclaim "That's a sin!" Perchik challenges this cultural practice that it is a sin for a man to dance with a woman. Perchik appeals to the Rabbi, the authorized representative of the community, who hesitantly admits that "it's not exactly forbidden." Tevye, the father of the bride then exclaims, "Well, there you see! It's not forbidden! And it's no sin." The wedding party and guests slowly begin to dance with one another (Jerry Bock et al., *Fiddler on the Roof* [New York: Limelight Editions, 2002], 99).

92   Coser, *The Functions of Social Conflict*, 70.

93   Milton J. Esman, *An Introduction to Ethnic Conflict* (Cambridge: Polity Press, 2004), 45.

94   Esman, *Introduction to Ethnic Conflict*, 45.

95   Esman, *Introduction to Ethnic Conflict*, 47. K. C. Hanson and Douglas Oakman observe, "In the first century, the Jesus group can be classified as a faction, as can the various Pharisee groups" (*Palestine in the Time of Jesus: Social Structures and Social Conflicts* [Minneapolis: Fortress, 2009], 182).

96   Malina and Neyrey, *Calling Jesus Names*, 37. Elsewhere Malina and Neyrey state: "Labeling has as its purpose to cut off the rule-breaker from the rest of society by invoking the socially shared presumption that one thus labeled is essentially and qualitatively different from other members of society, an 'outsider,' 'a special kind of person'" ("Conflict in Luke-Acts," 108). "In the case of Jesus and his disciples," Malina and Neyrey comment, "the publicly approved deviance-processing agencies are the Jerusalem elites and the local roman government. These agencies register deviance by defining, classifying, and labeling types of behavior or conditions deemed to be 'out of bounds'" ("Conflict in Luke-Acts," 104).

As we begin to analyze the function of labeling in the following chapters, we must bear in mind the following questions from John Barclay:

[1] 'Whose definitions of deviance are operative here?' and
[2], as a supplementary question, 'Whose interests do these definitions serve?'[97]

The reader should bear these questions in mind especially for Chapter Four, where we will answer them regarding the function of the dual labeling of Jesus as a "Jew" and as a "Samaritan" in the Gospel of John.

5   Conclusion

This chapter started with the distinction between the emic (insider sources) perspective and the etic (outsider researcher) perspective. Although members of ethnic groups routinely consider common ancestry as *sine qua non*, the etic social-scientific model determines that "it does not matter whether or not an objective blood relationship exists"; what matters is that the members of the group "entertain a subjective belief in their common descent."[98] Ethnicity is the framework by which we analyze and understand the ethnic groups in our sources. This framework takes into consideration ethnic groups' cultural traits while acknowledging that these cultural traits are used instrumentally by agents during interactions with one another as signals and emblems of their ethnic group identification. We briefly mentioned six features of ethnic identification that maybe made salient for identity construction and negations among and between members of ethnic groups. These ethnic features become points of contentions among factions within the group who claim the same particular ethnic identity.

Individuals learn to perform the accepted modes of behavior in the process of socialization, wherein individuals are instilled with their sense of the world. Part of understanding this sense of the world includes reproducing or performing roles and behaviors expected of them through inculcation and the establishment of "norms." However, the social world is hardly one of stasis. Destabilization may result through contact with a stranger—someone who is the product of a different socialization and who therefore performs to a different set of roles and expectations. As such, the stranger is inclined to

---

97   Barclay, "Deviance and Apostasy," 116.
98   Weber, *Economy and Society*, 1.389.

confront and question the "givenness" of their new social world. Similarly, the heretic presents an alternative choice pertaining to the established norms of the group. Particularly by offering an alternative interpretation of their group's cultural traits and, thus, what it means to be a member of the group.

We then distinguished between two ideal-types of labeling. Interactional labeling occurs as a natural phenomenon as we interact and address one another. Which category a person falls into and what label we attach to them determines how we will interact with that person. Institutional labeling, on the other hand, is a resource for social control by established institutions—representing "the way things are done"—against social deviants (such as factionalist and heretics). Institutional labeling functions to distance the perpetrator from the group and may even attempt to ban them. The function of these two types of labeling will be explicated in the following chapter as we turn our attention to the parting of the ways between Samaritans and Judeans, paying particular attention to how the Judeans label the Samaritans and how the Samaritans label the Judeans.

CHAPTER 3

Naming Narratives

Samaritans were (and are) not only members of a religious sect. They are also a people.[1]

Open hostilities were rare enough to have been recorded.[2]

∴

Introduction

Building on Chapter Two, this chapter will survey the discourse about Judeo-Samaritan relationships leading up to John's Gospel in order to understand how each group understands itself and the other group. In line with the previous chapter's discussion, we understand that foundational to ethnic groups is a subjective belief (from those both inside and outside) that they are an ethnic group. An ethnic group's cultural features signal identity during interactions and "become the dear symbols of the group's distinction from others."[3] John Hutchinson and Anthony Smith provide a list of six diagnostic cultural traits:

> 1) a common proper name to identify the group; 2) a myth of common ancestry; 3) a shared history or shared memories of a common past, including heroes, events and their commemoration; 4) a common culture, embracing such things as customs, language and religion; 5) a link with a homeland, either through actual occupation or by symbolic attachment to the ancestral land, as with diaspora peoples; and 6) a sense of communal solidarity.[4]

Since cultural features are used to signal identity according to the situational context, this list of cultural traits is not determinative for ethnic group identity.

---

1   Nathan Schur, *History of the Samaritans* (Frankfurt: Peter Lang, 1989), 13.
2   Alan D. Crown, "Redating the Schism between the Judeans and the Samaritans," *JQR* 82.1 (1991): 27.
3   Hughes, "The Study of Ethnic Relations," 92.
4   Hutchinson and Smith, "Introduction," 6–7.

© KONINKLIJKE BRILL NV, LEIDEN, 2019 | DOI:10.1163/9789004390706_005

NAMING NARRATIVES

The list is purely a diagnostic tool.[5] Accordingly, in each of the following instances, we must pay particular attention to the situational context (i.e. interactions) where ethnic identifications "are not *made* but are *made salient* ... [by] authors, orators, politicians."[6] In this chapter we will find how the social roles of Coser's "heretics" and Simmel's "strangers" come into play concerning how each group categorizes one another. By way of reminder, the Simmelian stranger and the Coserian heretic are societal categories, or roles, for individuals or groups that disrupt the givenness of host group's institutions.[7] These two social categories are an etic, modern sociological model, from which to understand the subject of analysis instead of relying upon the subject's emic understandings.[8]

This chapter will start with the Judeans and how, depending on the situational context, the cultural features listed by Hutchinson and Smith (hereafter H-S) are used to identify their group identity. We will look at texts of the Hebrew Bible and the meaning of the term יְהוּדִי ("Judean") and particularly how it was used in the post-exilic works of Esther and Ezra-Nehemiah. In this chapter, we translate יְהוּדִי as "Judean" and use the term "Judean" exclusively to refer to the ethnic group who: 1) inhabits the region of Judea, 2) shares an attachment with Judea as their ancestral homeland, or 3) shares an attachment to the cultural features developed therein.[9] We will then discuss the Judeans' labels for categorizing the Samaritans in the texts of the Hebrew Bible, namely, whether the Judeans' labels categorize the Samaritans in terms of Simmelian strangers, Coserian heretics, or neither.

Then we will look at the Samaritan textual evidence for the labels they used for their group identity and the labels they used for their social categorization of the Judeans. The earliest sources for the Samaritans' self-identifying label are two Greek inscriptions from the island of Delos. Next is the Samaritan

---

5   Esler has previously utilized Hutchinson-Smith's list of six cultural features in his *Conflict and Identity in Romans,* where he rightly emphasizes that these cultural traits are "'diagnostic' for, not constitutive of, the identity and boundary in question" (Esler, *Conflict and Identity in Romans,* 43).

6   Barclay, "Constructing Judean Identity After 70 CE: A Study of Josephus' Against Apion," 101; emphasis original.

7   In Chapter Two institutions are defined as "patterns of social practice identifying persons that have become established over time as the 'way things are done'" (Jenkins, *Rethinking Ethnicity,* 63).

8   The emic analysis "describe *what* and *how* the natives thought but not *why* [while the etic analysis] seek[s] to explain *why* the natives thought and behaved so and not otherwise" (John H. Elliott, *What Is Social-Scientific Criticism,* 39; emphasis original).

9   The advantage of translating יְהוּדִי as "Judean" is its stress on geography, which properly reflects its original use to identify the inhabitants of a geographical region (Edwin Yamauchi, "יְהוּדִי," in *NIDOTTE* 2.415–417).

Pentateuch, which, although void of labels for either self-identifying or categorizing, discloses the Samaritans' self-understanding by emphasizing the centrality of Mount Gerizim. (Recall in Chapter Two that we distinguished between "identifying," dealing with the self or the group, and "categorizing" which concerns the other outside of the group.) As we will see, Mount Gerizim is the defining cultural feature for Samaritan identity, as well as for their categorizing of the Judeans.

The works of Josephus will serve as a bridge in the discussion between the texts of the Hebrew Bible and the writings in the New Testament, specifically the Synoptic Gospels and Acts, for evidence of the Judean labeling tradition for the Samaritans. Given that the identity of the Samaritans in Josephus is a major research project in itself, we must limit the discussion to the labels Josephus applies to the Samaritans and what these labels reveal about how he categorized them (whether in terms of Simmelian strangers or Coserian heretics).

Finally, we will turn our attention to the Synoptic Gospels and their use of the "Samaritan" label. There is one reference to the Samaritans in the Gospel of Matthew concerning the mission of the twelve (Matt 10:5). The Gospel of Luke contains three references to the Samaritans: a Samaritan village refuses to receive Jesus (9:51–56), the parable of the Good Samaritan (Luke 10:25–37), and Jesus cleanses ten lepers (Luke 17:11–19). We will see that the Synoptic Gospels agree with Josephus: the Samaritans are Simmelian strangers in that they are foreigners (ἀλλογενεῖς Luke 17:18). Finally, Luke also uses the label "Samaritan" in Acts of the Apostles with Philip's evangelism to Samaria (Acts 8:5–25). Of particular note in Acts 8 is Philip's mission to "the people of Samaria" (8:9) and the person of Simon Magus. From these ancient sources, our conclusion for this chapter will be that for the Samaritans, those labeled "Judeans" are Coserian "heretics" but, for the Judeans those labeled "Samaritans" are Simmelian "strangers." In other words, the Samaritans viewed Judeans as disruptors from the inside and the Judeans viewed Samaritans as disruptors from the outside.

1 The Judeans' Narratives: the Label "Judean" in the Texts of the Hebrew Bible

In the Hebrew Bible, the Judeans are one of the tribes of Israel who settled in the promised land at the time of Joshua, and whose centralized cult at Shiloh (cf. Josh 18:1) was moved to Jebus/Jerusalem by David (cf. 2 Sam 6:12–16). The label "Judean" (יְהוּדִי is the gentilic form of Judah יְהוּדָה) means "belonging to

Judah, *Judean, Jewish*" (e.g. Zech 8:23; Esth 2:5; Jer 43:9; 1 Chr 4:18).[10] According to Edwin Yamauchi, the initial meaning for the label "Judean" (יְהוּדִי) "does not mean a descendant from the tribe of Judah, but originally an inhabitant of the area of Judah."[11] The geographic connotation is attested before the exile by the first canonical use of the gentilic form יְהוּדִי in 2 Kgs 16:6 and then in 25:25. We should be quick to note, however, that the label "Judean" is *not* limited to the actual residents in Judah. Examples of this include the Judeans whom Jeremiah mentions living in Moab, Ammon, and Edom (Jer 40:11–12), those living in Egypt (Jer 43:9; 44:1), and those in Babylon (Jer 52:28, 30).[12] In this context, Joseph Blenkinsopp suggests that the label "Judean" belongs "to the same category as Edomites, Syrians, and similar labels, which identify individuals politically and, given the existence of national patron deities, also to some extent religiously."[13]

From the start, we *must* recognize the false dichotomy between "Judean" as designating either "geographic," "ethnic" (that is, "ethnic" as it is primordially understood in terms of ancestral descent), or "religious." As we saw in Chapter Two, ethnic identity involves a myth of common ancestry (H-S#2), an attachment to a geographic homeland (H-S#5), as well as cultural components (H-S#4; such as religion), so that these three aspects are not completely separable in regards to ethnic identity. Rather, one or more of these cultural features are presented situationally during interactions. A prime example of Judean ethnic identity, without the typical religious attributes among the texts of the Hebrew Bible, is the Book of Esther. The following brief discussion of Esther will illustrate that applying the modern theories to the ancient texts is justified.

The book of Esther (composed c. 400–300 BCE[14]) is a "diaspora novella"[15] depicting Judean life outside of the land of Judah and uses the label "Judean" (יְהוּדִי) fifty-eight times. In particular, the label "Judean" is applied to the protagonist Mordecai, the son of Kish, a Benjaminite (Esth 2:5). The antagonist Haman is introduced when Mordecai refuses to "bow down or do obeisance"

---

10 "יְהוּדִי," *HALOT* 2.394; original emphasis.

11 Edwin Yamauchi, "יְהוּדִי," *NIDOTTE* 2.415.

12 This is keenly observed by Joseph Blenkinsopp, *Judaism The First Phase: The Place of Ezra and Nehemiah in the Origins of Judaism* (Grand Rapids: Eerdmans, 2009), 21. Blenkinsopp further adds: "So understood, Judeans were naturally not limited to those actually resident in Judah, no more than Englishmen resident in a foreign country cease to be English."

13 Blenkinsopp, *Judaism The First Phase*, 21.

14 Adele Berlin, *Esther: the Traditional Hebrew Text with the New JPS Translation; Commentary* (Philadelphia: Jewish Publication Society, 2001), xli.

15 For the term "diaspora novellas" see Daniel L. Smith, *The Religion of the Landless: The Social Context of the Babylonian Exile* (Bloomington, IN: Meyer-Stone Books, 1989), 153–61.

before Haman (Esth 3:5).[16] Haman earned the label "the enemy of the Jews" (Esth 3:10; 8:1; 9:10; 9:24) because he "plotted to destroy all the Jews" (Esth 3:6; cf. 3:13; 4:7; 8:5). However, through the intervention of Esther (Esth 7:3–6), the Judeans were spared and, in an ironic twist, Haman was hanged "on the gallows that he had prepared for Mordecai" (Esth 7:10). The novella's ironic twist climaxes in Esth 8:17 when the people who were once doomed to genocide are now to be feared.

Of particular interest is the fascinating statement in Esth 8:17b that highlights Judean group identity in the eastern Persian diaspora: "Furthermore, many of the peoples of the country professed to be Jews (מִתְיַהֲדִים), because the fear of the Jews had fallen upon them." The participle "professed to be Jews" (מִתְיַהֲדִים) has left translators and interpreters vexed as early as the Septuagint, Old Latin, and Targumim because it is a Hitpael participle, denominative from יְהוּדִי, and a *hapax legomenon*.

According to BHQ, "both Targums substitute [מִתְיַהֲדִים] with the more general 'converting' (becoming a proselyte [מתגיירין])" and the Septuagint adds "the verb 'circumcise' to the literal 'Judaize' [περιετέμοντο καὶ ἰουδάιζον]."[17] These renderings imply that Esth 8:17b is a record of a mass conversion to Judaism. Yet, according to Adele Berlin, "Religious conversion seems far-fetched in a book in which any mention of religious practice is studiously avoided. The emphasis here is not on religion, but on ethnic identification."[18] Although Berlin is certainly correct to note the emphasis is on ethnic identification, we must be careful not to separate "religion" from "ethnicity," given that religion is an indicium of ethnic identity (H-S#4). As Anne-Mareike Wetter states: "To argue that ethnic identity is what is left when we take away religion is to oversimplify the intricate nature of group identity."[19]

How is Judean ethnic identity presented in the Book of Esther? Firstly, the label "Judean" is used as a common name to identify the group (H-S#1). (To be

---

16   The text does not state the reason why Mordecai did not bow down to Haman, but Sidnie White Crawford suggests: "The fact that Haman is an Agagite is probably the best explanation; Mordecai will not bow to his hereditary enemy" (Crawford, "Esther," *Eerdmans Commentary on the Bible* [ed. James D. G. Dunn and John W. Rogerson; Grand Rapids: Eerdmans, 2003], 331).

17   *Biblia Hebraica Quinta, General Intro & Megilloth* (Van Der Schenker et al.; Peabody, MA: Hendrickson, 2004), 147*. Carey M. Moore observes: "While the LXX and the OL clarified *their* understanding of the word by adding 'they were circumcised,' they do not necessarily interpret it correctly" (*Esther* [AB 7B; Garden City, NY: Doubleday, 1971], 82; original emphasis).

18   Berlin, *Esther*, 80.

19   Anne-Mareike Wetter, "How Jewish is Esther? Or: How is Esther Jewish? Tracing Ethnic and Religious Identity in a Diaspora Narrative," *ZAW* 123 (2011): 597.

NAMING NARRATIVES

sure, this label implies a myth of common ancestry [H-S#2] from the epony-mous patriarch Judah, as well as link to a homeland [H-S#5] that bears Judah's name.) Secondly, in view of the outside threat to the Judean community, the book of Esther presents Judean ethnic identity in terms of "communal solidar-ity" (H-S#6).

For the books of Ezra and Nehemiah, however, their concern is an inside threat to the Judean community. In the Persian Yehud, according to Ezra-Nehemiah, the issue is not whether you identify yourself as a "Judean" but whether the Judean authorities accept your identification. As we will see, the Judean authorities distinguished between the two groups of "Judeans." There are the "Judeans" who are inhabitants of former Judah and there are the "Judeans" who are the descendants from a "golah-Judean" family who also adhere to the cultural practices developed in exile. The "*golah*-Judeans" are the Babylonian Judean exiles whom Ezra-Nehemiah label "*golah*" גּוֹלָה, "the deported, *exiles*"[20] (Ezra 1:11; 2:1; 6:21; Neh 7:6). For both Ezra and Nehemiah it is important to distinguish the *golah*-Judeans from the regional inhabitants of Judah/Yehud by providing a census of the *golah*-Judeans who "returned to Jerusalem and Judah, all to their own towns" (Ezra 2:1//Neh 7:6). The census is divided by the laity according to family (Ezra 2:3–20//Neh 7:8–25) and town (Ezra 2:21–35//Neh 7:26–38), by priests and temple personnel (Ezra 2:36–58// Neh 7:39–60), and then by those who could not prove whether they belonged to Israel by their families or descent (Ezra 2:59–63//Neh 7:61–65). The reason for recording this census of *golah*-Judeans is to solidify their identification as "the number of the Israelite people" (Ezra 2:2//Neh 7:7).

This census actually represents a shift in ethnic identification from the monarchic period to the post-exilic period. During the monarchic period, the label "Judean" was simply an ascriptive term for the people of Judah. In tradi-tional Yahwism of the land, also called "First Temple (National) Yahwism,"[21] the inhabitants of Judah were by birth and parentage Judeans who "would also be a devotee of Yahweh since Yahweh was from of old the national deity of Judah, resident in the Jerusalem temple, which was a national, dynastic shrine."[22] To be sure, the pre-exilic use of the label "Judean" is also found in Ezra-Nehemiah for members of an ethnic group whether they reside inside or outside of the province of Yehud.

---

20   "גּוֹלָה," *HALOT* 1:183

21   For the term "First Temple Yahwism" see Diana V. Edelman, "Introduction" in *The Triumph of Elohim: From Yahwisms to Judaisms* (ed. Diana V. Edelman: Grand Rapids: Eerdmans, 1996), 23–24.

22   Blenkinsopp, *Judaism The First Phase*, 32.

52   CHAPTER 3

This use of the label "Judean," however, appears only in the Aramaic sections in Ezra (Ezra 4:8–6:18) and is used in, or in association with, the citation of Persian letter documents. In the Aramaic section of Ezra, then, the label "Judean" is used for "one of many ethnic groups forming a distinct unit in the Persian Empire (Ezra 4:12, 23; 5:1, 5, 14; 6:7, 8, 14)."[23] The label "Judean" for members of an ethnic group is also used in Nehemiah whether they are inhabitants of the province (Neh 3:33–34 [4:1–2]; 13:23) or outside the province (Neh 4:6 [12]; 5:8). In Nehemiah, however, there is an additional use for the label "Judean" where it is also used to designate the social upper-class in the province of the Yehud (Neh 2:16, 5:17).[24] The label "Judean" is used to identify an ethnic group within the Persian Empire.

However, when the *golah*-Judeans returned to the land of Judah, ethnic identification shifted in that membership in an ethnic group was no longer synonymous with membership in "Israel" (unlike First Temple Yahwism). As Bob Becking observes, "The shift from the monarchic period to the Persian period provoked a change in self-understanding. 'Being Israelite' had changed from 'belonging to the Judean nation' to 'being part of a Jewish family' or 'being member of a guild, be it in Yehud or in the Diaspora.'"[25] This shift is particularly evident in Ezra-Nehemiah corpus which exclusively reserves the label "Israelite" for the *golah* group of returned Babylonian exiles and their families.

In his article on "יִשְׂרָאֵל" in *TDOT*, H.-J. Zobel succinctly observes Ezra-Nehemiah's identification of "Israelites" with the *golah* group:

> In the books of Ezra and Nehemiah, we observe the following: The exiles returning to Judah are called "Israel" (Ezra 2:59; Neh 7:61) and also are "Israel" (Ezra 6:17; 7:10; Neh 10:34[33]; 11:3; 13:3) or "all Israel" (Neh 7:73; 12:47), which hears the law of its God and must live by it. It is therefore evident that Yahweh should be called "God of Israel" (Ezra 1:3; 4:1, 3; 6:21; 7:6; 9:15; also 3:2; 5:1; 6:22; 7:15; 8:35; 9:4). "Israel" thus denotes membership in both the people and the cultic community. The two are identical,

---

23   Joseph Blenkinsopp, "Judeans, Jews, Children of Abraham," in *Judah and the Judeans in the Achaemenid Period: Negotiating Identity in an International Context* (ed. Gary N. Knoppers and Manfred Oeming; Wionna Lake, IN: Eisenbrauns, 2011), 467.

24   Joseph Blenkinsopp, *Ezra-Nehemiah: A Commentary* (OTL: Philadelphia: Westminster, 1988), 223–224 and 256.

25   Bob Becking, "Continuity and Discontinuity after the Exile: Some Introductory Remarks," 3. Although Becking and others use the term "nation," the term "ethnic group" is preferable in instances involving the ancient world so as to not impute notions of the modern "nation-state" into an ancient context.

NAMING NARRATIVES

so that aliens are "separated from Israel" (Neh 13:3). Others cannot even claim to belong to Israel, for this cultic community is all Israel.[26]

What Zobel here calls "the cultic community," Daniel Boyarin and others call "a confessional community."[27] This confessional community originated among "the exiles in Babylonia [who] had come to the conclusion that they had to build barriers of custom and religious practices in order to maintain their identity in a foreign country."[28] Ezra-Nehemiah brought the confessional community with them to Jerusalem/Judah so that "the in-group out-group mentality which originated in the diaspora situation assumed the form of a distinctive, segregated *golah* group *within* a Jewish ethnos itself."[29] In Ezra-Nehemiah, the result of this segregated *golah* confessional community is

> a three-tier model with an 'inner-group' with which the returning exiles identified credally and nationally, an 'in-group' (the 'people of the land') with which they were identified nationally but not credally (because their understanding of biblical monotheism was more rigid and extreme), and an 'out-group' with which they did not identify credally or nationally.[30]

According to the evidence from Ezra-Nehemiah, the label "Israelite(s)" is the inner-group consisting of the *golah*—the group returned from the Babylonian exile. Since the label "Judean" designates a member of an ethnic group in general across the Persian provinces, the "Judeans" are the in-group consisting of the "people of the land" *plus* the inner-group. Finally, there is the out-group designating the gentiles/*goyim*.[31] This model of Judean society also sets the

---

26   H.-J. Zobel, "יִשְׂרָאֵל," *TDOT* 6.418.

27   Boyarin, "The Ioudaioi in John and the Prehistory of 'Judaism'," 224. In his article, Boyarin follows Shemaryahu Talmon, "The Emergence of Jewish Sectarianism in the Early Second Temple Period," in *King, Cult and Calendar in Ancient Israel* [ed. Shemaryahu Talmon; Jerusalem: Magnes, 1986), 165–201; Talmon was following Max Weber, *Ancient Judaism* (Glencoe, IL: Free Press, 1952), 385–404.

28   Schur, *History of the Samaritans*, 30.

29   Blenkinsopp, *Judaism The First Phase*, 198; emphasis added. Talmon explains that "the traditional endogamy principle, which precludes intermarriage with ethnic foreigners, is now expanded to apply also to non-Judean Israelites whose version of the biblical faith was at variance with the returnees' understanding of biblical monotheism" (Talmon, "The Emergence of Jewish Sectarianism," 599).

30   Ashton, *Understanding the Fourth Gospel* (2d. ed), 72; also see: Boyarin, "The *Ioudaioi* in John," 225; Talmon, "The Emergence of Jewish Sectarianism," 599.

31   Accordingly, there was an inner-group of Judeans labeled "Israelites"; an in-group of Yahwists—"the people of the land"—"Judeans"; and an out-group of non-Yahwists

54 CHAPTER 3

stage for the clash between the inner-group of *golah*-Judeans and the in-group of local inhabitants called "the people of the land" in Ezra 4 and 9–10.

The interaction in Ezra 4:1–5 exemplifies the three-tier model. We should note here that the identification of the "people of the land" (עַם הָאָרֶץ; Ezra 4:4) and "the adversaries of Judah and Benjamin" (Ezra 4:1) as "Samaritans" is not in the text of Ezra even though, as we will see in section 3.0, it is found in Josephus (*Ant.* 11.19–30, 84–8). Instead, the people Ezra labels as "adversaries" (4:1) and "people of the land" (4:4) identify themselves as Yahwists who were brought into the region by King Esar-haddon (681–669 BCE) of Assyria (Ezra 4:2).[32] There are two important things to note. The first is that the group in Ezra 4:2, who identify with the Esarhaddon importation[33] which occurred after the fall of the Northern Kingdom of Israel in 722 BCE, cannot be directly identified with the people or the events in 2 Kgs 17:24–34 under Shalmaneser (727–722 BCE) or his usurper Sargon II (722–705 BCE).[34] This is significant because the account of the fall of Samaria in 2 Kgs 17 is the starting point for the "Samaritans" in Josephus. The second is the evidence that Yahwism continued in the former northern kingdom of Israel after 722 BCE. Yahwism in Samaria/Israel is evidenced in the reforms of the Judean kings Hezekiah and Josiah (2 Chr 30:1; 31:1; 34:6, 33) and in the prophetic literature describing a future reunited Israel (Isa 11:12–13; Jer 23:5–6; 31:17–20; 41:5; Ezek 37:15–28; Zech 8:13; 9:13; 10:6–12).[35] Consequently, "the people of the land" asked to share in the building of the Temple in Jerusalem because they too were Yahwists. Yet, the inner-group of the *golah*-Judeans (consisting of Zerubbabel the governor of Yehud, Jeshua the high priest, and the rest of the heads of families in Israel) rejected "the people of the land" having any part of the temple building (Ezra 4:3) because, even though "the people of the land" were Yahwists residing in the

---

gentiles. Also see Boyarin, "The *Ioudaioi* in John," 227–228; Talmon, "The Emergence of Jewish Sectarianism," 599.

32 The "people of the land" in the short section of Ezra 4:1–6 "presumably refers to 'the adversaries of Judah and Benjamin' who originally offered to participate in the building operations but became 'adversaries' when their offer was rejected (4:1–3)" (Shemaryahu Talmon, "Ezra and Nehemiah," in *The Literary Guide to the Bible* [ed. Robert Alter and Frank Kermode; Cambridge: Harvard University Press, 1987], 360).

33 For Esarhadon's Syrian campaign in 677/6 BCE see *ANET*, 290.

34 According to John A. Brinkman, "Shalmaneser was on the throne when Samaria fell to the Assyrians in 722 after a three-year siege (Babylonian Chronicle, I.28; 2 Kings 17.5–6, 18.9–10); but the subsequent deportation of the Israelites probably took place in 720 under his successor, Sargon II (722–705 BCE)" (John A. Brinkman, "Shalmaneser V," in *Oxford Companion to the Bible* [Oxford: Oxford University Press, 1993], 692).

35 Reinhard Pummer, "Samaritanism," *The Eerdmans Dictionary of Early Judaism* (ed. John J. Collins and Daniel C. Harlow; Grand Rapids: Eerdmans, 2010), 1187.

region, they did not share ancestrally with "the number of the Israelite people" (Ezra 2:2//Neh 7:7). The *golah*-Judeans' rejection of residential "people of the land" is significant because it indicates that Yahwism and indigeneity were no longer criteria for Israelite identity.[36]

The boundary created between "the people of the land" and the *golah*/Israelite community is further exemplified in Ezra 9–10 in the so-called mixed-marriage episode. The issue in Ezra 9–10 is that "the people of Israel" (i.e. the returned Judean exiles) "have not separated themselves" (Ezra 9:1) from "the peoples of the lands," but rather have intermarried with them. Ezra 9:1 categorizes "the peoples of the lands" as "the Canaanites, the Hittites, the Perizzites, the Jebusites, the Ammonites, the Moabites, the Egyptians, and the Amorites." Given that only the Ammonites, the Moabites, and the Egyptians still existed in the post-exilic period, the people groups listed are symbolic representations of Israel's archetypical enemies.[37] Accordingly, the ethnic labels in Ezra 9 invoke the "dormant ethnic boundaries between 'ancient' Israel and her archaic enemies ... to symbolically dichotomize between the *Golah* and the 'people of the land'."[38] As a result of categorizing the "people of the land" with Israel's archetypical enemies, Ezra states the entire assembly agreed to "separate themselves from the people of the land and from the foreign wives" (Ezra 10:11, 12).[39]

The episodes in Ezra 4:1–5 and Ezra 9–10 represent a transformation in Judean/Israelite identity in Judah/Yehud. Here we can note the contrast between "First Temple Yahwism" and the *golah*-Judeans' Yahwism. In "First Temple Yahwism," outsiders can become insiders. "A mixed crowd" (Exod 12:38) joined the Israelites' exodus from Egypt and the Israelites established rules for resident aliens' entry into Israel (Exod 12:48–49). Two other examples are Rahab and Ruth, who both gained entry into Israel (Josh 6:22–23; Ruth 4:10–11). In contrast, Ezra-Nehemiah promotes an exclusionary tiered identity in which neither indigeneity in the land or Yahwism (Ezra 4:2; 9–10) are sufficient criteria for Israelite identity. In the post-exilic era, a "Judean"

---

36   Gary N. Knoppers, "Ethnicity, Genealogy, Geography, and Change: The Judean Communities of Babylon and Jerusalem in the Story of Ezra" in *Community Identity in Judean Historiography: Biblical and Comparative Perspectives* (ed. Gary N. Knoppers and Kenneth A. Ristau: Winona Lake, IN: Eisenbrauns, 2009), 163.

37   Katherine Southwood, *Ethnicity and the Mixed Marriage Crisis in Ezra 9–10: An Anthropological Approach* (Oxford: Oxford University Press, 2012), 140–141. Also see Blenkinsopp, *Ezra-Nehemiah*, 175.

38   Southwood, *Ethnicity and the Mixed Marriage Crisis in Ezra 9–10*, 142.

39   Southwood rightly notes that "if any group of people qualify for the ascription 'foreign' it is not those who are currently living in post-exilic Yehud, but those who have been outside the land, that is, the 'children of the exile'" (Southwood, *Ethnicity and the Mixed Marriage Crisis in Ezra 9–10*, 142 n. 32).

may or may not reside in the Yehud or any former territory of Judah. Neither residency nor participation in the cultural activities of the Judeans are valid criteria according to the inner-*golah* group but only proper (that is, verifiable) ancestry. As we will see in the following section, the Samaritans cannot offer their lineage because, according to the Deuteronomist historian of 2 Kings, they were all exiled to Assyria.

1.1   *The Judean Label for "Samaritans" in the Texts of the Hebrew Bible*

The only occurrence of the label שֹׁמְרֹנִי "Samaritan" in the Hebrew Bible is 2 Kgs 17:29. Although this chapter plays a central role in later Judean anti-Samaritan polemics in Josephus and rabbinic literature, it is questionable whether the "Samaritans" named in 2 Kgs 17 are the same people group of "Samaritans" found in later Judean literature. Certainly, it is an invalid premise to start with Josephus's identification that the two groups were in fact identical and then read it back into the account of 2 Kgs 17. The text of 2 Kgs 17 is an account of the fall of the northern kingdom of Israel in 722 BCE to the Assyrian King Shalmaneser (2 Kgs 17:3).[40] Then, according to 2 Kgs 17:5–6, after besieging Samaria for three years, the Assyrian king "carried the Israelites away to Assyria. He placed them in Halah, on the Habor, the river of Gozan, and in the cities of the Medes." Then a Deuteronomic sermon (2 Kgs 17:7–23) occurs in order to explain not only why this event took place but also to offer a warning for the southern audience in Judah.[41]

The Deuteronomic Historian of 2 Kgs 17 names five people groups ("people from Babylon, Cuthah, Avva, Hamath, and Sepharvaim") who replaced "the people of Israel" (2 Kgs 27:24). The following sequence of events in particular formed the basis for the later Judean polemic against the later Samaritans. The readers are told that, since the new inhabitants "in the cities of Samaria do not know the law of the god of the land," the god of the land sent lions to kill them (17:26). In response to this crisis, the king of Assyria ordered one of the exiled priests to go back to teach the new inhabitants "the law of the god of the land" (17:27). So a priest returned to Bethel and "taught them how they should worship the LORD" (17:28). The lion attacks ceased because "they worshiped the LORD but also served their own gods, after the manner of the nations from among whom they had been carried away" (2 Kgs 17:33). This verse clearly indicates some kind of syncretism, but it is not clear how extensive it

---

40   For a detailed study see Bob Becking, *The Fall of Samaria: An Historical and Archaeological Study* (Leiden: Brill, 1992).

41   R. J. Coggins, *Samaritans and Jews: The Origins of Samaritanism Reconsidered* (Atlanta: John Knox, 1975), 14.

NAMING NARRATIVES

was. T. Raymond Hobbs observes that "the impression given here is that it was characteristic of the whole northern territory. This was an impression which remained embedded in Jewish memory."[42] For example, in the rabbinic tradition the Samaritans are labeled "lion converts" (*b. Qidd.* 75a) to reflect their ulterior motive for worshiping Yahweh. In later Jewish tradition, the inextricable focal point of 2 Kgs 17 is the syncretistic worship among the new inhabitants of Samaria who "to this day they continue to practice their former customs" (2 Kgs 17:34). *What this later interpretive tradition overlooks is the fact that the Deuteronomist actually does not label the new inhabitants "Samaritans."*

To be certain, the text of 2 Kgs 17 does *not* label the new inhabitants "Samaritans" because the new inhabitants worship their gods at "the shrines of the high places that the people of Samaria *had made*" (17:29). Rainer Albertz succinctly states:

> The wording of the polemical description in 2 Kings 17:24–41 of conditions in what was formerly the northern kingdom after its conquest by the Assyrians in 722 does not refer to the Samaritans. The term השמר־ נים, 'the Samarians' (v. 29), to which an appeal is frequently made, denotes the earlier Israelite population which in the view of Deuteronomist (vv. 6, 23) was deported in its entirety to Assyria.[43]

Since the text of 2 Kgs 17 is clear who the Samaritans (השמרנים) were, namely those deported, the Samaritans in this text of the Hebrew Bible were Israelites who inhabited the former northern kingdom of Israel. In fact, as we will see in the following section, the Samaritans to this day identify themselves as "Israelites."

---

42 T. Raymond Hobbs, 2 *Kings* (WBC 13; Waco, TX: Word Books, 1985), 238.

43 Rainer Albertz, *A History of Israelite Religion in the Old Testament Period* (Louisville: Westminster John Knox, 1994), 2.524. Historically, however, we know the entire northern population of Israel *was not* deported by the Assyrians. In an inscription, Sargon II (c.721–705 BCE) boasts: "I besieged and conquered Samaria (*Sa-me-ri-na*), led away as booty 27,290 inhabitants from it" ("The Fall of Samaria," translated by F. H. Weissback [*ANET*, 284–285]). According to Paul Stenhouse, "Estimates of the population of Samaria in the eighth century BCE range from 600,000 to 140,000. Extrapolating from known sites to numbers killed during the fighting to the numbers deported by Sargon, the reduction in population could be as high as 14%—leaving 86% of the pre-exilic population still in place" ("The Chronicle of Abu 'l-Fath and Samaritans Origins: 2 Kings, 2 Chronicles and Ezra-Nehemiah Viewed Through the Prism of Samaritan Tradition," in *The Samaritans and the Bible: Historical and Literary Interactions Between Biblical and Samaritan Traditions* [ed. Jörg Frey, Ursula Schattner-Rieser, and Konrad Schmid; Berlin: de Gruyter, 2012], 308).

CHAPTER 3

2 The Samaritan's Narrative: the Label "Israelite" for Self- or Group Identification

The first piece of hard evidence for the Samaritans' tradition of labeling themselves "Israelites" are two Greek inscriptions from the Greek island of Delos. The Samaritan Pentateuch (c. second–first century BCE[44]) supports the Samaritans self-identifying label but, more importantly, discloses the centrality of Mount Gerizim for Samaritan-Israelite identity. In this regard, it is important to note that while Josephus, Matthew, Luke, and John refer to this people group as "Samaritans," this was not their initial label for themselves. After this section, it will be important to observe how the people group we call "Samaritans" categorized and labeled the "Judeans."

2.1 Delos Inscriptions

In 1979, two marble stelae were discovered on the Greek island of Delos. In 1982, Philippe Bruneau published the stelae inscriptions.[45] On paleographic grounds, Bruneau dated the "the Sarapion Honorific" inscription to 150–50 BCE and "the Menippos Honorific" to 250–175 BCE.[46] The Menippos Honorific stele inscription consists of six lines. The first line and the continuation of the last word in the second line are of particular importance for this study. The opening line of the inscription reads:

[Οἱ ἐν Δήλῳ]
Ἰσραηλῖται οἱ ἀπαρχόμενοι εἰς ἱερὸν ἅγοιν Ἀρ–
γαριζείν

---

44 See Robert T. Anderson and Terry Giles, *The Samaritan Pentateuch An Introduction to Its Origin, History, and Significance for Biblical Studies* (Atlanta: Society of Biblical Literature, 2012), 43.

45 Philippe Bruneau, "'Les Israélites de Délos' et la Juiverie Délienne," *BCH* 106 (1982): 466–504.

46 The titles for the inscriptions are from L. Michael White, *The Social Origins of Christian Architecture: Vol. II, Texts and Monuments for the Christian domus ecclesiae in its Environment* (Valley Forge, PA: Trinity Press International, 1997), 340–341. Concerning the dating of the stele inscriptions, Bruneau states: "L'écriture procédant d'un savoir-faire implicite sujet à toute espèce d'aléas (age du graveur, rémanences de techniques surannées dans tel atelier, etc.), on ne saurait raisonnablement fonder des conclusions historiques fiables sur des datations issues du seul examen paléographique" (Bruneau, "'Les Israélites de Délos'"), 484. Concerning Bruneau's dating, Kartveit notes that "scholars have not come up with arguments against it, but seem to adopt it" (Magnar Kartveit, *The Origin of the Samaritans* [Leiden, Boston: Brill, 2009], 218).

NAMING NARRATIVES 59

[Those in Delos]
The Israelites who make offerings to hallowed, consecrated
Argarizein.[47]

The first two lines, with the continuation of the last word in the third line, of
the Sarapion Honorific reads much like the first stele:

Οἱ ἐν Δήλῳ ᾿Ισραελεῖται οἱ ἀ–
παρχόμενοι εἰς ἱερὸν ᾿Αργα–
ριζεῖν

The Israelites in Delos
who make offerings to hallowed
Argarizein.[48]

The key to identifying these Israelites in Delos is *Argarizein* for Mount Gerizim,
"since *Argarizein* [Αργαριζ(ε)ιν/הרגרזים] is an attested Greek rendering for the
sanctuary of Mt. Gerizim, the identity of the group as an enclave of Samaritans
is certain."[49]

Accordingly, if we follow Bruneau's dating for the "the Menippos Honorific,"
then as early as 250–175 BCE the people group known in the Gospel of John
as "Samaritans" self-identify and label themselves "Israelites." There is a hint
of the Samaritans identifying themselves as Israelites in John 4:20 when the
Samaritan woman appeals to their common descent: "*Our* ancestors worshiped on this mountain, but you ["Jews"] say that the place where people must
worship is in Jerusalem." The Samaritan woman's comment also implicitly

---

47   The text, translation, and title of the inscription are from White, *The Social Origins*, 340–
      341; original emphasis. We should also note the Delos inscriptions of Mount Gerizim as
      ᾿Αργαριζεὶν is also found in Josephus's *J.W.* 1.63. Other than this one occurrence, however,
      Josephus uses the orthography "Γαριζεῖν" for Gerizim in *Ant.* 5:235; 11:310, 340, 346; 12:7, 10,
      257, 259; 13:74, 78, 255; 14:100; 18:85; *J.W.* 3:307. The Septuagint, however, uses the orthogra-
      phy "Γαριζιν" for Gerizim in Deut 11:29; 27:12; Josh 9:2; Judg 9:7; 2 Macc 5:23; 6:2.

48   The text, translation, and title of the inscription are from White, *Social Origins*, 342; origi-
      nal emphasis.

49   White, *Social Origins*, 340. In his article, "ARGARIZIN: A Criterion for Samaritan
      Provenance?," Reinhard Pummer concurs that "there is no doubt that they are Samaritan
      inscriptions." However, Pummer cautions that "it is at least doubtful that the read-
      ing Αργαριζιν can at all times and in all writings where it is found be used as proof for
      Samaritan provenance or an underlying Samaritan tradition. It can only serve as one in-
      dicator among others. In itself it is insufficient to prove Samaritan provenance" (Reinhard
      Pummer, "ARGARIZIN: A Criterion for Samaritan Provenance?" *JSJ* 18 [1987]: 25).

60   CHAPTER 3

references Mount Gerizim as the Samaritans' sacred mountain. However, even before the first-century CE, the Samaritan Pentateuch evidences the centrality of Mount Gerizim as their defining indicium for the Samaritan Israelites' cultural traits and institutions.[50]

2.2   *The Samaritan Pentateuch and Mount Gerizim as Identity Indicator*

Before the discovery of the Dead Sea Scrolls, the Samaritan Pentateuch (hereafter, SP) could be compared only with the Masoretic Text (hereafter MT) and the Septuagint (hereafter LXX).[51] According to Emanuel Tov, this comparison "yielded mainly negative judgments regarding the characterization of [SP], since it ascribed to [SP] extensive changes of the earlier text."[52] Among the scrolls discovered at Qumran, however, is a group of texts named "pre-Samaritan."[53] The central feature of the pre-Samaritan Pentateuch and the SP is the tendency to harmonize alterations in order to make the text consistent from one passage to another.[54] These harmonizing alterations are principally accomplished by inserting parallel passages from Deuteronomy into earlier accounts of Exodus and Numbers.[55] By comparing the SP with pre-Samaritan texts, Tov and others detect what they call "the Samaritan ideology." For example, Sidnie White Crawford discerns that the Samaritans "added to [the

---

50   According to Pummer, "There is now a consensus among scholars that the Samaritan Pentateuch is an adaptation of a pre-Samaritan or harmonistic text known from Qumran that was produced in the 2nd or 1st century BCE" (Reinhard Pummer, "The Samaritans and Their Pentateuch," in *The Pentateuch as Torah: New Models for Understanding Its Promulgation and Acceptance* [ed. Gary N. Knoppers and Bernard M. Levinson; Winona Lake, IN: Eisenbrauns, 2007], 247).

51   The earliest SP manuscripts are medieval (e.g. Abisha Scroll c. 1150 CE), similar to the Masoretic Codex Leningradensis (c. 1008 CE).

52   Emanuel Tov, *Textual Criticism of the Hebrew Bible*, 3d ed. (Minneapolis, MN: Fortress, 2012), 79. Elsewhere Tov notes: "On the basis of a list prepared in the seventeenth century, the number of these differences [between the SP and the MT] is usually quoted as six thousand" (Emanuel Tov, "Proto-Samaritan Texts and the Samaritan Pentateuch" in *The Samaritans* [ed. Alan D. Crown; Tübingen: Mohr Siebeck, 1989], 401).

53   According to Sidnie White Crawford, "The Samaritan Pentateuch in fact contains an ancient edition of the Pentateuch, current in Palestine in the Second Temple period" (*Rewriting Scripture in Second Temple Times* [Grand Rapids: Eerdmans, 2008], 22). See also Tov, *Textual Criticism*, 91, who states: "The SP-group reflects a popular textual tradition of the Torah that circulated in ancient Israel in the last centuries BCE."

54   Pummer, "The Samaritans and Their Pentateuch," 244.

55   For example, compare Exod 20:19 MT with the pre-Samaritan text of 4QpaleoExod[m] and the SP that insert Deuteronomy 5:24–27 as part of the Israelites response to Moses. For a chart of forty harmonizing interpolations, see Anderson and Giles, *Samaritan Pentateuch*, 61–63.

NAMING NARRATIVES 61

pre-Samaritan texts] a thin veneer of sectarian edit[ing], bringing the text into line with their theology. This sectarian editing is easy to isolate."[56]

There are two main ideological changes to the pre-Samaritan text in the SP and both concern the central place of worship: Mount Gerizim הרגרזים (which is one word in the Samaritan orthography[57]). The first ideological change Tov identifies in the SP concerns the Samaritans' addition of an eleventh commandment to the Decalogue after Exod 20:14 and Deut 5:18. In this respect, it is important to note that the Samaritans enumerate the Ten Commandments differently than the Judean tradition. Both traditions count Exod 20:2–3// Deut 5:5–6 as the first commandment. However, whereas the Judean tradition counts Exod 20:4–6//Deut 5:7–10 as the second command, the Samaritans understand these verses as the explanation of the first command. The Samaritans' second commandment is the Judeans' third commandment and so on. After the Judean tenth commandment (the Samaritans' ninth), the SP includes a tenth commandment consisting of texts from Deuteronomy. The SP tenth commandment is a composite verse formed in the manner of the harmonistic alterations in the pre-Samaritan text type, but the Samaritan tenth commandment is *not* represented in the pre-Samaritan texts. The Samaritans' tenth commandment states:

> Exod 20:14a And when Shehmaa your Eloowwem will bring you to the land of the Kaanannee which you are going to inherit it. [cf. Deut. 11:29] 14b You shall set yourself up great stones and lime them with lime. And you shall write on them all the words of this law. 14c And when you have passed over the Yaardaan you shall set up these stones, which I command you today, in Aargaareezem. 14d And there you shall build an alter to Shehmaa your Eloowwem, an alter of stones. You shall lift up no iron on them. 14e And you shall build the altar of Shehmaa your Eloowwem of complete stones. 14f And you shall offer burnt offerings. Thereupon to Shehmaa your Eloowwem 14g And you shall sacrifice offerings and shall eat there. And you shall rejoice before Shehmaa your Eloowwem. [cf. Deut 27:2–7] 14h That mountain, in the other side of the Yaardaan, beyond the way toward the sunset, in the land of the Kaanannee who dwell in

---

56 Crawford, *Rewriting Scripture in Second Temple Times*, 22. Tov concurs with Crawford's assessment and notes: "It is now clear that the Samaritan layer is very thin, and that if this layer is 'peeled off', the proto-Samaritan basis of the Samaritan Pentateuch becomes visible" (Tov, "Proto-Samaritan Texts," 401).

57 Tov, *Textual Criticism*, 88.

62   CHAPTER 3

the prairie, before the Gaalgaal, beside the Aalone moora, before Ashkem
[cf. Deut 11:30].[58]

By including sections from Deut 11 and 27 into their tenth commandment, the
Samaritans solidify the significance of Mount Gerizim. This emphasis also appears in John 4:20, where Mount Gerizim was a decisive issue.

The second ideological change Tov identifies in the SP concerns the
Deuteronomic expression המקום אשר יבחר יהוה ("the site which the LORD *will*
choose"), with the future tense imperfect יבחר alluding to the future site of
Jerusalem. The SP, however, records the past tense Qal בחר ("*has* chosen"). The
reason for the SP past tense is that "from the Samaritan perspective, Shechem
had already been chosen at the time of the patriarchs (Gen 12:6; Gen 33:18–20),
and therefore they felt a need to change the tense."[59]

However, Stefan Schorch suggests that the Qal past tense בחר ("*has*
chosen") was the original reading and the Judeans' MT changed it to the imperfect future tense in order to cohere with their Jerusalem-centric ideology "and maybe even an anti-Samaritan correction."[60] According to Schorch's
hypothesis, Deuteronomy originated in the northern kingdom of Israel because "the only context within which the literary ambitions of Deut 27:4–8
are entirely understandable seems to be the cult on Mount Gerizim, with
the author of the text being a follower of the Gerizim cult."[61] Although MT

58   Unless otherwise indicated, all citations from the Samaritan Pentateuch are from
        Benyamim Tsedaka, *The Israelite Samaritan Version of the Torah: First English Translation
        Compared with the Masoretic Version* (Grand Rapids: Eerdmans, 2013).
59   Tov, *Textual Criticism*, 88. The Deuteronomic expression occurs twenty-one times:
        Deut 12:5, 11, 14, 18, 21, 26; 14:23, 24, 25; 15:20; 16:2, 6, 7, 11, 15, 16; 17:8, 10; 18:6; 26:2; 31:11.
60   Stefan Schorch, "The Samaritan Version of Deuteronomy and the Origin of Deuteronomy,"
        in *Samaria, Samarians, Samaritans: Studies on Bible, History and Linguistics* (ed.
        Jozsef Zsengeller; Berlin, Boston: de Gruyter, 2011), 32. In agreement with Schorch, Jan
        Dušek adds that "the original Deuteronomic formula 'the place which the Lord your
        God *has chosen* (בחר)', preserved in the Samaritan Pentateuch and some ancient Greek,
        Latin and Coptic translation, was in the Judean milieu modified, probably during the
        2nd century BCE, to 'the place which the Lord your God *will choose* (יבחר)', attested
        in the Masoretic text" (Jan Dušek, *Aramaic and Hebrew Inscriptions from Mt. Gerizim
        and Samaria between Antiochus III and Antiochus IV Epiphanes* [Boston, Leiden: Brill,
        2012], 90).
61   Schorch, "The Samaritan Version of Deuteronomy and the Origin of Deuteronomy," 29.
        Deuteronomy 27:4–8 MT states: "So when you have crossed over the Jordan, you shall set
        up these stones, about which I am commanding you today, on Mount Ebal, and you shall
        cover them with plaster. And you shall build an altar there to the LORD your God, an altar
        of stones on which you have not used an iron tool. You must build the altar of the LORD
        your God of unhewn stones. Then offer up burnt offerings on it to the LORD your God,

Deut 27:4–8 contains "Mount Ebal" and not "Mount Gerizim" as the site for the altar, Schorch is certainly correct that "due to its literary connections with Deut 12, Deut 27 does not designate the altar on Mount Gerizim as one possible cultic place *among others*, but as the *one and only* legitimate cultic place, delegitimizing all other cultic places including Jerusalem."[62] Schorch suggests that the Judean ideological corrections occurred only when the Judeans received the text after "the Assyrian conquest in the late 8th century BCE, when large parts of the Northern elite flew to the South."[63] In addition to the change in the Deuteronomic expression, the Judeans reinforced their Jerusalem-centric ideology with the texts of Samuel and Kings.[64]

James H. Charlesworth has identified another possible ideological change in Deut 27:4, involving the location of the stone altar, and also supporting the priority of SP. It was noted above that the MT Deut 27:4 contains Mount Ebal for the altar site instead of Mount Gerizim. Thus, the NRSV translates MT Deut 27:4: "So when you have crossed over the Jordan, you shall set up these stones, about which I am commanding you today, on *Mount Ebal*, and you shall cover them with plaster." However, in 2009, Charlesworth published a Dead Sea Scroll fragment of Deut 27:4b–6 and containing the reading בהרגוים ("on Mount Gerizim"), consistent with the SP בהרגר(י)זים ("on Aargaareezem"). Charlesworth notes that the majority of other textual witnesses read Mount Ebal instead of Mount Gerizim: "MT (and St. Petersburg Codex [also known as the Leningrad Codex]; Aleppo Codex begins at Deut 28:7): בהר עיבל; LXX: Γαιβαλ; Peshitta: ܓܒܠ. In Targum Onkelos: בטורא דעיבל."[65] Nevertheless, the central thrust of Charlesworth's article is that

---

make sacrifices of well-being, and eat them there, rejoicing before the LORD your God. You shall write on the stones all the words of this law very clearly."

62 Schorch, "The Samaritan Version of Deuteronomy and the Origin of Deuteronomy," 29; original emphasis.

63 Schorch, "The Samaritan Version of Deuteronomy and the Origin of Deuteronomy," 30. Concordantly, Israel Finkelstein observes "a major population shift in the hill country [of Judah] over a short period of time in the second half of the eighth century. The only possible reason for this is the fall of the northern kingdom and resettlement of Israelite groups from the area of southern Samaria, including Bethel, in Jerusalem and Judah" (*The Forgotten Kingdom: The Archaeology and History of Northern Israel* [Atlanta: Society of Biblical Literature, 2013], 155).

64 Regardless of whether one is persuaded by Schorch's hypothesis, Gary N. Knoppers helpfully reminds us that "It is not the case that one reading (SP) is somehow ideological while the other (the MT) is not. Each formulation expresses an election theology" (*Jews and Samaritans: The Origins and History of Their Early Relations* [Oxford: Oxford University Press, 2013], 187).

65 James Charlesworth, "What Is A Variant? Announcing A Dead Sea Scrolls Fragment of Deuteronomy," in *Maarav* 16.2 (2009): 201n3. The fragment is dated, according to

64   CHAPTER 3

we should keep in focus the possibility that a manuscript with a reading found in the Samaritan Pentateuch may not be the result of editing
by Samaritans; it may represent the original reading. Thus, the MT and
other related text types may represent anti-Samaritan motivated redaction by others, notably Jews in Judea especially after the burning of the
Samaritan 'altar' by John Hyrcanus in the late second century BCE.[66]

In his conclusion, Charlesworth proposes: "The original reading of Deuteronomy, 'on Mount Gerizim,' is preserved in this fragment. Thus, it should not be
labeled 'a variant'; the MT and related texts preserve the 'variant' and it looks
redactional and later."[67] With the support from Charlesworth's analysis of the
Deut 27:4 fragment from Qumran, Schorch's hypothesis discloses that what
Tov and others label a "Samaritan ideological" correction may actually in some
cases be a Judean anti-Samaritan motivated ideological redaction.

Although the debate concerning the original reading of "*will* choose" (יבחר)
versus "*has* chosen" (בחר), or "Mount Ebal" (MT) versus "Mount Gerizim" (SP),
will certainly continue, we are left with the Delos inscriptions and the SP (especially their Decalogue), which together witness some of the ethnic features
named by Hutchinson and Smith. According to the Delos inscriptions, the
Samaritans identify themselves under the common proper name "Israelites"
(H-S#1), as well as a link with their homeland (*Argarizein*) (H-S#5), even in
Delos, Greece. The SP further testifies to the Samaritans' Israelite identity as
a record of their common ancestry (H-S#2) [e.g. as descendants of the twelve
tribes of Israel], shared memories (H-S#3) [e.g. the exodus, wilderness wonder-
ings, and Moses], as well as identifying the Samaritans' central identity marker
as Mount Gerizim (H-S#4) [e.g. Deut 12 and 27].

2.3   *Who Are These "Samaritans" You Speak of?: Etymology of a Name*
The label "Samaritan" derives from Samaria/Σαμάρεια (cf. John 4:4, 5, 7) and
was originally the name of the city (Heb. שֹׁמְרוֹן, Aram. שָׁמְרַיִן) that Omri
founded (Omri reigned the kingdom of Israel c. 885–873 BCE).[68] According to
1 Kgs 16:24, Omri "bought the hill of Samaria [שֹׁמְרוֹן] from Shemer for two tal-
ents of silver; he fortified the hill, and called the city that he built, Samaria,
after the name of Shemer, the owner of the hill." (Then, c. 27 BCE, the city

---

paleography, "perhaps to 175 BCE and later forms that date from around 50 and even
conceivably to 30 BCE (but we cannot ascertain when such forms first appeared)"
(Charlesworth, "What Is A Variant," 202).

66   Charlesworth, "What Is A Variant," 208.
67   Charlesworth, "What Is A Variant," 209–210.
68   Mary Joan Winn Leith, "Samaria," in *Oxford Companion to the Bible*, 670.

NAMING NARRATIVES

of Samaria was renamed Sebaste Σεβαστή by Herod the Great in honor of Augustus [Josephus, *Ant.* 15.7.7; *J.W.* 1.403].[69]) Although 1 Kgs 16:24 is a plausible derivation (Samaria from Shemer), another possibility is that Samaria (שֹׁמְרוֹן) derives from the verb שמר ("to keep or watch over") "and in this case the word would mean something like mountain for watching, observation point."[70] The latter etymological possibility, as we will see, is important for the Samaritans' labeling themselves "the keepers."

Regardless of whether the label "Samaritan" derives from an eponymous Shemer or from the locality (the hill of Samaria [שֹׁמְרוֹן]), we should perhaps note that the people group we have called the "Samaritans" reluctantly accept this name for themselves today.[71] (We are using the term "Samaritan" principally because it is the one used in the Gospel of John [Σαμαρίτης/Σαμαρῖτις John 4:9, 39; 8:48].) Paul Stenhouse suggests that the reason Samaritans reject this name for themselves is because it was the Judeans who first "called them 'the Samarians,' השמרנים, with all the pejorative overtones that term carried from 2 Kgs 17:24ff."[72]

Given that the earliest Samaritan literature is the SP, we must turn to the medieval Samaritan Chronicles for information concerning their self-labeling practices. Paul Stenhouse notes that in the Samaritan Chronicle *The Kitāb al-Tarīkh of Abu 'l-Fath*[73] (hereafter AF), the Samaritans instead prefer to

> call themselves 'the sons of Israel,' 'the tribes of Israel,' 'the family of Israel,' 'the sons of Israel the observant ones,' 'the sons of Israel who

---

69 BDAG notes the region of "Samaria" "included the region from the Plain of Jezreel southward to the border of Judea" ("Σαμάρεια," 912).

70 "שֹׁמְרוֹן," *HALOT* 4.1587. Accordingly, Aharoni Yohanan observes: "The choice of Samaria was most propitious because of its excellent strategic position on a high and isolated hill in Mount Ephraim" (*The Land of the Bible: A Historical Geography Revised and Enlarged Edition*, [Philadelphia: Westminster, 1979], 334).

71 Moses Gaster, *The Samaritans: Their History, Doctrines and Literature* (London: Oxford University Press, 1923), 5. According to Benyamim Tsedaka, the Samaritan-Israelites "never adopted the name *Samaritans*. Our forefathers only used the name when speaking to outsiders about our community" (Benyamim Tsedaka, "Who are *The Keepers*?," http://www.israelite-samaritans.com/life/keepers-israelite-samaritan-identity/; original emphasis.

72 Paul Stenhouse, "The Chronicle of Abu 'l-Fath and Samaritans Origins: 2 Kings, 2 Chronicles and Ezra-Nehemiah Viewed Through the Prism of Samaritan Tradition," in *The Samaritans and the Bible: Historical and Literary Interactions Between Biblical and Samaritan Traditions* (ed. Jörg Frey, Ursula Schattner-Rieser, and Konrad Schmid; Berlin: de Gruyter, 2012), 305.

73 All citations from the *The Kitāb Al-Tarīkh of Abu 'L-Fath* are from Paul Stenhouse, *The Kitāb Al-Tarīkh of Abu 'L-Fath* (Sidney: University of Sidney, 1985).

66   CHAPTER 3

possess the truth,' 'the family of Phinehas,' 'the tribe of Joseph,' 'the family of Ephraim,' 'the family of Phinehas,' 'the observant ones,' and 'the Samaritans.'[74]

Of all the labels listed by Stenhouse, the only designation not found in the texts of the Hebrew Bible is the label "the observant ones," also translated "the keepers." The rest of the labels listed here represent the Samaritans' constructed identity that they are indeed Israelites—the remnants of the tribes of Israel who settled the north in the time of Joshua and survived both the divided monarchy and its fall to Assyria.

Although the Samaritan Chronicles are merely illustrative of how the Samaritans constructed their identity into the medieval and modern period, Pummer notes that "it is not certain when [the Samaritans] first used this term ["the keepers"]."[75] In fact, Knoppers suggests that "there may be a much earlier allusion [to the Samaritans as "the keepers"] in late biblical lore."[76] Although the Samaritan texts that apply the label "the Observers/Keepers" (שמרים) to themselves are medieval and modern, the early church fathers as early as Origen were aware of the Samaritan self-labeling tradition. For this reason, it may prove instructive for how the Gospel of John, or at least some of its earliest interpreters, understood the Samaritans' identity. For example, as we noted in Chapter One, Augustine appeals to the tradition that "Samaritan means keeper" for his comments on John 8:48 that Jesus is a "Samaritan."[77]

---

74   Stenhouse, "The Chronicle of Abu 'l-Fath and Samaritans Origins," 305. For a complete list of the Samaritans self-identifying labels and their citations in AF see: Paul Stenhouse, "Abu'l-Fath as Editor: His Use of His Sources," *The Kitab al-Tarikh of Abu'l-Fath* (3 vol. Ph.D. diss., The University of Sydney, 1980), 2.4–5.

75   Pummer, *The Samaritans in Flavius Josephus*, 6.

76   Knoppers, *Jews and Samaritans*, 16 n. 21. In particular, Knoppers adds: "In the Chronistic depiction of the dual monarchies, King Abijah of Judah pointedly announces to this northern counterparts and enemy in battle, 'Jeroboam and all Israel': 'Indeed we are observing (שמרים אנחנו) the charge (את־משמרת) of YHWH our God' (2 Chr 13:11). It would seem that Chronicles is punning on a traditional self-designation of the Samaritans, insisting that the southern Israelites, and not the northern Israelites, are properly keeping the responsibilities YHWH entrusted to his people."

77   See page 15n40 and Augustine, *Homilies on Gospel of John* 43.2 (*NPNF* 7.307). Other early church fathers who appealed to "Samaritan = Guardian/Keeper" tradition are Origen (c. 185–c.254 CE), Epiphanius of Salamis (c. 315–403 CE), and Jerome (c. 347 or 348–420 CE). For texts, translation, and commentary, see Reinhard Pummer, *Early Christian Authors on Samaritans and Samaritanism: Texts, Translations and Commentary* (Tübingen: Mohr Siebeck, 2002), 74 (28), 156 (66), 193 (77), 201 (95). Pummer's page numbers are followed by his excerpt number in parenthesis.

NAMING NARRATIVES

2.4 The Samaritan Labels for the "Judeans": the Categorization of Judeans

The Samaritan Chronicles are the only evidence of the Samaritans' labels for the "Judeans." If the Samaritans are "the keepers," then the "Judeans" are categorized as those who do not keep the Torah. This is, according to Stenhouse, exactly how AF labels the "Judeans" as "the people of error," "the sons of Israel the erroneous ones" and, "in a word, 'rebels' or 'heretics'."[78] Thus, this Samaritan chronicler does not label the "Judeans" in terms of another ethnic group.[79] Rather, the Samaritans construct the "Judeans" in the category that Coser would later define as "heretics" for erroneously following Eli's choice for an alternative sanctuary at Shiloh.

3 Labeling the Samaritans in Josephus

The study of the Samaritans in Josephus is a field of its own accompanied by vast research.[80] Accordingly, we will approach the passages in Josephus's works concerning the labeling of Samaritans only insofar as it enlightens the reading of John 4 and 8.

It is first important to note that Josephus connects the names of people groups to geographic locations. In particular, concerning the group we have been calling the "Judeans," Josephus states, "This name ['Ιουδαῖοι], by which they have been called from the time when they went up from Babylon, is derived from the tribe of Judah; as this tribe was the first to come to those parts, both the people themselves and the country have taken their name from it" (Josephus, *Ant.* 11.173 [Marcus, LCL]). Josephus makes three observations concerning the label "Judean." First, the label "Judean" started in the post-exilic period.[81] Second, the label derives from the tribe of Judah. Third, since the

---

78   Stenhouse, "The Chronicle of Abu 'l-Fath and Samaritans Origins," 305–306.

79   The anthropologist Monika Schreiber notes: "The animosity between Samaritans and Jews is traced back to rivalry between the offspring of Joseph and the children of Judah. While certainly opponents, they are nevertheless kin: in Samaritan eyes, the Jews are apostates, but still Israelites in terms of descent. For this reason the Judahites still have the option to repent and to reunite with their brother tribes—under the condition, improbable as it may be, that they abandon Jerusalem, throw away their holy books and legal compendia, and join the cult of the Josephites on *Hargrizim*" (Monika Schreiber, *The Comfort of Kin: Samaritan Community, Kinship, and Marriage* [Boston, Leiden: Brill, 2014], 34).

80   The most recent review is Kartveit, *The Origin of the Samaritans.*

81   This usage is reflected in Josephus's works where "the term 'Israelite' occurs 186 times in the first eleven books of the *Antiquities*, but nowhere else in his writings. The term

68

CHAPTER 3

tribe of Judah was first to inhabit the region, both the country and its people take their name from Judah. Thus, for Josephus, as we will see, ethnic labels are defined geographically.

Concurrent with this observation, Joachim Jeremias makes two claims in his entry on Σαμάρεια in *TDNT*.[82] The first claim is that, according to Jeremias, "the first century was thus a time of very strained relations between Jews and Samaritans. The old antithesis of North and South, of Israel and Judah, was revived in all its sharpness."[83] The "old antithesis" is indeed an important aspect, as we will see. The second claim is that, "In practice the Samaritans were put on a level with the Gentiles in the first century."[84] This claim is overstated. According to Josephus's constructed identity for the "Samaritans," they were not on the level of gentiles, but rather a separate ethnic group (from the "Judeans") who claimed Israelite descent.[85] There are at least three separate occasions where Josephus refers to the Samaritans as an ἔθνος (*Ant.* 10.184, 17.20, 18.85), not an αἵρεσις (the word Josephus uses for "sects" [cf. *Ant.* 13.171]).[86] In fact, Louis H. Feldman observes,

> An exhaustive examination of Josephus' use of this word [ἔθνος] indicates that he generally reserves it for either the Jewish nation or the Jewish people, whether in Judea or in the Diaspora (253 times); or for other nations (124 times)—Idumaeans, Arabs, Gauls, Parthians, Pamphylians, Africans, Philistines, Alani, Medes, Cappadocians, Ethiopians, Moabites, Canaanites, Amalekites, Sikimites, Assyrians, Ammanites, Syrians, Ituraeans, and Germans. He speaks (*Ant.* 17.20) of someone's Samaritan origin 'ethnos,' where the term implies a categorization that depends

---

Ἰουδαῖος, by contrast, occurs 582 times after *Ant.* 11.173, but only 65 times in the first half of the *Antiquities*" (Miller, "The Meaning of *Ioudaios* and its Relationship to Other Group Labels in Ancient 'Judaism,'" 102).

82   J. Jeremias, "Σαμάρεια," *TDNT* 7:90.

83   J. Jeremias, "Σαμάρεια," *TDNT* 7:90.

84   J. Jeremias, "Σαμάρεια," *TDNT* 7:91.

85   This view, however, was not shared by Sirach who states: "Two nations my soul detests, and the third is not even a people [ἔθνος]: Those who live in Seir, and the Philistines, and the foolish people that live in Shechem" (Sir 50:25–26).

86   Louis H. Feldman notes that while Josephus "uses the word 'ἔθνος' very frequently— 401 times to be exact—he never employs it to refer to one of the sects of Judaism— whether Pharisees, Sadducees, Essenes, or Fourth Philosophy—or any other religious grouping" ("Josephus' Attitude Toward the Samaritans: A Study in Ambivalence" in *Studies in Hellenistic Judaism* [New York: Brill, 1996], 118).

NAMING NARRATIVES 69

upon birth in a nation not upon adherence to a creed or a set of practices, hence, not as a variety of Judaism.[87]

In Feldman's analysis, Josephus understood the Samaritans as a matter of ethnicity (of how they understood the qualities or affiliations of ethnic groups) and *not* as a matter of heterodoxy within "Judaism." However, we are again reminded that ethnicity is an umbrella concept consisting of multiple cultural features—such as religion (H-S#4) and geography (H-S#5)—that are attributes of an ethnic group's identity, and are used situationally to differentiate their group from others. This is an etic model analysis for interactions between ethnic groups. Consequently, although Feldman is certainly correct in his observations about Josephus's terminology, he offers an emic analysis that "describe[s] *what* and *how* the natives thought but not *why* ... [while the etic analysis] seek[s] to explain *why* the native thought and behaved so and not otherwise."[88] Therefore, given that our interests lie in *why* Jesus is labeled both a "Jew" and a "Samaritan" by different groups and in different situations, we must be careful to not separate religion, or religious aspects, from ethnic identity and vice versa.

Returning to Feldman's terminological observations we see that, unlike the Samaritans who constructed the identity of the "Judeans" as Israelites but in the category of Coserian "heretics," Josephus constructed the "Samaritan" identity as a distinctly separate ethnic group. In this regard, Ingrid Hjelm notes, "This problem of ethnicity forms the central core of Josephus's struggle with the Judean-Samaritan relationship."[89] Yet, even though Josephus's central origin story (which is told three times; see below) heightens the Samaritans' ethnic distinction (namely, his accounts of Samaritans as Cutheans), his other two accounts of Samaritan origins, as we will see, disclose a certain ambivalence towards the Samaritans.

3.1 Josephus's Three Samaritan Origin Stories

Josephus places the origins of the Samaritans at the fall of the northern kingdom of Israel to Assyria in 722 BCE (retelling of 2 Kings 17 in *Ant.* 9.277–291). In Josephus's account, every Israelite is deported to Media and Persia and replaced by the nations from Chuthos.[90] Josephus explains that the name "Chuthaioi"

---

87   Feldman, "Josephus' Attitude Toward the Samaritans," 117–118.
88   Elliott, *What Is Social-Scientific Criticism?*, 39; emphasis original.
89   Ingrid Hjelm, *The Samaritans and Early Judaism: A Literary Analysis* (Sheffield: Sheffield Academic, 2000), 194.
90   Josephus, *Ant.* 9.278–9.

"is the name by which they have been called to this day because of having been brought over from the region called Chutha, which is in Persia, as is a river by the same name."[91] (Note that the ethnic label is defined geographically.) The salient ethnic feature in Josephus *Ant.* 9.277–291 is H-S#1: a common proper name to identify the group. The Samaritans are labeled by another "common name" not shared by the Judeans and, additionally, Josephus uses the labels "Cutheans," "Sidonians," "Shechemites," or "Samaritans" in order to construct their identity as separated from the "Judeans." The purpose of these labels is to emphasize that the Samaritan ἔθνος derives from another place and particularly outside of the land of the Judeans' ancestors.

Accordingly, when the Cutheans were settled in Samaria, in the country of the Israelites, they also "brought along [their] own god, and, as they reverenced them accordance with the custom of their country."[92] As punishment for worshiping other gods, "a pestilence" came upon them.[93] Thus far, Josephus has followed the presentation of 2 Kgs 17. Intriguing is the fact that Josephus's account differs from 2 Kgs 17 with the introduction of Yahwism. According to Josephus, the Samaritans themselves, in response to the pestilence, took the initiative to learn the worship of "the Most High God" and "worshipped Him with great zeal, and were at once freed of the pestilence."[94] Absent in Josephus's account is the continued worship of "their own gods" in addition to Yahweh (2 Kgs 17:33). Josephus had an opportunity to exploit this aspect of religious syncretism so as to distance the Samaritans further from himself (and the Yahwism of the Judeans), but at this point Josephus omits any notion of religious syncretism among the Samaritans. Instead of attacking their religious practices, Josephus asserts that "even to this day" the Samaritans continue to use "these same rites" in which they "worshipped Him [Yahweh] with great zeal."[95] If Josephus is not critical of the Samaritans' Yahwism (H-S#4: a common culture, embracing such things as religion), what is the crux of the matter?

For Josephus, the problem with the Samaritans is not their religious practices (H-S#4) but rather their inconsistent association with the Judeans to the

---

91   Josephus, *Ant.* 9.288 (Marcus, LCL). Josephus also remarks: "those who are called Chuthaioi (Cuthim) in the Hebrew tongue, and Samareitai (Samaritans) by the Greeks" (Josephus, *Ant.* 9.290 [Marcus, LCL]).

92   Josephus, *Ant.* 9.288 (Marcus, LCL).

93   Josephus, *Ant.* 9.288 (Marcus, LCL).

94   Josephus, *Ant.* 9.290 (Marcus, LCL).

95   Josephus, *Ant.* 9.290 (Marcus, LCL).

south (i.e. for their lack of "communal solidarity" [H-S#6]).[96] For example, Josephus's central criticism against the Samaritans is that "they alter their attitude according to circumstance."[97] When the Judeans are prospering, the Samaritans "call them their [relatives] (συγγενεῖς)" and recall how they are descendants of Joseph.[98] Yet, when the Judeans are in trouble, the Samaritans "say that they have nothing whatever in common with them (Judeans)... and they (Samaritans) declare themselves to be aliens (μετοίκους) of another race (ἀλλοεθνεῖς)."[99] According to Josephus, the Samaritans identify themselves in terms of Simmelian "strangers" when they declare themselves to be μέτοικοι— "settler[s] from abroad, alien resident[s] in a foreign city, denizen[s]."[100] Although the Samaritans were accommodated into their new surroundings,[101] and even finding an identity for themselves as descendants of Joseph in the Israelites' "shared memories of a common past" (H-S#3), the Samaritans are nevertheless alienated from the indigenous inhabitants they encounter from Judea.

In spite of Josephus's prejudice against the Samaritans, there is no implication that he denied either the conversion of the Cutheans to Yahwism when they came into the land of Israel or that they continued in the same faith until his day. In this section, Josephus does not attack their orthodoxy or even suggest that they are heterodox; he attacks their opportunistic identification with Judean ethnic identity. For Josephus, the Samaritans were strangers from Chutha in Persia but became Yahwistic Samaritan-Israelites who were even able to claim "that they are descended from Joseph."[102] What was troublesome to Josephus was their dual-ethnic identity which could be turned to their advantage when necessary—a luxury the Judeans in the south did not

---

96   According to Kartveit, "This is emphasized three times in the form of comments on the stories of [the Samaritans'] origin and constitutes [Josephus's] *Tendenz* in this connection" (*The Origin of the Samaritans*, 82).

97   Josephus, *Ant.* 9.291 (Marcus, LCL). That this forms Josephus' main criticism is supported by the fact that "it forms the climax to Book 9 of the *Antiquities* and is thereby given special prominence" (Richard J. Coggins, "The Samaritans in Josephus" in *Josephus, Judaism and Christianity* [ed. Louis H. Feldman and Gohei Hata; Leiden: Brill, 1987], 259). Perhaps even more so, however, is the fact that "it is repeated almost *verbatim* in *Ant.* 11.341 and 12.257, and, with the same meaning, in a variant form in 11.85" (Hjelm, *The Samaritans and Early Judaism*, 194–195).

98   Josephus, *Ant.* 9.291 (Marcus, LCL).

99   Josephus, *Ant.* 9.291 (Marcus, LCL). Given the observations made in Chapter Two about the concept of "race," Whiston's translation is preferable here: "They declare that they are sojourners that come from other countries" (Josephus, *Ant.* 9.291).

100   "μέτοικος," LSJ, 1121.

101   Josephus, *Ant.* 9.290.

102   Josephus, *Ant.* 9.291 (Marcus, LCL).

have. Accordingly, the Judeans treated the Cutheans/Samaritans in terms of Simmelian "strangers" who came into their Judean cultural framework. Even though the Samaritans settled into their context and learned how to be good Yahwists they were nonetheless "treated as alien by the autochthones."[103]

When Josephus retells the beginning stages of the rebuilding of the temple in Jerusalem at the beginning of *Ant.* 11, there is a brief mention of the Samaritans. Josephus does not call them "Samaritans" but "Cuthean" and adds a reminder that they were the people who were settled into Samaria when the Israelite people were deported.[104] Josephus picks the story up again at *Ant.* 11.84 when he explicitly identifies "the adversaries of Judah and Benjamin" (Ezra 4:1) with "the Samaritans" (*not* Cutheans). Here, the Samaritans asked the *golah*-Judeans if they might participate in the rebuilding of the temple in Jerusalem.[105] While Josephus's identification of "the adversaries of Judah and Benjamin" with the Samaritans may appear as an awkward interpolation, given the centrality of Mount Gerizim for the Samaritans, there is perhaps some merit to this claim in light of Jer 41:5, which states that "eighty men arrived from Shechem and Shiloh and Samaria ... bringing grain offerings and incense to present at the temple of the LORD."[106] This would certainly cohere with the reason for the Samaritans' request to help (Josephus, *Ant.* 11.85; cf. Ezra 4:2). Here, the Samaritans assert that they are in fact genuine converts to Yahwism since the days of their arrival in the land, which Josephus does not deny.

In this story, the Samaritans were acting in the role of a Coserian heretic in that they were presenting a choice to the recently returned *golah*-Judeans. Those who faced this choice were "Zorobabelos and the high priest Jesus and the chiefs of the Israelite families" (i.e. the Judean authorities) for whom "only those who had gone through the experience of the Babylonian exile ... were the true heirs of the promises to the forefathers."[107] In Josephus's text, the Judeans are now faced with a choice about what to do with the Samaritans.

---

103 Fuhse, "Embedding the Stranger," 652. It is, however, ironic that Josephus should view the Samaritans as Cuthean strangers in the land given that the next place they are mentioned (in *Ant.* 11.1–119) is when the Judeans return to the land from the Babylonian exile (retelling the events of Ezra-Nehemiah). From the Samaritan perspective, the recently re-inhabited *golah*-Judeans are the strangers in the land.

104 Josephus, *Ant.* 11.19.

105 Josephus, *Ant.* 11.84.

106 The "temple of the Lord" is not specified but, presumably, these eighty men from the north would be traveling to the site of the destroyed temple in Jerusalem. Joseph Blenkinsopp, however, contends that the temple destination refers to Bethel. See Joseph Blenkinsopp, "The Judean Priesthood during the Neo-Babylonian and Achaemenid Periods: A Hypothetical Reconstruction," in *CBQ* 60 (1998): 25–43.

107 Coggins, "The Samaritans in Josephus," 260.

NAMING NARRATIVES

When the Samaritans arrived with an offer to assist in rebuilding the Judean temple it presented alternatives to the Judeans' notion of what it meant to be Yahwists. The confessional community of *golah*-Judeans was forced to create "new institutional structures centering on the enforcement of ... new rules and laws."[108] According to Josephus's account, the Judeans in fact established a new rule for relations with the Samaritan people; namely, "the only thing which [the Samaritans] might, if they wished, have in common with [the Judeans], as might all other men, was to come to the sanctuary and revere God."[109] In Josephus's account of Ezra 4, the new Judean establishment (consisting of *golah*-Judeans) explicitly pushed the Samaritans outside of the realm of the Judean-Israelite community by placing the Samaritans alongside "all other peoples" who might "come to the sanctuary and revere God."[110]

Not surprisingly, Josephus records that "on hearing this, the Chuthaeans— it is by this that the Samaritans are called—were indignant" (Josephus, *Ant.* 11.88 [Marcus, LCL]). The Samaritans were, after all, Yahwists too. Why should they be denied co-religionist status and placed alongside "all other peoples"? It may be a coincidence, but it is at this very time period, in the mid-fifth century BCE, that the Samaritans built their temple on Mount Gerizim (*contra* Josephus who, as we will see, places it in the late fourth century BCE at the time of Alexander the Great).[111] The Judean rejection of the Samaritans marks a turning point in Judean-Samaritan relations and escalated the tensions between the two Yahwist groups.

Josephus addresses the Samaritans again at the end of *Ant.* 11, in which he repeats his main criticism from *Ant.* 9.291 concerning the opportunistic "nature of the Samaritans, as we have already shown somewhere above."[112] Here we find Sanaballetes desiring to build a temple on Mount Gerizim[113] and, according to Josephus, this occurred when Alexander the Great was on the move through Palestine. Alexander gave his consent and the temple on Mount Gerizim began. However, problems for the Samaritans emerged when, after a

---

108 Coser, *The Functions of Social Conflict*, 126.
109 Josephus, *Ant.* 11.87 (Marcus, LCL).
110 Josephus, *Ant.* 11.87 (Marcus, LCL).
111 According to Yitzhak Magen, "The coins from the Persian period, the pottery vessels, and Carbon 14 (C-14) testing at the site enable us to ascribe the first phase of the temple to the mid-fifth century BCE. This temple was active for approximately 150 years, until the establishment of the new temple in the Hellenistic period" ("The Dating of the First Phase of the Samaritan Temple on Mount Gerizim in Light of the Archaeological Evidence" in *Judah and the Judeans in the Fourth Century BCE* [ed. Oded Lipschits, Gary N. Knoppers and Rainer Albertz; Winona Lake, IN: Eisenbrauns, 2007], 162–164).
112 Josephus, *Ant.* 11.341 (Marcus, LCL).
113 Josephus, *Ant.* 11.310.

grand reception of Alexander in Jerusalem, the Samaritans, hoping to profit from the Judeans good fortune, found Alexander outside of Jerusalem and "decided to profess themselves Jews."[114] At this point, Josephus remarks, when times are good for the Judeans, the Samaritans "suddenly grasp at the connection with [the Judeans], saying that they are related to them and tracing their line back to Ephraim and Manasseh, the descendants of Joseph."[115]

By Josephus's own account, however, it is not outside of the realm of possibilities for the Samaritans to legitimately assert this claim of lineage. For example, in his second origin story, Josephus comments that the Samaritans' chief city during that time was "Shechem, which lay beside Mount Gerizim and was inhabited by apostates from the Jewish nation (ἔθνους)."[116] (To be sure, Josephus does *not* state that Shechem was inhabited only by Judean apostates, but that the Judean apostates represent a segment of that population.) These apostates were Judean deserters, as Josephus later explains: "Whenever anyone was accused by the people of Jerusalem of eating unclean food or violating the Sabbath or committing any other such sin, he would flee to the Shechemites, saying that he had been unjustly expelled."[117] If so, then Shechem, the city built around Mount Gerizim, was inhabited with descendants of Judeans, which certainly would lend credence to their claim of Israelite lineage.

We should also note Josephus's connection of the Samaritans with the label "Shechemites." The label "Shechemite" occurs in *Ant.* 5.240–1, 243, 247, 248, 250–1, where Josephus records the events of Abimelech's Shecemite kingdom (cf. Judg 9), and so there were "negative associations to the name 'Shechemites' from early on."[118] The fact that Josephus refers to the Samaritans as Shechemites, instead of Cutheans, seems to imply that "the Samaritans had a connection to the original inhabitants of the city, and this runs counter to his first story that they are immigrants."[119] Thus, while the label "Cuthean" seems to categorize the "Samaritans" in terms of Simmelian "strangers," the label "Shechemites" designates the "Samaritans" in the category of Coserian "heretics" who "claim to uphold the group's values and interests only proposing ... variant interpretations of the official creed."[120]

---

114 Josephus, *Ant.* 11.340 (Marcus, LCL).
115 Josephus, *Ant.* 11.341 (Marcus, LCL).
116 Josephus, *Ant.* 11.340 (Marcus, LCL).
117 Josephus, *Ant.* 11.346–347 (Marcus, LCL).
118 Kartveit, *The Origin of the Samaritans*, 94. Also see Timothy Thornton, "Anti-Samaritan Exegesis Reflected in Josephus Retelling of Deuteronomy, Joshua, and Judges," *JTS* 47 (1996): 125–130.
119 Kartveit, *The Origin of the Samaritans*, 94.
120 Coser, *The Functions of Social Conflict*, 70.

NAMING NARRATIVES   75

In the midst of his second origin story, the Samaritans as Judean apostates among the Shechemites, Josephus records yet another origin of the Samaritans: "the Sidonians of Shechem."[121] As we will see, this phrase "brings to mind a Phoenician origin."[122] Since this section in Josephus contains several labels for the Samaritans, it is best to cite it in full.

> Thereupon [Alexander] promised to grant this request another time when he should come back to them, but, when they asked him to remit their tribute in the seventh year, saying that they did not sow therein, he inquired who they were that they made this request. And, when they said that they were Hebrews but were called the Sidonians of Shechem, he again asked them whether they were Jews. Then, as they said that they were not, he replied, 'But I have given these privileges to the Jews. However, when I return and have more exact information from you, I shall do as I think best.' With these words, then, he sent the Shechemites away.[123]

In this passage, the Shechemites approach Alexander and identify themselves as "Hebrews" and "the Sidonians of Shechem." Returning to the Samaritans' identification as "Hebrews" in a moment, who are these "the Sidonians of Shechem"? As with the label "Shechemites," we should understand the label "Sidonians" in light of how it is used elsewhere in Josephus as well as in the texts of the Hebrew Bible. Hjelm succinctly summarizes this tradition:

> Sidonians in biblical tradition are identical with the worst of idol worship that caused the partition of the kingdom, resulting from Yahweh's punishment of Solomon's worship of "Ashtoret the goddess of the Sidonians, Kemosh the god of Moab and Milkom the god of the children of Ammon" (1 Kgs 11:5, 33; 2 Kgs 23:13).... the Sidonians, who in tradition had become synonymous with ever-hated "Canaanites."[124]

Why would the Shechemites, then, go under the name of "the Sidonians of Shechem"? The likeliest reason for this identification is Josephus's opportunistic

---

121   Josephus, *Ant.* 11.344.
122   Étienne Nodet, *A Search for the Origins of Judaism: From Joshua to the Mishnah* (translated by Ed Crowley; Sheffield: Sheffield Academic, 1997), 140.
123   Josephus, *Ant.* 11.343–344 (Marcus, LCL).
124   Hjelm, *The Samaritans and Early Judaism*, 221. For example, notice Mark's "Syrophoenician" woman (Mark 7:26) and Matthew's "Canaanite" woman (Matt 15:22).

76   CHAPTER 3

criticism against the Samaritans "even to the extent that they profess themselves Sidonians if they consider this opportune."[125]

In regards to the Samaritans identifying themselves as "Hebrews," it is important to be clear about what, according to Josephus, the Samaritans are claiming and denying in this exchange. The Samaritans assert that they *are* "Hebrews" and use this label to identify themselves with the "ethnic name for an Israelite."[126] Although the Samaritans may have "decided to profess themselves Jews" in *Ant.* 11.340, they do not, and instead call themselves "Hebrews." Thus, the Samaritans only deny being identified with those Yahwists to the south who had rejected them when the Judeans had returned to the land and rebuilt the temple in Jerusalem. As a result, the Samaritans were forced to find another identification, and they found one in the connection with their geographical territory in "Ephraim and Manasseh, the descendants of Joseph,"[127] who were, after all, *not* "Jews" or "Judeans" but "Hebrews." The Samaritan identification with the sons of Joseph no doubt derives from the fact that Mount Gerizim and the city of Shechem, the burial site of Joseph (Josh 24:32), were in the tribal territory of Ephraim. Therefore, the Samaritan identification with Joseph (a Hebrew) and his sons Ephraim and Manasseh, whose tribes settled the region of northern Israel, solidifies their identification with the north. The "Samaritans" are an insidious danger to the construction of Judean identity because they identify themselves as "Hebrews" from the tribes of "Ephraim and Manasseh, the descendants of Joseph" (*Ant.* 11.341), which evokes (H-S#2) a myth of common ancestry with the Judeans.

In the face of the Maccabean revolt against the Seleucids, Josephus returns to the Cuthean origin story and his opportunistic criticism of the Samaritans in *Ant.* 12.257.[128] As with the first two renderings, Josephus's comments on the nature of the Samaritans have no parallel in the texts of the Hebrew Bible or the Maccabean accounts. Josephus places this account of the Samaritans after the abomination of desolation (cf. 1 Macc. 1:54) and initial persecution of the pious Judeans (cf. 1 Macc. 1:57–64). According to Josephus, upon seeing the misfortune of the Judeans, the Samaritans "would no longer admit that they were their kin or that the temple on Gerizim was that of the Most Great God, thereby acting in accordance with their nature."[129] Ingrid Hjelm postulates that the point of Josephus's criticism is "the hypocrisy of the Samaritans" and,

---

125   Kartveit, *The Origin of the Samaritans*, 98.
126   "Ἑβραῖος," BDAG, 269.
127   Josephus, *Ant.* 11.341 (Marcus, LCL).
128   Also see Josephus, *Ant.* 9.291 and *Ant.* 11.341.
129   Josephus, *Ant.* 12.257 (Marcus, LCL); cf. *Ant.* 9.291; *Ant.* 11.341.

NAMING NARRATIVES 77

given that these "accounts state that they are not Jews, which, in consideration of their hypocrisy, should imply that they in fact are Jews and therefore should partake in the fate of the Jews whether good or bad."[130] Hjelm's postulation, however, needs to be nuanced. The Samaritans, as presented by Josephus, do not identify themselves as "Jews" or "Judeans" because, as we have seen, these terms imply, for Josephus, an identification with the southern region of Israel principally inhabited by the tribe of Judah.[131] Rather, the Samaritans identify themselves with the labels "Hebrews" or "Israelites" (cf. Delos inscriptions), who share kinship with the Judeans via the tribes of Jacob who settled to the north. Accordingly, the Samaritans do not identify themselves with the label "Jews/Judeans" because they rather consistently identified with the tribes of Joseph in the north.[132]

Nonetheless, according to Josephus, when the Samaritans began to suffer in the Seleucid persecution of the Judeans, they appealed once more to their status as "colonists from the Medes and Persians and they are, in fact, colonists from these peoples."[133] The Samaritans wrote to Antiochus Epiphanes as "the Sidonians in Shechem" about their situation, expressing how they came to practice Yahwism in a manner similar to that of the Judeans.[134] So similar are their Yahwistic practices that "the king's officers, [are] in the belief that we [Samaritans] follow the same practices as they [Judeans] through kinship with them ... whereas we are Sidonians by origin."[135] According to Josephus, the Samaritans once again do not deny being Yahwists; they only qualify their association with the Judeans. While "the king's officers" (Apollonius and Nicanor) cannot distinguish between the two groups, the Samaritans assert that they "are distinct from them both in race [γένει] and in customs [ἔθεσιν]."[136]

As part of the Samaritans' petition to Antiochus Epiphanes, Josephus includes a request "that the[ir] temple without a name be known as that of Zeus Hellenios."[137] Josephus's account parallels the renaming of the temple at

---

130   Hjelm, *The Samaritans and Early Judaism*, 208.

131   Josephus, *Ant.* 11.173.

132   See AF, 68 [57]; 54 [46]; Josephus, *Ant.* 9.291; *Ant.* 11.341.

133   Josephus, *Ant.* 12.257 (Marcus, LCL).

134   Josephus, *Ant.* 12.258–259.

135   Josephus, *Ant.* 12.261 (Marcus, LCL).

136   Josephus, *Ant.* 12.261 (Marcus, LCL). Here again, Whiston's translation is preferable than LCL in light of the concept of "race" outline in Chapter Two. Whiston's translation is, "Since we are aliens from their nation, and from their customs" (Josephus, *Ant.* 12.261). Philip Esler, in his article on Josephus' *Against Apion*, observes that γένος "generally means 'birth' or 'descent,' or it refers to a group of people who are related to one another by the fact of physical descent" ("Judean Ethnic Identity in Josephus' Against Apion," 78).

137   Josephus, *Ant.* 12.261 (Marcus, LCL).

Mount Gerizim in 2 Macc 5–6, which records the persecution of the Samaritans alongside of the Judeans; only here, the Samaritans are in fact identified as the same γένος (2 Macc 5:22–23), and the Judeans' temple in Jerusalem is also renamed (2 Macc 6:2 "the temple of Olympian Zeus"). Josephus, however, completely omits the renaming of the Jerusalem temple in order to denigrate the Samaritans who "successfully petitioned Antiochus, claiming that they were not responsible for the unrest and were not kin to the Judeans."[138] Hjelm explains that "the non-naming of the temple falls within Jewish tradition. Because God has no name, a dedication of the temple would be to 'the only god, creator of heaven and earth'."[139] Concerning the naming of the Samaritan temple on Mount Gerizim, Hjelm accordingly states, "The naming, not the name, is essential to Josephus's account. If the Jews were forced to accept the naming, it was an inevitable fate, but if the Samaritans themselves had asked for the naming and its protection, it was treachery!"[140] Here again is Josephus's central critique about the opportunistic hypocrisy of the Samaritans. As Yahwists, the Samaritans should share in the fate of their co-religionists to the south, and yet they do not. Therefore, the Samaritans are another people group (ἔθνος) altogether. It is, after all, "the living of a common life and the facing of common problems" that stimulates the development of a common ethnic identification.[141] Given that the Samaritans denied Judean identification when faced with "common problems"[142] (e.g. Antiochus Epiphanes), it is not surprising that this is Josephus's central criticism against the Samaritans and not their similar—if not at times identical—ethnic indicia (e.g. Yahwistic cultic practices).

We conclude that, according Josephus's accounts of the Samaritans' origins, the Samaritans continued in their Yahwism until the return of the exiled *golah*-Judeans. Upon their return, the *golah*-Judeans rejected the Samaritans and said they were no better than anyone else who may come to worship at the temple in Jerusalem. This event, probably more than anything else, was the impetus for the Samaritans in solidifying their own Yahwism and identification with the land (i.e. the sons of Joseph/northern Israel). Accordingly, the Samaritans built their own temple on Mount Gerizim and developed their own scriptural tradition in the Samaritan Pentateuch. These developments did

---

138 Knoppers, *Jews and Samaritans*, 176.
139 Hjelm, *The Samaritans and Early Judaism*, 209–210.
140 Hjelm, *The Samaritans and Early Judaism*, 211.
141 Hughes, "The Study of Ethnic Relations," 92.
142 Hughes, "The Study of Ethnic Relations," 92.

NAMING NARRATIVES   79

not occur overnight, but came about over time through the growing tensions
between the Samaritans in the north and the Judeans in the south.

3.2   *Narratives of Judeo-Samaritan Antipathy in Josephus*

There are three events recorded by Josephus that are taken as evidence of commonplace hostility between Judeans and Samaritans: 1) Hyrcanus's destruction
of the Samaritans' temple; 2) the Samaritans scattering bones in the Jerusalem
temple; and 3) the battle between Samaritans and Galileans/Judeans. The first
event is Josephus's account of John Hyrcanus's destruction of the Samaritans'
temple (c. 128 BCE).[143] Josephus's account is included as part of his summary of John Hyrcanus's capturing Medaba, Samoga, and then Shechem. Of
particular note is that the Samaritans are referred to as the Cuthaean nation
(γένος) who lived near the temple on Gerizim.[144] The temple was deserted as
a result of Hyrancus's capturing of Shechem/Gerizim.[145] Josephus does not
linger long on this event and states neither Hyrcanus's purpose for, nor the
Samaritans' reaction to, the desolation of the Gerizim temple.[146] Nonetheless,
this event is often designated as the beginning of the parting of the ways
between Samaritans and Judeans[147] in which "there can be little doubt that the
events of the second century soured relations between the two communities
for centuries to come."[148]

Perhaps the most well known story about the Samaritans in Josephus, other
than his Cuthean origin story, is the story of Samaritans secretly entering the
Jerusalem temple and scattering bones during Passover (Josephus, *Ant.* 18.30).
According to Jeremias, this episode reveals that "the old hatred became more
implacable than ever."[149] Since Josephus states *when* this event took place but

---

143   Josephus, *J.W.* 1.63//*Ant.* 13.255.

144   Josephus, *J.W.* 1.63//*Ant.* 13.255.

145   Kartveit has observed that Josephus does not use a word for "destruction" in regards to
       the Samaritan temple only that it "'became desolate' either from destruction or aban-
       donment" (*The Origin of the Samaritans*, 102). See also Hjelm, *The Samaritans and Early
       Judaism*, 226.

146   Coggins suggests the reason for Josephus' brevity concerning the destruction of the
       Samaritans' temple on Mount Gerizim could be "that this was not a subject upon which
       Josephus would have wished to expatiate, with the destruction of the Jerusalem Temple
       so recent a memory and with the constant ambiguity of the Samaritans' own position"
       (Coggins, "The Samaritans in Josephus," 266).

147   For example see Pummer, *The Samaritans in Flavius Josephus*, 210; Pummer, *Early
       Christian Authors*, 2; Kartveit, *The Origin of the Samaritans*, 102; Knoppers, *Jews and
       Samaritans*, 212–214.

148   Knoppers, *Jews and Samaritans*, 174.

149   Jeremias, "Σαμάρεια," *TDNT* 7:90.

80   CHAPTER 3

says nothing about *why* it occurred, it is prudent "to refrain from seeing the passage as one more of Josephus's anti-Samaritan texts."[150] Regardless, there is not much that can be learned about the label "Samaritan" in this passage.

Josephus records the next Samaritan episode twice and, as we will see, this is the preeminent account for comments on Samaritans in Matthew and Luke. In 52 CE, a battle broke out between Galileans/Judeans and Samaritans.[151] It was first reported in *J.W.* 2.232–44 where the battle between Judeans and Samaritans ensues after a Galilean pilgrim was murdered. However, in Josephus's second treatment of this event in *Ant.* 20.118–136, the Samaritans slew a great number of Galilean pilgrims. According to Josephus, "hatred also arose between the Samaritans and the Jews for the following reason … On one occasion … certain of the inhabitants of a village called Ginaë … joined battle with the Galileans and slew a great number of them."[152] Josephus's report that on *one* occasion *some* Samaritans of *one* village fought Galilean pilgrims can hardly represent the *Zeitgeist*. Although Jeremias cites this singular event as characteristic of Judeo-Samaritan relations in the first-century CE,[153] the incident is, in fact, an exception rather than the rule.[154] If Josephus is correct that it was the Galileans' custom to travel through Samaria for Jerusalem festivals,[155] then "the enmity or hatred between Jews and Samaritans at that time can therefore not have been as general and all-pervading as it is often made out to have been."[156] This is not to deny that hostilities could and did occur between Galileans/Judeans and Samaritans, but to suggest that it was antipathy, rather than enmity, as the norm between Judeans and Samaritans.

In conclusion, Josephus constructs the "Samaritans'" identity in the category of Simmelian "strangers." This understanding is reinforced by the Judeans labeling the Samaritans as "Cutheans"—a label "designed to perpetuate their

---

150   Pummer, *The Samaritans in Flavius Josephus*, 230.
151   For combining Galileans (Γαλιλαῖοι) with Judeans (Ἰουδαῖοι), Steve Mason argues that "the Galilean should be understood as one of the Judeans: since it is a pilgrimage festival, many Judeans are going to Jerusalem; this incident happened to a Galilean. As Josephus' *Life* shows clearly (e.g. 26–27, 63–66, 188–98), Galilean culture of the time was Judean" (Steve Mason, *Flavius Josephus: The Judean War* 2 (Vol. 1B) [Leiden: Brill, 2008], 189 n. 1449).
152   Josephus, *Ant.* 20.118 (Feldman, LCL).
153   Joachim Jeremias, *Jerusalem in the Time of Jesus: And Investigation into Economic and Social Conditions During the New Testament Period* (Philadelphia: Fortress, 1978), 353 n. 5.
154   Pummer, *The Samaritans in Flavius Josephus*, 261.
155   Josephus, *Ant.* 20.118.
156   Pummer, *The Samaritans in Flavius Josephus*, 262.

NAMING NARRATIVES

pagan origin as the descendants of Cutha."[157] The last occurrence of this label in Josephus's *Antiquities* occurs during the Persian period.[158] Starting in the Hellenistic period, Josephus labels the Samaritans as "Sidonians of Shechem"[159] and "Shechemites."[160] Both of these labels harken back to Israel's past, specifically referencing the Canaanites and Phoenicians. In the Roman period, Josephus uses the label "Samaritan" exclusively in *Antiquities*, although he does use the label "Cutheans" for the Samaritans once in *War*.[161] Thus, the more recent the events are to Josephus's writing, the fewer social distancing labels (such as "Cutheans") he uses for the Samaritans. Nonetheless, the Samaritans represent, for Josephus, a distinct ethnic group from the Judeans.[162] Therefore, although the Samaritans share a number of common cultural traits, for the Judeans the label "Samaritan" in Josephus is a "foreigner" or "stranger" who compromises their own ἔθνος[163] and who are not a Judean αἴρεσις "sect."

4   Labeling the Samaritans in the Synoptic Gospels and Acts

We turn now to portrayals of Samaritans in the New Testament outside of the Gospel of John.

4.1   *Gospel of Matthew*
In the Gospel of Matthew, the label "Samaritan" occurs in the context of the mission of the twelve disciples: "These twelve Jesus sent out with the following instructions: 'Go nowhere among the Gentiles (εἰς ὁδὸν ἐθνῶν μὴ ἀπέλθητε), and enter no town of the Samaritans (εἰς πόλιν Σαμαριτῶν μὴ εἰσέλθητε) but go rather to the lost sheep of the house of Israel (οἴκου Ἰσραήλ)'" (Matt 10:5–6). What does the label "Samaritan" mean in context with "the gentiles (ἔθνοι)" and "house of Israel"? Klaus Haacker concludes that Matt 10:5 unequivocally demonstrates that the Samaritans are not "Israelites" by reading "gentiles" and "Samaritans"

---

157   Aryeh Kasher, "'The Enclave of Cutheans'—A Factor in Jewish-Samaritan Relations in Antiquity," in *Proceedings of the Fifth International Congress of the Societe D. Etudes Samaritaines* (ed. Haseeb Shehadeh and Habib Tawa; Paris: Geuthner, 2005), 206.

158   Josephus, *Ant.* 11.302.

159   Josephus, *Ant.* 11.344; 12.258, 262.

160   Josephus, *Ant.* 11.342, 344, 347.

161   In Josephus' account of John Hyrcanus: "He thus captured Medabe and Samaga with the neighbouring towns, also Šii In iii and Argarinin, besides defeating the Cutheans, the race inhabiting the country surrounding the temple modeled on that at Jerusalem" (Josephus, *J.W.* 1.63 [Thackeray, LCL]).

162   Feldman, "Josephus' Attitude Toward the Samaritans," 118.

163   Josephus, *Ant.* 10.184, 17.20, 18.85.

as parallels in juxtaposition to "the house of Israel."[164] W. D. Davies and Dale Allison similarly conclude that "Matt 10:5 dispels any doubt. The Samaritans are not Jews; treat them like Gentiles."[165] Davies and Allison arrive at this premise because "one fact remains undisputed": "Before the time of Jesus and Matthew hostility between Jews and Samaritans was commonplace."[166] Yet, the previous section demonstrated that the evidence for regional conflicts between Judeans and Samaritans is, in fact, limited. First, Josephus is our only source of information for open hostilities between Galileans/Judeans and Samaritans in first-century Palestine. Second, Josephus records only two events of hostilities between Galileans/Judeans and Samaritans (*Ant.* 18:30; 20:118//*J.W.* 2.232). We ought to be cautious about taking limited evidence as representing commonplace occurrences.[167] Instead, as suggested earlier, Josephus represents antipathy (i.e. a dislike or aversion) between Galileans/Judeans and Samaritans that could and did turn into open hostilities but this hardly appears to have been commonplace.

Haacker's and Davies-Allison's examination overlooks the geographic referents of Matt 10:5 where Jesus prohibits the disciples from taking "a *road* that leads to the Gentiles" and from going "into Samaritan *cities*."[168] For, rather than reading the label "Samaritans" in terms of Jew versus gentile, Jesus's command to the disciples represents a geographic limitation of their mission. Yet, even if the geographic reading is not persuasive, we should still understand the label "Samaritan" as referring to a category of its own. The fact that the Samaritans are named separately from the gentiles in Matt 10:5b indicates that they were not equivalent with the gentiles—the Samaritans may not be part of the "lost house of Israel" but they were not gentiles either.[169] Even though the

---

164   K. Haacker, "Samaritan, Samaria," *NIDNTT*.

165   W. D. Davies and Dale Allison, *A Critical and Exegetical Commentary on the Gospel According to Saint Matthew* (3 vols.; ICC; Edinburgh: T&T Clark, 1991), 2.166.

166   Davies and Allison, *The Gospel According to Saint Matthew*, 2.166.

167   For example, as we noted earlier, "open hostilities [between Samaritans and Judeans] were rare enough to have been recorded" (Crown, "Redating the Schism between the Judeans and the Samaritans," 27).

168   Ulrich Luz, *Matthew 8–20* (Minneapolis: Fortress, 2001), 2.73; emphasis added. Also, Benjamin Witherington: "This seems to mean avoid the roads that lead to Gentile territory and avoid Samaritan territory" (Benjamin Witherington, *Matthew* [Macon, GA: Smyth & Helwys, 2006], 219). *Contra* Haacker: "Matt. 10:5f. is not to be understood as a purely geographical limitation of the mission of the disciples to Galilee" (K. Haacker, "Samaritan, Samaria," *NIDNTT*).

169   See Knoppers, *Jews and Samaritans*, 221; wherein Knoppers: "The Samaritans are a *tertium quid*—neither Jews nor Gentiles, but rather something in between." For examples of the Samaritans as a *tertium quid* see Justin Martyr, *First Apology* 53 (*ANF* 1.281) and *m. Qidd* 4:3

NAMING NARRATIVES   83

Samaritans do not share the same status as gentiles, it appears that in the brief reference in Matt 10:5b–6 the Gospel of Matthew constructed the "Samaritans'" identity as Simmelian "strangers," rather than Coserian "heretics," because they are not part of Israel (even the part considered lost).[170]

4.2   Luke-Acts

There are three occurrences of the label "Samaritan" in the Gospel of Luke. The first (9:52) and last (17:16) involve Jesus's and his disciples' interactions with Samaritan(s) while the second (10:33) occurs in a parable. The first encounter between Jesus and the Samaritans starts Luke's travel narrative (Luke 9:51–19:48) when Jesus "set his face to go to Jerusalem" (9:51). For Jesus's first stop, he sent messengers ahead of him to make arrangements for lodging in the Samaritan village (9:52). The Samaritans, however, did not receive Jesus as a guest "because his face was set toward Jerusalem" (9:53). This rejection coheres with the attitudes of some of the Samaritan villagers towards Galileans traveling to Jerusalem.[171] Since Jesus is one of the Judeans who are loyal to Jerusalem, he too is traveling to Jerusalem via Samaria.[172] In light of our discussion on the Judeo-Samaritan relationship, it is possible that the reason the Samaritans reject Jesus for going to Jerusalem is that it violated their "basic value orientation"[173] of a centralized cult on Mount Gerizim which is their dear symbol of Israelite-Samaritan identity (cf. Delos inscriptions and SP Deut 11; 27).

In response to the Samaritans, the disciples James and John ask "to command fire to come down from heaven and consume" the Samaritan village (9:54). Rather than admonishing the Samaritans, Jesus instead "turned and rebuked" his disciples and "then they went on to another village [in Samaria?]" (Luke 9:54–56). In this account, the Samaritan villagers show only an aversion or antipathy towards the traveling Judeans; it is James and John who display open hostility. As we will see in the parable of the Good Samaritan, Jesus does not condone wholesale negative categorization towards non-Judeans and, for

---

F–G (Jacob Neusner, *The Mishnah: A New Translation* [New Haven: Yale University Press, 1988], 496).

170   See John P. Meier, "The Historical Jesus and the Historical Samaritans: What can be Said?" *Bib* 81.2 (2000): 221.

171   Josephus *Ant.* 18:30; 20:118//*J. W.* 2.232. Also see the Gospel of John's parenthetical aside in John 4:8 where there is an absence of Samaritan hostility when the disciples went into the Samaritan city of Sychar to buy food.

172   This was their custom according to Josephus *Ant.* 20.118.

173   Barth, "Introduction," 14.

84   CHAPTER 3

this reason, James and John are the ones to receive Jesus's rebuke and not the
Samaritan villagers.

The second reference to Samaritans in Luke is in the parable of the Good
Samaritan (Luke 10:25–37). The parable is a response to the lawyer's question
"Who is my neighbor?" (10:29). The lawyer is asking a question about bound-
aries: "Where does one draw the line?" Who are our neighbors (i.e. Judean-
Israelites) and who are excluded (i.e. non-Israelites). In this parable, the
Samaritan is a foil to the priest and Levite (10:31–32) who were two respected
members of the Jewish community.[174] More than this, however, we should see
the first two characters as the first two categories in the traditional Judean tri-
partite division of society: "the priests, the Levites, and all the people of Israel."[175]
In this case, the expected third character would be an Israelite layman and
not a Samaritan, whom Luke later categorizes as a "foreigner" (ἀλλογενής;
Luke 17:18). However, as this parable illustrates, Luke does not portray the
Samaritan as a foreigner in the sense of gentiles but rather as non-Judean
Israelites who had their "own text [i.e. SP] and interpretation of the law
of Moses."[176]

In response to the lawyer's question, Jesus begins the parable with a man
leaving Jerusalem heading towards Jericho. On his way the man was attacked
by robbers "who stripped him, beat him, and went away, leaving him half dead"
(10:30). Fortunately for the man both a priest and a Levite come along but,
unfortunately, they both passed him by on the other side of the road. Until the
introduction of the Samaritan, the parable centers on the question of whether the priest and Levite were justified in not treating the half-dead man as a
neighbor.[177]

One reason the priest could be justified for not assisting the victim, although not the Levite, concerns the purity laws of corpse impurity.[178] For
example Leviticus 21:1 states, "No one shall defile himself for a dead person
among his relatives." However, given that the priest was not "among his relatives," "an unattended corpse in the country side does not come under this

---

174   Joseph A. Fitzmeyer, *The Gospel According to Luke I–IX* (AB 28; New York: Doubleday,
       1981), 827.
175   See Michel Gourgues, "The Priest, the Levite, and the Samaritan Revisited: A Critical Note
       on Luke 10:31–35," *JBL* 117.4 (1998): 709–713.
176   Pummer, *The Samaritans in Flavius Josephus*, 31 n. 131.
177   Philip Esler, "Jesus and the Reduction of Intergroup Conflict: The Parable of the Good
       Samaritan in the Light of Social Identity Theory," *BibInt* 8.4 (2000): 341.
178   Richard Bauckham, "The Scrupulous Priest and the Good Samaritan: Jesus' Parabolic
       Interpretation of the Law Of Moses," *NTS* 44.4 (1998): 475–489.

NAMING NARRATIVES

law."[179] Nonetheless, a possible justification for the priest passing the victim by would be the expansion of the purity laws to outside of the temple. Supporting this is the fact that "The appropriate action of a priest finding a corpse by the road was apparently not self-evident, but was discussed by the Tannaim in the period following Yavneh."[180] In particular, there is the debate in *m. Nazir* 7.1 between rabbi Eliezer and the sages concerning whether a high priest or a Nazirite should "contract corpse uncleanness on account of a neglected corpse" (7.1 B). Therefore, according to this interpretation, Jesus's use of a priest in this parable probably reflects the divided opinion between interpreting the Law of Moses—singular Torah or a plural written *and* oral Torah.

When the Samaritan is introduced in the parable some commentators tend to portray the Samaritans in the worse possible light in order to make Jesus's comparison with the priest and Levite all the more poignant. For example, Daryl Bock states:

> For a Jew, a Samaritan was among the least respected people. Eating with Samaritans was equated with eating pork (*m. Seb.* 8.10; *b. Sanh.* 57a). Such people were unclean and to be avoided. The Samaritan would be the last type of person the lawyer would expect to be the climactic figure who resolves the story.[181]

However, Bock only offers a decidedly one-sided reading of the rabbinic traditions concerning Samaritans.[182] In fact, the very passage that Bock cites from the Mishnah reveals more than one opinion concerning Samaritans. According to *m. Seb.* 8.10, Rabbi Akiba is asked what Rabbi Eliezer meant that the "one who eats bread [baked by] Samaritans is like one who eats pork" to which Rabbi Akiba responded, "Shut up [dummies]! I will not tell you what R. Eliezer meant by this."[183] Furthermore, concerning Bock's assertion that

---

179   James G. Crossley, *The Date of Mark's Gospel: Insight from the Law in Earliest Christianity* (Edinburgh: T&T Clark, 2004), 117.

180   Thomas Kazen, "The Good Samaritan and a Presumptive Corpse," *SEÅ* 71 (2006): 140–141.

181   Darrell L. Bock, *Luke* (BECNT 3; Grand Rapids: Baker Academic, 1994), 2.1031.

182   According to Lawrence Schiffman, "a number of Tannaitic passages regarding the Samaritans ... reveal an ambivalent attitude towards them on the part of the Tannaim" ("The Samaritans in Tannaitic Halakah," *JQR* 75.4 [1985]: 349). Concurrent with Schiffman's conclusion, Schur also observes: "The Samaritans are also mentioned at great length in the Talmudic literature. The line taken there is not a consistent one and shows a slow change taking place in the Jewish attitude towards them" (Schur, *History of the Samaritans*, 47).

183   Klyne Snodgrass rightly observes that "the extreme statement of Rabbi Eliezer in *m. Seb* 8.10 is explicitly rejected by Rabbi Akiba in the same passage" (*Stories with Intent:*

86   CHAPTER 3

Samaritans were unclean, we note Rabbi Simeon b. Gamaliel statement that "Every precept which Cutheans [i.e. Samaritans] have adopted, they observe it with minute care, [even] more than the Israelites" (*b. Qidd.* 75b).

Accordingly, the issue is *not* that Samaritans were perpetually unclean[184] or were in the same category as gentiles. Rather the Samaritans are a particular type of Law keeper who is compared to the Sadducees in "follow[ing] after the ways of their fathers" (*m. Nidd.* 4.2).[185] The Samaritans, like the Sadducees, did not accept the plurality of *Torot* (i.e. both written and oral Torah).[186] This is not to deny that the Samaritans had their own halakahic traditions (or Oral Torah) "but they maintain that the tradition is only a help in knowing what the Torah requires, and is not to be considered part of the Torah itself."[187]

Rather than purity shaming the Samaritan in light of rabbinic traditions in order to sharpen the contrast with the priest and Levite, it is prudent to focus on the point of the parable; namely, on *being* a neighbor rather than categorizing *who* is a neighbor. This is made evident by Jesus's rephrasing the question from "Who is my neighbor" (10:29) to "Which of these three, do you think, *was a neighbor* to the man who fell into the hands of the robbers?" (10:36). The lawyer's answer to who was a neighbor demonstrates that the neighbor

---

    A Comprehensive Guide to the Parables of Jesus [Grand Rapids: Eerdmans, 2008], 347). Similarly, in regards to *m. Seb* 8.10, Hjelm comments that "R. Akiba was a former pupil of R. Eliezer (First-Second Century CE) and he did not want to speak with disrespect about his teacher, as the continuation in *m. Seb* 8.11 clearly shows" (*The Samaritans and Early Judaism*, 105 n. 7).

184   *Contra* Bauckham, "The Scrupulous Priest and the Good Samaritan," 488.

185   See Emil Schürer comment: "Basically, therefore, their [Samaritans'] observance of the Torah could be compared to that of the Sadducees" (*A History of the Jewish People in the Time of Jesus Christ* (Peabody, MA: Hendrickson, 1994), 2.20. Schürer also cites the interesting statement from Epiphanius's *Panarion* (16,1 16) that "Sadducees, meaning 'most righteous,' who were descended from the Samaritans" (Epiphanius, *The Panarion of Epiphanius of Salamis, Book I (Sects 1–46)*, trans. Frank Williams (Leiden; Boston: Brill, 2009), 12.

186   According to Rory M. Bóid, "It seems that the Sadducean and Samarian view of the theory of the relationship between Torah and tradition is largely identical" ("The Samaritan Halakah," *The Samaritans*, ed. Alan David Crown [Tübingen: Mohr Siebeck, 1989], 646).

187   Bóid, "The Samaritan Halakah," 645. Bóid adds that "although [Samaritans] are content to accept that much of the halakah can only be known by tradition, they are most emphatically opposed to the Rabbanite version of the concept of Oral Torah" ("The Samaritan Halakah," 644). Also see Alan David Crown, "Qumran, Samaritan Halakah and Pre-Tannaitic Judaism," in *Boundaries of the Ancient Near Eastern World: A Tribute to Cyrus H. Gordon*, ed. Cyrus H Gordon et al. (Sheffield: Sheffield Academic, 1998), 420–441; and Hjelm, *The Samaritans and Early Judaism*, 115 and 271–272.

NAMING NARRATIVES   87

is not someone who must be loved (because they are members of the Judean-Israelites), but the neighbor is "the one who showed him mercy" (Luke 10:37).[188]

The priest and the Levite represent the concern of the lawyer who is interested in categorizing who his neighbors are in light of Lev 19:18. The Samaritan, presumably, represents Jesus's concern which is identifying yourself as a neighbor and then "do likewise" (10:37) in light of Lev 19:18.[189] Thus, as Pummer rightly concludes, "the parable showed that someone who disagrees with the religious authorities in Jerusalem, has his own text and interpretation of the law of Moses, and, strictly speaking, does therefore not belong to one's own faith group, acted correctly."[190] This portrayal of the Good Samaritan's actions is concurrent with the final occurrence of "Samaritan" in Luke's Gospel.

The final occurrence of Samaritans in the Gospel of Luke is 17:11–19 where Jesus cleanses the ten lepers. Jesus is on his way to Jerusalem and, while passing between Samaria and Galilee (17:11), he encounters and heals ten lepers. Only one of the ten returned to thank Jesus "and he was a Samaritan" (17:16). In addition to Luke identifying the healed leper as a Samaritan is Jesus's statement in Luke 17:18: "Was none of them found to return and give praise to God except this foreigner (ἀλλογενής)?" Luke's use of ἀλλογενής is a *hapax legomenon* in the New Testament but it occurs thirty times in the LXX for "of another race, foreign; stranger; layman."[191] (Perhaps the most well known occurrence of ἀλλογενής is "the famous Jerusalem temple inscription μηδένα ἀλλογενή εἰσπορεύεσθαι."[192]) Jesus's identification of the Samaritan as a foreigner

---

188   Gourgues, "The Priest, the Levite, and the Samaritan Revisited," 712.

189   According to Paul Stenhouse the Parable of the Good Samaritan, "put simply, the message of the parable, intended for the lawyer and the bystanders, would run something like this: 'You ask questions about the meaning of the Torah. Then, when they are answered you ask yet another question. Instead of talking about the Torah, dissecting it and weakening its effects on people's lives, observe it, as the Samaritan does. Be like the שמר. Do this and you shall live" ("Who Was the Man Who Fell Among Robbers on the Jericho Road?," in *Proceedings of the Fifth International Congress of the Société d'Études Samaritaines: Helsinki, August 1–4, 2000: Studies in Memory of Ferdinand Dexinger* [Paris: Librairie orientaliste Paul Geuthner, 2005], 203).

190   Pummer, *The Samaritans in Flavius Josephus*, 31 n. 131.

191   "ἀλλογενής," LEH, 27. Also, ἀλλογενής occurs seventeen times in the apocrypha: 1 Esd 8:66–67, 80, 89–90; 9:7, 9, 12, 17–18, 36; Jdt 9:2; 1 Macc 3:36, 45; 10:12; Sir 45:13; Pss. Sol. 17:28. The word "ἀλλογενής" also occurs once in Josephus (*J.W.* 2.417) and four times in Philo (*Somn.* 1.161; *Spec. Laws* 1.124, 4.16; *Virt.* 1.147).

192   "ἀλλογενής," BDAG, 46. Josephus references the temple inscription but "the word denoting the foreigner in the inscription is ἀλλογενής ["another race"] and the words used by Josephus are ἀλλοεθνής ["another nation"] (*Ant.* 15.417) and ἀλλόφυλος ["another tribe"] (*J.W.* 5.194). These three words are used in the Septuagint to translate the Hebrew נכרי 'foreigner'" (Dušek, *Aramaic and Hebrew Inscriptions*, 116).

presents the same comparison as in the parable of the Good Samaritan in which the proper response this Samaritan "foreigner" contrasts the other nine (presumably Judean "insiders"). The Gospel of Luke does not portray the Samaritans as foreigners in the same sense as gentiles but rather acknowledges that the Samaritans are non-Judean Israelites.

There is one other occurrence of the label "Samaritan" in the New Testament. In the Acts of the Apostles 8:4–25 is the account of Philip's interaction with the people of Samaria. According to Luke, Jesus foretold the mission to Samaria immediately before his ascension; saying that they "will be my witnesses in Jerusalem, in all Judea and Samaria, and to the ends of the earth" (Acts 1:8). The impetus for the Samaritan mission was Saul's persecution against the church in Jerusalem "when all except the apostles were scattered throughout the countryside of Judea and Samaria" (Acts 8:1). We are told that, as one of those who were scattered, Philip "went [the/a] city of Samaria and proclaimed the Messiah to them" (Acts 8:5). There is a textual variant in regards to the presence or omission of the definite article before "city of Samaria." If the article is present, "*the* city of Samaria" presumably means the capital city of Sebaste (the city of Samaria in the Hebrew Bible; cf. 1 Kgs 16:24).[193] The reading without the article is an unspecified city in the territory of Samaria which is consistent with the indefinite "in that city" of Acts 8:8. Although the external manuscript evidence for the article is strong, the internal context supports its absence.[194] Some scholars have suggested that the unspecified city in Samaria in Acts 8:5 was Shechem (later Neapolis and modern Nablus), which was the center of the Samaritan people near Mount Gerizim (e.g. Josephus's reference of Samaritans as Shechemites).[195] Another possibility is the village of Gitta because, according to Justin Martyr, this was the hometown of Simon Magus (*1 Apol.* 26) with whom Philip, John, and Peter engage.[196] Regardless, Luke is less interested in the city's location than the evangelist's (Philip) and apostles'

---

193   See, for example, Bruce J. Malina and John J. Pilch, *Social-Science Commentary on the Book of Acts* (Minneapolis: Fortress, 2008), 62 and Hans Conzelmann, *Acts of the Apostles* (Hermeneia; Philadelphia: Fortress, 1987), 62.

194   For this reason, according to Metzger, the article is enclosed brackets in NA/UBS texts (Metzger, *Textual Commentary*, 311). The article is present in P74, ℵ, A, B, 181, 1175, 2344 and omitted in C, D, E, Ψ, 33, 81, 323, 614, 945, 1241, 1505, 1739, *Byz.* For a thorough discussion of the textual issues involved in Acts 8:5 see V. J. Samkutty, *The Samaritan Mission in Acts* (London: T&T Clark, 2006), 86–96.

195   F. F. Bruce, *The Acts of the Apostles* (NICNT; Grand Rapids: Eerdmans, 1990), 216 and Ernst Haenchen, *The Acts of the Apostles: A Commentary* (Oxford: Blackwell, 1971), 301–302.

196   F. J. Foakes Jackson, Kirsopp Lake, and Henry Joel Cadbury, *The Beginnings of Christianity* (Grand Rapids: Baker Book, 1979), 4.89.

NAMING NARRATIVES

(John's and Peter's) interaction with the Samaritans as a people group (τὸ ἔθνος τῆς Σαμαρείας: Acts 8:9).[197]

Luke begins with a summary of Philip's activities in Samaria that upon his arrival, Philip proclaimed the Messiah (8:5) and gained an eager audience by hearing and seeing the signs that he did (8:6) so that there was great joy in that city (8:8). Some scholars suggest that Philip's proclaiming "the Messiah" (instead of "Jesus Christ") was deliberate so as to appeal to the Samaritans' version of a messianic figure—the Taheb ("the returning one").[198] In the Samaritan tradition, the Taheb was the eschatological prophet like Moses (promised in MT Deut 18:15 and the Samaritan Tenth Commandment) who would restore "the Era of Divine Favor" which ended when Eli "the erroneous" violated the statutes of the centralized cult on Mount Gerizim and ushered in "the Era of Disfavor."[199] Although it is possible that these Samaritan concepts lay behind Luke's presentation of Philip in 8:5–7, this is an awful lot to hang upon Philip preaching "the Messiah" instead of "Jesus Christ."

In Acts 8:9–11, Luke provides a flashback to Simon in the time before the arrival of Philip in order to lay the framework for the competition to follow between Philip/Peter and Simon. Philip's activities caught the attention of a magician named Simon who, according to Luke, previously "amazed the people of Samaria, saying that he was someone great" (8:9; cf. Theudas who claimed to be somebody in 5:36). Luke does not indicate the kind of things that Simon did, in contrast to his presentation of Philip in 8:7, but does state the affect that Simon had on the Samaritan people; Simon had "the Samaritans openmouthed with wonder."[200] Consequently, although Simon said of himself that

---

197   In this regard, C. K. Barrett asserts: "The fact is that Luke has no interest in, and perhaps no knowledge of, precise geographical location; his concern is with the events that took place, and took place in a Samaritan environment" (Barrett, *Acts*, 402–403). Also see Ben Witherington, *The Acts of the Apostles: A Socio-Rhetorical Commentary* (Grand Rapids: Eerdmans, 1998), 282 and Aaron Kuecker, *The Spirit and the 'other': Social Identity, Ethnicity and Intergroup Reconciliation in Luke-Acts* (London: T&T Clark International, 2011), 158.

198   See Witherington, *Acts*, 282; James D. G. Dunn, *The Acts of the Apostles* (Valley Forge, PA: Trinity Press International, 1996), 108; Craig S. Keener, *Acts: An Exegetical Commentary* (Grand Rapids: Baker Academic, 2012), 2.1497. In fact, James Dunn suggests that "Luke's report may be sufficient indication that this hope [i.e. the Taheb] was already lively among the Samaritans and that Philip made his evangelistic appeal by claiming that his hope had now been realized in Jesus" (*Beginning From Jerusalem* [Grand Rapids: Eerdmans, 2009], 281).

199   For the Taheb, the "Era of Divine Favor," and the "Era of Disfavor" see Ferdinand Dexinger, "Samaritan Eschatology," in *The Samaritans* (ed. Alan David Crown; Tübingen: Mohr Siebeck, 1989), 266–292.

200   Haenchen, *Acts*, 302.

"he was someone great" (8:9), Luke states that it was the people of Samaria who said of Simon: "This man is the power of God that is called Great" (8:10). Hence, according to Luke, before the Samaritans eagerly listened (προσεῖχον) to Philip (8:6), they were followers (προσεῖχον) of Simon (8:11).[201]

At this point we turn to the discussion of Simon Magus with whom some Johannine scholars have connected their comments on John 8:48.[202] The issue here is whether the "Samaritans," as a whole people and/or region, were explicitly or implicitly associated with the demonic so that "to call someone a 'Samaritan' is an accusation and insult equivalent to denouncing him as possessed by a demon."[203] To support this thesis, scholars have referenced: Justin, *First Apology* 26,[204] Justin, *Dial.* 69 and Origen, *Cels.* 6.11; 8.8,[205] and Origen, *Cels.* 7:9.[206] In particular, let us note Justin Martyr's *First Apology* 26, which states that Simon was a Samaritan from the village of Gitta who "did mighty acts of magic, by virtue of the art of the devils operating in him.... And almost all the Samaritans, and a few even of other nations, worship him, and acknowledge him as the first god."[207] The logic behind appealing to Justin's comments on Simon Magus for labeling Jesus a "Samaritan" in John 8:48 is a syllogism: since Justin, who is also a Samaritan (cf. *Dial.* 120),[208] reports that "almost all" Samaritans worshiped Simon, and Simon was demon possessed, then the Samaritan people, region, and religion must also be demonic.

For substantive support for this reasoning, some scholars (e.g. Haenchen; Conzelmann; Fossum) work backwards to fit Simon's title ("the power of God that is called Great" Acts 8:10) into a Samaritan setting. To begin with, Lukan additions are identified and removed from Simon's title. Two parts are removed, "that is called" (ἡ καλουμένη) and "of God,"[209] which leaves the original

---

201 Luke employs προσέχω three times in Acts 8. BDAG defines προσέχω as: "to play close attention to something, *pay attention to, give heed to, follow*" ("προσέχω," 879–880). According to Luke Timothy Johnson, προσέχω in Acts 8:6 is used in "the sense of mental attentiveness.... [While] in verses 10–11, it has more the sense of commitment of the heart" (Luke Timothy Johnson, *The Acts of the Apostles* [SP: Collegeville, MN; Liturgical Press, 1992], 145).

202 Bauer, *Das Johannesevangelium*, 67; Beasley-Murray, *John*, 136; Michaels, *The Gospel of John*, 523.

203 Dunn, *Beginning From Jerusalem*, 280 n. 164.

204 Michaels, *The Gospel of John*, 523 n. 103.

205 Barrett, *Gospel According to St. John*, 350.

206 Bultmann, *The Gospel of John*, 299 n. 4.

207 Justin Martyr, *First Apology* 26 (ANF 1:263).

208 Justin Martyr (circa 100 to circa to circa 165 CE), "was born of pagan parents at Flavia Neapolis ('Nablus'), the ancient Shechem in Samaria" ("Justin Martyr," in *The Oxford Dictionary of the Christian Church* [ed. F. L. Cross and E. A. Livingstone; Oxford: Oxford University Press, 2005]).

209 Conzelmann, *Acts*, 63; Jarl Fossum, "Sects and Movements," 363–364.

Samaritan statement for Simon as: "This one is the Great Power (οὗτός ἐστιν ἡ μεγάλη δύναμις)."[210] It is then noted that since the Hebrew אל "God" can be substituted by חילה "the Power" in the Samaritan Targum (e.g. Gen 17:1) the title "the Great Power" is a Samaritan title for Yahweh.[211] Accordingly, then, Fossum can conclude, "When Simon claimed to be the 'the Great Power', this amounted to a claim to be the divine Glory, the manifestation of God in human form."[212]

These conclusions are then understood as representing the Samaritan culture (H-S#4) in the first-century, in which to be associated with or labeled a "Samaritan" was equivalent to possessing a demon. There is, however, no evidence for this denotation in the texts of the Hebrew Bible, Josephus's presentation of Samaritans in *Antiquities* or *J.W.*, or even in the rabbinic tradition until *b. Sot.* 22a (c. 400–500 CE), where the Samaritans are included in a list with "magicians" for someone who learned "Scripture and Mishnah but did not attend upon Rabbinical scholars."[213] It is therefore necessary to reassess the syllogism.

For the first premise, that the Samaritans worshiped Simon, Luke states only that the Samaritan people "listened eagerly to" or followed (προσεῖχον[214]) Simon (8:11). Although Luke includes the Samaritans' title for Simon (be it "the Great Power" or "the power of God that is called Great") it is unclear how expansive Simon's following was. Does Luke mean the entire Samaritan people (Acts 8:9) or only the Samaritan people in one particular city (Acts 8:5) were followers of Simon the magician? Also, although Simon is recorded in later Samaritan tradition, it is rather uneventful and it notes only "that he was a contemporary of Dositheus (Dusis) and Philo of Alexandria, and that he opposed Christianity."[215] Additionally, in light of the fact that Samaritan literature "shows no certain signs of Simonian impact,"[216] it is almost certain that Justin

---

210   Fossum, "Sects and Movements," 364.

211   Haenchen, *Acts*, 303; Conzelmann, *Acts*, 63; Fossum, "Sects and Movements," 364.

212   Fossum, "Sects and Movements," 371.

213   Isidore Epstein, *The Babylonian Talmud: Translated Into English With Notes, Glossary, and Indices* (London: Soncino Press, 1961), 3.109–110. According to earlier rabbinic accounts, however, Samaritans were only of doubtful status (*m. Qidd* 4:3 F–G) and, although some rabbis said to treat Samaritans like gentiles, others said to treat them as Israelites (*t. Ter.* 4:12).

214   BDAG defines προσέχω as: "to play close attention to something, *pay attention to, give heed to, follow*" ("προσέχω," 879–880).

215   Stanley Isser, "The Samaritans and Their Sects," in *CHJ* 3.594. For Simon in the Samaritan tradition see Stenhouse, AF 219–222 [169–171].

216   Isser, "The Samaritans and Their Sects," 594. Also see Ingrid Hjelm, "Simon Magus in Patristic and Samaritan Sources: The Growth of Traditions," in *The Samaritans and the Bible* (et. al., Jörg Frey; Berlin: de Gruyter, 2012), 263–284.

92   CHAPTER 3

exaggerated his statement that "almost all the Samaritans" worshiped and
recognized Simon as a god (*1 Apol.* 26).

For the second premise, that Simon was demon possessed, we return to
Luke's statement that the Samaritan people followed Simon because "he had
amazed them with his magic (μαγεία)" (8:11).[217] First, let us note that Luke's
portrayal of Simon, then, is *not* that of a prophet or a messiah/Taheb but magician "and Luke uses the episode to demonstrate Christianity's difference
from, superiority to and triumph over magic (*mageia*—8:11)."[218] The point
of introducing Simon in Acts 8 is not to characterize the Samaritan people
en masse as demon possessed but rather concerns Luke's contrast between
Simon's supposed magical prowess versus the Gospel.[219] Second, it is not as
if the Samaritans alone were prone to figures like Simon Magus for this to be
thought of as characteristic of only Samaritans.[220] After all, Luke includes two
stories of Jewish magicians in Acts (13:6–11; 19:13–14) and yet these figures are
not taken to be representative of Judeans. Therefore, we must reject this notion that the Judeans in general associated the Samaritan people and region
with the demonic *tout court*.[221]

In Acts, as in Josephus, the Samaritans are their own people (ἔθνος) and
not a Judean sect (αἵρεσις). Luke's presentation of the Samaritans in Acts 8,
as a separate people group (ἔθνος) than the Judeans, is again consistent with
Josephus's accounts of the Samaritans. Although the Samaritan people are
outside of Judean ethnic boundaries (cf. Luke 17:18), the Samaritan people are
nevertheless portrayed as Yahwists. As Eckhard Schnabel explains:

---

217   BDAG defines μαγεία as: "a rite or rites ordinarily using incantations designed to
      influence/control transcendent powers, *magic*" ("μαγεία," 608).
218   Dunn, *Beginning From Jerusalem*, 285. Accordingly, Samkutty concludes that "Luke's inter-
      est lies more in the nature of the Samaritan mission than in Simon himself. The central
      argument here is that Luke uses Simon not to tell a story about him, but to portray the
      legitimacy of Samaritan Christianity and to show that it is a mission on a par with the
      Jewish mission. That means Simon is only a vehicle for Luke to authenticate Samaritan
      Christianity" (*The Samaritan Mission in Acts*, 215).
219   F. Scott Spencer explains that "in the narrative world of Luke-Acts, the performance
      of miraculous signs implies a channeling of authentic, divine power for altruistic ends
      in contrast to the demonic origin and fraudulent intent of the practice of magical arts.
      'Miracle' is a positive term; 'magic' is pejorative" (*Journeying through Acts: A Literary-
      Cultural Reading* [Peabody, MA: Hendrickson, 2004], 96).
220   See Keener, *Acts*, 2.1513.
221   In any case, that some Samaritans were followers of Simon makes them no more demon-
      ic than the Judeans who followed the "imposter" Theudas (Josephus *Ant.* 20.97) or the
      Egyptian "charlatan" (Josephus *J.W.* 2.261) ("γόης," LSJ, 356).

Since the missionary preaching of Philip focused on Jesus as Messiah, his listeners obviously were worshipers of Yahweh. He could presuppose faith in the one true God, and he does not preach repentance from idolatry and turning to the only true God. Philip is not engaged in missionary work among Gentiles.[222]

As in Matthew 10:5, the Samaritans are again represented as a *tertium quid* between the Judeans and gentiles.

Accordingly, the Synoptic Gospels and Acts of the Apostles are consistent with the interactions recorded in Josephus that the label "Samaritan" represented a category for particular people group of foreigners and outsiders—Simmelian "strangers." Yet, this "Samaritan" category, as Matt 10:5b–6 and Acts 8:5–25 disclose, was also not the same as gentile outsiders. It was a *tertium quid*. In his Gospel, Luke particularly uses the label "Samaritan" as a foil for the Judean ethnic identity and its boundary line separating them (the insiders) from gentiles (outsiders) and the Samaritans (those in between). Luke's portrayal of Jesus's and Philip's interaction with Samaritans reveals the broadening of the tacit, or "misrecognized," Judean boundary line. As we will see in the following chapter, this is the same purpose of Jesus in the Gospel of John and his interactions with both the Samaritan woman and the group known as "the Jews."

5   Conclusion

The Samaritans identified themselves as Israelites (cf. Delos inscriptions) who have remained faithful to the Mosaic covenant, especially the Deuteronomic command for the centralized temple on Mount Gerizim, and thus (in their own literature) they label themselves "the Keepers." The Samaritans use the label "Judean" to represent those who are a rebellious dissension from this Mosaic (Samaritan) tradition and therefore are Coserian "heretics" who present a choice. This choice, however, does not undo their ancestry as Israelites, specifically as descendants of the tribe of Judah. The Judeans are simply Israelites who have deviated from the primacy of Mount Gerizim as authorized by the Mosaic Pentateuch.

For the Judeans, however, the label "Samaritan" represents a people group of non-Israelites. According to their account in 2 Kgs 17, all former inhabitants of

---

222   Eckhard J. Schnabel, *Early Christian Mission* (Downers Grove, IL: InterVarsity Press, 2004), 1.677.

the northern kingdom of Israel were deported by the Assyrians and replaced by foreigners. Consequently, only the Judeans are the inheritors of Israel's traditions and, specifically, the Judeans who constitute the *golah*-confessional community. Josephus's accounts of the Samaritans' origins in *Antiquities* accentuate their status as foreigners by labeling them "Cutheans." For Josephus, and indeed later Judean traditions, the Samaritans are truly Simmelian "strangers"—outsiders living among them, representing an opposition to their "misrecognized" Judean boundary line.

At times, representatives of each group participated in open hostilities towards the other. If Josephus is any indication, these open hostilities were rare occurrences. Indeed, the Synoptics' accounts use the Judeans' negative categorization of the Samaritans for the purpose of broadening the boundary lines between insiders and outsiders. Similarly, in the following chapter, we will see that the Gospel of John uses ethnic labeling for the purpose of developing a trans-ethnic identity for the followers of Jesus.

CHAPTER 4

Labeling an Ethnic Jesus

Introduction

In the last chapter we saw that the people group named "Samaritans" in the Gospel of John identify themselves, in the evidence outside the Gospel, as Israelites—the descendants of the Hebrews who settled in the northern kingdom and heirs of their Mosaic tradition, which emphasizes Mount Gerizim. In light of the Mount Gerizim tradition, the Samaritans constructed the identity of their Judean neighbors to the south as dissenters (i.e. Coserian heretics) for deviating from the cultic centralization commandment in Deut 12. For the Judeans, since the entire population of the northern kingdom of Israel was deported by Assyria (at least according to the Deuteronomist Historian of 2 Kgs 17), the people group claiming Israelite heritage are foreigners in the land and, therefore, are disinherited from Israelite descent and Mosaic tradition. That the Judeans categorized the Samaritans in this manner is consistent with Zerubbabel's, Jeshua's, and the rest of the heads of families' (Ezra 4:2–3) ostracizing treatment towards the "People of the Land" (i.e. non-*golah* Judeans). The issue for this chapter is how labeling Jesus with either ethnic group functions to broaden ethnic categories into the trans-ethnic identity called the "children of God."[1]

Sections 2 and 3 are structured by setting the context for the labeling event in John 4 and 8 followed by an analysis of Jesus's discourse with his interlocutors. After establishing the parameters for the social context and examining the content of the discourse, we then discuss the specific function of the ethnic labels in that particular chapter of John. Then, in section 4.0, we turn our attention to the function of the dual ethnic labeling in the Gospel of John and note intratextual features between John 4 and 8. For these reasons, there will be repetitions of not only themes but of the subject matter as well.

When addressing the labeling of Jesus with a particular ethnic group, first in John 4 by the Samaritan woman and then in John 8 by "the Jews," we see both the Samaritan woman (John 4) and "the Jews" (John 8) interact with Jesus from

---

1 In this book, the definition for trans-ethnic identity is an identity that binds its members by their faith/belief in Jesus. Although the believers in Jesus are still recognized as Judeans, Galileans, Samaritans, etc., their belief in Jesus transcends the importance of those distinctions.

© KONINKLIJKE BRILL NV, LEIDEN, 2019 | DOI:10.1163/9789004390706_006

their particular view of humanity—one that is divided into ethnic groups. The dual ethnic labeling functions as a social foil for the establishment of the trans-ethnic identity the "children of God" (1:12–13; 11:52). Although "the world of men,"[2] as Bultmann calls it, continues to categorize the "children of God" in terms of ethnic groups (e.g. the Samaritan woman is still a *Samaritan* woman as well as Jesus and his disciples are still Jews), the self-identity of the "children of God" is no longer restricted by the categories of "the world of men." In other words, the self-identity of all who believe is united into a fictive kinship as "children of God" that is embedded in Judean ethnic categories.

1   The Father, the Son, and the Children of God

From the start, the Gospel of John presents a contrast between two kinds of people groups. John 1:11–12 not only summarizes the Prologue but also the whole of the Gospel of John."[3] John 1:11 addresses those of Jesus's "own people" and 1:12 addresses those who are able to "become children of God." The people group of Jesus's "own people" (1:11) are an ethnic group, such as the Samaritans or Judeans, whose criteria of membership one can gauge by the six indicia provided by Hutchinson-Smith. By contrast, however, John 1:12 reveals another people group whose primary criterion of membership is belief in Jesus (cf. John 20:31). Those who believe in him become the "children of God" and are described as having trans-ethnic identity, namely those "who were born, not of blood or of the will of the flesh or of the will of man, but of God" (1:13).[4]

In 1:11, Jesus's ethnic group is indicated by the use of "his own" twice: "He came to what was his own [τὰ ἴδια], and his own people [οἱ ἴδιοι] did not accept him." The first occurrence of ἴδιος is neuter so it is a reference to "*his homeland, his own country.*"[5] The second occurrence of ἴδιος, however, is masculine making it a reference to "his own people."[6] Yet Bultmann argues that both

---

2   Bultmann, *The Gospel of John*, 56.

3   According to Raymond Brown, John 1:11–12 not only provides a summary for the Prologue but also "the flow of the Gospel by describing the activity of the Word" (*An Introduction to the Gospel of John*, 80).

4   I note here that in the Gospel of John "son" is used *only* of Jesus and "children" only for his followers.

5   John F. McHugh, *A Critical and Exegetical Commentary on John 1–4*, ICC (London: T&T Clark, 2009), 41; original emphasis.

6   Louw and Nida define οἱ ἴδιοι here as "persons who in some sense belong to a so-called 'reference person'—'his own people'" ("ἴδιος," L&N 10.12).

LABELING AN ETHNIC JESUS   97

references to "his own" in John 1:11 refer "to the world of men."[7] Bultmann's
stated reason for this interpretation is the context of the Prologue, which is concerned with the ἄνθρωποι and the κόσμος (cf. 1:9, 10). Consequently, Bultmann
asserts: "It is impossible ... to take τὰ ἴδια (or οἱ ἴδιοι) to mean Israel or the
Jewish people."[8] Although Bultmann's stated reason is contextual, Bultmann's
premise may be influenced by his understanding of "the Jews" in John. In his
footnote comment on John 4:22 ("for salvation is from the Jews"), Bultmann
affirms that John "1:11 already made it clear that the Evangelist does not regard
the Jews as God's chosen and saved people."[9] Thus, for Bultmann, it is impossible that "the Jews" could be the reference for "his own" possession or people
in John 1:11.[10]

An issue with Bultmann's interpretation that Jesus came "to the world of
men" in general as "his own," is the Gospel of John's focus on the people living in the land of Israel. Bernard, in making this point, suggests, "in coming to
Palestine, rather than to Greece, the Word of God came to His own home on
earth. Israel were the chosen people; they formed, as it were, an inner circle in
the world of men; they were, peculiarly, 'His own.'"[11] In this regard, Exod 19:5
is frequently referenced for describing Israel as YHWH's "treasured possession out of all the peoples."[12] Hence, as we will see, in the Gospel of John both
the Samaritans and the Judeans identify their people group to be peculiarly
God's own.

To be sure, the Gospel of John portrays Jesus's "own people" (1:11; i.e. "the
Jews" [cf. 4:9; 18:35]) as their own ethnic group in the same way that both
Josephus and Luke-Acts portrayed the Samaritans as an ethnic group. Based
upon the diagnostic features from H-S#1–6 we can collect the ethnic data from

---

7   Bultmann, *The Gospel of John*, 56. In a footnote Bultmann clarifies that "τὰ ἴδια cannot
       here mean 'home, homeland' as in 16:32; 19:27; Acts 21:6, but only 'property, possession'.
       The ἴδιοι are 'his own', who belong to him as their creator" (Bultmann, *The Gospel of John*,
       56 n. 1).

8   Bultmann, *The Gospel of John*, 56 n. 1. Rudolf Schnackenburg similarly concludes, "There
       is no compelling reason to believe that he had Israel in mind" (*The Gospel According to
       St. John*, 1.260).

9   Bultmann, *The Gospel of John*, 189 n. 6. Bultmann's comment is also cited by Grundmann,
       Jesus der Galiläer und das Judentum, 225 n. 5.

10   In this regard, we recall Boyarin identifying Bultmann's paradigm as the "attempt to en-
       hance the anti-Judaism of the New Testament at every turn" (Boyarin, "The Ioudaioi in
       John and the Prehistory of 'Judaism'," 223 n. 24).

11   Bernard, *The Gospel According to St. John*, 1.15. Bernard further observes: "It is not said that
       Israel did not 'know' Him, as is said of the 'world' (v. 10); but Israel did not receive Him in
       welcome."

12   For example, Brown, *Gospel According to John*, 10; Beasley-Murray, *John*, 13; Köstenberger,
       John, 37.

the Gospel of John about this ethnic group. The Gospel of John identifies this group by a common proper name ("the Jews"; H-S-#1).[13] They share "a myth of common ancestry" (H-S#2; 8:33, 39). They share a "collective memory" of a common past such as heroes, events, commemorations, or festivals (H-S#3). The prime example of this in the Gospel of John is the eight references to the commemoration of the Passover event (John 2:12, 23; 6:4; 11:55; 12:1; 13:1; 18:28, 39; 19:14). "The Jews" in the Gospel of John also share a "common culture" (H-S#4) such as customs, language, religion, etc. An example of participating in a common culture is the observance of the Sabbath (5:9, 10, 16, 18; 6:59; 7:22, 23; 9:14, 16; 19:31; 20:1, 19). As an ethnic group, "the Jews" have an attachment to their ancestral homeland (H-S#5). This link to the homeland is evidenced in pilgrimages made to Jerusalem such as Galilean Jews in John 4:45 as well as "the Jews" in Galilee (6:41, 52). Finally, we see "communal solidarity" (H-S#6) in the response of the chief priests and Pharisees, as rulers of "the Jews" (e.g. 3:1; 7:26, 32, 45, 48), who plotted Jesus's death in order to protect their people (ἔθνος; "nation") against the Romans (John 11:48).[14]

Based upon the same diagnostic features (H-S#1–6) we can also collect ethnic data from the Gospel of John about Jesus as a member of this ethnic group. Jesus is categorized as a member of "the Jews" (H-S-#1) by the Samaritan woman and Pilate (4:9; 18:35). However, Jesus was also categorized as a "Jew" (albeit tacitly) in John 8 since he was allowed to enter the Court of Women, which strictly forbade non-Jews. Furthermore, it is possible that Jesus is included in the appeal of "the Jews who had believed in him" (8:31) to be "descendants of Abraham" and therefore sharing "a myth of common ancestry" (H-S#2; 8:33). Jesus also shares the "collective memories" (H-S#3) and participates in the commemorations and festivals of "the Jews" (John 2:23; 4:45; 5:1; 7:10; 12:12; 13:1). Although Jesus sometimes deviates from the practices of "the Jews" in terms of a shared "common culture" (H-S#4), such as how he observes the Sabbath, he decisively sides with and champions the religion of "the Jews" (4:22). Jesus, too, has an attachment to the ancestral homeland (H-S#5) of "the Jews," evidenced by his pilgrimages to Jerusalem with other Galilean Jews (4:45; 7:10). Finally, we see Jesus's "communal solidarity" (H-S#6) with "the

---

13   The Gospel of John uses Ἰουδαῖος seventy times but only seven are spoken by characters in the narrative. The Samaritan woman (4:9), the disciples (11:8), and Pilate (18:35) use the label "Jew" once while Jesus speaks the remaining four other occurrences (4:22; 13:3; 18:20, 36).

14   Esler explains that "the strength of ethnic group solidarity is revealed when an attack launched on one section of an ethnic group leads to other members of that group mobilizing themselves against the enemy" ("From *Ioudaioi* to Children of God," 123).

LABELING AN ETHNIC JESUS

Jews" for fulfilling Caiaphas's prophecy "to die for the nation (ἔθνος)" (11:51; cf. 18:14) and "to gather into one the dispersed children of God" (11:52).

For these reasons, Raymond Brown is certainly correct that "the Jews were Jesus' 'own' (ἴδιοι) people."[15] If this is the case, then according to John 1:11 Jesus's original in-group ("the Jews") "did not accept him" and "by implication they have now become an out-group."[16] However, we must exercise caution here concerning what the Gospel of John is stating. To be clear, just because a person was a member of Jesus's own people (namely "the Jews") does *not* automatically mean that they are part of Jesus's out-group[17] (e.g. "the Jews" who believed in him; 8:30–31; 11:45; 12:11). Instead, the Gospel of John is making the inverse point that just because a person is a member of a certain ethnic group (e.g. Jesus's own people "the Jews") does not automatically mean they are "of God" (e.g. 8:42, 47).[18] As we will see later in this chapter, this is the very source of the conflict between Jesus and "the Jews" in John 8:31–59. When conflict appears in the Gospel of John, such as when Jesus deviates from "the Jews'" accepted mode of conduct (e.g. Sabbath regulations), Jesus is performing the role that Coser would later categorize as a "heretic"; namely, as someone who "claims to uphold the group's values and interests only proposing different means to this end or variant interpretations."[19] From this perspective, Jesus is a factionalist "Jew" who presents an alternative choice of interpretation from *within* his ethnic group ("the Jews") and whose followers are identified as "children of God" (τέκνα θεοῦ; 1:12).

That the Gospel of John promotes the "children of God," as the broadening of the Judean ethnic group identity, is explicit in 1:13, which describes the "children of God" as "born, not of blood or of the will of the flesh or of the will

---

15 Brown, *An Introduction to the Gospel of John*, 171.

16 Esler, "From *Ioudaioi* to Children of God," 126. Elliott defines the term "in-group" as "any set of persons whose members perceive themselves as sharing the same distinctive interest and values and as constituting a collective 'we' over against nonmembers or 'out-groups' designated as 'they,' often with negative valuation" (Elliott, *What is Social-Scientific Criticism?*, 130).

17 Elliott defines "out-groups" as "any set of persons that is perceived by members of an in-group as holding different or competing interests and values from those of the in-group and that is designated by in-group members as 'they,' often with negative valuation" (Elliott, *What is Social-Scientific Criticism?*, 132).

18 Herman N. Ridderbos explains that "the privilege of being children of God is special and exclusive. It is not a natural quality that every human being has as a creature of God; nor is it the inalienable right of Israel as 'his own' (cf. 8:42)" (*The Gospel According to John: A Theological Commentary* [Grand Rapids: Eerdmans, 1997], 46).

19 Coser, *The Functions of Social Conflict*, 70.

of man, but of God."[20] The three consecutive negatives in 1:13 indicate that the "children of God" are presented as an alternative kinship group, which social scientists call "fictive kinship."[21] In terms of a fictive kinship, the "children of God" is capable of including anyone so long as they believe in him (1:12) which is in contrast to the ethnic definitions of the Samaritans or "the Jews" who (at least partially) defined their people group in terms of being "descendants of Jacob" (4:12) and "descendants of Abraham" (8:33, 39, 53) (H-S#2).[22] Already then, the "children of God" is a kind of people group that one is not born (H-S#2) or socialized (H-S#3, 4) into but who are born into a fictive kinship that transcends ethnic identity via belief in Jesus.

Similarly, Peder Borgen describes the Gospel of John's portrayal of Jesus as "the cosmic broadening of ethnic ideas" and this has affinity to the "internationalization" trends in Hellenism.[23] An example of "cosmic broadening"[24] is Isocrates's statement in *Panegyricus 50*: "she [Athens] has brought it about that the name 'Hellenes' suggests no longer a race but an intelligence, and that the title 'Hellenes' is applied rather to those who share our culture than to those who share a common blood."[25] The cosmic broadening is achieved by shifting the unifying factor from the narrower limits of ancestral descent (H-S#2) to the much broader boundary of sharing a disposition from a common culture (H-S#4). Similarly, the Johannine Jesus broadens the criterion for being "(chil-

---

20   Accordingly, Neyrey observes that "membership in the clan or family normally occurs by birth ('born of blood'), then by entrance rituals such as circumcision ('born of the will of the flesh') or by adoption ('born by the will of man'). But none of these can achieve the kinship described here [1:13], for those who calibrate kinship according to the three modes just mentioned 'did not accept him'" (*The Gospel of John*, 40–41).

21   David deSilva defines "fictive kinship" as "the application of the roles and ethos of family to people who are not related" (*Honor, Patronage, Kinship & Purity*, [Downers Grove, IL: InterVarsity Press, 2000], 195). Also see Bruce J. Malina and Richard L. Rohrbaugh, *Social-Science Commentary on the Gospel of John* (Minneapolis: Fortress, 1998), 32–33.

22   Lincoln, *Gospel According to St John*, 103.

23   Borgen, "The Gospel of John and Hellenism," 111. Borgen adds that the Gospel of John's broadening of ethnic ideas "is parallel to the Hellenistic movement from the perspective of the city—state to more universal perspectives. It may even be said that the cosmic broadening of ethnic ideas in John corresponds to the cosmic broadening of the ideas of the city—state (πόλις) to the view that the whole cosmos is a πόλις, in habited by gods and men" ("The Gospel of John and Hellenism," 113).

24   Borgen, "The Gospel of John and Hellenism," 111.

25   Isocrates, *Panegyricus 50* (George Norlin LCL). Jonathan M. Hall, offers the following nuanced translation of Isocrates, *Panegyricus 50*: "The result is that the name of the Hellenes no longer seems to indicate an ethnic affiliation but a disposition. Indeed, those who are called 'Hellenes' are those who share our culture rather than a common biological inheritance" ("Ethnicity," in *The Oxford Encyclopedia of Ancient Greece and Rome* [Oxford: Oxford University Press, 2010], 112).

dren) of God" (e.g. 1:12–13; 8:42, 47) from being narrowly defined in terms of ancestral descent (H-S#2) to being broadly defined as a fictive kinship designated the "children of God," who are those that share the disposition of receiving and believing in Jesus (1:12).[26]

1.1 Jesus and the Gathering of "His Own"

Examples of the Gospel of John's broadening ethnic ideas are found in its theme of gathering in 10:16 and 11:45–53. In the Good Shepherd discourse Jesus says: "I have other sheep that do not belong to this fold (αὐλή). I must bring them also, and they will listen to my voice. So there will be one flock (ποίμνη), one shepherd" (John 10:16). While the Johannine Jesus uses the imagery of God's shepherd gathering his people from exile (e.g. Jer 3:15; 24:3–6; Ezek 34:23–24), which might point to the gathering of Jews from the diaspora, the fact that Jesus has already drawn Samaritans to himself precludes the narrower focus of calling only diaspora Jews into the flock.[27] Instead, Jesus is distinguishing between the sheep who remain in the "fold" (αὐλή) and the sheep, wherever and whoever they are, who "hear his voice" and "follow him" (cf. 10:3–4).[28] Accordingly, Jesus has already caused a division in the fold (cf. 7:43; 9:16) as well as already gathering others from outside the fold of "the Jews" (cf. the Sycharian Samaritans 4:39–42).[29] There are sheep from different folds (i.e. ethnic groups) and those who hear his voice (i.e. believe in Jesus; 10:26–27) are gathered into one flock. Yet the flock is not naturally bound together through their ethnic social ties (H-S#1–6) but gathered together by belief in Jesus into another flock and united by one shepherd.[30]

The second example of the Gospel of John's broadening ethnic ideas in the theme of gathering is John 11:45–53. Johannes Beutler has insightfully observed that John 11:47–53 illustrates "two ways of gathering," with 11:47 beginning "with 'συνήγαγον οὖν', referring to the High Priests and the Pharisees,

---

26   According to Malina and Rohrbaugh, "Those who believe 'into' (are embedded in, remain loyal to) Jesus' name will be made God's kinfolk" (*Social-Science Commentary on the Gospel of John*, 32).

27   Michaels, *The Gospel of John*, 588–589 n. 90.

28   Hence, Paul Rainbow statement: "Gentiles who believe will be full members of the flock. People who do not believe, even if their blood is Jewish, are not his sheep (Jn 10:26)" (*Johannine Theology: the Gospel, the Epistles, and the Apocalypse* [Downers Grove, IL: InterVarsity Press, 2014], 372).

29   In fact, given that "in the Fourth Gospel there is no stress on blood continuity with Israel," the way is open "to all who receive him" (1:12) to be "gathered from the whole world into one (11:52)" (Brown, *An Introduction to the Gospel of John*, 227).

30   Barrett, *Gospel According to St. John*, 376.

102   CHAPTER 4

and leads to the 'συναγάγῃ εἰς ἕν' towards the end (v.52)."[31] The first gathering
occurred because of the High Priests' and the Pharisees' fear that the Romans
would take away from them "both our holy place and our nation" (11:48). In
John's presentation, then, "this Jewish body ... seems to be mainly interested in
the maintenance of its own power."[32] Indeed, it is for this reason that Caiaphas
the high priest asserts his political savvy: "You do not understand that it is better for *you*[33] to have one man die for the people (λαός) than to have the whole
nation (ἔθνος) destroyed" (11:50). Caiaphas's advice to the chief priests and the
Pharisees, then, is to safeguard the "nation" (ἔθνος), "referring to the Jewish
people and its institution."[34]

At this point, the evangelist breaks into the narrative to present the second mode of gathering, of which Beutler remarks, "His death is no longer considered politically but soteriologically."[35] The Evangelist interprets Caiaphas's
statement as a prophecy "that Jesus was about to die for the nation (ἔθνους),
and not for the nation only (ἔθνους μόνον), but to gather into one the dispersed
children of God" (11:51–52). According to the evangelist's prophetic interpretation, Caiaphas "spoke of Jesus' death as the only way in which the people could
be saved."[36] Jesus dies for the people (ὑπέρ τοῦ λαοῦ; 18:14) and for the Jewish
nation (ὑπέρ τοῦ ἔθνους; 11:51–52).[37] Yet, as Barrett observes, "those of the nation

---

31   Johannes Beutler, "Two Ways of Gathering: The Plot to Kill Jesus in John 11:47–53," NTS 40
     (1994): 400.

32   Beutler, "Two Ways of Gathering," 401. Beutler rightly adds that "The 'holy place' (the
     temple, the house of God) and the 'people' (of God) are considered as objects of posses-
     sion which can be taken away by the Romans if Jesus goes on in his activity and arouses
     suspicion." Also see Beasley-Murray, *John*, 196.

33   Caiaphas's advice "for *you*" are the gathered High Priests and Pharisees in John 11 but this
     gathering is identified later as "the Jews" in John 18:14 when the evangelist reminds his
     readers that "Caiaphas was the one who had advised the Jews that it was better to have
     one person die for the people."

34   Francis J. Moloney, "Israel, the People and the Jews in the Fourth Gospel," in *Israel und
     seine Heilstraditionen im Johannessevangelium: Festgabe für Johannes Beutler SJ zum 70.
     Geburtstag*, ed. Michael Labahn, Klaus Scholtissek, Angelika Strotmann, and Johannes
     Beutler (Paderbron: Ferdinand Schöningh, 2004), 354.

35   Beutler, "Two Ways of Gathering," 402.

36   Ridderbos, *Gospel According to John*, 410.

37   According to John A. Dennis, "But this very death will bring about the birth of a 'new
     his own' (1:12), the true Israel or the τέκνα (τοῦ) θεοῦ (1:12; 11:52). This is particularly clear
     in 11:51–52 where Jesus' death *for* others is said to *effect* the gathering of the dispersed
     children of God into one" (*Jesus' Death and the Gathering of True Israel: The Johannine
     Appropriation of Restoration Theology in the Light of John 11:47–52*, WUNT 217 [Tübingen:
     Mohr Siebeck, 2006], 342; original emphasis).

LABELING AN ETHNIC JESUS

who believed in him did not perish (καὶ μή ... ἀπόληται) but received eternal life (3.16)."[38]

Accordingly, in the Good Shepherd discourse, before Jesus spoke of "other sheep that do not belong to this fold" (10:16), he said "I will lay down my life for the sheep" (10:15). The message from 10:15–16 and 11:51–52 is that Jesus will die for his sheep from the fold of "his own people" (1:11) as well as "the dispersed children of God" (11:52) who are his "other sheep" (10:16), and both groups are being united together into one flock as the "children of God" (1:12–13).[39]

Confirming this view is the continuing theme of a broader gathering is John 12 when, after Jesus's entry into Jerusalem, the Pharisees say: "the world has gone after him!" (12:19). The arrival of the Greeks to see Jesus follows (12:20–21).[40] However, this is not the final gathering. The presence of the Greeks signal that "the hour has come for the Son of Man to be glorified" (John 12:23) which Jesus later explains, "I, when I am lifted up from the earth, will draw all people to myself" (12:32).[41]

In 10:16, we can understand the one flock representing a fictive kinship that consists of sheep from other folds/ethnic groups who are being gathered and united by their belief in Jesus.[42] This gathering represents the "cosmic broadening" of Judean ethnic identity. Although this fictive kinship is not restricted by a perceived physical ancestral descent (H-S#2), it is thoroughly embedded within Judean ethnic identity. Jesus broadens Judean ethnic identity, such as

---

38   Barrett, *Gospel According to St. John*, 406–407.

39   "Jesus collects those who belong to him within and without Judaism, and lays down his life for them" (Barrett, *Gospel According to St. John*, 407–408).

40   Johannes Beutler, "The People of God," in *Judaism and the Jews in the Gospel of John* (Roma: Pontificio Istituto Biblico, 2006), 143. According to Moloney, "The theme of a universal gathering, from the Jewish and non-Jewish world, is explicit. In proof of the movement of the whole world toward Jesus as the passion approaches, Greeks arrive, and ask to see Jesus (12:20–31)" ("Israel, the People and the Jews in the Fourth Gospel," 356).

41   Moloney notes that "Whatever might be thought of the many sheep in 10:16 or those scattered abroad in 11:52, Jesus' words in 12:32 are unambiguous: when he is lifted up from the earth, he will draw everyone (πάντας) to himself. The Greek expression can mean only 'all people,' not 'all things'" (Francis J. Moloney, *Love in the Gospel of John: An Exegetical, Theological, and Literary Study* [Grand Rapids: Baker Academic, 2013], 92).

42   For ethnic categories fading in significance, Brown argues that "even if John would never deny that salvation is from the Jews, the time has come when the argument over the proper place of worship that distinguished Samaritans from Jews has been resolved by worship in Spirit and truth (4:21–23)" (Brown, *An Introduction to the Gospel of John*, 181 n. 74).

104   CHAPTER 4

collective memories (H-S#3); common culture and religion (H-S#4); and links
to the homeland (H-S#5), by means of giving them variant interpretations.[43]

1.2   *Broadening Horizons*

The gathering of the disciples in John 1:35–51 illustrates the embeddedness of
Jesus's fictive kinship ("children of God") in Judean ethnic identity as well as
the convergence with Jesus's broadening alternative interpretation of Judean
ethnic identity. For example, the one flock is united under the one shepherd
whom they believe is the Jewish Messiah (1:41), "about whom Moses in the law
and also the prophets wrote" (1:45), and who Nathanael addresses "Rabbi, you
are the Son of God! You are the King of Israel!" (1:49; H-S#4). Yet Moloney, followed by Beutler, have rightly observed a "tension between the messianic expectations of the Palestinian Jews and the true dignity of Jesus according to
John's faith community."[44] Nathaniel's confession (1:49) is not fully adequate
because it is qualified by Jesus's response that they will see still "greater things"
(1:50). Regarding the Gospel of John's purpose statement ("so that you may
come to believe that Jesus is the Messiah, the Son of God"; 20:31), Moloney
observes the subtle modification that "Jesus's being the Christ is entirely conditioned by the greater truth: he is the Son of God."[45] The confessions proclaimed
by Jesus's followers in the Gospel of John are not wrong, but rather not fully adequate because they have yet to be broadened by Jesus's variant interpretation.

1.3   *Children of God*

Those who receive and believe in Jesus will become "children of God" (1:12)
regardless of their descent (1:13). They are gathered from ethnic groups, such
as the Samaritans or Judeans, whose criteria of membership we have gauged
in terms of the six indicia provided by Hutchinson-Smith. Jesus's interaction
with members from both of these ethnic groups, as we will see, disrupts the

---

43   Jesus is portrayed in a role that Coser defines as the "heretic" (*The Functions of Social
      Conflict*, 70).

44   Beutler, "The People of God," 140. For example, Moloney notes that "these disciples' un-
      derstanding of the person of Jesus ... does not match the understanding of the reader,
      provided by the prologue (1:1–18) and the witness of John the Baptist (1:19–36)" (Moloney,
      Love in the Gospel of John, 40).

45   Moloney, *The Gospel of John*, 544. Moloney adds that: "Jesus is the Christ, but the Christ
      who is the Son of God. A belief that reaches beyond all human, historical, and cultur-
      al conditioning accepts that Jesus is the long-awaited Christ, but only insofar as he has
      come from God and returns to God and is the Son of God, the Sent One of the Father,
      the one who has made God known. Eternal life is possible for those who come to know
      God through Jesus Christ, the one whom God has sent (cf. 17:3)" (Moloney, *The Gospel of
      John*, 543–544).

LABELING AN ETHNIC JESUS

seemingly static nature of how their identity (as God's peculiar people) is constructed. This disruption elicits both a positive and a negative response that functions as a social foil revealing the nature of the "children of God" as transcending the primacy attached to ancestral descent in their ethnic identity.

2 Jesus "the Jew"

In this section of Chapter Four, we find that Jesus is labeled as a member of "the Jews" (H-S-#1) by the Samaritan woman (4:9). Confirming the Samaritan woman's categorization of Jesus as a "Jew" is Jesus's participation in the Galilean Jews' custom of pilgrimage (4:45; 7:10; cf. Josephus, *Ant.* 20.118) to their ancestral homeland (H-S#5) in order to participate in the Judean festivals (H-S#3) in Jerusalem (2:23, 4:45).[46] Jesus is labeled a "Jew" by the Samaritan woman for deviating from established rules of interaction between the two people groups (cf. 4:9b). However, in this section we will see that Jesus's deviation coheres with his variant interpretation of Judean ethnic identity that is broadened to include "other sheep" (10:16) not of his fold.

2.1 *Setting the Scene: Jacob's Well*
John 4:1–6 sets the scene for Jesus's interaction with the Samaritan woman (4:7–26) and subsequently the Samaritan villagers (4:39–42). Jesus leaves Judea for Galilee because the Pharisees had heard he was making and baptizing more disciples than John the Baptist (4:1). It is possible that since the last account concerning the Pharisees involved their questioning of John the Baptist (1:24) as well as their absence in Galilee (in the Gospel of John), Jesus is seeking to avoid similar lines of questioning by going to Galilee.[47] Jesus departs for Galilee from somewhere in the "Judean countryside"[48] (3:22) but he "*had to* [ἔδει] go through Samaria" (4:4), which used the route known as the "National

---

46   John P. Meier has observed that, "For all the supposed anti-Judaism of John's Gospel, it is in this story [John 4] that Jesus is most directly identified as 'a Jew'—as distinct from another monotheistic religious groups of Semites in Palestine—and that he clearly vindicates the stance of the Jews vis-à-vis the Samaritans on the proper place for the public, communitarian worship of God ('we [Jews] worship what we know', v. 22)" ("The Historical Jesus and the Historical Samaritans," 229–230).

47   Michaels, *The Gospel of John*, 231.

48   BDAG notes that Ἰουδαῖος with "γῇ [in] J 3:22 is to be taken of Judea in the narrower sense (s. Ἰουδαία 1), and means *the Judean countryside* in contrast to the capital city" ("Ἰουδαῖος," 478). The narrower sense of Ἰουδαία is defined as "the southern part of Palestine in contrast to Samaria, Galilee, Perea and Idumea, *Judea*" ("Ἰουδαία," BDAG, 478).

Highway," "Ridge Route," or "Watershed Route."[49] For Brown, however, the reason Jesus "*had to* [ἔδει] go through Samaria" (4:4) was not due to a topographic necessity but because it was divine necessity for Jesus's mission (4:32, 34).[50] In addition, Brown has observed that if Jesus's starting point was in proximity to John the Baptist (3:22–23), locating Jesus somewhere in the Jordan River Valley, the obvious route to Galilee was the Jordan Rift/Valley Road,[51] which circumvented Samaria.[52] Yet, given that there are three different sites suggested for John the Baptist's location "at Aenon near Salim" (3:23),[53] we should not too readily discount topographical necessity without knowing the location of Jesus's starting point. Instead of reading John 4:4 as either topographic necessity or divine necessity, J. Eugene Botha suggests that "the use of ἔδει at first only serves to help set the scene for the subsequent dialogue and

---

49   According to Carl Rasmussen, the first day of this route started from the north of Jerusalem to Lebonah, which was south of the Judea's northern border at Anuathu Borcaeus and Acrabeta. The second day, after passing through Mount Ebal and Mouth Gerizim, ended at Geba. The third day led to Ginae on the southern side of the Valley of Esdraelon and northern boundary of Samaria and then crossing into Galilee (*Zondervan Atlas of the Bible* [Grand Rapids: Zondervan, 2010], 215). The stops between Jerusalem and Ginae are based upon Josephus's statement that this route took three days (*Life* 260).

50   Brown, *The Gospel According to John*, 1.169. Also see Beasley-Murray, *John*, 59; Keener, *The Gospel of John*, 1.590; Lincoln, *Gospel According to Saint John*, 171.

51   The "Jordan Rift/Valley Road" led from Galilee through Scythopolis into Perea in the Transjordan, then south in the Rift Valley along the Jordan River, and then back west through Jericho and onto Jerusalem (Peter Richardson, *Herod: King of the Jews and Friend of the Romans* [Minneapolis: Fortress, 1999], 143). Anson F. Rainey and R. Steven Notley note a third route between Galilee and Judea not mentioned in connection with Jesus's travels that "led along the foothills of Mount Ephraim to Antipatris and ascended the Beth-horon ridge to Jerusalem" (*The Sacred Bridge: Carta's Atlas of the Biblical World*, 2d ed. [Jerusalem: Carta, 2014], 363).

52   Brown, *The Gospel According to John*, 1.169. For the route from Galilee through Samaria to Jerusalem, known as the "National Highway," "Ridge Route," or "Watershed Route," see David Dorsey, *The Roads and Highways of Ancient Israel* (Baltimore: Johns Hopkins University Press, 1991), 117–146; also, Rainey and Notley, *Sacred Bridge*, 363.

53   The three sites are: 1) Sapsaphas north-east of the Dead Sea in the Transjordan (Madeba Map); 2) Tel Salim seven miles south from Scythopolis/Beth-Shean (Eusebius' *Onomasticon*); 3) the modern-day Arab village of Salim three miles east of Shechem in the interior of the hill country of Samaria. For further discussion see Rainey and Notley, *Sacred Bridge*, 350–351 and Urban C. Von Wahlde, Archaeology and John's Gospel," in *Jesus and Archaeology*, ed. James H. Charlesworth (Grand Rapids: Eerdmans, 2006), 555–556.

LABELING AN ETHNIC JESUS

that it is purely informative."[54] It is only as the narrative progresses that "it will become clear that the entire narrative is subject to divine necessity."[55]

Upon arriving in Samaria, Jesus comes to the Samaritan city of Sychar (4:5), which is near the place Jacob gave Joseph (4:5) and Jacob's well (4:6). The site of the city of Sychar is the present day city of Askar,[56] although Brown contends Sychar should be identified as Shechem.[57] Regardless of the site's identification, what is important for the Gospel of John is that "Sychar" forms part of a geographical unit that included Jacob's field and well.[58] In the Hebrew Bible there are two references to Jacob in this region. The first is Jacob's purchase of the field near Shechem (Gen 33:18–20) and the second is Joseph's burial there (Josh 24:32). In fact, Joseph's burial "at Shechem" is specifically linked with "the portion of ground that Jacob had bought" (Joshua 24:32). Still more importantly, Joshua 24:32 specifically states that the site "became an inheritance of the descendants of Joseph." The Samaritan people, being descendants from the tribe of Joseph (cf. Josephus, *Ant.* 11.341), could claim the site as an inheritance for themselves.

Although the texts of the Hebrew Bible do not reference the existence of Jacob's well, the Gospel of John nevertheless "presupposes that this well … was revered by the Samaritans as having been used by Jacob (4:12)."[59] Thus, the Gospel of John sets the stage for Jesus's interaction with the Samaritan woman at the geographic unit that represents the "primordial attachments" or

---

54   J. Eugene Botha, *Jesus and the Samaritan Woman: A Speech Act Reading of John 4:1–42* (Leiden: Brill, 1991), 103.

55   Hendrikus Boers, *Neither on This Mountain Nor in Jerusalem: A Study of John 4* (Atlanta: Scholars Press, 1988), 155.

56   W. R. F. Browning, "Sychar," *Oxford Dictionary of the Bible* (Oxford: Oxford University Press, 2009), 345. Browning further notes that Sychar "was a central settlement for Samaritan inhabitants between the destruction of Shechem (*c.* 107 BCE) and the foundation of Neapolis by the Romans in 70 CE."

57   Brown, *Gospel According to John*, 1.169. The textual manuscript evidence is overwhelmingly in favor of Συχάρ with only the Syriac manuscripts Sinaitic (Syr^s) and Curetonian (Syr^c) supporting Shechem (ܫܟܝܡ). Jerome, however, thought "Συχάρ" was a corrupt form of Συχέμ ("Συχάρ," BDAG, 979).

58   Clemens Kopp, *The Holy Places of the Gospels* (New York: Herder and Herder, 1963), 162. Neyrey suggests that "the well in John 4:12 might be called Jacob's well simply because it lies in Jacob country, at Shechem" ("Are You Greater than Our Father Jacob?," in *The Gospel of John in Cultural and Rhetorical Perspective* [Grand Rapids: Eerdmans, 2009], 109).

59   McHugh, *Critical and Exegetical Commentary on John*, 266. Knoppers points out that even though it is not mentioned in the texts of the Hebrew Bible, Jacob's well "was an important site in Samaritan and Jewish (and later Christian and Muslim) tradition" (*Jews and Samaritans*, 2–3). An example of Jacob's Well as an important site in later tradition is its inclusion in the Madaba Map (c. sixth-century CE).

"givenness" for the Samaritans' sense of ethnic identity (e.g. ancestral descent, language, region, religion, customs, etc. [H-S#1–6]) that are situationally reproduced during interactions as indicia of their ethnic groups' identity.

2.2   *Setting the Labeling Context: if You Only Knew*

The entire discourse (4:7–26) and the Samaritan mission (4:1–42) is the result of Jesus's request for a drink (4:7). In fact, according to Cyril of Alexandria, the purpose for Jesus's request was "in order then that the woman may exclaim, and that His unwonted conduct may invite her to ask Who He is, and whence, and how He despises the Jewish customs."[60] In John 4:7, Jesus asks for a drink from "a Samaritan woman" (lit. a woman of/from Samaria: γυνὴ ἐκ τῆς Σαμαρείας).[61] The woman's identity, in fact, is emphasized by being named three times as a Samaritan (an inhabitant of Samaria) in the span of two verses (John 4:7, 9); twice the narrator calls her a "Samaritan" and once she uses it as a self-identifying label. The remainder of their exchange, however, centers on Jesus's identity: a "Jew," as "greater than Jacob," a "prophet," and as "Messiah."

In John 4:9, which is the focus of the following section, the Samaritan woman asks how Jesus, as a "Jew," can ask her for a drink. Jesus's response in John 4:10a ("If you knew the gift of God, and who it is that is saying to you") is asking "the woman to reassess her perception of the present situation."[62] Jesus challenges the Samaritan woman's knowledge of his identity and the "gift of God," which prompts her question "Are you greater than our ancestor Jacob?" (4:12).[63] Jerome Neyrey suggests that Jacob traditions, found in the Palestinian Targumim *Neofiti* and *Pseudo-Jonathan*, are implied in the Samaritan woman's

---

60   Cyril of Alexandria, *Commentary on the Gospel of St. John* (trans. Philip Edward Pusey; London: James Parker & Co., 1874), 1.206.

61   When Herod renamed the capital city from "Samaria" to "Sebaste" in 27 BC, the name "Samaria" was transferred to the region spanning from the Plain of Jezreel in the north to Anuathu Borcaeus (the northern boundary of Judea [Josephus, *J.W.* 3.51] ("Σαμαρίτης," BDAG and Jeremias, "Σαμαρίτης," *TDNT*). In 6 CE Samaria was incorporated with Judea and Idumea to form the Roman province of Judea but after the destruction of the Jerusalem temple in 70 CE, "the Romans changed the name of the province from Judea to Palestina, the Greek term for Philistia, on the Mediterranean coast" (Aaron Demsky, "Judah," *The Oxford Dictionary of the Jewish Religion*, 2d. edited by Adele Berlin and Maxine Grossman [Oxford: Oxford University Press, 2011]).

62   Gail R. O'Day, *Revelation in the Fourth Gospel: Narrative Mode and Theological Claim* (Philadelphia: Fortress, 1986), 60. O'Day adds, "She assumes that she is in conversation with a thirsty Jew; this Jew informs her that if she knew both the gift of God and the identity of the person with whom she was speaking, should recognize that she herself was the thirsty one."

63   O'Day states: "The woman's question in v. 12 focuses directly on Jesus's identity when she asks, 'Are you greater than our father Jacob?" (*Revelation in the Fourth Gospel*, 62).

questions in 4:11–12.[64] In particular, Neyrey notes that *Tg. Ps.-J.* Gen 28:10 references five miracles performed by Jacob and the fourth one was "*that the well flowed, and the waters came up before him and continued to flow all the days that he was in Haran*" (cf. Gen 29:10).[65] Therefore, in light of the Samaritan woman's observation that Jesus has no bucket, "the only alternative would be to perform a miracle, like Jacob's."[66] Although Neyrey's interpretation is possible, it is not probable because the *Pseudo-Jonathan* traditions may well be too late[67] in addition to the absence of the Jacob miracle traditions in the known Samaritan literature (e.g. Samaritan Pentateuch, *Samaritan Targum*, or Samaritan Chronicles). Instead, the Samaritan woman likely understood Jesus's offer of "living water" (4:11) as a reference to the spring that fed into the well (πηγή: 4:5) and therefore asks how he could get living water from the well (φρέαρ) without a bucket (4:11).[68]

Regardless, the Samaritan woman's question reveals that she understood the "gift of God" as "Jacob's well" that was, after all, the gift that Jacob gave to Joseph (4:5) and his descendants (4:12). The Samaritan woman responds out of her social reality, wherein it was a "misrecognized" givenness "that the giver of the gift was Jacob, and that he cannot be surpassed."[69] Accordingly, the Samaritan woman asks Jesus with the expectation of a negative answer,

---

64   Neyrey, "Are You Greater than Our Father Jacob?," 106. Also see José Ramón Díaz, "Palestinian Targum and New Testament," *NovT* 6 (1963): 75–80; Martin McNamara, *Targum and Testament Revisited: Aramaic Paraphrases of the Hebrew Bible* (Grand Rapids: Eerdmans, 2010), 220–221.

65   *Pseudo-Jonathan* Gen 28:10 (Michael Maher, ArBib 1B); original emphasis. This event took place in Gen 29:10, which *Tg. Ps.-J.* Gen 29:10 states: "And when Jacob saw Rachel, the daughter of Laban, his mother's brother, <and the flock of Laban, his mother's brother>, Jacob drew near and, *with one of his arms,* rolled the stone from the mouth of the well; *and the well began to flow, and the waters came up before him,* and he watered the flock of Laban, his mother's brother; *and it continued to flow for twenty years*" (*Tg. Ps.-J.* Gen 29:10 [ArBib 1B]; original emphasis).

66   Neyrey, "Are You Greater than Our Father Jacob?," 109.

67   Keener, *The Gospel of John*, 1.604.

68   For a cistern (φρέαρ) with an underground spring (πηγή) see: Morris, *The Gospel According to John*, 228; Carson, *Gospel According to John*, 217; Köstenberger, *John*, 151. Louw and Nida explain that "if there was a relatively ready flow of water, a well could very appropriately be called a πηγή, 'spring,' 1.78 (and this may be the reason for πηγή, in John 4:6), but if water only gradually seeped into the well from surrounding areas or was collected in the well from surface drainage, it would be more appropriately called φρέαρ. However, both terms are used interchangeably in certain contexts; compare, for example, πηγή, in John 4:6 and φρέαρ in John 4:11, both referring to Jacob's well at Sychar" ("φρέαρ," L&N 7.57).

69   Moloney, *The Gospel of John*, 118.

"Are you greater than our ancestor Jacob?" (4:12).[70] Here we must note that just as the Samaritan labels Jesus a "Jew" (4:9) and "the Jews" label Jesus a "Samaritan" (8:48), both interlocutors also ask Jesus the same question, "Are you greater than our father?" (4:12a//8:53a). These intra-textual links will be examined in more detail in section 4.0 but, as Hans Förster has insightfully observed, "in beiden Fällen wird die Identität durch die Genealogie zum Ausdruck gebracht."[71] In this regard, then, the Samaritan woman's question is more than a patriotic defense of Jacob or ancestral water[72] because it is a claim about kinship, that the Samaritan people are descendants from Jacob—Israel himself (cf. Josephus *Ant.* 11.341) and therefore Israelites (cf. Delos inscriptions and the Samaritan Chronicles). We recall that from the Samaritan perspective, although the Judeans are Israelites (the children of Judah), the Samaritans categorized the Judeans as what Coser would later define as "heretics" because the Judeans are erroneously beholden to Jerusalem and the prophets (Nevi'im) (cf. AF, 56–57 [48]). Therefore, the Samaritan woman's statement about "*our father Jacob*" is an acknowledgement of their common ancestry (H-S#2).

Yet, there is more than appeal to genealogical "kinship" here; there is ethnicity.[73] In particular we note that the Samaritan woman says "our father Jacob who gave *us* [i.e. the Samaritans] the well" (4:12).[74] This well, as part of "the plot of ground that Jacob had given to his son Joseph" (4:5), was the in-

---

70   According to Jürgen Zangenberg, "There was enough reason, therefore, for both Samaritans and Jews to be present at a site ["the plot of ground that Jacob had given to his son Joseph" (4:5)] so charged with religious significance and to underscore their position over against competing claims on the heritage of the patriarchs and the right way to worship the God of Israel" ("Between Jerusalem and the Galilee: Samaria in the Time of Jesus," in *Jesus and Archaeology* [Grand Rapids, Eerdmans, 2006], 417).

71   Hans Förster, "Die Begegnung am Brunnen (Joh 4.4–42) im Licht der 'Schrift': Überlegungen zu den Samaritanern im Johannesevangelium," *NTS* 61.2 (2015): 212. Förster also suggests: "Dass Jesus dann im Johannesevangelium seitens der Juden als 'Samaritaner' bezeichnet wird, könnte einen potentiellen intratextuellen Verweis von Joh 8.48 auf die gegenständliche Passage darstellen, welche die Frage der Genealogien (und ihrer damit verbundenen Identitätsaussagen bezüglich Juden und Samaritanern) zu einem zentralen Thema macht" (Förster, "Die Begegnung am Brunnen," 211 n. 75).

72   O'Day, *Revelation in the Fourth Gospel*, 62; Teresa Okure, *The Johannine Approach to Mission: A Contextual Study of John 4:1–42* (Tübingen: Mohr Siebeck, 1988), 99.

73   For issues of kinship in the New Testament, see deSilva, *Honor, Patronage, Kinship & Purity*, 199–40; Hanson and Oakman, *Palestine in the Time of Jesus*, 19–56.

74   See Michaels: "The merits of the well become for the woman a matter of ethnic pride. What water source could be greater or more satisfying than that which 'our father Jacob' left for his Samaritan children?" (*The Gospel of John*, 241). Similarly, Tertullian states: "The Samaritans were always pleased with themselves, about mountains, and ancestral wells ... although the Samaritans also are Israelites" (*Adversus Marcionem* 4.35, trans. Ernest Evans [Oxford: Clarendon, 1972], 463).

LABELING AN ETHNIC JESUS

heritance given to Joseph (cf. Gen 48:22) and his children (cf. Joshua 24:32). Accordingly, there is more at work than a genealogical claim (H-S#2); there is also claim to an ancestral homeland (H-S#5), collective memories (H-S#4) [i.e. the giving of land to Joseph], and shared culture (as Yahwists) (H-S#4), albeit at Mount Gerizim and not Jerusalem.[75] The basis of her appeal to Jacob, as common ancestor and benefactor of this land to Joseph, are representative of the tacit "misrecognition" of her social reality and, as such, informs her question to Jesus with the expectation that his answer is "no" (4:12).

Jesus's response shifts to the future tense in order to move her beyond the negative expectations from "misrecognized" categories.[76] Also, this will eventually lead her in overcoming the past divisions between "Samaritans" and "Jews" and into his flock of "children of God." In response to the Samaritan woman's question, Jesus offers a comparison between thirsting again and again (4:13) in contrast to a potential future of never being thirsty (4:14).[77] In so doing, Jesus answers the Samaritan woman's question (4:11–12) in the affirmative that he is greater than Jacob.[78] In response, the Samaritan woman asks Jesus for his living water (4:10) that quenches thirst forever (4:14).

---

75   It is also possible that the Samaritan woman's appeal to "our father Jacob" represents communal solidarity (H-S#6) for, as deSilva states, "The expressions 'house of Jacob,' 'house of Israel,' 'children of Jerusalem' ... and the like were *verbalizations of the corporate solidarity* of the Jews on the basis of a notion of extended kinship" (deSilva, *Honor, Patronage, Kinship & Purity*, 164; emphasis added).

76   Martina Böhm, *Samarien und die Samritai bei Lukas* (Tübingen: Mohr Siebeck, 1999), 144. Also see McHugh who similarly notes, "Her mindset is locked in the past (see also 4:20), so Jesus from this point onwards begins to speak only about the future" (*Critical and Exegetical Commentary on John*, 271).

77   The Johannine Jesus expresses the givenness of thirsting in 4:13 by using a present participle to indicate the repeated and habitual practice of drinking water from Jacob's well versus the potential of drinking ($\delta\varsigma$ $\dot{\alpha}\nu$ $\pi\acute{\iota}\eta$) his water and never thirsting again. This potential is expressed as a conditional relative clause and could be rendered: "If anyone should drink water I give then they will never thirst again." See "$\dot{\alpha}\nu$," 1.b. and 1.b.α. BDAG, 56; and BDF §380.1. For the transition and contrast of drinking in 4:13 to 4:14, see O'Day, *Revelation in the Fourth Gospel*, 63 and Moloney, *The Gospel of John*, 123.

78   John Chrysostom insightfully observes that Jesus established a comparison of superiority so that instead of saying, "'Yea, I am greater,' (for He would have seemed but to boast, since the proof did not as yet appear,) but by what He saith He effecteth this. For He said not simply, 'I will give thee water,' but having first set that given by Jacob aside, He exalteth that given by Himself, desiring to show from the nature of the things given, how great is the interval and difference between the persons of the givers, and His own superiority to the Patriarch" (*Hom. Jo. 32* [*NPNF* 14:177]).

    Also, if Palestinian traditions about Jacob's well are being evoked in John 4:12–14, then Jesus's promise of water forever is in contrast to water "for twenty years as in the Jacob's

Consequently, the Samaritan woman's statement (4:15) recognizes that the water from the one who had asked her for a drink (4:10) is in fact greater than the water from their patriarch Jacob (4:12).[79] However, the second part of her reasoning, "so that I may never ... have to keep coming here to draw water" (4:15), reveals that she is still using the "misrecognized" categories formed out of her daily experiences of socialization in the world.[80] The Samaritan woman understands that Jesus's promise of living water negates the necessity of habitually returning to Jacob's well for water, and therefore that Jesus offers a water source greater than Jacob's.[81] However, Jesus's identity remains that of a "Jew" and nothing more at this point because the Samaritan woman does not know who it is that asked her for a drink (4:7, 10a). Accordingly, while 4:10–15 concerned the gift of God and living water, the topic shifts to address Jesus's identity in 4:16–26.[82]

Jesus broaches the topic of his identity by revealing special knowledge about the Samaritan woman (4:16–18). In particular, Jesus reveals that he knows the Samaritan woman has had five husbands and that the one she lives with is not her husband (4:18). Hoskyns and Davey interpret the Samaritan woman's marital life as an allegory reflecting the history of Samaria so that her five husbands

---

story [cf. *Tg. Ps.-J.* Gen 29:10]. So Jesus is really greater than Jacob" (Díaz, "Palestinian Targum and New Testament," 76–77).

79   According to Birger Olsson, "By her reply the woman admits that Jesus' water is better than Jacob's. She is prepared to abandon Jacob's well, if she receives the water which slakes all thirst. Thus the woman has partly understood Jesus' will: she asks Jesus for water, she sets a positive value on his water, she believes it can slake thirst for evermore" (*Structure and Meaning in the Fourth Gospel: A Text-Linguistic Analysis of John 2:1–11 and 4:1–42* [Lund: Gleerup, 1974], 182–183). For Chrysostom as well, the Samaritan woman "having gained a clearer insight, but not yet fully perceiving the whole ... she for the time preferreth Him to Jacob. 'For' (saith she) 'I need not this well if I receive from thee that water.' Seest thou how she setteth Him before the Patriarch? This is the act of a fairly-judging soul. She had shown how great an opinion she had of Jacob, she saw One better than he, and was not held back by her prepossession" (*Hom. Jo.* 32 [*NPNF* 14:172]).

80   According to Brown, the Samaritan woman asking Jesus for water in 4:15 fulfills "one part of Jesus' challenge mentioned in vs. 10. However, another part of the challenge remains to be answered, for the woman has not yet recognized who Jesus is. She understands that he is speaking of an unusual type of water, but her aspirations are still on the level of earth" (Brown, *The Gospel According to John*, 1.177).

81   Craig R. Koester suggests: "The woman asks for the water, though she seems to have no idea what it is—she seems to think of it as a plumbing miracle, which will eliminate the need to haul water from the well each day" (*The Word of Life: A Theology of John's Gospel* [Grand Rapids: Eerdmans, 2008], 61). Similarly, Frederick Dale Bruner states that "she misunderstands Jesus's promise of Living Water as the promise of a miraculous water facet or of a divine fire hydrant" (*The Gospel of John*, 252).

82   Moloney, *The Gospel of John*, 117.

LABELING AN ETHNIC JESUS

are a reference to the five gods of Samaria and the sixth is Yahweh who the Samaritans live with as "the god of the land" (2 Kgs 17:26).[83] Yet, according to 2 Kings 17, the five nations that were placed in Samaria (2 Kgs 17:24) worshiped seven gods (2 Kgs 17:30–31), not five.[84] A further problem with this reading is that, according to 2 Kings 17, the Judeans were just as guilty of worshiping multiple deities as the Israelite-Samaritans were. Plus, as we saw in Chapter Three, Josephus does not criticize the Samaritans for heterodox worship in his accounts of the Samaritans' origins but rather their lack of communal solidarity (H-S#6) with the Judeans. Finally, the allegorized reading of the Samaritan woman's husbands cannot account for how Jesus, as a "Jew" making disparaging comments about her people's history (4:18), would lead her to perceive him as a prophet (4:19).

The point of 4:16–18 is that the Samaritan woman who, based upon the special knowledge Jesus has demonstrated about her, perceives that Jesus is *a* prophet (4:19) and then possibly the Messiah (4:29). Previously in the Gospel of John, when Jesus revealed special knowledge about how he knew Nathanael (1:48), Nathanael proclaimed "Rabbi, you are the Son of God! You are the King of Israel!" (1:49). In both instances, Jesus's identity is expressed in terms of the givenness of their ethnic group's categories and both, therefore, are not fully adequate.[85] Here, the Samaritan woman perceiving Jesus as a prophet (4:19) is an acknowledgement of his gift and revelation of special knowledge (4:17–18).[86]

Yet we should call attention to the fact that "for the Samaritans there was, and could be, no prophet after Moses, with one exception, their Messiah or Taheb, the prophet like Moses promised in Deut 18:18."[87] Accordingly, in recognizing Jesus as some sort of a prophet in 4:19 is more significant than from a "Jew" (e.g. 9:17) because the Samaritan woman "has been certain that her people are on the correct side of the religious divide between Samaritans and Jews, but now she has met a Jewish prophet, and cannot accommodate this

---

83   Hoskyns and Davey, *The Fourth Gospel*, 242–243.

84   Beasley-Murray rightly states, "This exegesis is not to be countenanced; 2 Kings 17:30f. mentions seven gods, not five, but more importantly the Evangelist does not allegorize in this manner" (*John*, 61).

85   See Section 1.0 for comments concerning Nathanael's confession in 1:49 as not fully adequate.

86   Klaus Haacker correctly recognizes that the focus is "on a special charismatic gift of Jesus and eliciting a corresponding confession (cf Jn 1:49; 4:19). The woman's belief that in Jesus she was being confronted by a prophet is to be understood from her standpoint only in the light of v. 18. One should not read into it any eschatological expectations, e.g. those derived from Deut. 18:15, 18" ("Samaritan, Samaria," *NIDNTT*.)

87   Bowman, "Samaritan Studies," 299 n. 5.

114   CHAPTER 4

anomaly into her belief system."[88] Therefore the Samaritan woman, again categorizing Jesus as a "Jew" and fellow Israelite in contradistinction to the Samaritan-Israelites (cf. 4:12), must test the would-be prophet.[89]

Since each group had a particular place (τόπος) where they "must worship" (προσκυνεῖν δεῖ; 4:20), the Samaritan woman appeals to Jesus's prophetic prowess to answer the centuries old debate between the two mountains (Gerizim and Jerusalem/Zion).[90] In Chapter Three we noted that Mount Gerizim is the central identifying marker for the Samaritans who even include it in their Decalogue.[91] "The Jews" were no less concerned with their place (τόπος; cf. 11:48). Essentially, then, the Samaritan woman is asking who has the proper place (τόπος) where Israel "must worship"?[92] The response from the would-be prophet would then indicate "whether Jesus will speak as just another

---

88   Keener, *The Gospel of John*, 1.610.
89   Hence, Michaels: "Prophet he may be, but Jesus is still 'a Jew,' and she 'a Samaritan woman' (v. 9)" (*The Gospel of John*, 248).
90   Josephus, in fact, writes about a debate taking place in the presence of Ptolemy Philometor (180–145 BCE) between Judeans and Samaritans in Alexandria concerning their respective temples (*Ant.* 13.74–79). The debates between Judeans and Samaritans about the place for worship continued for centuries to come. Origen of Alexandria (185–254 CE), for example, states that "even to the present day, if Samaritans and Jews agree to a discussion with one another, each will then object, and the Samaritan will make the speech to the Jew that is recorded of the woman here, 'Our fathers worshipped on this mountain,' pointing to Garizim, 'but you say in Jerusalem is the place to worship'" (*Comm. Jo.* 13.80 [FC, 84]). Another example of the continued debate is found in *Gen. Rab.* 81.3 when a Samaritan asked R. Ishmael b. R. Yose, who was going to Jerusalem to worship, "Wouldn't it be better for you to pray on this holy mountain [i.e. Gerizim] and not on that dunghill? [R. Ishmael] said to him, 'I shall tell you, what are you like? You are like a dog lusting after carrion. So, because you know that idols are hidden under that mountain, in light of this verse, 'and Jacob hid them [idols] under the oak which was near Shechem' [cf. Gen 35:4], therefore you lust after that mountain" (Jacob Neusner, *Genesis Rabbah: The Judaic Commentary to the Book of Genesis: a New American Translation* [Atlanta: Scholars Press, 1985], 161). It is perhaps worth nothing that *Gen. Rab.* 81.3 refers to the "Samaritans" in a nonderogatory manner, as "Samaritans" and not "Cutheans" or "lion converts."
91   Josephus observed that Mount Gerizim is "regarded by them as the most holy of mountains" (*Ant.* 18.85).
92   Knoppers notes that, "in line with the demands of the Torah (Deuteronomy 12), both the Samaritans and Jews advocated centralization—the firmly held tenant that the God of Israel *had to be worshiped only at one location*—but differed strongly about where that worship was to be centered (Mt. Gerizim vs. Mt. Zion)" (*Jews and Samaritans*, 1; emphasis added). The obsession with "place" is also evidenced in John Hyrcanus's destruction of the Mt. Gerizim temple in 112–111 BCE when "he ended the existence of the chief Yahwistic competitor to the Jerusalem sanctuary within the land" (Knoppers, *Jews and Samaritans*, 212).

LABELING AN ETHNIC JESUS   115

partisan Jew, or as a true 'prophet' whose words she can take seriously."[93] Here again, as in 4:9 and 12, the Samaritan woman's question derives from the givenness of her "misrecognized" categories that Yahwistic worship must be at *either* the Samaritans' Gerizim *or* the Judeans' Jerusalem and this is something that Judeans of the period also reflected.

The Samaritan woman is correct to perceive that Jesus is a prophet (4:19) for revealing special knowledge but she is also correct in another way. In Chapter Two we noted that the prophetic role was known for its confrontation against the "misrecognized" givenness of social reality (e.g. Jer 26:8–11, 28:3–4, 38:2–6; Isa 30:10; Amos 7:9–13). Jesus's response that true worship will be *neither* here *nor* there (4:21) but instead "in spirit and truth" (4:23, 24), as fulfilling the cultic worship command of Torah, is a performance of the prophetic role, which violates the perceived facticity that the cultic worship must be at either Gerizim or Jerusalem.[94]

The Samaritan woman spoke of the greatness of our father Jacob (4:12) and our fathers who worshiped on this mountain (4:20).[95] In contrast, Jesus speaks of worshiping *the* Father (4:21) "in spirit and truth" (4:23).[96] Thus, as Schnackenburg observes: "Jesus uses the term 'Father', not just because it is his usual way of speaking of God in the fourth Gospel, but because he is describing the new relationship of the true adorer to God (cf. 1:12; 3:5f.; 1 Jn 3:1f)."[97] Jesus introduces God as "the Father" to denote that his people (the "children of God" 1:12) are of a different kind (1:13), one that broadens traditional ethnic categories that consist of ancestral descent (H-S#2), common culture (H-S#4), geographic homeland (H-S#5), etc.[98] The phrase "in spirit and truth," as Moisés Silva keenly notes, "is often taken to mean 'inwardly and sincerely,' but the

---

93   Michaels, *The Gospel of John*, 248.

94   For example, recall the distinction we noted in Chapter Three between the MT Deuteronomic command to worship at "the place I will choose" verses the SP "the place I have chosen."

95   For example, both Abraham (Gen 12:7) and Jacob (Gen 33:20) erected alters to YHWH there and Mount Gerizim was the site of blessing and curses (Deut 11:29; 27:12).

96   On reconfiguring sacred space see deSilva, *Honor, Patronage, Kinship & Purity*, 291–294. In particular, deSilva states: "In John's Gospel, Jesus is even more explicit about the reconfiguration of sacred space. Jesus sets aside limited locales of sacred spaced (the fixed centers both of Jerusalem and Mount Gerizim, the sacred site for Samaritans) in favor of sacred space that opens up wherever people worship God 'in spirit and truth' (Jn 4:21–23)" (*Honor, Patronage, Kinship & Purity*, 292).

97   Schnackenburg, *The Gospel according to St. John*, 1.436–437.

98   According to deSilva, "A transition between natural kinship and the fictive kinship of the community of disciples is facilitated by the concept of God as Father" (*Honor, Patronage, Kinship & Purity*, 196). Also see Schnackenburg, *The Gospel according to St. John*, 1.438.

116   CHAPTER 4

Samaritans are not criticized for lacking sincerity. True worship is that which accords with reality."[99] These are the kind of people, whoever and wherever they are, that "the Father seeks ... to worship him" (4:23) and Jesus gathers "into one the dispersed children of God" (11:52) and for whom the disciples are sent to harvest (4:35–38).

In response, the Samaritan woman expresses a belief in the coming Messiah who "will proclaim all things to us" (4:25).[100] Pummer suggests that 4:25 "means that the Messiah will reveal hidden or lost *truths*.... And in fact, the oldest function of the Taheb is to reveal the truth."[101] However, it is frequently noted that the Samaritan woman knows of a coming "Messiah" (with Davidic/Judaic overtones), instead of the "Taheb" (the Samaritan name for the prophet-like-Moses).[102] The reason for using "Messiah" instead of "Taheb" is that the title "Taheb" only came into use in the fourth-century CE Samaritan literature. Nonetheless, as Meier has rightly observed, "The Samaritan woman's expectation of a Messiah who is a prophet, teacher, or revealer figure (v. 25) confirms for the first-century what we learn from later Samaritan sources: the Samaritans awaited an eschatological figure called the Taheb."[103] Regardless of the terminology used, Jesus here identifies himself as the expected Messiah/ Taheb for the first time in the Gospel of John (4:26).

The disciples arrive at the scene at Jacob's well (4:27), prompting the Samaritan woman to head back to the city (4:28). Unlike the Samaritan woman who was surprised that Jesus the "Jew" would ask a woman of Samaria for a drink (4:9), the disciples were surprised that Jesus the man was talking with

---

99   Silva, "ἀλήθεια," *NIDNTTE* 1.237. Also see C. H. Dodd who rightly observed: "The ἀληθινοὶ προσκυνηταὶ are those who are aware that God is πνεῦμα and accordingly worship Him ἐν πνεύματι: and they are contrasted with those who by confining His presence to Jerusalem or to Gerizim show that they do not realize His nature as πνεῦμα" (*The Interpretation of the Fourth Gospel* [Cambridge: Cambridge University Press, 1953], 175).

100   It is uncertain whether her reference to "us" means Samaritans or to all Israelites including Judeans.

101   Reinhard Pummer, "The Mosaic Tabernacle as the Only Legitimate Sanctuary: The Biblical Tabernacle in Samaritanism," in *The Temple of Jerusalem: From Moses to the Messiah*, ed. Steven Fine (Leiden, Brill, 2011), 138. Pummer comments that "the formula 'the Taheb will reveal the truth' occurs three times in *Tibat Marqe* (also known as *Memar Markah*)."

102   As Brown notes: "The Samaritans did not expect a Messiah in the sense of an anointed king of the Davidic house. They expected a Taheb (*Ta'eb* = Hebrew verb *šûb* = the one who returns), seemingly the Prophet-like-Moses. This belief was the fifth article in the Samaritan creed" (*Gospel According to John*, 1.172). Also see comments from Bowman, "Samaritan Studies," 299.

103   Meier, "The Historical Jesus and the Historical Samaritans," 230.

LABELING AN ETHNIC JESUS   117

a woman—regardless of her ethnicity.[104] Due to the disciples' astonishment, they did not ask Jesus "What do you want [seek]?" (4:27).[105] Earlier, in 4:23, Jesus told the Samaritan woman that "the Father seeks" "true worshipers [who] will worship the Father in spirit and truth." The answer to the disciples' unarticulated question, then, is that Jesus seeks people who—regardless of their ethnic identity or gender—worship the Father in spirit and in truth.

At this point the Samaritan woman, turned apostle to Sychar, enacts the calling narratives from John 1:40–51. Instead of calling only one or two people (such as Andrew and Philip) she called the entire city.[106] The Samaritan woman's invitation parallels the calling stories of the first disciples. She tells the Sycharians to "come and see" (4:29) as in Phillip's invitation to Nathanael (1:46) but, while Andrew's testimony is definitive ("We have found the Messiah"; 1:41), her testimony is in the form of a question expecting a negative response ("He cannot be the Messiah, can he?"; 4:29).[107] Given that the Samaritan woman's question expects a negative response, it is possible that she does not have complete faith in Jesus.[108] Another possibility is that the Samaritan woman's question is a rhetorical strategy rather than an indication of the incompleteness of her faith testimony.[109] The Samaritan woman goes into Sychar presenting the possibility in order that they would not "trust only her own report but to come and make a judgment about Christ for themselves."[110] The Samaritan woman's

---

104   According to Bultmann, "the extent to which this [the question of "the Jews" and the Samaritans] has become insignificant is shown by v. 27; the disciples are not surprised that Jesus is talking to a Samaritan, but that he is talking to a *woman*" (Bultmann, *The Gospel of John*, 179 n. 3).

105   Earlier in the Gospel of John, Jesus asked Andrew and another disciple "What do you [pl] seek?" (1:38) but now the disciples cannot bring themselves to ask Jesus "What do you [sg] seek?"

106   Chrysostom, *Hom. Jo.* 34.1 (FC, 332). According to Origen, "He [Jesus] also uses the woman as an apostle, as it were, to those in the city" (*Commentary on John*, 13.169 (FC, 104]).

107   According to BDAG, μήτι is "a marker that invites a negative response to the question that it introduces" ("μήτι," 649). Additionally, in reference to John 4:29, BDAG suggest "in questions in which the questioner is in doubt concerning the answer, *perhaps*."

108   Brown, *Gospel According to John*, 1.173; Moloney, *The Gospel of John*, 135. According to Schnackenburg, however, "the μήτι does not demand absolutely a negative answer, but can express a cautious opinion" (*The Gospel According to St. John*, 1.444).

109   Theodore of Mopsuestia, *Commentary on John*, 43; Chrysostom, *Hom. Jo.* 34 (FC, 332).

110   Chrysostom, *Hom. Jo.* 34.1 (FC, 332). Also see John Wesley: "She does not doubt of it herself, but incites them to make the inquiry" (*Explanatory Notes Upon the New Testament*, 12d. [New York: Carlton & Porter, 1857], 223); and Michaels: "But here the remarkable thing is that she is even raising such a question, so that the effect is not to rule anything out, but on the contrary to introduce a possibility not considered before" (*The Gospel of John*, 259 n. 106).

118   CHAPTER 4

strategy evidently worked because, even before these Samaritans from Sychar
had met Jesus at Jacob's well, many of them "believed in him because of the
woman's testimony" (4:39). When the Samaritans did meet Jesus, they asked
him to remain with them. Jesus obliged them for two days (4:40), resulting
in "many more" who believed him "because of his word" (4:41). While many
Samaritans believed in Jesus because of the Samaritan woman's testimony,
they confessed that, having heard Jesus for themselves, they "know that this is
truly the Savior of the world" (4:42). As a result, the Samaritans are part of "the
dispersed children of God" (11:52) who are gathered into the "one flock [with]
one shepherd" (10:16). Regardless of their physical kinship (H-S#2) or cultural
heritage (H-S#4), the "children of God" are those who receive and believe in
him (1:12).[111]

2.3   *How Jesus the "Jew" Asks for a Drink*

As we have just seen, the Johannine Jesus broadens traditional ethnic group
identity in order to gather "all who received him, who believed in his name"
into fictive kinship in the trans-ethnic identity "children of God." In this section we examine how the Samaritan woman's ethnic labeling of Jesus as a
"Jew" structured their interaction with one another, as well as how Jesus over-
came the ethnic label's social distance. We will first address the issues pertaining to the narrative aside in John 4:9b before addressing the function of the
Samaritan woman's ethnic labeling.

As noted in Chapter One, the majority of analysis of John 4:9 concerns the
parenthetical aside: "Jews do not share things in common with Samaritans."
The central issues concern whether the statement was original to the text and
whether συγχρῶνται means "dealings with" or "common use with." Although
John 4:9b is absent in Codex Sinaiticus (but added by a later corrector) and
omitted in both the Greek and Latin folios of Codex Bezae, there is overwhelm-
ing evidence to support its inclusion in the text.[112] If John 4:9b is original,
then what does it mean when it says "Jews do not share things in common

---

111   Accordingly, Moloney states, "As John the Baptist was prepared to decrease that Jesus
       might increase, so are the Samaritans prepared to abandon all debates of Gerizim or
       Jerusalem, and place their trust in Jesus as the savior of the world. The Samaritans' open-
       ness to the world of Jesus transforms them; they become examples of authentic Johannine
       belief" (*The Gospel of John*, 148).

112   For example, the following manuscripts contain John 4:9b: P[63], P[66], P[75], P[76], ℵ, A, C,
       L, W[supp], Δ, Θ, Ψ, as well as cited by Origen, Chrysostom, Cyril, Jerome, and Augustine.
       For the relationship between Sinaiticus and Bezae in John 1:1–8:39 see Gordon Fee,
       "Codex Sinaiticus in the Gospel of John: A Contribution to Methodology in Establishing
       Textual Relationships," NTS 15.2 (1968): 23–44.

LABELING AN ETHNIC JESUS 119

(συγχράομαι) with Samaritans"? A popular proposal is David Daube's rendering of συγχράομαι as: "Jews do not use—*scil.* vessels—with Samaritans."[113] However, the broader meaning of συγχράομαι as *"have dealings with"*[114] is more likely in light of the nature of Judeo-Samaritan relations, as discussed in Chapter Three, and particularly Josephus's prominent portrayal of the "Samaritans" for their lack of "communal solidarity" (H-S#6).[115]

The problem with this rendering is that the "disciples had gone to the city to buy food" (4:8) and so were "having dealings with" the Samaritans. Yet, as BDAG explains in their definition of συγχράομαι, the Judeans and Samaritans do not "associate on friendly terms with"[116] one another. That is, as we saw in Chapter Three, the nature of the relationship between Judeans and Samaritans was aversion or antipathy, instead of the deep-seated enmity that is often presented. Therefore, Judeans and Samaritans did not negate all dealings with one another as a matter of practicality (e.g. 4:8).[117] Regardless of how 4:9b is translated, we must not lose sight of the explanatory comment's purpose, which is to point out that Judeans and Samaritans had established rules for interaction and that Jesus violated them.[118]

---

113   Daube, "Jesus and the Samaritan Woman," 139; followed by Barrett, *Gospel According to St. John*, 230, 232–33; Brown, *Gospel According to John*, 1.170; Morris, *The Gospel According to John*, 229; Carson, *Gospel According to John*, 218; Moloney, *The Gospel of John*, 121.

114   "συγχράομαι," BDAG, 953–954; original emphasis. This rendering is followed by Schnackenburg, *The Gospel according to St. John*, 1:425 n. 18; Lindars, *The Gospel of John*, 181; Haenchen, *John*, 240; Beasley-Murray, *John*, 58.

115   Köstenberger also notes that "the explanatory aside, 'For Jews have no dealings with [συγχρῶνται] Samaritans', probably is broader than the mere refusal to share drinking vessels" (*John*, 149 n. 30). Ridderbos states, seemingly in exasperation, that the Evangelist "does not breath a word" about the Jewish laws of purification (*Gospel According to John*, 154 n. 147).

116   "συγχράομαι," BDAG 953–954. Similarly, Böhm states that John 4:9b "spiegelt eine gewisse Distanz und Reserviertheit zwischen den beiden Gruppen" (*Samarien und die Samritai bei Lukas*, 143).

117   According to Knoppers, "How much Jews and Samaritans distinguished between holding strictly to their theological tenets and dealing practically with the realities of ordinary life also varied. A Samaritan could express hostility toward the Jerusalem temple and yet have practical dealings with contemporary Jews. Similarly, a Jew might firmly hold to the notion that Jerusalem was elect of God and still do business with his Samaritan neighbors" (*Jews and Samaritans*, 227). For further evidence of practical dealings between Samaritans and Jews Knoppers observes: "There would not be debates registered in the Mishnah, the Tosefta, and in the Palestinian and Babylonian Talmuds (including within the minor rabbinic tractate *Masseket Kutim*) about these issues [i.e. intermarriage, trade, etc.] if this were not the case" (*Jews and Samaritans*, 227 n. 22).

118   Accordingly, Boers is correct when he states, "Whatever interpretation one accepts of the expression [John 4:9b], as far as the meaning of the text is concerned, it is clear that

120   CHAPTER 4

The following analysis contributes to our understanding of the narrative a perspective on the social dynamics of Jesus's "gathering" (cf. 10:16; 11:53). In particular we see that Jesus is functioning in ways that Coser describes as a "heretic," which is *not* an abandonment of Judean ethnic identity but a broadening of particular ethnic categories for the gathering of non-Judeans into the flock. In terms of ethnicity, which we defined in Chapter Two as a framework for understanding the classification, affiliation, and cultural traits of ethnic groups, we understand that the Samaritan woman is, in a very real way sociologically representative of her people group. As we will see later in section 4.0, the application of this method discloses a particular perspective onto the discussion of "the Jews" in John 8. Just as the Samaritan woman is a representative of her ethnic group when confronted by Jesus, so too, as we will see, are "the Jews" in John 8. In section 4.0 we will further address the issue of the Samaritan woman and "the Jews" in terms of labeling theory. In particular, we will address Barclay's questions concerning the role of deviance in social contexts, as well as intratextually comparing the functions of labeling by the Samaritan woman in John 4 with that of "the Jews" in John 8 in section 4.0.

2.4 *Labeling Jesus a "Jew"*

In John 4:9, our particular issue is the function of the Samaritan woman's ethnic labeling. As we noted in Chapter One, some scholars have understood the Samaritan woman's question as insulting Jesus, in which case labeling Jesus a "Jew" enforces their distinctions.[119] Yet, we also noted in Chapter One and verified in Chapter Three that, outside of the Gospel of John, there is no known evidence for using "Jew" *or* "Samaritan" as a term of abuse (i.e. an ethnic slur).[120] Rather than insulting and further distancing Jesus from herself, the Samaritan woman's labeling of Jesus as a "Jew" is an interactive labeling that acknowledges the boundary's existence.[121]

     Jesus violated an important custom which regulated association of Jews and Samaritans" (*Neither on This Mountain Nor in Jerusalem*, 149–150).

119   Bernard, *The Gospel According to St. John*, 1.137; Brown, *Gospel According to John*, 1.177.

120   Bultmann, *The Gospel of John*, 178–179 n. 7. Luke T. Johnson, in his "The New Testament's Anti-Jewish Slander and the Conventions of Ancient Polemic," noted that, "There remains perhaps surprisingly little direct evidence of polemic against Samaritans by Judeans, even though the fact that 'Jews have no dealing with Samaritans' (John 4:9 [RSV]) is axiomatic" (*JBL* 108.3 [1989]: 437).

121   For example, Botha argues that "she is actually not being impolite but ... [simply] reminding him of the traditions and customs" (*Jesus and the Samaritan Woman*, 118).

     Chrysostom speculates that if it was the Samaritan woman's purpose to insult Jesus, then she would have said, "as though speaking to an alien (ἀλλόφυλον) and an enemy

LABELING AN ETHNIC JESUS

As an interactive labeling, when the Samaritan woman first saw Jesus at Jacob's well he inevitably found a place in an already defined category.[122] For the Samaritan woman, as a member of the Samaritan people, the social category "Jew" existed as the result of the socialization processes wherein "institutions, roles, and identities exist as objectively real phenomena in the social world."[123] Once these social categories attain the status of objective reality then they become "misrecognized" as the things people know, but do not know that they know.[124] The Samaritan woman's categorization of Jesus as a "Jew," then, immediately imposes a predefined set of interactional patterns with Jesus as a person who would have not associated on friendly terms with a Samaritan (4:9b).

Although Judeo-Samaritan relations had established a "basic value orientation"[125] towards one another (i.e. no friendly dealings; 4:9b), Jesus challenges the "misrecognized" facticity of these social relations in order to transcend their ethnic group's boundaries.[126] Jesus presents a choice that confronts the Samaritan woman's "misrecognition" of the way things are done in exchange for "one in which the barrier she has mentioned plays no role."[127] Although the ethnic categories of "Samaritan" and "Jew" frame their entire dialogue (4:7–26; e.g. the emphatic pronouns "we" and "you"), by the end of it "Jesus challenges both Jewish and Samaritan tradition, calling for a higher worship that transcends geographical (hence also, in this context, ethnic) particularities (4:21)."[128]

(ἐχθρὸν), 'Far be it from me to give to thee, who are a foe and a stranger to our nation'" (Chrysostom, *Hom. Jo.* 31.107 [*NPNF* 14.168]).

122 Recall Robert Ezra Park's conclusion: "Every individual we meet inevitably finds a place in our minds in some category *already* defined" ("The Bases for Race Prejudice," 232; added emphasis). Also see Ridderbos's statement that "she immediately recognizes this stranger as a Jew" (*Gospel According to John*, 154).

123 Berger, *The Sacred Canopy*, 13.

124 Jacques Berlinerblau, "Toward a Sociology of Heresy, Orthodoxy, and *Doxa*" in *The History of Religions* 40:4 (2001): 346. Clifford Geertz describes the phenomenon as the assumed givens of social existence ("The Integrative Revolution," 259).

125 Barth, "Introduction," 14. Botha rightly observes that, "in terms of the social context, the woman behaves correctly but Jesus does not" (*Jesus and the Samaritan Woman*, 120).

126 In this regards, Botha proposes that "the author is preparing the readers to answer the following questions: *first*, is Jesus in the wrong or are the accepted social customs perhaps wrong?; *secondly*, is the belief correct in that Samaritans are to be avoided?" (*Jesus and the Samaritan Woman*, 120; original emphasis).

127 Ridderbos, *Gospel According to John*, 155. Ridderbos adds: "If she knew the gift of God and, in that connection, who the stranger was who was speaking with her, she would no longer trouble herself about problems between Jews and Samaritans but would ask him for water and he would give it to her: living, running, water (again, whether she was a Samaritan or not)."

128 Keener, *The Gospel of John*, 1.617.

122   CHAPTER 4

In this regard it is important to observe that Jesus's ethnic identity as a "Jew" (4:9, 20, 22) does *not* change throughout John 4:1–42 but instead changes in significance. The Gospel of John does not say how the Samaritan woman was able to categorize Jesus as a Judean, although, in Chapter One, we noted the possibilities that it was by Jesus's clothes and/or dialect.[129] A frequently overlooked reason she recognized that Jesus was a "Jew" was simply that he would have been one of the many festival pilgrims who customarily traveled through Samaria between Galilee and Jerusalem (cf. Josephus, *Ant.* 20.118).[130] Moreover, as a festival pilgrim, the Galilean Jesus (John 1:45; 7:41, 52) demonstrates that he is a "Jew" (᾿Ιουδαῖος).[131]

Yet, by the end of the interaction between Jesus and the Samaritan woman (4:7–26), he has transcended the boundaries established by the label "Jew" (᾿Ιουδαῖος) and reduced the previously understood social distance between them (cf. John 4:29, 39–42). The answer to the Samaritan woman's question ("How is it that you, a Jew, ask a drink of me, a woman of Samaria?"; 4:9a) was that it presented Jesus with the opportunity to provide an alternative interpretation of their shared descent (H-S#2) and culture (H-S#4) in order to both broaden ethnic group boundaries. As a result of this event, Jesus gathered her and the Sycharian Samaritans into receiving him and becoming "children of God" (1:12–13) that "ultimately transcends ethnic allegiances."[132]

The Samaritan woman's "misrecognized" categories for Jesus (a "Jew"; as "greater than Jacob"; "a prophet"; "messiah"), as well as Jesus's disciples (e.g. Nathanael 1:49: "Rabbi," "Son of God," "King of Israel"), are all based upon their ethnic groups' cultural traditions (H-S#1–6). The Johannine Jesus challenges people's "misrecognized" ethnic categories in order to reveal to the Samaritan

---

129   For example Chrysostom, *Hom. Jo.* 31.107 (*NPNF* 14.167); Bernard, *The Gospel According to St. John*, 1.137; Michaels, *The Gospel of John*, 239 n. 33; as well as Frédéric Louis Godet noted the hypothesis of Rudolf Stier that the Samaritan woman identified Jesus by his dialect and specifically his pronunciation of שׁ *shin* instead of שׂ *sin* (*Commentary on John's Gospel*, 422).

130   Lütgert, "Die Juden im Johannesevangelium," 152. Sean Freyne suggests: "It might be hypothesized that the very intensity of the animosity that our sources indicate was due to the fact that, at least in the eyes of the Samaritans, Galileans were being deeply disloyal in not supporting them rather than the Judean/Jerusalem center, when social and religious experiences might be presumed to have dictated differently" ("Behind the Names: Galileans, Samaritans, Ioudaioi," in *Galilee Through the Centuries: Confluence of Cultures*, ed. Eric M. Myers [Winona Lake, IN: Eisenbrauns, 1999], 49).

131   According to Yardenna Alexandre, "By the end of the late Hellenistic period the definition of the '*Galilaioi*' as 'northern *Ioudaioi*' seems to be established (Josephus, *J.W.* 2.232)" ("Galilee," in *The Oxford Encyclopedia of the Bible and Archaeology*, ed. Daniel M. Master [Oxford: Oxford University Press, 2013], 430).

132   Keener, *The Gospel of John*, 1.617.

LABELING AN ETHNIC JESUS

woman (as well as to his disciples and "the Jews") the alternative possibility for the group identification of the people of Israel (4:20) as "the children of God" (1:12–13; 11:52).

3   Jesus the Samaritan

Throughout the Gospel of John, Jesus is portrayed as repeatedly attempting to challenge the importance his interlocutors place in their ethnic groups' cultural traits. Jesus's challenges, such as in 4:7, are in the form of deviant behavior for "not adhering to the conventions."[133] This phenomenon is also manifested in what has been characterized as Jesus's dissociation from "the Jews"/Judaism, such as, according to Adele Reinhartz, when Jesus "declares that he is not bound by the Sabbath laws because of his unique relationship to the Father" (5:17).[134] Reinhartz proposes that "Jesus' discourses employ such a sharp dichotomy between Jesus and believers on the one hand, and the unbelieving Jews on the other, that the term 'Jew' cannot comfortably be used to describe the Jesus we find in this Gospel."[135] Yet, the prophetic corpus in the texts of the Hebrew Bible contains accounts of prophets who also employed such a sharp dichotomy between themselves (as aligned with YHWH) and the people of Israel that they were banished (e.g. Amos 7:10–13) and had their lives threatened (e.g. Jer 26:8). By the Second Temple period, Israel's rejection of their prophets had become a trope (e.g. Dan 9:6, 10; Neh 9:26, 30). Since the Gospel of John states that Jesus had caused "division" (σχίσμα; 7:43; 9:16; 10:19) among "his own people" (1:11), it might be more accurate to say that Jesus is portrayed as a factionalist "Jew" among "the Jews." The central issue concerned who had the right to be thought of as being "(the children) of God"—those "who received him, who believed in his name" (1:12) or those among "his own people [who] did not accept him" (1:11). The issues about what constitutes being "(children) of God" (1:12; 8:47) are at the crux in the following section of the Gospel of John.

---

133   Botha, *Jesus and the Samaritan Woman*, 119.

134   Adele Reinhartz, *Befriending the Beloved Disciple: A Jewish Reading of the Gospel of John* (New York: Continuum, 2001), 63. Instead of "dissociation," Brown uses the term "alienation" to describe this phenomenon: "The Johannine Jesus is portrayed as sharing this alienation, so that at times he speaks as if he himself were not a 'Jew'" (*An Introduction to the Gospel of John*, 168–169).

135   Adele Reinhartz, "How 'the Jews' Became Part of the Plot," in *Jesus, Judaism, and Christian Anti-Judaism: Reading the New Testament after the Holocaust*, ed. Paula Fredriksen and Adele Reinhartz (Louisville: Westminster John Knox, 2002), 103.

124   CHAPTER 4

3.1 Setting the Scene: Jesus in the Jerusalem Temple

The Samaritan woman had labeled Jesus a "Jew" (cf. 4:9, 20) but "the Jews"
label Jesus as "Samaritan" (8:48) and, as we will see in this section, in a context
of intra-ethnic factionalist conflict. At the beginning of John 7, we see Jesus
as a Jewish festival pilgrim leaving from Nazareth for Jerusalem to attend "the
Jewish festival of Booths" (7:2, 10). Then, in John 8, Jesus is "teaching in the
treasury (γαζοφυλάκιον) of the temple" (8:20) and this is the setting for the discourse in 8:31–59 with "the Jews."[136] In addition to Jesus being a Jewish festival
pilgrim, Jesus is further shown as one of "his own people" (1:11; i.e. "the Jews") by
being in the Temple treasury. The treasury was not part of the Temple proper
(i.e. ναός) but rather the Temple complex (called the ἱερόν) and was located in
the Court of Women[137] (not far from the inner Court of the Israelites where
the Sanhedrin met). This is important to note because the Court of Women
was open for *all Jews* to gather,[138] yet, before entering it from the Court of
gentiles, there were signs warning "foreigners" (ἀλλογενεῖς) not to enter.[139] The

---

136   According to BDAG: "It is quite probable that John [8:20] may be using the term
      γαζοφυλάκιον loosely of the area generally known as the 'treasury'" ("γαζοφυλάκιον," 186).
      Although, Louw and Nida suggest that the term γαζοφυλάκιον in John 8:20 "designates the
      offering boxes rather than the treasury itself…. If one interprets the term γαζοφυλάκιον in
      John 8:20 as the offering boxes, then one may translate 'he spoke these words near where
      the offering boxes were'" ("γαζοφυλάκιον," L&N 7.33).

137   D. H. Madvig, "γαζοφυλάκιον," NIDNTT. Also Beasley-Murray notes: "γαζοφυλάκιον
      can mean a receptacle in which 'treasure' can be placed, i.e., a collecting box (as in
      Mark 12:41), or a place where treasure is kept. Josephus speaks of several rooms in the tem-
      ple where valuables were kept, but it is likely that the hall in which the thirteen trumpet-
      shaped collection boxes stood was so named; it was evidently in the court of the women,
      since they had access to it, and is here mentioned to identify the scene for the utterance
      of v. 12" (Beasley-Murray, *John*, 125).

138   Certain restrictions, however, were enforced in order to enter particular courts in the
      temple complex. Josephus describes the restrictions: "The outer court [Court of Gentiles]
      was open to all, foreigners included; women during their impurity were alone refused
      admission. To the second court [Court of Women] all Jews were admitted and, when un-
      contaminated by any defilement, their wives; to the third [Court of Israelites] male Jews,
      if clean and purified; to the fourth [Court of Priests] the priests robed in their priestly
      vestments" (*Ag. Ap.* 2.103–104 [Thackeray, LCL]).

139   For the Jerusalem Temple Warning Inscription see Jack Finegan, *The Archeology of the
      New Testament: The Life of Jesus and the Beginning of the Early Church* (Princeton, NJ:
      Princeton University Press, 1992), 197. See Philo's comments: "Still more abounding and
      peculiar is the zeal of them all for the temple, and the strongest proof of this is that death
      without appeal is the sentence against those of other races [πάντας τῶν οὐχ ὁμοεθνῶν] who
      penetrate into its inner confines. For the outer are open to everyone where they come
      from" (*Embassy*, §212 [F. H. Colson LCL]).

LABELING AN ETHNIC JESUS 125

enforcement of the warning required temple guards to be stationed near the gates of the temple "to check on Jewishness and purity."[140] According to John 8, then, Jesus was allowed to enter into the Court of Women as a "Jew" and he had yet to be thought of as being out of place, that is a "foreigner" or a "Samaritan," upon entering the inner temple complex.

3.2 Setting the Labeling Context: You Are Your Father's Children

The discourse with "the Jews" who will label Jesus a "Samaritan" begins with Jesus addressing "the Jews who had believed in him" (8:31) and ends with them attempting to stone Jesus (8:59).[141] In John 8:31, Jesus addresses "the Jews who had believed in him" from the preceding verse. In direct contrast to the Samaritan woman in John 4, however, John 8:31–59 "details a progressive unraveling of the 'faith' of these 'believing Jews.'"[142] The "progressive unraveling" is generally structured by the rhetorical pattern of statement— misunderstanding—clarification, in which Jesus makes a statement that is misunderstood, leading him to clarify and speak further.[143] According to Neyrey, this rhetorical pattern

---

140 E. P. Sanders, *Judaism: Practice and Belief 63 BCE–66 CE* (Philadelphia: Trinity Press International, 1994), 82. Sanders references Philo's *Spec. Laws* 1.156 that states: "Some of [the temple attendants] are stationed at the doors as gatekeepers at the very entrances, some within in front of the sanctuary to prevent any unlawful person from setting foot thereon, either intentionally or unintentionally. Some patrol around it turn by turn in relays by appointment night and day, keeping watch and guard at both seasons. Others sweep the porticoes and the open court, convey away the refuse and ensure cleanliness" (Colson LCL).

141 We should perhaps note there are contrasting opinions concerning the unity of John 8. For example, John Ashton notes: "In some respects chapter 8 is a rag-bag. Even after excluding the inauthentic story of the woman taken in adultery, Bultmann splits it into ten fragments, a couple of them no longer than one verse a piece, and scatters them liberally around 250 pages of his commentary" (*Understanding the Fourth Gospel*, 85). C. H. Dodd, on the other hand, states: "The long dialogue in John 8:31–59, one of the most powerful and most carefully composed in the Fourth Gospel … is held together by recurrent references to Abraham" ("Behind a Johannine Dialogue," *More New Testament Studies* [Grand Rapids: Eerdmans, 1968], 41).

142 Michaels, *The Gospel of John*, 503. Similarly, Gail O'Day and Susan Hylen observe: "The tone becomes more adversarial as the conversation proceeds, and the dialogue concludes with an attempt to kill Jesus (v. 59). Yet it begins with those who 'had believed in him' (v. 31). To these, Jesus offers a gift to those who 'continue in [his] word' to know the truth (v. 31)" (*John* [Louisville: Westminster John Knox, 2006], 93).

143 Neyrey, *Gospel of John*, 13. Also see Neyrey, "Secrecy, Deception, and Revelation: Information Control in the Fourth Gospel," in *The Gospel of John in Cultural and Rhetorical Perspective* (Grand Rapids: Eerdmans, 2009), 252–281.

126 CHAPTER 4

functions in two ways. When Jesus engages in catechetical instruction, he tolerates initial misunderstanding in order to produce an enlightened climax (e.g., the Samaritan woman). But at other times Jesus's speech distances people and proves their incapacity to comprehend him (e.g., 8:21–58).[144]

Noting this structuring device will help us to track the movements of "the Jews'" "misrecognized" social categories. We should also note, Neyrey's observation of how John 4 and 8 connect through rhetorical strategy.

Since "the Jews" believed in him (8:30), Jesus states what it means to be his true disciples. First, the potential disciple must continue to remain in his word (8:31) and then, second, they will know the truth that makes them free (8:32). Jesus's statement is then misunderstood and prompts "the Jews who had believed in him" to reply that they are already free because they are "descendants (σπέρμα) of Abraham and have never been slaves to anyone" (8:33). In response, Jesus clarifies his initial statement: "Everyone who commits sin is a slave to sin" (8:34). He then makes another statement (8:35–38) that is also misunderstood (8:39a).

What is initially misunderstood by the potential disciples (8:31) is that it is "the truth" (ἀλήθεια) that "will make you free" (8:32) and without understanding "the truth" (ἀλήθεια) they misunderstand freedom. In his *TDNT* article, Bultmann defined ἀλήθεια in John as the "divine reality."[145] Schnackenburg rightly clarifies that "ἀλήθεια is not simply 'divine reality' ... because Jesus not only reveals the truth in this words and actions, but also embodies it in his person, God's reality becomes manifest in him" (cf. 1:14; 14:6).[146] The Johannine Jesus, therefore, both manifests and reveals "truth"—"divine reality"—"in contrast to whatever the situation may seem to look like on the surface."[147]

The truth that Jesus reveals, particularly in 8:31–59, is that Judean ethnic identity (as based upon Abrahamic descent) is not sufficient in itself as the sole criterion for being "(children) of God" (1:12, 8:47).[148] By remaining in

---

144 Neyrey, *Gospel of John*, 78.

145 Bultmann, "ἀλήθεια," *TDNT* 1.245.

146 Schnackenburg, *The Gospel according to St. John*, 2.228. Louw-Nida also observed: "In John 8:32 ἀλήθεια is used to refer to the revelation of God that Jesus brings or, perhaps, to Jesus himself for what he actually is as the revelation of God" ("ἀλήθεια," L&N 72.2).

147 Silva, "ἀλήθεια," *NIDNTTE* 1.236–237. Silva earlier stated: "The view adopted in this article is that John uses ἀλήθεια regularly in the sense of reality in contrast to falsehood or mere appearance, but that this in no way provides evidence of Greek affinities of ideas, or of disregard for the OT tradition" (1.235).

148 Moloney observes that "to believe in ... Jesus Christ gives one power to become a child of God (cf. 1:12–13). But Judaism taught that the study of the Law made people free ... and

LABELING AN ETHNIC JESUS

Jesus's word, the potential disciple will learn this reality, and knowing this reality sets them free from sin. Consequently, the fact that "the Jews who had believed in him" (8:31) already think they are free, as Abraham's descendants (H-S#2), demonstrates that they do not know this divine reality. They misunderstand Jesus because he is "conceived in the ['misrecognized'] categories of worldly thought."[149]

Jesus affirms that he knows "the Jews" are "descendants (σπέρμα) of Abraham" (8:37) but yet they are looking to kill him (cf. 8:59). The plot to kill Jesus is first introduced in a narrative aside in 5:18 and, according to 7:1, Jesus was aware of it before he came to Jerusalem.[150] At this point, Jesus makes it known why there is a plot to kill him (8:37) and it is "because my word is not progressing among you" (my translation).[151] If they knew God's reality (ἡ ἀλήθεια) and if they progressed in Jesus's word as potential disciples (8:31), then they would know that there is more to being "(children) of God" (1:12; 8:47) than being Abraham's descendants (σπέρμα; H-S#2). In this regard, Beutler rightly notes, "Already at this point, we notice a difference of perspective: for 'the Jews' what is important is physical descent from Abraham. However, this descent is not enough for Jesus."[152]

    Targum Neofiti on Gen 15:11 even promises delivery of the wicked 'in the merits of their father Abram'.... This promise is transcended by the words of Jesus as he tells "the Jews" that through acceptance of his revelation of God (ἡ ἀλήθεια) they will be set free" (*The Gospel of John*, 275–276). Similarly Beasley-Murray points out that "It was the boast of rabbis, 'All Israelites are sons of kings' (i.e., of Abraham, Isaac, and Jacob), and in their view the merits of Abraham covered all their demerits, hence the dictum, 'The circumcised do not go down to Gehenna' *Exod. Rab.* 19.81c'" (Beasley-Murray, *John*, 134).

149   Rudolf Bultmann, *Theology of the New Testament* (New York: Charles Scribner's Sons, 1955), 2.45. Also see Schnackenburg who states: "The Jews immediately make an objection which depends on a misunderstanding and reveals their incomprehension" (*The Gospel According to St. John*, 2.207).

150   Schnackenburg suggests that at this point "the desire to kill Jesus need no longer be taken as referring to a particular occasion (cf. 5:18; 7:19); it becomes a permanent feature of John's narrative (cf. 7:1, 25: 8:59; 10:31, etc.)" (*The Gospel According to St. John*, 2.210).

151   This translation is based upon BDAG's rendering, "my word makes no headway among you," for χωρέω in John 8:37. BDAG defines χωρέω as "to make an advance in movement, *be in motion, go forward, make progress*" ("χωρέω," 1094). Similarly, Louw and Nida note that, although it is possible to interpret χωρέω in John 8:37 as "as referring to an adequate place," they render χωρέω "figuratively in the statement ὁ λόγος ὁ ἐμὸς οὐ χωρεῖ ἐν ἐμῖν 'my word makes no progress in you'" ("χωρέω," L&N 15.13).

152   Beutler, "Abraham," in *Judaism and the Jews in the Gospel of John* (Roma: Pontificio Istituto Biblico, 2006), 65. Similarly, Lincoln notes "they appear to show more concern about the ethnic aspect of their identity—*We are descendants of Abraham*—than about being followers of Jesus" (*Gospel According to Saint John*, 270; original emphasis).

128   CHAPTER 4

3.3   *True Disciples*

Jesus finishes his discourse on true disciples by telling "the Jews who had believed in him" (8:31) "the revelation which is directly available to him through 'seeing' in the Father's presence."[153] For this reason, Jesus tells "the Jews," "You should do what you have heard from the Father" (8:38). However, John 8:38 is riddled with textual variants and particularly the appearance of pronouns for "my Father" and "from your father,"[154] so the issue is whether Jesus is already introducing the contrast between fathers from John 8:41–44.[155] Given that Jesus is still addressing potential disciples (i.e. "the Jews who believed in Him" in 8:31) and the possessive pronouns were likely later scribal additions, then "Jesus is still trying to convince his audience to obey the real Father, God" (8:38).[156] (Thus, the NRSV rendering: "you *should* do what you have heard from the Father"; added emphasis.)

"The Jews," however, misunderstand the one whom Jesus calls "the Father" so they reassert their ethnic identity on the basis that their father is Abraham since they are his descendants (H-S#2). According to Brown, "If the reference there is to Jesus's Father, then here the Jews are saying that they want nothing to do with his 'father' for they have Abraham."[157] In light of "the Jews" misunderstanding of Jesus's Father and their assertion that Abraham is their father (8:39a), Jesus clarifies his statement about how they should do what they have heard from the Father (8:38). Jesus gives them a paternity test: "If you were Abraham's children (τέκνα), you would be doing what Abraham did" (8:39b). Jesus agreed that they were indeed Abraham's "descendants" (σπέρμα) (8:37) but now distinguishes it from "Abraham's children (τέκνα)."[158] To belong to a

---

153   Schnackenburg, *The Gospel According to St. John*, 2.210–211.

154   Notably, ℵ and D contain the pronouns μου and ὑμῶν for "my" and "your" father while B, P66, and P75 do not contain the pronouns.

155   Michaels suggests that the pronouns "were introduced by scribes who were in a hurry to get to the controversy that surfaces in verses 41–44 between having God and having the devil as 'father'" (*The Gospel of John*, 509–510). Also see Metzger, *Textual Commentary*, 192. Brown comments that "it seems too early in this section of the discourse for the introduction of the theme of the devil as the father of the Jews; it makes the development in 41–44 senseless" (*Gospel According to John*, 1.356).

156   Brown, *Gospel According to John*, 1.356. Bruner also interprets 8:38 as "the second straight attempt to get them to take his Word seriously" (*The Gospel of John*, 539).

157   Brown, *The Gospel According to John*, 1.356.

158   Similarly Philo states: "In the court where truth presides, kinship is not measured only by blood, but by similarity of conduct and pursuit of the same objects" (*Virt.* 195 [F. H. Colson, LCL]). Beasley-Murray (*John*, 134) references *Beṣa* 32b that states: "for it is written, *And* [*He will*] *show thee mercy and have compassion upon thee*, [teaching that] whoever is merciful to his fellow-men is certainly of the children of our father Abraham, and whosoever is not merciful to his fellow-men is certainly not of the children of our father Abraham."

LABELING AN ETHNIC JESUS — 129

particular ancestral lineage was one thing but, according to deSilva, "both Greek and Jewish writers stressed … that one's behavior reflects on one's parentage."[159] Given that "the Jews" do not and have not denied their murderous intent (8:37, 39), they cannot be Abraham's or God the Father's children. Although "the Jews" bring up the topic of Abraham (8:33, 39), Jesus "utilizes it rather *ad hominem*: if 'the Jews' claim to be children of Abraham, then they must act like Abraham."[160] Twice Jesus implored them to "do what you have heard from the Father" (8:38) and to do "what Abraham did" (8:39) but instead Jesus brings to their attention that they are "doing what your father does" (8:41).[161]

Although it is possible that Jesus is contrasting paternity in 8:39, depending upon the scribal additions of possessive pronouns, he explicitly contrasts their paternity in 8:41. In fact, if we do not read the later hostility (8:41–59) back into the earlier part of the dialogue (8:31–40), then "the Jews'" statement "*We* are descendants of Abraham" (8:33) and "Abraham is *our* father" (8:39) could include Jesus in their (self-) identification. Jesus, after all, has passed the threshold exclusively for Jews in the Temple's Court of Women. Just as the Samaritan woman misunderstood Jesus and appealed to their common ancestor Jacob, so too "the Jews" misunderstood and appealed to their common ancestor Abraham. Until 8:41, Jesus addressed them as potential disciples to think about the nature of their action and to do the things their father (be it God or Abraham) does/did.[162] It is only when they do not comprehend Jesus's teaching that he explicitly turns to contrastive parentage: "You are indeed doing what your father does" (8:41a).

For the third time "the Jews who had believed in him" do not receive Jesus's teaching and, rather than be led into truth, they can assert only what they have known all along because it is the "misrecognized" facticity that has been

---

159   deSilva, *Honor, Patronage, Kinship & Purity*, 187. deSilva adds that the idea is that there is "likeness between parents and their children, a 'wondrous likeness both of mind and form' (4 Macc 15:4). This likeness was held to extend beyond physical appearance to emotions, predispositions and moral character." Hence, Neyrey states: "A true son of Abraham will prove to be a chip off the old block by imitating his father, who offered hospitality to strangers from heaven; false sons 'try to kill me'" (*The Gospel of John*, 161).

160   Beutler, "Abraham," 66. Beutler adds that even though "descent form [sic.] Abraham does not seem to have a positive or decisive role for Jesus … The relevance of descent from Abraham for salvation is neither confirmed nor denied."

161   Michaels calls attention to the fact that "the Gospel writer's memorable words, 'He came to what was his own, and his own did not receive him' (1:11), are beginning to come true before the reader's very eyes" (*The Gospel of John*, 514).

162   Ridderbos, *Gospel According to John*, 312.

130 CHAPTER 4

ingrained into the core of their social reality.[163] Accordingly, out of this facticity, they state that they already are the children of God[164] and "not illegitimate children" (ἐκ πορνείας) (8:41b). Since at least the time of Origen, it was suggested that "the Jews'" statement "We are not illegitimate children" was an accusation concerning Jesus's illegitimate birth.[165] However, the second part of "the Jews'" defense strategy, which switches from Abraham as their father to God, suggests that "Jesus, in effect, has accused them of disobedience or infidelity toward God."[166] The imagery of fornication was used in the Hebrew Bible to describe Israel's infidelity to Yahweh (e.g. "They are children of whoredom," Hos 2:4).[167] Therefore, in light of the context of John 8 and the allusion to the texts of Hebrew Bible, the reference to "illegitimate children" (8:41b) is unlikely a reference to Jesus's birth.[168] Instead, 8:41 is an accusation that Jesus is the one

---

163   For a similar point see O'Day and Hylen who state: "Like the believers with whom Jesus began this conversation in verse 31, the dilemma for them, too, will be to resist the temptation to allow their prior understanding of their identity as God's chosen ones to close them to the ongoing work of listening to Jesus's words" (*John*, 95).

164   Since Jesus interprets their claim to have "Abraham as their father" to mean they are "children of Abraham" (8:37), we can safely infer that their claim to have "God as their father" is a claim to be "children of God" (8:41).

165   In Origen *Against Celsus* 1.28, Celsus presents the following scenario: "After this he represents the Jew as having a conversation with Jesus himself and refuting him on many charges, as he thinks: first, because *he fabricated the story of his birth from a virgin* ... he says that *she was driven out by her husband, who was a carpenter by trade, as she was convicted of adultery*" (Origen, *Contra Celsum* translated by Henry Chadwick [Cambridge: Cambridge University Press, 1953], 28). Also in the *Acts of Pilate* 2.3, "the elders of the Jews answered and said to Jesus: ... you were born of fornication" (*NTApoc* 1.453). Brown suggests that this interpretation is a distinct possibility because, after all, "Were there not rumor about [Jesus's] own birth? Was there not some question of whether he was really the son of Joseph? ... The Jews may be saying, '*We* were not born illegitimate [but you were]'" (Brown, *The Gospel According to John*, 1.357; original emphasis). However, as early as these stories of Jesus's illegitimate birth may be, John P. Meier has shrewdly observed, "Most likely such a story does not date earlier than [the middle of the 2d century CE], since Justin Martyr argues with Trypho the Jew at great length over the virginal conception, without Trypho ever being represented as replying with the charge of illegitimacy" (*A Marginal Jew: Rethinking the Historical Jesus* [New York: Doubleday, 1991], 1.223).

166   Meier, *A Marginal Jew*, 1.228. Brown also notes the possibility that, "When in 41 the Jews deny that they are children of fornication, they are denying that they have wandered from the truth path of the worship of God" (Brown, *The Gospel According to John*, 1.364).

167   Hos 2:6 LXX "τέκνα πορνείας"; also see Hos 1:2; 4:46; 4:15; 5:4; Ezek 16:15, 33–34. Additionally, according to Philo, "those who know not the one true God" are "figuratively called by the law 'the children of a harlot' [ἐκ πόρνης]" (*Spec. Laws* 1.332 [Colson LCL]). Also see Silva, "πορνεύω," *NIDNTTE* 4.113.

168   Meier concludes that "to see a hidden reference to Jesus' physical illegitimacy in vv. 39–41 is, in my opinion, highly imaginative" (Meier, *A Marginal Jew*, 1.228). Also see Beasley-Murray, *John*, 135 and, in particular, Schnackenburg who notes: "(1) The expression ἐκ

who is being unfaithful to God[169] because he challenges their faithfulness to God and therefore their status as children of God.[170] According to this reading, Jesus is deemed a heretic, like the Israelite prophets before him, for confronting the "misrecognized" facticity of the people of Israel and, as a result, Jesus faces the same fate.[171]

Throughout the dialogue, where paternity determines behavior, Jesus tells "the Jews who had believed in him" that they are incapable of accepting his words because "you are from your father the devil" (44a) and "are not from God" (47b) while "whoever is from God" (i.e. the children of God) accept the words of God (47a). The concluding point Jesus makes with "the Jews who had believed in Him" (8:31) is that there are two categories of people in the world but the categories are no longer Jew and non-Jew (Abraham's descendants and everyone else) but now those who are "of God" and those who are not of God (regardless of their ancestral and ethnic lineage).[172] In this way, then, "the Jews'" assessment of Jesus functions as the social foil for the trans-ethnic identity for the followers of Jesus who are labeled the "children of God."[173]

πορνείας (on the wording cf. Gen 38:24) is adequately explained by Hos 1:2; 2:6 (LXX) τέκνα πορνείας; (2) The continuation, 'we have one father', shows that the Jews are defending themselves and do not follow up the hypothetical charge; (3) Jesus too does not mention it, but only deals with the Jews' claim to have God as their father (v. 42)" (*The Gospel According to St. John*, 2.212).

169 Within the Gospel of John, Michaels suggests that "the phrase, 'not born of unlawful intercourse,' evokes other expressions in this Gospel, such as 'born not of blood lines, nor of fleshly desire, nor a husband's desire, but of God (1:13), 'born form above' (3:3), 'born of water and Spirit' (3:5), 'born of the flesh' and 'born of the Spirit' (3:6, 8), all with the construction 'to be "born"' or 'begotten' *of*, of *from* someone or something" (*Gospel of John*, 515; original emphasis).

170 See Bultmann's statement: "Jesus' reproof assumes what was common knowledge, namely that the Jews call themselves children of God and that they call God their Father. Jesus challenges their right to do so" (Bultmann, *The Gospel of John*, 315–316).

171 For example, Isaiah also confronted the Judeans as "rebellious children" (בָּנִים סוֹרְרִים; Isa 30:1) who "are a rebellious people, faithless children, children who will not hear the instruction of the LORD" (Isa 30:9). Jesus also shares the fate of Jeremiah, who also having preached in the Temple, was told "You shall die!" by "the priests and the prophets and all the people" (Jer 26:8).

172 Moloney, *The Gospel of John*, 281.

173 Similarly, Wes Howard-Brook states: "They ['the Jews who had believed in Him'] want to affirm Jesus without giving up their privileged status of membership in the Chosen People by virtue of their ancestry. This conflict occupies the rest of the chapter and is at the very core of the fourth gospel's challenge. Just as the Samaritan woman was told that true worship took place on neither Samaria's nor Judea's 'holy mountain,' now the believing Judeans face the most difficult implication of Johannine discipleship: to give up their claim to inherited national pride in favor of receiving the authority to become

3.4 Failed Paternity Test

In the following section (John 8:48–59), "the Jews" are no longer identified as those "who had believed in Him" (v. 31) but are now simply identified as "the Jews" (three times; v. 48, 52, 57). The new introduction indicates "a formal change of interlocutor" in which Jesus is now addressed by "the Jews" as a broader group.[174] Instead of denying what Jesus has just said about them (8:42–47), "the Jews" in this section interrogate Jesus and assert statements of fact (8:48, 52–53, 57) beginning by confidently asserting ("Are we not right in saying? … ") that Jesus is a "Samaritan" and has "a demon" (8:48).[175] Jesus does not respond to the accusation of being a Samaritan (8:49), not because it was the same thing as having a demon, but because Jesus minimizes the importance people place in ethnic categories. Thus, as Bernard observed, Jesus being labeled a "Samaritan" "was not so offensive to Him as it was intended to be, for He looked to the day when the rivalries between Jews and Samaritans would disappear (4:21)."[176] "The Jews'" defense against Jesus's accusation of being children of the devil (8:44) was to label Jesus a "Samaritan"[177] and demon possessed while Jesus's defense against their accusations was to appeal to his

---

God's children by means of belonging to a loving community of discipleship" (*Becoming Children of God: John's Gospel and Radical Discipleship* [Maryknoll, NY: Orbis Books, 1994], 203).

174   Stephen Motyer, *Your Father the Devil?: A New Approach to John and 'the Jews'* (163). *Contra* Bennema who finds this view "mistaken since 8:31–59 refers to one group—the same Ἰουδαῖοι who initially 'believe' turn against Jesus when they grasp the implications of his teachings" ("The Identity and Composition of *hoi Ioudaioi* in the Gospel of John," 258). Dunn rightly places 8:48 within the larger context of John 7–8. In particular, Dunn states: "Throughout chapter 7 the 'Jews'/'the crowd' debate back and forth the significance of Jesus, with many believing or responding positively (7:31, 40), but others skeptical (7:35), and the end result 'a division (σχίσμα) among the people' (7:43). In chapter 8 the debate among 'the Jews' continues, some believing (8:31) and others rejecting (8:48)" (Dunn, "The Embarrassment of History: Reflections on the Problem of 'Anti-Judaism' in the Fourth Gospel," in *Anti-Judaism and the Fourth Gospel: Paper of the Leuven Colloquium 2000*, Bieringer et al. [Assen; Royal Van Gorcum, 2001], 57).

175   Moloney, *The Gospel of John*, 283. According to Michaels, "the expression, 'Do we not say well?' hints that "the Jews" are not saying this for the first time. In the two instances in which Jesus uses such an expression, it is in relation either to something someone has just said, or something said repeatedly or customarily [cf. 4:17; 13:13]" (*The Gospel of John*, 522). Also see Chrysostom: "And even though the Evangelist did not mention before this that they called Him a Samaritan, it is probable, in the light of this speech, that they often used this epithet" (*Hom. Jo.* 55.1 [FC, 77]).

176   Bernard, *The Gospel According to St. John*, 2.317.

177   Remember that we are using the term "Samaritan" because it is the one used in the Gospel of John (Σαμαρίτης/Σαμαρῖτις John 4:9, 39; 8:48) while, according to the Delos inscriptions, they called themselves "Israelites."

honoring of "my Father" (8:49). Although Jesus's response retains the diverging paternity, Jesus nevertheless continues to appeal to them to keep his word so that they "will never see death" (8:51).[178]

In the previous section of dialogue (8:31–47), "the Jews who had believed him" appealed to their common ancestor with Jesus in attempting to understand how Jesus's teaching coherers with their understanding (cf. the Samaritan woman in 4:15, 19–20). Jesus's appeal in 8:51, however, is confirmation for "the Jews" from 8:48 that Jesus has a demon (8:52a) and their reasoning is sound: for, if Abraham as well as the prophets died then Jesus must be claiming to be greater than them.[179] Since the Samaritans adhere only to the Law of Moses and none of the prophets after Moses,[180] it is interesting to note "the Jews" inclusion of "the prophets" in their accusation (8:52–53), for it serves as an indicium between Judean and Samaritan ethnic identity. "The Jews" shrewdly include "the prophets" into their inquiry (8:53; cf. 4:12) in order to determine whether, and to what degree, Jesus is in agreement with the Samaritans over against themselves, "the Jews."[181] Far from being "the Jews who had believed in Him" (8:31), "the Jews" in 8:48–59 progressively question Jesus's allegiance to Judean ethnic identity.[182]

Jesus's defense is that he is "glorified" by "*my* Father" about whom "the Jews" claim "He is *our* God" (8:54). Jesus now makes explicit that his Father is the one whom they claim as their God (cf. 8:41b) and yet, they have "not known him but I know him" (8:55). It is important to note that "Jesus does not say that they serve another God but that they do not know the one they call their God."[183]

---

178   In 8:31 Jesus promised that they would be free if they remained in his word and now that point is reiterated in a different way. See Beasley-Murray: "The promise relates to one who 'keeps' the word of Jesus, i.e., who believes it, holds on to it, carries out its demands, and so lives by it; it is the equivalent to 'abiding' in his word (v. 31) and is common in Johannine writings" (*John*, 137).

179   Beasley-Murray, for example, states: "The craziness of the saying is emphasized by the Jews in adducing the holiest of their forefathers, Abraham, and all who have spoken in God's name, as men who yet experienced death like the rest of humankind" (*John*, 137).

180   Bowman, "Samaritan Studies," 299 n. 5.

181   Accordingly, Meier states that "by questioning the Jerusalemite Jews' status as the true children of Abraham, Jesus, in their minds, is aligning himself with the 'heterodox and schismatic' Samaritans, who question the Jews' status as the only children of Abraham and Jerusalem's status as the one true place of temple worship (cf. John 4:20)" (Meier, *A Marginal Jew*, 1.228–229).

182   This progression may also explain why "the Jews" know where Jesus is from in 6:41–42; 7:27–28; 41–42 but no longer know where he comes from in 9:29.

183   Ridderbos, *Gospel According to John*, 320. In this regard, Lincoln has observed that "nearly all of the accusations Jesus makes in John 8 were made by Yahweh against Israel in Isaiah. Their lack of knowledge (8:14, 19, 55; cf. Isa 48:8), their being from below (8:23; cf. Isa 55:9),

134   CHAPTER 4

Jesus is suggesting that "the Jews" are adhering to opinions and traditions other
than those of their God, his Father. In this regard, Cyril of Alexandria suggests
that Jesus "all but utters against them that which was declared through the
Prophet: for 'then' He said, 'This people draweth nigh to Me, with their lips
they do honor Me, but their heart is far from Me' [Isa 29:13]."[184] Cyril, however,
omits the final clause of Isa 29:13, that "their [i.e. the Judeans'] worship of me
[YHWH] is a human commandment learned by rote." Yet, this is the very point
Jesus was trying to make since 8:31 and "it is loyalty to God *as they know him*
that leads ["the Jews"] to reject Jesus."[185] Here again, we note that Jesus is in
the social role of prophet/heretic recalling the prophetic critique of YHWH's
people not knowing YHWH (e.g. Jer 4:22; 9:3; Hos 4:1, 6; 5:4).

Although Jesus fulfills the social role of a prophet/heretic, he is more than
a prophet (cf. 4:19) because, unlike the prophets before him, Jesus tells "the
Jews," "Your ancestor Abraham rejoiced that he would see my day; he saw it
and was glad" (8:56). It has been noted since the time of Cyril of Alexandria
that, "[Jesus] in one place removes them from relation with Abraham [8:37]...
but now again calls them Abraham's sons [8:39, 56]."[186] Yet, in 8:37 Jesus
does not actually exclude them from kinship. He exhorts "the Jews who had
believed in him" to do the works of Abraham if they claim to be children of
Abraham. Accordingly, in light of his previous exhortation, it is possible that
in 8:56 Jesus is urging "the Jews" (who claim to be children of Abraham) to re-
joice as Abraham had done.[187] Regardless, in saying "Abraham rejoiced that he
would see my day," the Johannine Jesus challenges the prominence they placed
on Abrahamic descent, but not in a manner that relegates it to irrelevance.
Instead, Jesus asserts that truly being a child of Abraham is to receive God's
messenger.

---

their being slaves because of sin (8:33, 34; cf. Isa 50:1), and their not hearing (8:43, 47;
cf. Isa 42:18, 20) are indicted in both places" (Lincoln, *Truth on Trial*, 400–401).

184   Cyril of Alexandria, *Commentary on the Gospel of St. John* (trans. Philip Edward Pusey),
1.675. Brown observes that, "unlike Mark 7:6, John does not cite Isa 29:13 to the effect
that the hearts of the people of Israel are far from God although they honor God with
their lips; yet this theme goes all through Jesus' arguments with "the Jews" in the Fourth
Gospel" (Brown, *An Introduction to the Gospel of John*, 133).

185   Rodney A. Whitacre, *Johannine Polemic: The Role of Tradition and Theology* (Chico, CA:
Scholars Press, 1982), 76; added emphasis.

186   Cyril of Alexandria, *Commentary on the Gospel of St. John* (trans. Philip Edward Pusey),
1.680.

187   For example, Keener notes that "if they claim Abraham as their father (8:56)—and Jesus
does not deny that Abraham is their father ethnically (8:37)—then they ought to embrace
Jesus' revelation joyfully as their ancestor Abraham did (8:56; cf. 8:39–40)" (*The Gospel of
John*, 1.767).

LABELING AN ETHNIC JESUS   135

For the third time since 8:48, "the Jews" are identified as responding to Jesus
and, because they limit themselves to the assumed facticity (i.e. "misrecognition") of their ethno-cultural categories, they yet again misunderstand what
Jesus has said: "You are not yet fifty years old, and have you seen Abraham?"
(8:57).[188] In his final response to "the Jews" in John 8, Jesus makes his most
pronounced statement to them: "Very truly, I tell you, before Abraham was,
I am" (8:58). According to Theodore of Mopsuestia, "at a bare minimum he is
referring here to his divine nature ... [and] since the Jews could not stand these
words, they [8:59] *picked up stones to throw at him*."[189] Reinhartz rightly demonstrates that "the Jews" attempted to stone Jesus because they recognized
Jesus as a false prophet who was leading Israel astray (specifically in reference
to Deut 13:1–5, 10 as well as *b. San* 43a and 107b).[190] By the end of the dialogue
in John 8:31–59 it is clear there is a clash "between two differing understandings of the way in which God is made known."[191]

3.5   Labeling Jesus a "Samaritan"

In the beginning of John 8:48, where Jesus is labeled a "Samaritan," Jesus's dialogue partners are no longer identified as "the Jews who had believed in Him"
(8:31). They now are simply identified as "the Jews." In 8:48, "the Jews'" riposte
places Jesus's charges back upon him; namely, that his paternity (as a descen-
dant/child of Abraham) was questionable (if he was a "Samaritan") and that
he was the one under the control of the devil.[192] According to Luke Timothy
Johnson, that "Jews have no dealings with Samaritans" (4:9b) "is axiomatic"
but the link between the label "Samaritan" and "having a demon" in 8:48 is "as
though these automatically went together!"[193] Consequently, as we noted in
the Introduction and Chapter One, "the Jews'" labeling of Jesus as a "Samaritan"

---

188   Two important textual witnesses (P[75] and ℵ*) read: ἑώρακέν σε ("Has Abraham seen you?").
      There is stronger witness for reading ἑώρακας ("you [i.e. Jesus] have seen Abraham") in-
      cluding, for example, P[66], ℵ[c], A, B* (ἑόρακες) B[c] and D. In support of the reading ἑώρακας,
      Metzger states: "[It] is more fitting on the part of the Jews, who, assuming the superior-
      ity of Abraham (ver 53), would naturally represent Jesus as seeing Abraham rather than
      Abraham as seeing Jesus" (*Textual Commentary*, 193).
189   Theodore of Mopsuestia, *Commentary on John*, (translated by Marco Conti), 83.
190   Reinhartz, *Befriending the Beloved Disciple*, 94.
191   Moloney, *The Gospel of John*, 276.
192   Brooke Foss Westcott, *The Gospel according to St John: The Authorized Version with
      Introduction and Notes* (Grand Rapids: Eerdmans, 1971), 138. Also see Malina and
      Rohrbaugh, *Social-Science Commentary on the Gospel of John*, 162.
193   Johnson, "The New Testament's Anti-Jewish Slander and the Conventions of Ancient
      Polemic," 437.

136   CHAPTER 4

and demon-possessed are generally held as synonymous.[194] Barrett, for example, states that "To this suggested equivalence the best parallel that can be offered is ... Simon Magus."[195] In Chapter Three, however, we observed that it is
problematic to infer from Justin Martyr's account of Simon Magus that the
Judean ethnic group closely associated the Samaritan region and people group
with demons. Rather than equating the Samaritan people with demons, Dunn
suggests instead that "to call someone a 'Samaritan' is an accusation and insult equivalent to denouncing him as possessed by a demon."[196] In this way,
then, the labels "Samaritan" and "demon-possessed" themselves are not synonymous; the insult of each label is equivalent to one another.

In regard to whether the labels themselves or their insults were equivalent,
let us note the following about "the Jews" using the label "Samaritan" as an
insult in 8:48. First, it will be recalled from Chapter One that neither ethnic epithet ("Samaritan" or "Jew"), by themselves, was used as a term of abuse based
on the available evidence.[197] If there was a Jewish ethnic term of abuse against
the Samaritans, it was the label "Cuthean," which emphasized their status as
foreigners rather than the label "Samaritan." Second, instead of being a characteristic trope in Jewish anti-Samaritan polemics, Pummer has observed that
"nowhere else do these two terms, Σαμαρίτης and δαιμόνιον, occur together."[198]
Therefore, the most that can be said of the two charges in 8:48 is that they reinforce one another in the minds of "the Jews" in 8:48.[199] Third, since Abraham
is the topic of discussion in 8:31–59, we must address the relationship between
"the Jews'" labeling of Jesus as a "Samaritan" to the topic of Abraham.[200] The
charges in 8:48 reinforce one another because they are *in response to* Jesus's

---

194   For example, see Haacker, "Samaritan, Samaria," *NIDNTT*: "For the majority of exegetes
      the two halves of the question in v. 48 are materially related or even mean the same thing,
      and the answer in v. 49 refers to the whole question as a *pars pro toto*."
195   Barrett, *Gospel According to St. John*, 350.
196   Dunn, *Beginning From Jerusalem*, 280 n. 164.
197   See Bultmann, *The Gospel of John*, 299 n. 4; *contra* Walter Bauer, "Über die Spannung
      zwischen Juden und Samaritern, die 'Samariter' im Munde der Juden zum Schimpfwort
      macht" (*Das Johannesevangelium*, 130). Pummer also has observed that Σαμαρίτης is not
      "used anywhere as a term of abuse" (*The Samaritans in Flavius Josephus*, 36).
198   Pummer, *The Samaritans in Flavius Josephus*, 36. Also, in light of Pummer's observation
      "that the two terms, Σαμαρίτης and δαιμόνιον, do not occur anywhere else together," we
      must caution against the advice that it is "better to follow most exegetes in saying that the
      two parts of the question in John 8:48 are materially related or even mean the same thing"
      (Silva, "Σαμαρίτης," *NIDNTTE* 4.249).
199   Michaels, *The Gospel of John*, 523. For Michaels, however, this is the *least* that can be said
      of the two charges in 8:48.
200   Böhm, *Samarien und die Samritai bei Lukas*, 146.

LABELING AN ETHNIC JESUS

questioning "the Jews" as children of Abraham (8:39) and the accusation that they are children of the devil (8:44).

For these reasons, our focus concerns the function of the "the Jews'" labels (8:48) within the context of 8:31–59. Along these lines, Bultmann and others, suggest that the label "Samaritan" could be understood as "heretic"[201] or "apostate."[202] One of Beasley-Murray's suggested possibilities for the label "Samaritan" in 8:48, is that the "Samaritans were viewed by the Jews as heretics, since they rejected the worship at Jerusalem and asserted their own as God ordained."[203] However, we must clarify the concepts of the "heretic" and "apostate" in light of our etic social-scientific analysis from Chapter Three, in which we noted that both Josephus and the Synoptic Gospels portrayed the Samaritans as neither "heretics" nor "apostates" but as "foreigners." Also, according to our etic social-scientific analysis, since the Judeans (insiders) constructed the Samaritans' identity as foreigners (outsiders) who lived among them, they are categorized as Simmelian "strangers." This is not simply because the Samaritans were viewed as "foreigners" but rather because the "Samaritans" challenged the givenness of Jewish exclusivity as Israel, heirs of Abrahamic descent, and Mosaic tradition.

Also bearing in mind that, for Josephus, the problem with the Samaritans was not their religious practices (H-S#4) but their lack of "communal solidarity" (H-S#6) with the Judeans to the south, labeling Jesus a "Samaritan" could signify that he is being disloyal to "the Jews'" sense of ethnic solidarity (H-S#6). In this regard, Pummer suggests that "the accusation of being a Σαμαρίτης hurled at Jesus expresses only that Jesus belongs to another camp within Israel, just like the Samaritans."[204] Yet, since the Johannine Jesus is a "Jew" (4:9; 18:35), according to our etic social-scientific analysis, he is performing in a role that Coser defines as a "heretic" who proposes alternative means of understanding his own group's identity. In this regard, then, Bultmann's suggestion that the label "Samaritan" in 8:48 means something like "heretic" or "apostate" is correct. In terms of labeling theory, the purpose for "the Jews'" labeling of Jesus

---

201   See Bultmann, *The Gospel of John*, 299 n. 4; Schnackenburg, *The Gospel According to St. John*, 2.218.

202   See Lincoln, *Gospel According to Saint John*, 274; Köstenberger, *John*, 268.

203   Beasley-Murray, *John*, 136.

204   Pummer, *The Samaritans in Flavius Josephus*, 36. Similarly, Bernard comments: "Jesus had been combating their claim to be the true children of Abraham (vv. 39, 40), and had thus challenged their boasted spiritual privileges. This was a principal point with the Samaritans, who would never allow that the Jews had any exclusive right to the promises made to Abraham and his seed. And so, observing, as they thought, that Jesus agreed with their despised Samaritan neighbors, they said contemptuously, 'You, after all, are only a Samaritan'" (*The Gospel According to St. John*, 2.316).

138

as a "Samaritan" was an act of institutional labeling that categorized Jesus as "not one of us" and placed him outside the boundaries of the Judean ethnic identity. In the minds of "the Jews" in 8:48–59, although Jesus may belong to another camp within Israel (like the Samaritans), he is not a member of their ("the Jews'") ethnic group (ἔθνος).

As we have shown, there is more involved in the social dynamics in John 8:31–59 than a reciprocal exchange of invectives. The "Samaritan" label functions to stigmatize Jesus (and his followers) as deviating from the prioritizing of the importance of the Abrahamic descent of "the Jews." Jesus's labeling of "the Jews" functions in the same way, so that in calling them the children of the devil (8:44) he stigmatizes those who prioritize ethnic identities rather than receiving and believing in him (1:12). Thus, the ethnic labeling of Jesus as a "Samaritan" not only distances him from the boundaries of themselves (i.e. "the Jews") but, for the broader scope and purposes of the Gospel of John, it also further demonstrates that "the Jews" are *still* thinking only in terms of ethnic identities and categories. "The Jews" retain their ethnic social categories instead of Jesus's teaching that their ethnic identity and categorizations have strayed from "the truth" (i.e. Jesus's revelation of God's reality). Those who come "to believe in Him" become a member of the trans-ethnic identity called "the children of God" (1:12–13) who are those who worship of the Father "in spirit and in truth" (4:23). This is in contradistinction from "the Jews" who worship in the Jerusalem Temple, which strictly maintains ethnic categorizations by not allowing foreigners (ἀλλογενεῖς) to enter under penalty of death.[205]

4   Intra-textual Labeling of an Ethnic Jesus

In this section, we will look at the Samaritan's woman's labeling of Jesus as a "Jew" in John 4 and what it contributes to how we understand "the Jews'" labeling of Jesus as a "Samaritan" in John 8. Finally, how this intratextual ethnic labeling functions to broaden both the Samaritans' and the Judeans' ethnic categories into the trans-ethnic identity called the "children of God" will be examined.

---

205   In this way, to label Jesus a "Samaritan" could also be a means of testing him to see if he qualifies for the "death penalty" in passing from the Court of Gentiles and into the Court of Women. In other words, it is possible that labeling Jesus a "Samaritan" in the Court of Women is one way that "the Jews" are seeking to kill him (8:37, 40). Jesus is marked as being out of place in two ways: 1) ideologically, for deviating from "the Jews" norms and mores and 2) physically, by being in the inner Court of Women.

In sections 2.2 and 3.4 we noted that the Samaritan woman and "the Jews" use the same construction that expects a negative response. In both instances, the Samaritan woman and "the Jews" assert that Jesus could not be greater than "our father Jacob" (4:12) or "our father Abraham" (8:53). The purpose of their question is to express their ethnic identity in terms of genealogy (H-S#2).[206] In both instances, Jesus's social deviation from established norms prompts their questions. Yet, in each instance, Jesus's interlocutors had different reactions. The Samaritan woman asked for his offer of living water (4:15). "The Jews," however, did not ask for his offer of "never seeing death" (8:51) and instead became convinced that Jesus had a demon (8:52a) and was leading Israel astray.

Consequently, Jesus was able to transcend the expectations of "being a Jew" (4:9a) with the Samaritan woman by deviating from social conventions (4:9b), but among "his own people" (1:11) he was not able to broaden "the Jews'" ethnic boundary into the trans-ethnic children of God. In other words, in John 4 Jesus's deviation from social conventions exposed their "misrecognized" state that allowed for a recategorization of the people of God (4:42); but in 8:31–59 his challenge about the "misrecognized" givenness of Judean ethnic identity (especially as descendants/children of Abraham) only reinforced their ethnic distinction, even to the point of labeling Jesus a "Samaritan" and thus not (truly) one of them.

Reacting to Jesus's request for a drink (4:7), the Samaritan woman asks Jesus: "How is it possible that you, being a Jew, are asking for a drink from me, being a woman who is a native of Samaria" (my own translation).[207] The Samaritan woman's question ("How is it possible?") discloses her judgment that Jesus is deviating from established associations (4:9b). Similarly, after Jesus says "the truth will make you free" (8:32), "the Jews who had believed in him" (8:31) ask "how is it possible ... ?" (8:33; my own translation). Both the Samaritan woman and "the Jews'" recognition of Jesus's deviance raises the important labeling questions pointed out by Barclay: "'Whose definitions of deviance are operative here?' and (as a supplementary question) 'Whose interests do theses definitions serve?'"[208] The definitions of deviance for both the Samaritan woman and "the Jews" are not their own but rather their society who makes the rules.[209]

---

206   See Förster, "Die Begegnung am Brunnen," 212.

207   BDAG translate πῶς here as "How is it possible" ("πῶς," 901) and Louw and Nida translate Σαμαρίτιδος, from Σαμαρῖτις, as "a woman who is a native of Samaria" ("Σαμαρῖτις," L&N 93.570).

208   Barclay, "Deviance and Apostasy," 116.

209   Recall Howard Becker's sociological insight: "*Social groups create deviance by making the rules whose infraction constitutes deviance*" (*Outsiders*, 9; original emphasis).

140   CHAPTER 4

Hence the Samaritan woman did not create the boundaries and rules of interaction between herself and Jesus. Instead, group identification (of the self) and categorization (of the other), as well as the social roles and rules for interactions, are things "learn[ed] early, deeply, and usually irrevocably"[210] that form the individual's "habitus."[211] In Chapter Two we noted that this process of socialization, and the stasis of cultural reproduction, accounts for the "misrecognized" facticity of the social world. Accordingly, the definitions of deviance operative for the Samaritan woman are *not* her own but are the result of her habitus—the internal definitions and practices she learned as a member of her ethnic group.[212]

When Jesus is labeled a "Jew" (4:9a) who deviates from having "no dealings" with the Samaritan woman (4:9b), we may ask: "Whose interests do these definitions of deviance serve?"[213] The definition of deviance serves to reinforce in-group identity by categorizing others into out-groups.[214] The maintenance of these social boundaries preserves the social order and, as a result, the definitions of deviance ultimately serve those in legitimated roles who define Us/Them. An etic term for those in legitimated roles within their social group is the "elites." To be sure, John 4 does not mention the Samaritans' "elites" but elsewhere in the Gospel of John, the "elites" can be identified as the chief priests and the Pharisees (7:32, 45; 11:49–51)[215] as well as other "gatekeepers"[216] such as the Levites (1:24) and the "temple police" (7:32, 45–46; 18:3, 12, 18, 22; 19:6). This system of cultural reproduction is so effective that it is a facticity, for both the

---

210   Hughes, "The Study of Ethnic Relations," 91.

211   "Habitus" is Bourdieu's term for the internal disposition that "tends to reproduce those actions, perceptions, and attitudes consistent with the conditions under which it was produced" (Swartz, *Culture & Power*, 103).

212   In this way, the Samaritan woman is not only symbolic of the Samaritan people but in a very real way, sociologically, she is representative of her people group.

213   Barclay, "Deviance and Apostasy," 116.

214   Hence Richard Jenkins: "The process of defining 'us' demands that 'they' should be split off from, or contrasted with, 'us'; group identification is likely to proceed, at least in part, through categorizing others, whether positively or negatively" (Jenkins, *Rethinking Ethnicity*, 59).

215   The chief priests and the Pharisees represent the "elites" in the Gospel of John because they are represented, for example, as having authority to send others (1:24, 7:32); to excommunicate (9:22, 12:42, 16:2); to gather a hearing (11:45–53).

216   A "gatekeeper" is defined as "an individual—or possibly a group—able to control access to goods and/or services" (Susan Mayhew, "gatekeeper," in *A Dictionary of Geography* (Oxford: Oxford University Press, 2009). Consequently, since gatekeepers "can control access to goods, services, or information ... they therefore wield power far in excess of their formal authority" (John Scott, "gatekeeping," in *A Dictionary of Sociology* (Oxford: Oxford University Press, 2014).

LABELING AN ETHNIC JESUS   141

societal elites and non-elites, and therefore is *"misrecognized"* as legitimate by
both. The state of "misrecognition" is a tacit, but nonetheless absolute, recognition of legitimacy for the status quo of social existence (e.g. social order [such
as class/status] or social categories [such as identities]).[217]

Accordingly, in the state of "misrecognition," the Samaritan woman categorized and labeled Jesus "a Jew" because she was taught that there is such
a thing as an objective category of us/Samaritans and them/Judeans; hence
the we/you pronouns used throughout their dialogue. Of course, the inverse
is true for Jesus and his disciples who no doubt knew that "Jews have no dealings with Samaritans" (4:9b; my own translation). For the Samaritan woman,
the particularity of her and Jesus's social interaction is a facticity because she
has internalized the givenness of cultural practices (i.e. habitus) as legitimated
by her Samaritan leaders (the "elites"), to recognize Jesus's infraction of cultural customs. After labeling Jesus a "Jew" (Ἰουδαῖος), the Samaritan woman
discloses what she was taught the label to mean. In particular, that the label
"Jew" describes a descendant of the patriarchs (i.e. an Israelite from the tribe
of Judah; 4:12) but who is beholden to the Jerusalem-centric traditions (4:20)
developed in Judea in contrast to those in Samaria to the north.[218] That this is
an important distinction to the Samaritan woman is evidenced by her question to Jesus in John 4:20 where she yet again categorizes Jesus as a "Jew" ("you
[people] say that the place where people must worship is in Jerusalem"). Yet
the Johannine Jesus, like the prophets in the texts of the Hebrew Bible, challenges the status quo's reproduction of cultural practices for having deviated
from the ways of YHWH.[219] Accordingly, the Johannine Jesus deviated from
the cultural practices for interactions between Jews and Samaritans in order to
transcend their ethnic divide and led the Samaritan woman and the Sycharian
Samaritans into his fictive-kinship as "children of God" (1:12–13; 11:52).

---

217   Pierre Bourdieu aptly summarizes this analytical perspective that, "The most successful
      ideological effects are those which have no need for words, and ask no more than com-
      plicitous silence" (Bourdieu, *Outline of a Theory of Practice*, 188).

218   The Judean's Jerusalem-centric tradition is not found in the MT Pentateuch (Torah) but
      only in the Prophets (Nev'im) and Writings (Ketuvim) is Jerusalem identified as "the site
      which the LORD *will* choose" (cf. MT Deut 12:5, 11, 14, 18, 21, 26; 14:23, 24, 25; 15:20; 16:2, 6,
      7, 11, 15, 16; 17:8, 10; 18:6; 26:2; 31:11).

219   For example, Isaiah criticizes "these people" whose "worship of [YHWH] is a human
      commandment learned by rote" (Isa 29:13) and Jeremiah bluntly criticizes the remnant
      in 42:19–21: "The LORD has said to you, O remnant of Judah, Do not go to Egypt. Be well
      aware that I have warned you today that you have made a fatal mistake. For you yourselves
      sent me to the LORD your God, saying, 'Pray for us to the LORD our God, and whatever
      the LORD our God says, tell us and we will do it.' So I have told you today, but you have
      not obeyed the voice of the LORD your God in anything that he sent me to tell you."

142   CHAPTER 4

After addressing the Samaritan woman in terms of Barclay's questions, we now turn to "the Jews" in John 8:31–59. We have already observed that in both John 4 and 8 Jesus's deviant behavior is marked by his interlocutors' question "how is it that you … ?" (4:9; 8:33; my own translation). Also in both instances, the definitions of deviance are not the interlocutors' own definitions but belong to their ethnic group's cultural milieu. The interlocutors are able to recognize deviant behavior, even if they are not a member of the "elites" or a "gatekeeper" (such as the Samaritan woman), because they were socialized into norms of acceptable practices of their ethnic group. Accordingly, "the Jews who had believed him" (8:31) knew that as "descendants of Abraham" they "have never been slaves to anyone" (8:33) and, in their "misrecognized" state of cultural reproduction, ask Jesus how he can say "they will be free?" (8:33). In this regard, we can observe that "the Jews" having "never been slaves to anyone" (8:33) was as much a facticity for them as "Jews have no dealings with Samaritans" (4:9b my own translation) was for the Samaritan woman.

We have also already observed that the definitions of deviance serve the interests of the "elites" whose social position grants them a "misrecognized" legitimacy among the members of their ethnic group.[220] The exception, however, is the ethnic factionalist who challenges the "elites'" legitimacy to represent their ethnic group. In John 8:31–59 we see "the Jews who had believed in him" identifying Jesus's deviance for suggesting that they are not already free (8:31–47). As a result of his deviancy, "the Jews" label Jesus a "Samaritan" and "demon-possessed" (8:48–59), which functions to maintain their ethnic identity.[221] In John 8:31–59, "the Jews (who have believed him)" (8:31, 48, 52, 57) express their ethnic identity in terms of "descendants of Abraham" (8:33, 37), "children of Abraham" (8:39, 56), and "children of God" (8:41) who "have never been slaves to anyone" (8:33; perhaps meaning served an idol[222]) or apostates ("not illegitimate children"; 8:41). Based upon their self-identification as a particular expression of their ethnic identity, we may infer the following. First, we note that from the perspective of "the Johannine Jews, belief in Jesus is the

---

220 Barclay, "Deviance and Apostasy," 116. Hence the Samaritan woman who knew Jesus had deviated from the rules of interactions between Samaritans and Jews because it was something she learned as a member of the Samaritan ethnic group.

221 In particular, Bruce J. Malina and Jerome H. Neyrey note that "from the viewpoint of negative labelers, then, deviance refers to those behaviors and/or conditions perceived and assessed to jeopardize the interests and social standing of persons who negatively label the behaviors and/or conditions" (*Calling Jesus Names*, 39–40).

222 Reinhartz suggests translating δεδουλεύκαμεν ("we have been slaves") in 8:33 as "to serve," which in terms of worship, "the Jews who had believed in him" (8:31) are declaring that "they have never served any being other than God" (*Befriending the Beloved Disciple*, 92).

path *not* to the God of Israel but away from God to idolatry"[223] (8:33; 41). This perspective, that Jesus is a false prophet leading "the Jews" (and the people) astray from YHWH,[224] is also found in 7:12, 47. However, from the perspective the Johannine Jesus in John 8, "the Jews" have already been "led astray" because, although they say "we have one father, God himself" (8:41) and "He is our God" (8:54), Jesus asserts they "do not know him" (8:55).[225] Second, we can view "the Jews (who have believed him)" through the lens of ethnicity as referring "to those who at a particular point in time represent and act in the name of their ethnic community."[226] From this perspective, Jesus is an ethnic factionalist for challenging "the Jews'" representation of their shared Judean ethnic identity as primarily expressed in terms of ancestral descent (8:33, 37, 39, 56; H-S#2). In other words, for both the Samaritan woman and "the Jews," it is a "misrecognized" facticity that their ethnic identity is expressed by genealogical descent from the patriarchs (4:12//8:53). Instead, in the Gospel of John, "physical descent from Abraham has little importance" because "the children of God" are now identified as those who do what Abraham had done by receiving God's divine messenger Jesus (1:12; 8:47).[227]

The Johannine Jesus, then, is either a false prophet (cf. Deut 13:1–5, 10) or a divine/heavenly messenger sent to "the Jews" just as they were sent to their father Abraham (cf. Gen 18:1–18). In this way, John 8:31–59 represents an intra-ethnic conflict with the Johannine Jesus representing an ethnic factionalist who "compete(s) for influence and support among members of [his Jewish] community, for the right to control its institutions and collective resources, to speak authoritatively on its behalf, and to represent it to outsiders."[228] The

---

223 Reinhartz, *Befriending the Beloved Disciple*, 93; original emphasis. Reinhartz later adds: "The words assigned to the Jews in John 8:31–59 suggest that the basic issue at stake is whether or not Jesus and the claims made for him are an enhancement of monotheism, that is, a 'new and improved' but fundamentally recognizable revelation or, conversely, a radical infringement on this basic Jewish belief" (Reinhartz, *Befriending the Beloved Disciple*, 95).

224 Reinhartz suggests that Jesus "bears a striking resemblance to the deceitful prophet as described in [Deut 13:1–5, 10]" (Reinhartz, *Befriending the Beloved Disciple*, 94).

225 In fact, the prophetic critique in Hosea 4 of the people not knowing YHWH (Hosea 4:1, 6) is due to their having been led astray (Hosea 4:12).

226 Esman, *Introduction to Ethnic Conflict*, 45.

227 Beutler, "Abraham," 68. Beutler adds: "To the sonship of Abraham is opposed that which is from God, whether that of Jesus himself or that of those who believe in him. The role of Abraham is reduced to that of witness alongside Moses, the prophets and John the Baptist."

228 Esman, *Introduction to Ethnic Conflict*, 47.

144 CHAPTER 4

Johannine Jesus, then, was a factionalist Jew who caused "division" (σχίσμα; 7:43; 9:16; 10:19) among "his own people" (1:11)—"the Jews."[229]

Among "his own people" (1:11), Jesus attempted to broaden their ethnic group's boundary into the trans-ethnic "children of God" (1:12–13). In John 8:31–59, Jesus reveals that "the Jews'" ethnic social conventions (e.g. H-S#1–6) were not an adequate view of reality because there is more to "being of God" (8:47) than being Abraham's descendants/children (8:33, 39).[230] In fact, this is the very same point Jesus argued with the Samaritan woman that subsequently led the Sycharian Samaritans to confessing that Jesus "is truly the Savior of the world" (4:42). Yet, in response to Jesus's factionalist challenge, "the Jews" label him as both a "Samaritan" and "demon-possessed," which socially distances Jesus from them by underscoring the differences between them.[231]

5   Conclusion

The Johannine Prologue discloses two contrasting types of people in the world: those who did not receive Jesus (those among his own people—"the Jews"; 1:11) and those who did ("children of God"; 1:12). The Samaritan woman and the Sycharian Samaritans represent the gathering of "the dispersed children of God" (11:52). Although the Samaritans were "foreigners" and outside of Jesus's "own people" (1:11; "the Jews"), they listened to the shepherd's voice and entered into the "one flock, [with] one shepherd" (10:16). This is the truth (God's reality) that Jesus, performing the role that Coser calls "heretic," presents and it elicits a choice. In contrast, when confronted by this truth, "the Jews" in John 8:31–59 choose to reinforce their ethnic identity, especially by Abrahamic descent (which, from an emic perspective, is the *sine qua non* of ethnic identity), and they do not receive him (1:11).

---

229   Beasley-Murray rightly states, "The Evangelist rejects neither Moses and the prophets, nor Judaism as such; it is the unbelieving leaders of Israel against whom he polemizes" (*John*, 62).

230   For example, in 8:39 Jesus says, "If you were Abraham's children, you would be doing what Abraham did" and the Sycharian Samaritans, in fact, had done what Abraham did—they received Jesus, as God's messenger, and offered him hospitality by inviting Jesus to stay with them (cf. Gen 18). In this way, the Samaritans claim to be children of Abraham/Jacob are true because they did the works of Abraham.

231   Malina and Neyrey, *Calling Jesus Names*, 37. Elsewhere Malina and Neyrey state: "In the case of Jesus and his disciples, the publicly approved deviance-processing agencies are the Jerusalem elites and the local roman government. These agencies register deviance by defining, classifying, and labeling types of behavior or conditions deemed to be 'out of bounds'" (Malina and Neyrey, "Conflict in Luke-Acts," 104).

In both of these instances, when Jesus addresses the members of an ethnic group, he is labeled an outsider. For this reason, Barrett suggested that "in this world [Jesus] is never anything but a stranger."[232] Yet, as we have noted before, Jesus is not labeled a "stranger" as if he were an unknown entity or ethereal figure but rather a stranger within a known ethnic identity. Also, we have observed in this chapter that labeling Jesus with an ethnic identity was not mere happenstance but was a particular social function ensuing from the immediate social interaction. While both labeling occasions mark Jesus as outside of the labeler's ethnic boundary, the Samaritan woman (in John 4) simply acknowledged the boundary line while "the Jews" (in John 8) sought to push Jesus outside of their ethnic boundary line; which, to a certain extent, worked because he left the temple's segregated area for Jews only (the Court of Women). The larger purpose of these labeling events in the Gospel of John is to function as a social foil, revealing the nature of the children of God who transcend their ethnic identity.

In this chapter, we demonstrated how ethnic identities and categories impact the assessment of Jesus's identity. In the next chapter, we apply the findings of the study thus far to the contentious question of the identity of "the Jews" in the Gospel of John.

---

232   Barrett, *Gospel According to St. John*, 232.

CHAPTER 5

Ethnic Assessments in the Gospel of John

> Once in a while you get shown the light, in the strangest of places if you look at it right.[1]

> 'Johannine Christianity' does not explicitly define itself over against 'the other', either of Jewish or of Gentile culture and practice. Instead, its incipient concern [is] with the articulation of belief.[2]

∴

Introduction

We recall from Chapter One that only non-Jews label Jesus a "Jew" in the Gospel of John (John 4:9; 18:35) while "the Jews" label Jesus a non-Jew (a Samaritan in 8:48). In Chapter Four we saw that, in both instances of Jesus's ethnic labeling (4:9; 8:48), he is marked as an outsider to the labelers' ethnic group either by acknowledgment (interactive) or by force (institutional). We concluded the previous chapter by noting that the dual ethnic labeling events in the Gospel of John functioned as a social foil for the followers of Jesus who, by their belief in him, became "children of God" (1:12)—a fictive-kinship group (1:13) embedded in Judean heritage (4:22). This chapter will apply the significance of these prior insights concerning ethnic identity in the Gospel of John for the contentious problem of the identity of "the Jews."

We begin this chapter with a brief overview of studies on the identity of "the Jews" in the Gospel of John and conclude that no single meaning of "the Jews" can account for all of the occurrences in the Gospel. The following section, then, examines the implications of the Gospel of John's employment of ethnic terms in this debate, and particularly instances of interactions with Jesus and others where ethnic categories impact assessment of identity. In addition to the aforementioned instances of the Samaritan woman of John 4 and "the

---

1　Robert Hunter, "Scarlet Begonias," *A Box of Rain* (New York: Penguin Books, 1993), 197.
2　Judith Lieu, *Christian Identity in the Jewish and Greco-Roman World* (Oxford: Oxford University Press, 2004), 138.

Jews" of John 8, this section discusses other occurrences of ethnic assessments including "the Jews'" assessments of John the Baptist (1:19–28) as well as the disciples' assessments of Jesus (1:35–51). The next section addresses ethnic implications for the proposed identities of "the Jews" in reference to John 6 and John 7. We will conclude the chapter by arguing that, although there is more than a single meaning for the Gospel of John's use of "the Jews," what they all have in common is a relationship to an ethnic group.

Chapter Four argued that "the children of God" neither reject their existing ethnic identity nor do they adopt of another one.[3] The Sycharian Samaritans remain Samaritans though they confess Jesus as "the Savior of the world" (4:42). The "children of God" transcend the primacy attached to their ethnic identity with being "of God" (8:47; cf. 4:20–24). In this sense, and regardless of their ethnic identity, they are connected to the Judeans' heritage through their belief in Jesus by the fact that "salvation is from the Jews" (4:22).[4]

Consequently, this chapter will conclude that both "the Jews" and Jesus are concerned with being "of God" (8:47) but diverge in how this is understood. For "the Jews" who do not believe in Jesus, to be "of God" is understood in terms of a Judean ethnic identity that foregrounds being descendants of Abraham (8:33) and disciples of Moses (9:28). We also saw in Chapter Four that for the Samaritans to be "of God" was to a member of the Samaritan ethnic group, that is, descendants of Abraham (4:12) who worship on Mount Gerizim (4:20). These indicia of ethnic group identity are not "replaced"[5] by Jesus in the Gospel of John. What changes is *how* they are significant in light of Jesus who "has made [the Father] fully and clearly known" (1:18).[6] In the Samaritan and Judean heritage, Moses is the decisive revealer of God for the children of Abraham, but in the Gospel of John both Moses and Abraham are in a subordinate role as witnesses to Jesus as "God the only Son" (1:18; cf. 5:46; 8:56). For Jesus, to be "(children) of God" is therefore to believe in him and abide in "the truth" (of God's reality), which ultimately transcends ethnic group boundaries

---

3   Cornelis Bennema, "The Ethnic Conflict in Early Christianity," *JETS* 56.4 (2013): 755.

4   Marianne Meye Thompson, *John: A Commentary* (Louisville: Westminster John Knox, 2015), 204.

5   In his commentary on the Gospel of John, Raymond Brown speaks of Jesus's "replacing Jewish institutions, feasts, and customs" (Brown, *The Gospel According to John*, 2.895). However, we must note that Brown's understanding the "the Jews" in the Gospel of John developed from the time of his commentary on John in 1966 until his death in 1997 and his posthumously published works. For full discussion on this matter see Sonya Shetty Cronin, *Raymond Brown, 'The Jews', and the Gospel of John* (LNTS 504; London: Bloomsbury, 2015).

6   "ἐξηγέομαι," L&N 28.41. Louw-Nida further defines the meaning of ἐξηγέομαι in John 1:18 as "to make something fully known by careful explanation or by clear revelation."

148 CHAPTER 5

(including "the Jews," Samaritans, Greeks, etc.) while remaining thoroughly rooted in the heritage of "the Jews" (e.g. 1:45; 4:22; 5:39, 46; etc.).

1 Who Are "the Jews" in the Gospel of John? A Retrospective

According to John Ashton, the identity of the "the Jews" is generally discussed in terms of their referent (i.e. their historical existence outside of the text) or in terms of their sense (i.e. the role they play inside of the text).[7] As a referent, "the Jews" are understood in a seemingly simplistic geographic identification as the inhabitants of Judea (Lowe)[8] or an ethnic group (Mason).[9] In terms of their role in the Gospel of John, "the Jews" are identified as the enemies of Jesus (Bultmann; Reinhartz)[10] or their role (as opponents to Jesus) is limited by their status as the "Jewish authorities" (von Wahlde).[11] The following section highlights aspects of each of these positions that are pertinent to the present argument.

1.1 *"The Jews" as Judeans*
Malcolm Lowe proposes that, "rather than a merely religious denotation," there is also a geographical understanding of "the Jews" in the Gospel of John as Judeans.[12] According to Lowe, the first geographical designation of "Jews" (Ἰουδαῖοι) appears in 2 Kings 16:6 for the inhabitants of Judah, which the NRSV translates "Judeans," in distinction from other inhabitants of Israel.[13] Although this usage occurs long before the time of Jesus, Lowe cautions that "it should not be thought ... that the geographical sense of Ἰουδαῖοι quickly died out, since

---

7   John Ashton, "The Identity and Function of the Ἰουδαῖοι in the Fourth Gospel," *NovT* 27.1 (1985): 40–75.
8   Malcolm Lowe, "Who Were the ΙΟΥΔΑΙΟΙ?," *NovT* 18.2 (1976): 101–130.
9   Mason, "Jews, Judeans, Judaizing, Judaism," 457–512.
10 Bultmann, *The Gospel of John,* 54–56, 86–87; Reinhartz, *Befriending the Beloved Disciple,* 61–70.
11 Von Wahlde, "The Terms for Religious Authorities in the Fourth Gospel," 33–60.
12 Lowe, "Who Were the ΙΟΥΔΑΙΟΙ?," 101.
13 Lowe, "Who Were the ΙΟΥΔΑΙΟΙ?," 103 n. 4. We also noted this use in Chapter Three and added that the label "Judean" is *not* limited to the inhabitants Judah but includes Judeans living in Moab, Ammon, and Edom (Jer 40:11–12), those living in Egypt (Jer 43:9; 44:1), and those in Babylon (Jer 52:28, 30). We also called attention to Joseph Blenkinsopp's suggestion that the label "Judean" belongs "to the same category as Edomites, Syrians, and similar labels, which identify individuals politically and, given the existence of national patron deities, also to some extent religiously" (*Judaism The First Phase,* 21).

ETHNIC ASSESSMENTS IN THE GOSPEL OF JOHN

they are clearly attested by Josephus."[14] Consequently for Lowe, the two central meanings of "Jews" (Ἰουδαῖοι) in the time of the New Testament are geographical and religious, with the former as its primary meaning.[15] The reason for geographic primacy, as Lowe observes, is that "in the ancient Mediterranean world almost every people had its own national religion, so that to be a member of that religion was in a sense to have that nationality."[16] The secondary religious sense of "Jews" (Ἰουδαῖοι), Lowe argues, did not become its basic meaning until "Palestine gradually ceased to be looked upon as the home of an ἔθνος τῶν Ἰουδαίων."[17] Concerning "the Jews" in the Gospel of John, Lowe more recently concludes that "the word *Ioudaioi* does not have a peculiar theological sense in John but is used as in other ancient texts."[18]

Steve Mason is another proponent of translating "Jews" (Ἰουδαῖοι) as "Judeans." However, Mason's primary interest is the ancient Greco-Roman world in general rather than the Gospel of John specifically. Mason argues that within the broader Greco-Roman world "the *Ioudaioi* were understood until late antiquity as an ethnic group comparable to other ethnic groups, with their distinctive laws, traditions, customs, and God. They were indeed Judeans."[19] Mason's conclusion is the result of his emic approach that seeks to understand the ancient categories used when discussing "Jews" (Ἰουδαῖοι) in Greco-Roman

---

14 Lowe, "Who Were the ΙΟΥΔΑΙΟΙ?," 104. As we discussed in Chapter Three, Josephus makes three observations concerning the label "Judean" in Josephus, *Ant.* 11.173. According to Lowe, Josephus can use Ἰουδαῖοι in a geographical sense to indicate inhabitants of a territory or in an ethnic sense to distinguish Ἰουδαῖοι from gentiles but can also use Ἰουδαῖοι "in *different* senses in the *same* passages, supposing that the reader can easily guess the correct sense from the context" (Lowe, "Who Were the ΙΟΥΔΑΙΟΙ?," 104–105; original emphasis).

15 In his follow-up article, Lowe states: "Here the key passage is Dio Cassius, *R.Hist.* XXXVII, xvi.5–xvii.1, which (in effect) says precisely this" (Malcolm Lowe, "ΙΟΥΔΑΙΟΙ of the Apocrypha: A Fresh Approach to the Gospels of James, Pseudo-Thomas, Peter and Nicodemus" *NovT* 23.1: 56 n. 3).

16 Lowe, "Who Were the ΙΟΥΔΑΙΟΙ?," 107. For ancient support, Lowe cites Cicero, *Pro Flacco*, 69: "Every city, Laelius, has its own religious observances and we have ours" (Coll MacDonald, LCL). Consequently, Lowe asserts that "even when non-Judean converts began to call themselves Ἰουδαῖοι the word would probably have retained a connotation of Judea in the [geographical] sense, since they had become members of the religion *of* the latter area" (Lowe, "Who Were the ΙΟΥΔΑΙΟΙ?," 109; original emphasis).

17 Lowe, "Who Were the ΙΟΥΔΑΙΟΙ?," 109. Lowe then adds that the geographic meaning gradually began to fade "following the Bar-Kochba revolt, whose result was to eliminate or expel most of the Jewish population of Judea."

18 Malcolm Lowe, "Concepts and Words," *Jew and Judean: A MARGINALIA Forum on Politics and Historiography in the Translation of Ancient Texts* (Timothy Michael Law and Charles Halton, eds.; Los Angeles, CA: The Marginalia Review of Books, 2014), 33.

19 Mason, "Jews, Judeans, Judaizing, Judaism," 457.

literature and particularly in Josephus.[20] An important aspect of Mason's emic approach is that, since the modern concept of religion "lack[s] a taxonomical counterpart in antiquity,"[21] it cannot be used in determining who the "Jews" (Ἰουδαῖοι) were in the Greco-Roman world. Instead, Mason finds that ancient Greco-Roman writers "employed *ethnos* and its usual companions as an exceptionally robust taxonomy for classifying the social phenomena they saw around them."[22]

Mason offers a compelling argument for how those living in the Greco-Roman world categorized one another in relationship to their ethnic group. Yet, Lowe has recently identified a flaw in Mason's ethnic proposal. Lowe correctly states that "we should beware of assuming that if a word or use of a word is not found in ancient authors, then those authors did not have the concept denoted by that word."[23] Consequently, although Mason is correct about the absence of the word for "religion" in the Greco-Roman world, this does not mean that the ancients did not express concepts that we know as religion/religious.[24] This does not negate Mason's overall thesis that the ancient concept of *ethnos* is an umbrella concept for categorizing social phenomena. Rather, it recognizes that elements that we would understand as religious are incorporated into it.

1.2 *"The Jews" as the Enemies of Jesus*

Bultmann lays the foundation of his symbolic reading of "the Jews" in his discussion of the Johannine Prologue, even before the first appearance of "the Jews" in John 1:19. In his comments on John 1:1, Bultmann states: "The idea of the election of the nation, and of the covenant of God with it, does not occur at all either, and nowhere in the Gospel does the Israelite-Jewish nation appear to be raised decisively above the rest of the world."[25] Still, even in view of the fact that Jesus was a "Jew" (4:9; 18:35), as well as positive statements about "the

---

20 Mason, "Jews, Judeans, Judaizing, Judaism," 459. In sum, Mason's emic approach asks, "How did *they* understand the phenomena their world presented to them, and what do their terms reveal about their values and assumptions?" (458).

21 Mason, "Jews, Judeans, Judaizing, Judaism," 480.

22 Mason, "Jews, Judeans, Judaizing, Judaism," 483. As we noted in Chapter Two, according to Mason, "each *ethnos* had its distinctive nature or character (φύσις, ἦθος), expressed in unique ancestral traditions (τὰ πάτρια), which typically reflected a shared (if fictive) ancestry (συγγενεία); each had its charter stories (μῦθοι), customs, norms, conventions, mores, laws (νόμοι, ἔθη, νόμιμα), and political arrangements or constitution (πολιτεία)" (Mason, "Jews, Judeans, Judaizing, Judaism," 484).

23 Lowe, "Concepts and Words," 34.

24 Lowe, "Concepts and Words," 35.

25 Bultmann, *The Gospel of John*, 21.

ETHNIC ASSESSMENTS IN THE GOSPEL OF JOHN

Jews" (which he cites as John 4:22; 5:39ff.),[26] Bultmann declares "the Jews" to be "the representatives of unbelief"[27] and "the representatives of the 'world,'"[28] which he defines as "that which stands over against God."[29]

Similarly, according to Reinhartz, Jesus and his followers are not explicitly "Jews" in the Gospel of John, which "allows this term to be identified tightly with the opposition to Jesus."[30] Then, more recently in her article "The Vanishing Jews of Antiquity," Reinhartz states that "despite some neutral or even positive occurrences, the *Ioudaioi* figure most prominently as the opponents of Jesus."[31] Reinhartz further emphasizes this point by noting that "the seventy-fold repetition of the term does not allow readers to ignore or make light of this hostile portrayal."[32]

1.3 *"The Jews" as the Religious Authorities*

Urban C. von Wahlde proposes there are two categories of occurrences of "the Jews" in the Gospel of John. The first category is the "neutral" occurrences that designate the inhabitants of Judea, "the Jews" as a nation, or their customs or feasts.[33] Von Wahlde designates the second category as "the Johannine use." According to von Wahlde, "the Johannine use" occurs when "the word ["Jews"] is used in a way that does not indicate simply nationality nor even regional affiliation (i.e. 'Judean') but seems to refer to a certain class (or classes) of persons within Palestinian society."[34] For this reason, von Wahlde proposes that

---

26   Bultmann, *The Gospel of John*, 21 n. 5.

27   Bultmann, *The Gospel of John*, 86.

28   Bultmann, *The Gospel of John*, 21 n. 5.

29   Bultmann, *The Gospel of John*, 54–55.

30   Reinhartz, *Befriending the Beloved Disciple*, 63. Reinhartz does note that John 4:9 is the exception for Jesus's identification as a "Jew" (Reinhartz, *Befriending the Beloved Disciple*, 63). The result of the "Compliant Reading" is that "the Johannine Jews constitute a vehicle through which the Beloved Disciple illustrates the negative response to his gift" (Reinhartz, *Befriending the Beloved Disciple*, 64).

31   Adele Reinhartz, "The Vanishing Jews of Antiquity," *Jew and Judean: A MARGINALIA Forum on Politics and Historiography in the Translation of Ancient Texts* (Timothy Michael Law and Charles Halton, eds.; Los Angeles, CA: The Marginalia Review of Books, 2014): 9.

32   Adele Reinhartz, "The Vanishing Jews of Antiquity," 9.

33   Von Wahlde's identified neutral occurrences of "the Jews" are the "twenty-three times the term is used to refer to the Jews as a nation, to their customs or feasts: 2:6, 13; 3:1, 25; 4:9 (twice), 22; 5:1; 6:4; 7:2; 11:55; 18:20, 33, 35, 39; 19:3, 19, 20, 21 (three times), 40, 42. Nine occurrences refer to the common people with no connotation of hostility toward Jesus; this is a neutral sense such as 'inhabitants of Judea': 10:19; 11:19, 31, 33, 36, 45, 54; 12:9, 11. One instance refers to the land of Judea: 3:22" (von Wahlde, "The Terms for Religious Authorities," 233).

34   Von Wahlde, "The Johannine 'Jews,'" 35. The identified "Johannine use" verses are as follows: 1:19; 2:18, 20; 5:10, 15, 16, 18; 6:41, 52; 7:1, 11, 13, 15, 35; 8:22, 31, 48, 52, 57; 9:18, 22 (twice);

"the Johannine use" signifies "the religious authorities," which he further supports with the four following points. The first is that John uses "the Jews" interchangeably with other terms for the authorities (e.g. 1:19–24; 7:32–36; 9:13–41; 18:3–14).[35] The second point is that, since the Jewish people are said to "fear the Jews," this denotes "the Jews'" position of authority (e.g. 7:13; 9:22). The third point for von Wahlde is that "the Jews" "are able to pass formal edicts of excommunication ... a function of religious authorities" (e.g. 9:22).[36] The fourth is that the term "the Jews" is used in 18:12–14 for the same people who were earlier identified as Pharisees and chief priests in 11:46–52. The occurrence of "the Jews" where this view is explicitly problematic is John 6:41, 52, which not only takes place in Galilee but where "the Jews here seem to be identified with a group which had previously been described as the 'crowd' (*ochlos*) (6:2, 5, 22, 24)."[37] Consequently, von Wahlde concludes that "the Jews" as the authorities in John 6:41, 52 is "an 'exception' possibly due to editorial activity."[38] Apart from these two verses, von Wahlde asserts "there is little or no reason for seeing the Johannine Jews as common people."[39]

1.4 *The Gospel of John's Jewish Occurrences*

The Gospel of John uses Ἰουδαῖος seventy-one times. According to Bultmann, the Gospel of John's seventy-fold use of "Jew(s)" is always negative because they are no longer God's chosen people, which are evidenced by their rejection of Jesus. Reinhartz also reinforces this reading of "the Jews" in the Gospel of John.[40] The problem with both Bultmann's and Reinhartz's reading of "the Jews" are the instances when there is not only an absence of hostility towards

---

      10:24, 31, 33; 11:8; 13:33; 18:12, 14, 31, 36, 38; 19:7, 12, 14, 31, 38; 20:19 ("The Terms for Religious Authorities," 233).

35   Von Wahlde, "The Terms for Religious Authorities," 234.

36   Von Wahlde, "The Terms for Religious Authorities," 234.

37   Von Wahlde, "The Terms for Religious Authorities," 234 n. 11. Yet, since there is "the same note of hostility" in 6:41, 52 as is found elsewhere, von Wahlde asserts that "even here the terms are probably intended to refer to authorities and it is from this point of view that the verses will be treated in this study."

38   Von Wahlde, "The Johannine 'Jews'," 45.

39   Von Wahlde, "The Johannine 'Jews'," 54.

40   For example in "'Jews' and Jews in the Fourth Gospel," Reinhartz states: "The two contrasting states of being, while described in universal terms at certain points within the Gospel, are therefore also made concrete in the form of Jesus' followers on the one hand and the Jews on the other hand" (in *Anti-Judaism and the Fourth Gospel*, ed. R. Bieringer, Didier Pollefeyt, and F. Vandecasteele-Vanneuville [Louisville, Ky: Westminster John Knox Press, 2001], 216).

Jesus, but also when "the Jews" believe in Jesus (e.g., John 7:11; 8:31; 10:19; 11:19, 31, 33, 36; 12:9, 11).[41]

Furthermore, although the Gospel of John is known for its binary dualism, the negative dualism does *not* extend to "the Jews" collectively or exclusively. For example, both Craig Koester and Paul Anderson have observed the Gospel of John's negative portrayal is not limited to "the Jews" but also extends to Jesus's disciples as well. In particular the disciples who had been following Jesus (6:60, 66) and of course Judas Iscariot "a devil" (6:70; cf. 6:71; 12:4; 13:2, 26; 18:2–5). Accordingly, Koester states that "the influence of the evil one is not limited to one group"[42] and Anderson that "close followers of Jesus are not portrayed with general positivity, and Jewish actants within the narrative are not portrayed with pervasive negativity."[43]

Instead of the singular meaning required of the dualistic reading of "the Jews" in the Gospel of John, von Wahlde proposed two meanings or uses of "Jew(s)" that form a "neutral" and a "Johannine use." Von Wahlde's conclusion is that "the Johannine use" specifically refers to the Judean leadership opposed to the entire population of Judea. What is perhaps most revealing concerning von Wahdle's analysis is that only fifty percent of the occurrences of "Jew(s)" account for "the Johannine (hostile) use."[44] Necessarily, then, the other fifty percent of the occurrences of "Jew(s)" in the Gospel of John are neutral.[45] In addition to these "neutral" occurrences in the Gospel of John are the overall

---

41   Walter Gutbrod, "Ἰουδαῖος, Ἰσραήλ, Ἑβραῖος," *TDNT* 3.378.

42   Koester, *Word of Life*, 81.

43   Paul N. Anderson, "Anti-Semitism and Religious Violence as Flawed Interpretations of the Gospel of John," in *John and Judaism a Contested Relationship in Context*, ed. R. Alan Culpepper and Paul N Anderson (Atlanta: SBL Press, 2017), 285.

44   Similarly, Wendy E. S. North, states: "For while it is true that the so-called hostile references tend to stick in the mind, in reality they account for only 40% of the total and John's expression 'the Jews' does duty in a variety of others way: some instances occur purely in descriptions of Jewish festivals and rites (e.g. 2:6, 13; 6:4; 7:2; 19:31, 40), while others refer to 'Jews' who are *not* hostile but instead fall into the category of the well-meaning but mystified (e.g. 6:41–42; 7:35–36; 8:22; 11:19, 36–37; 12:9). Yet more positively, we note that John has no difficulty in identifying Jesus as a 'Jew' (4:9, cp. 18:35), or as 'the King of the Jews' from the Passion tradition (18:33, 39; 19:3, 19, 21 [*bis*]) and, finally, that he has Jesus himself announced that 'salvation is of the Jews' (4:22)" ("'The Jews' in John's Gospel," in *A Journey Round John: Tradition, Interpretation and Context in the Fourth Gospel* [London; New York: Bloomsbury T & T Clark, 2015], 151).

45   Von Wahlde defines the "neutral" use of "Jew(s)" as 1) "a distinct religious/political/cultural grouping"; or, 2) "one part of Palestine and its inhabitants are distinguished from another" ("The Johannine Jews," 46).

154 CHAPTER 5

forty-four references to Jewish culture (H-S#1–6)[46] that Jesus actively participates in and is therefore indicative of Jesus's relationship with "his own people" (1:11). Since Jesus came into "the world of men,"[47] according to the Gospel of John, there are social implications for "this world's" assessments of Jesus and why "the world did not know him" (John 1:10).

2 "Misrecognizing" Jesus in the World

We noted in Chapters Two and Four that social beliefs and customs are understood to exist as givens in ethnic groups in a "misrecognized" state. As we have shown in the case of the Samaritan woman, it was an assumed given that "Jews have no dealings with Samaritans" (4:9b my own translation) and that, for "the Jews," as descendants of Abraham, they "have never yet been enslaved to anyone" (8:33). In Chapter Four we also noted that this givenness is both legitimated and maintained by those whose interests are served by the status quo—the elites. Bourdieu summarizes this social-scientific principle as follows:

> The conservation of the social order is decisively reinforced by ... the orchestration of categories of perception of the social world which, being adjusted to the divisions of the established order (and, therefore, to the interest of those who dominate it) and common to all minds structured in accordance with those structures, impose themselves with all appearances of objective necessity.[48]

Accordingly, when people come into contact with Jesus and interact with him, they inherently categorize him according to their ethnic group's "categories of perception"[49] (e.g. Jesus is a "Jew" [4:9; 18:35], the son of Joseph [6:42], from

---

46 In the Gospel of John, there are in total eighteen references to Jewish festivals (John 2:23; 4:45 [twice]; 5:1; 6:4; 7:2, 8 [twice], 10, 11, 14, 37; 10:22; 11:56; 12:12, 20; 13:1, 29); thirteen to the Law of Moses (John 1:17, 45; 7:19, 23, 49, 51; 8:5, 17; 10:34; 12:34; 15:25; 18:31; 19:7); eleven to the Sabbath (John 5:9, 10, 16, 18; 7:22, 23 [twice]; 9:14, 16; 19:31 [twice]); and two about purification (2:6; 3:25).

47 Bultmann, *Gospel of John*, 56. Elsewhere Bultmann states, "For John the κόσμος means primarily the world of men" (Bultmann, *Theology of the New Testament*, 2.15). Silva also notes that "human beings are so much a part of the world that κόσμος in John almost always refers to humanity" (Silva, "κόσμος," *NIDNTTE* 2.735).

48 Bourdieu and Wacquant, *An Invitation to Reflexive Sociology*, 13.

49 Bourdieu and Wacquant, *An Invitation to Reflexive Sociology*, 13. See Park's statement that "every individual we meet inevitably finds a place in our minds in some category *already* defined" (Park, "Bases," 232; added emphasis).

ETHNIC ASSESSMENTS IN THE GOSPEL OF JOHN

Nazareth [1:45] or Galilee [7:52], the messiah [1:41; 7:41], the prophet [6:14; 7:40], or a false prophet [7:12, 47], etc.). Conflict, however, arises when Jesus deviates from the givenness of his ethnic group's "basic value orientations."[50] For example, conflict arises when Jesus defies "the Jews'" interpretation of Sabbath practices (John 5:10, 16, 18; 7:22–23; 9:16). Another example that is particularly problematic for the "religious authorities" are the occasions when Jesus claims to be more than a man but (the Son of) God incarnate (5:18; 10:33; 19:7), which would challenge their status as authorized agents of God's people. Likewise, we can understand that the sending of a prophet John the Baptist and Jesus as the Son was deemed unnecessary by those who dominate the established order (i.e. the elites)[51] as well as by other members of the elites' social group who share in its collective representation (i.e. the crowd in Galilee [John 6] and in Jerusalem [John 7]).[52] However, for the purposes of this chapter, it is not the socially deviant Jesus that is of interest but rather the responses of "the Jews"[53] to this factionalist Jew named Jesus who is both is one of them (4:9) and not one of them (8:48).

3 Ethnic Assessments in the Gospel of John

According to the Gospel of John, Jesus is a man from Nazareth (1:46; 7:42, 52) and the son of Joseph (1:45; 6:42) but, as Larry Hurtado succinctly states, "to define Jesus simply with reference to his earthly family and origins is to fall far short of an adequate perception of him."[54] This is to "judge by appearances" (7:24) and "judge by human standards" (8:15) but, for those who believe

---

50   Barth, "Introduction," 14.

51   D. Moody Smith, *The Theology of the Gospel of John* (Cambridge: Cambridge University Press, 1995), 83.

52   Bourdieu and Wacquant explain that the social-scientific explanation for this is that "categories of understanding are collective representations, and the underlying mental schemata are patterned after the social structure of the group" (*An Invitation to Reflexive Sociology*, 12).

53   This also necessarily includes the disciples and the crowds in Galilee and Jerusalem given that they identify themselves with "the Jews as a nation defined by a set of religious beliefs, cultic and liturgical practices, and a sense of peoplehood" (Reinhartz, *Befriending the Beloved Disciple*, 74).

54   Larry Hurtado, *Lord Jesus Christ: Devotion to Jesus in Earliest Christianity* (Grand Rapids: Eerdmans, 2003), 395. Also, as Malina and Rohrbaugh note: "In John's Gospel, Jesus' opponents feel they know all there is to know about him by simply identifying his lineage: 'Is not this Jesus, the son of Joseph, whose father and mother we know?' (6:42). They naturally assume that to know from what family Jesus comes and where the family lives is to know all that is worthwhile to know about him. Note the frequency with which

156   CHAPTER 5

in him, "Jesus is the Messiah, the Son of God" (20:31; cf. 1:18). This is the perspective promoted by the Gospel of John and the one that finds adherents
among the disciples and the Sycharian Samaritans, as well as some among the
crowds (7:31), "the Jews" (11:45), and the authorities (12:42). The dividing line
for the Gospel of John is *not* between Jesus and "the Jews" but rather those who
believe in Jesus (1:12–13) and those among "his own people [who] did not accept him" (1:11).

   In other words, strictly speaking, the issue is not "the Jews'" ethnic identity
or categories but whether the significance they attach to them persist in light of
God sending Jesus into the world (cf. 6:29).[55] Accordingly, the following section
addresses instances of the Judean ethnic group's "categories of perception"[56]
as the disciples, the crowds, and "the Jews" make assessments about Jesus.

   In this section we examine "the Jews" who inquire about John the Baptist.
This is the first occurrence of "the Jews" in the Gospel of John and provides an
example of "the Jews'" social categories. The second example is Nathanael's
objection that Jesus cannot be the "Messiah" because Jesus's coming "out of
Nazareth" (1:46), which illustrates how Nathanael's already defined category of
Messiah does not cohere with his initial assessment of Jesus.[57] The third example concerns "the Jews" in the synagogue at Capernaum who grumbled among
themselves that they *already* know Jesus as the son of Joseph (6:42). The fourth
example is the division Jesus creates in John 7 and the objection that he is
known to be from Galilee (7:41, 52). These examples involve a mixed reaction
from both the people in general as well as the authorities. *Consequently "the
Jews" who believed in Jesus from among the crowd as well as among the authorities illustrate that there was not a singular assessment of Jesus.*

3.1   *First Occurrence of "the Jews"—Ethnic Assessments of John the Baptist*

John starts his narrative with John the Baptist's testimony to a delegation of
priests and Levites from Jerusalem who were sent by "the Jews" (1:19). The

---

this issue is raised in John's Gospel: 7:27, 34; 8:14; 9:29; 13:36; 14:4; 16:5; 19:9" (*Social-Science Commentary on the Gospel of John*, 165).

55   Hurtado suggests that "the references to Jesus' earthly origins by characters in the narrative can signal their failure to perceive the full truth of his person and significance (e.g.,
Nathanael's disdainful remark about Nazareth in 1:46; the crowd's claim to know his
origins in Galilee in 7:27, 41–44, and to know his family in 6:42)" (Hurtado, *Lord Jesus
Christ*, 395).

56   Bourdieu and Wacquant, *An Invitation to Reflexive Sociology*, 13.

57   In Chapter Four we noted Beutler's observation of the "tension between the messianic
expectations of the Palestinian Jews and the true dignity of Jesus according to John's faith
community" (Beutler, "The People of God," 140).

ETHNIC ASSESSMENTS IN THE GOSPEL OF JOHN

delegation asks John the Baptist "Who are you?" for the purpose of determining the legitimacy of his ministry, particularly as a ministry that operates outside of the purview of the religious authorities.[58] John the Baptist denies his
identity as the Messiah. In response, the delegation asks whether he is Elijah
or the prophet (1:20–21), which he also denies. According to Barrett, with this
triad of denials, John the Baptist "corresponds to no known character within
the framework of Jewish religion."[59] Since John the Baptist does not identify
himself with one of these prescribed social categories, the delegation press-
es him "to state his identity in his own terms"[60] because they need to "have
an answer for those who sent us" (1:22). John the Baptist identifies himself as
"the voice of one crying out in the wilderness, 'Make straight the way of the
Lord'" (1:23). However, John the Baptist's answer hardly legitimates his ministry for the delegation of priests and Levites who further press him for answers
(1:24–25).[61] The Baptist's final response to the delegation is that "the one who
is coming after me" (i.e. the Lord; cf. 1:23), who they do not know, is already
standing among them (1:26–27).[62]

After explaining his ministry to the delegation in 1:26, John the Baptist
explains it again the following day to an unknown audience. He says, "I
came baptizing with water for this reason, that [Jesus] might be revealed to
Israel" (1:31).[63] Yet, like the delegation from "the Jews," John the Baptist "did not
know him" (1:31, 33) until he saw Jesus coming towards him and it was revealed
to him by the Spirit descending and remaining on Jesus (1:32–33). John the

---

58   Bultmann, *Gospel of John*, 87. Köstenberger rightly observes: "The very fact that emissar-
      ies from the Jerusalem authorities show up on John's doorstep serves as a show of power
      and as a signal that the authorities will not tolerate in the long run a ministry that runs
      counter to their own purposes" (Köstenberger, *John*, 59).

59   Barrett, *The Gospel According to St. John*, 173.

60   Michaels, *The Gospel of John*, 100. Keener notes "that John's interlocutors must provide
      an answer to those whose agents they are (1:22) underlines their official character in this
      text" (*The Gospel of John*, 1.433).

61   Barrett rightly phrases the delegations' question in 1:25 as: "Why do you perform what
      appears to be an official act if you have no official status?" (Barrett, *The Gospel According
      to St. John*, 174). Indeed, according to Jerome Neyrey, "Why do those in the 'center,' priests
      and Levites, come to the 'periphery'? They are the people most likely to be threatened
      by a figure who performs purificatory rites apart from the Temple and who talks about
      a person whose potential role is higher than theirs. Their questions, then, are hardly
      an impartial search for knowledge but rather attempts to challenge John" (*The Gospel of
      John*, 59).

62   According to Moloney, the Baptist's response indicates that "the expected messianic crite-
      ria are being eclipsed as the Baptist points forward to 'the Lord'" (*The Gospel of John*, 52).

63   Beasley-Murray observes: "The audience is unnamed, but the mention of 'the next day'
      shows that the embassy has departed and John speaks to the people about him" (*John*, 24).

158   CHAPTER 5

Baptist concludes his second day of testimony by saying: "I myself have seen and have testified that this is the Son of God" (1:34).

The first occurrence of "the Jews" in the Gospel of John is 1:19 when "the Jews" send "priests and Levites" from Jerusalem to ask about the identity of John the Baptist.[64] Given that they have no reason to believe yet, it is unlikely that "the Jews" in 1:19–28 are already representative of unbelief (cf. Bultmann).[65] Instead, "the Jews" here may be "Judeans" in the strict geographical sense of being from Judea (cf. Lowe). However, by sending a delegation of priests (as purification specialists) and Levites (who were used as temple police; cf. 7:32, 45), "the Jews" in 1:19 are portrayed as possessing a certain amount of authority/ status (cf. von Wahlde).[66] In this instance, therefore, the Gospel of John's employment of the ethnic label "the Jews" cannot refer to the entire ethnic group; it refers to their leadership. The Judeans' authorities disclose their interest in maintaining the legitimacy of their authoritative status (cf. 7:32, 45; 11:45–52) by sending the delegation in order to determine the legitimacy of John the

---

64   There are perhaps unanswerable questions concerning the aside in 1:24: "Now they had been sent from the Pharisees." For example, according to Urban C. von Wahlde, "the phrase *ek tōn Pharisaiōn* is ambiguous. It could mean either that those sent were Pharisees or that they were sent by the Pharisees" (*The Gospel and Letters of John* [Grand Rapids: Eerdmans, 2010], 2.37). First, does the Gospel of John imply that only some of the delegation were Pharisees (Beasley-Murray, *John*, 19n.c; Köstenberger, *John*, 63; Ridderbos, *The Gospel According to John*, 66 n. 10; Schnackenburg, *The Gospel According to St. John*, 1.292) or the entire delegation (Brown, *The Gospel According to John*, 1.44; Köstenberger, *John*, 63 n. 24; Moloney, *The Gospel of John*, 52)? Second, was the delegation sent by "the Jews" who are the Pharisees (Lincoln, *The Gospel According to Saint John*, 112; Michaels, *The Gospel of John*, 101) or are "the Jews" (1:19) and Pharisees (1:24) working in conjunction with one another (von Wahlde, *The Gospel and Letters of John*, 2.35; cf. 7:32)?

65   Bultmann, *Gospel of John*, 86. Ashton cautions, "We should be careful not to read into this passage the overtones of mistrust and hostility that the term οἱ Ἰουδαῖοι carries almost everywhere in the body of the Gospel. The priests and Levites in this story were conscientiously discharging a perfectly proper function, and it would be wrong to assume, from what we know elsewhere of the attitudes of the Pharisees, that his was done with any malevolent intent" (Ashton, *Understanding the Fourth Gospel*, 168).

66   Regarding John 1:19 there is a confluence of interpretation with Lowe and von Wahlde. According to Lowe, "as senders of emissaries from Jerusalem to John the Baptist, ["the Jews"] probably means the authorities" (Lowe, "Who Were the ΙΟΥΔΑΙΟΙ?," 124). Whilst for von Wahlde "the identification of these *Ioudaioi* as being from Jerusalem groups them with other, similar instances where 'Judeans' are from, or near, Jerusalem. This indicates that the term is the 'neutral' use that properly means 'Judeans'" (von Wahlde, *The Gospel and Letters of John*, 2.34–35).

Baptist's ministry (1:19, 22, 25) because it is separate from the synagogue and the Temple services.[67]

In terms of ethnic factionalism, then, John the Baptist's testimony in the Gospel of John discloses "the Jews" as the faction who are in charge their ethnic community's institutions and collective resources.[68] However, John the Baptist makes way for a dissenting faction of Judeans who are "committed to gaining support among their fellow ethnics."[69] In other words, John the Baptist's testimony reveals a different meaning (what Jesus will call "truth") in the Judean ethnic traditions and practices (H-S#1–6) than those maintained by those in authority (be they Temple priests or the Pharisees). According to the Gospel of John, John the Baptist was sent by God (1:6) to "make straight the way of the Lord" (1:23) and "revealed to Israel" (1:31) that Jesus is the Son of God (1:34). John the Baptist's testimony places Jesus *within* Judean—Israelite traditions even though Jesus evidently does not fall within *expected* Judean categories (e.g. 7:40–42). In this way, as we noted in Chapter Four, there is a "tension between the messianic expectations of the Palestinian Jews and the true dignity of Jesus according to John's faith community."[70]

3.2 First Occurrence of Belief—the Disciples' Ethnic Assessments of Jesus

John 1:35–51 is the story of Jesus gathering his first disciples. Two former disciples of John the Baptist approach Jesus to follow him as a "'Rabbi" (1:38).[71] One of these disciples is identified as Andrew (1:40), who then tells his brother Simon "We have found the Messiah" (1:41). After Jesus calls Philip to "Follow me" (1:43), Philip tells Nathanael that "We have found him about whom Moses in the law and also the prophets wrote, Jesus son of Joseph from Nazareth" (1:45). Breaking the mold of the previous disciples who immediately responded,

---

67 Also, Johannes Beutler, commenting on John 5:41–44, states: "Apparently, the hesitancy of the leading Jews of Jerusalem to accept and confess faith in Christ has to do with their social situation and their wish to maintain it" ("Faith and Confession: The Purpose of John," *Word, Theology, and Community in John* [eds. John Painter, R. Alan Culpepper, and Fernando F. Segovia: St. Louis: Chalice, 2002], 21).

68 Esman, *An Introduction to Ethnic Conflict*, 48.

69 Esman, *An Introduction to Ethnic Conflict*, 48.

70 Beutler, "The People of God," 140.

71 In his "The Gospel of John as a Source for First-Century Judaism," Craig Koester proposes that "the way each of them [i.e. John the Baptist and Jesus] is called rabbi shows the growing tendency to identify the title with teaching, and especially with teachers who had groups of disciples that engaged in discussion over belief and practice" (R. Alan Culpepper and Paul N Anderson, eds., *John and Judaism: A Contested Relationship in Context*. [Atlanta: Society of Biblical Literature, 2017], 67–68).

160   CHAPTER 5

Nathanael objects "Can anything good come out of Nazareth?" (1:46). For those who persist in seeing Jesus only in the "misrecognized" categories of their ethnic group (i.e. "world of men"[72]), then the answer is no. "At this point," Koester observes, "Philip might have tried to marshal a collection of Scripture passages to answer Nathanael's objection, but he does not do so. Instead he repeats the invitation, 'Come and see' (1:46)."[73] In spite of his objection, Nathanael goes to see Jesus and, while approaching him, "Jesus hails him as one truly representative of Israel" (1:47).[74] Nathanael asks Jesus how he knows him, and Jesus revealed that he saw him before Philip called him (1:48). Here, as we saw in our earlier discussion of the Samaritan woman (4:17–18), Jesus's supernatural knowledge leads Nathanael to belief (1:50); after all, Jesus knows his own and they know him (cf. 10:14, 27; 18:37).

The calling of Jesus's disciples contains two motifs. First, the disciples demonstrate their belief that Jesus fulfills their messianic expectations (1:41, 45), while Jesus broadens these expectations so that they can see greater things.[75] Second, the disciple Nathanael exemplifies not only the scandal of the incarnation when not met with faith (1:46; cf. 6:42; 7:41–42, 52), but also "that only faith overcomes all objections and recognizes the divine origin of Jesus in spite of his earthly lowliness"[76] (1:49). The scandal of the incarnation, however, remains when Jesus is understood only in terms of their ethnic group's preconceived categories (e.g. the Prophet [7:40] or the Davidic Messiah [7:41–42]), and in this case, Jesus does make himself God as he will later (5:18; 10:33; 19:7).

Before addressing the Judean ethnic group's preconceived categories in John 6 and 7, we must not lose sight of the following social-scientific principles. First is the fact that the givenness Jesus confronts in the Gospel of John is legitimated and enforced by the elites (cf. 1:19–28), whose interest is in preserving their positions in society by maintaining the status quo (cf. 11:45–52; 18:14).[77] Second, the givenness experienced in "the world of men," is shared by everyone

---

72   Bultmann, *The Gospel of John*, 56. Hence, as Moloney rightly observes, "Philip's mistake, which attempts to understand Jesus in terms of his physical and geographical origins (cf. v. 45: 'of Joseph,' 'from Nazareth'), persist" (*The Gospel of John*, 55).

73   Koester, *The Word of Life*, 165.

74   Brown, *The Gospel According to John*, 1.86. Also see: Bultmann, *The Gospel of John*, 104 n. 4; McHugh, *Commentary on John 1–4*, 161; Schnackenburg, *The Gospel According to St. John*, 1.316.

75   Moloney, *The Gospel of John*, 57.

76   Schnackenburg, *The Gospel According to St. John*, 1.315.

77   Peter Berger states: "One may say, then, that the facticity of the social world or of any part of it suffices for self-legitimation as long as there is no challenge. When a challenge appears, in whatever form, the facticity can no longer be taken for granted" (*The Sacred Canopy*, 31).

ETHNIC ASSESSMENTS IN THE GOSPEL OF JOHN

in the social group due to the fact that, "being born in a social world, we accept a whole range of postulates, axioms, which go without saying and require no inculcating."[78] These social-scientific principles explain why John the Baptist, from the delegations' perspectives, had to be assessed in terms of messianic, Elijanic, or prophetic categories. Similarly, the following section will show that the authorities do not have to impose their view of the ethnic group because it is already accepted as a given (or an "objective necessity"[79]) by those socialized into the Judean ethnic group.

3.3 "The Jews" as Judeans in Galilee

In the "bread of life discourse" (6:22–59), Jesus's interlocutors rightly restate his words that "I am the bread that came down from heaven" (6:41) and "I have come down from heaven" (6:42). This restatement is identified as the grumblings of "the Jews" (6:41) who, from among the crowd who were gathered in the Capernaum synagogue (6:59), were saying among themselves "Is not this Jesus, the son of Joseph, whose father and mother we know?" (6:42, 43).[80] The interlocutors' identification as "the Jews" (6:41, 52) are the only instances of "the Jews" in Galilee (and hence outside of Judea) in the Gospel of John. Consequently, the two occurrences of the ethnic labels "the Jews" in John 6 are used to argue against the proposals set forth by Lowe ("the Jews" as "Judeans") and von Wahlde ("the Jews" as authorities).

Concerning Lowe's proposition that "the Jews" are "Judeans," Herman Ridderbos states that "the Jews" in John 6:41 are "obviously Galileans" and therefore "is proof that Ἰουδαῖοι does not refer in the Fourth Gospel just to 'Judeans.'"[81] Brown also objects to Lowe's proposal, stating, "When Jesus asks 'the Jews' in 10:34, 'Is it not written in your own Law?' John is referring not to Judeans specifically but to the Scriptures shared by all Jews."[82] The objection

---

78 Bourdieu and Wacquant, *An Invitation to Reflexive Sociology*, 168.

79 Bourdieu and Wacquant, *An Invitation to Reflexive Sociology*, 13.

80 According to Stanley Porter, "in these two instances [John 6:41, 52], the Jewish leaders— or at any rate a group of Jews capable of being distinguished from others—are apparently being referred to, since they are defined as a portion of the crowed that heard Jesus' words (6:22)" ("Jesus, 'the Jews,' and John's Gospel," in *John, His Gospel, and Jesus: In Pursuit of the Johannine Voice* [Grand Rapids: Eerdmans, 2015], 168). Additionally, John Painter has noted: "The Jews of 6:41, 52 can hardly be identified with the many disciples of 6:60, 66 or 'the twelve' of 6:67, 71. If these terms distinguish different groups it seems clear that the crowd is to be distinguished from the Jews also" (*The Quest for the Messiah: The History, Literature and Theology of the Johannine Community* [Edinburgh: T&T Clark, 1993], 278).

81 Ridderbos, *The Gospel According to John*, 231 and 231 n. 124.

82 Brown, *An Introduction to the Gospel of John,* 162. Brown cites "the Jews" in John 6 among the "serious objections to any dominant geographical thesis"; specifically, "Why is Jesus

Brown raises here, however, is due to his misreading of Lowe's geographic thesis. Lowe does *not* suggest that the Scriptures belong solely to Judean Jews. Instead, the Scriptures belong to all Judeans in that "to be a member of that religion was in a sense to have that nationality."[83] To return to Ridderbos's objection, "the Jews" in Galilee is an excellent illustration of Judeans outside of Judea. For although "the Jews" in 6:41 "can scarcely be anything other than Galileans," since they know Jesus's father and mother (6:42), "the term οἱ Ἰουδαῖοι is just as proper a designation for the inhabitants of Galilee as it is for the Jewish communities of, say, Antioch or Alexandria."[84] Therefore, "the Jews" in John 6 support Lowe's geographical and Mason's ethnic proposal that "the Jews" are "Judeans" (i.e. members of the Judean ethnic group). Yet, "the Jews" who are grumbling among themselves, are distinguished from other Jews who are present; namely, the crowd in general and Jesus's disciples in particular who are also members of the Judean ethnic group.

The appearance of "the Jews" in Galilee also illustrates the difficulty of identifying "the Jews" as "the religious authorities." Earlier in this chapter we noted that von Wahlde himself acknowledges that "the Jews" were "identified with a group which had previously been described as the 'crowd' (*ochlos*) (6:2, 5, 22, 24)."[85] Von Wahlde's proposal, that "the Jews" are the religious authorities instead of the Jewish people *en masse*, could benefit from understanding "the Jews" in 6:41–43 as referring to a segment of the crowd present.[86] For example, von Wahlde recently stated:

> I am convinced that even here [6:41, 52] 'the Jews' are intended to represent the official position of Judaism over against those who believe in

---

speaking to Judeans in a Galilean (Capernaum) synagogue and how do they know his family who live at Nazareth (6:41, 42, 52, 59)?" (*An Introduction*, 163).

83   Lowe, "Who Were the ΙΟΥΔΑΙΟΙ?," 107. Lowe's point here is congruous to Mason's discussion of ethnic group identity.

84   Ashton, *Understanding the Fourth Gospel*, 67. Similarly for Brown, "the Jews" in 6:41 cannot be "visiting leaders from Jerusalem (as in Mark 7:1) because they know the local details of Nazareth village life" (Brown, *The Gospel According to John*, 1.270).

85   Von Wahlde, "The Terms for Religious Authorities," 234 n. 11. Yet, since there is "the same note of hostility" in 6:41, 52 as is found elsewhere, von Wahlde asserts that "even here the terms are probably intended to refer to authorities and it is from this point of view that the verses will be treated in this study" (von Wahlde, "The Terms for Religious Authorities," 234 n. 11).

86   Also, von Wahlde would not have to resort to 6:41, 52 as "an 'exception' possibly due to editorial activity" (von Wahlde, "The Johannine 'Jews'," 45).

ETHNIC ASSESSMENTS IN THE GOSPEL OF JOHN 163

Jesus. Thus, in my view, it is correct to say that 'the Jews' in the Gospel represent the official *religious* opposition to Jesus by Jewish officials.[87]

While this certainly represents an aspect of how the Gospel of John uses "the Jews," it cannot be determinative of every occurrence (such as the neutral uses) or perhaps even every hostile occurrence depending on what one considers as hostile.[88] Von Wahlde is correct in observing that in some interactions "the Jews" are Jewish officials (such as the chief priests) but, nevertheless, "the Jews" encompass more than their leaders especially given that Jesus is one of them (4:9; 18:35).[89]

We must also caution against Bultmann's construction of Jesus versus "the Jews"[90] given that not all of the unbelievers in the Gospel of John are labeled "the Jews" (e.g. Jesus's brothers 7:5); additionally the fact that there are many of "the Jews" who do believe in him (cf. 12:11). *Thus, there simply is not a direct correlation between the ethnic label ("the Jews") and their status as either believers or unbelievers in the Gospel of John.* Instead, what we can say is that the Gospel of John uses the ambivalence among "the Jews" collectively (that is, those who believe and do not believe) in order to point beyond ethnic identities towards the trans-ethnic "children of God" (1:12–13; 11:52).

The phrase, in 6:41–42, "the Jews began to complain (ἐγόγγυζον) about him" (6:41), alludes to the Israelites who grumbled against Moses in the wilderness.[91] The Gospel of John uses the ethnic label "the Jews" for this segment of the crowd in Galilee, in order to frame the interaction in terms of their shared ethnic traditions (H-S#3; shared historical memories) so that, just as their forefathers complained against Moses, so now "the Jews" complain against Jesus.[92]

---

87 Von Wahlde, *The Gospel and Letters of John*, 1.215; original emphasis.

88 In fact, according to Porter, "There are a variety of factors at play in the analysis of the use of οἱ Ἰουδαῖοι, and that the linguistic situation is too complex simply to categorize usage on the basis of whether there is purported hostility or not indicated, especially when there is a thoughtful concern for the larger literary context. The determination of hostility is simply too nebulous to provide a firm criterion for assessing what the phrase means" ("Jesus, "the Jews," and John's Gospel," 157–158).

89 Von Wahlde, *The Gospel and Letters of John*, 1.145.

90 See Bultmann's statement that "Jesus stands over against the Jews" (*Gospel of John*, 86).

91 According to Silva, "more than half of the uses of this word group [γογγύζω] are found in two narrative sections, Exod 15–17 and Num 14–17, which record the grumbling of the Israelites against their leaders (Moses and Aaron) and ultimately, therefore, against the Lord" (Silva, "γογγύζω," *NIDNTTE* 1.591).

92 Köstenberger, *John*, 213. Also see Ruth Sheridan, *Retelling Scripture: 'The Jews' and the Scriptural Citations in John 1:19–12:15* (Leiden, Boston: Brill, 2012), 135–157.

164   CHAPTER 5

Accordingly, the label "the Jews" is used to allude to their shared ethnic traditions, and not simply because their response to Jesus was negative or hostile.[93]

In fact, when "the Jews" say among themselves, "Is not this Jesus, the son of Joseph, whose father and mother we know?" in 6:42, they implicitly acknowledge that they know Jesus is one of their own—a Jew. In particular, the form of "the Jews'" complaint against Jesus in 6:42 is what deSilva terms a "segmented genealogy." According to deSilva, the appeal to a "segmented genealogy" (such as in the synagogue of Nazareth in Mark 6:3) is due to the fact that:

> The status that Jesus is claiming by means of his actions and words, and the role he has begun to play as teacher, prophet and miracle worker is dissonant with the status ascribed him by birth. The way [Jesus] is located in Judean culture becomes problematic for the acceptance of his message.[94]

The segmented genealogy "the Jews" construct is at variance with Jesus's claims to "come down from heaven" (6:41b). In this regard, Köstenberger raises an insightful comparison: "The Jews here object not to the notion that a man (like Jesus) could receive a divine calling, or even that someone like Elijah might appear on earth and dwell among human beings, but to Jesus' claim of descent from heaven in fact of his obvious (or so it seemed) human origin."[95] For "the Jews," the social categories already exist for someone being Elijah or "the prophet" (cf. 1:21) but they were not prepared for someone being the "Son of God" (20:31), in terms of "God the only Son" (1:18), coming in the flesh and living among them (1:14).

According to the Gospel of John, for those who categorize Jesus in terms of external appearances (cf. 7:24; 8:15; i.e. ethnic reality), Jesus can only be Joseph's

---

93   According to Sheridan, "The Galilean crowd is here called 'the Jews' and this *strongly demonstrates* that whenever the Gospel text 'moves towards hostility, it moves towards the use of οἱ Ἰουδαῖοι'" (*Retelling Scripture*, 144; emphasis added). The issue with Sheridan's statement, however, is her omission of the first part of Judith Lieu's comment, which states: "Yet, on the whole—and, *again one of the problems is that we can only say 'on the whole'* (cf. 4:22)—whenever the narrative moves toward hostility it also moves towards the use of *hoi ioudaioi* ("Anti-Judaism, the Jews, and the Worlds of the Fourth Gospel," *The Gospel of John and Christian Theology* [eds. Richard Bauckham and Carl Mosser; Grand Rapids: Eerdmans, 2008], 171; emphasis added). For Sheridan this instance "strongly demonstrates" every occurrence of "the Jews" is hostile, or moves towards hostility, whereas Lieu is far more cautious and does not allow the hostile occurrences of οἱ Ἰουδαῖοι to stand in place of every occurrence.

94   deSilva, *Honor, Patronage, Kinship & Purity*, 162.

95   Köstenberger, *John*, 213.

ETHNIC ASSESSMENTS IN THE GOSPEL OF JOHN

son (cf. 6:42). For those who believe in him, however, are described as "no longer conditioned by the world" (John 17:16).[96] Thus Jesus is a Jew, but he is more than that ethnic identity, just as his disciples are Jews and the Sycharians are Samaritans, because they are being gathered into fictive kinship the "children of God" (11:52) as one flock with one shepherd (10:16).

3.4 "The Jews" as the Religious Authorities—Fear and Division of "the Jews"

In section 3.1 we observed that "the Jews" have an authoritative status by their ability to send a delegation to John the Baptist (1:19–28). This authority to send a delegation also occurs in John 7:32–36 when the chief priests and Pharisees send temple police to arrest Jesus (7:32). Their subsequent discussion further discloses their concern, not so much with Jesus "leading the people astray" (7:12, 47), as with their superior status to determine that this is what Jesus is doing (7:48–49). Consequently, von Wahlde draws upon John 7 to support his proposal that "the Jews" are the religious authorities; in particular, that the term "the Jews" is interchangeable with other terms for the authorities (7:32–36) and that that the people "fear the Jews."

Before Jesus attends the Festival of Booths in Jerusalem, he was staying in Galilee because "the Jews" in Judea were seeking to kill him (7:1). The Gospel of John does *not* use the ethnic label "the Jews" to mean that every Jew in Judea was seeking to kill him given that the context limits "the Jews" here to those who have the authority to kill (i.e. the Jewish leadership).[97] At Jerusalem, "the Jews" are looking for Jesus (7:11), that is, "the Jews" who want to kill him in 7:1.[98] Before Jesus arrives in Jerusalem to participate in the Jewish festival (as one of "the Jews" himself) the crowds gathered there were debating their perceptions of Jesus (7:12). Some of the crowd said "He is a good man" while others thought of Jesus as a false prophet who was leading people astray.[99] Regardless of the

---

96 Silva, "κόσμος," *NIDNTTE* 2.735.

97 We must note that although "the Jews" in John 7:1 are the official representatives of the ethnic group (those who represent Jesus's "own nation" 18:35) they do not speak for everyone within their ethnic group (such as John the Baptist and Nicodemus).

98 Moloney observes: "'The Jews' are looking for him (*ezētoun auton*). This search is ominous, as it recalls 5:18 and 7:1 where the same verb (*zēteō*) was used for their designs on his life" (Moloney, *The Gospel of John*, 240).

99 In regards to leading the people astray, Beasley-Murray comments that the "charge is a serious one in Jewish law, and if established could lead to capital punishment. It is early exemplified in Deut 13:1–6 (LXX), which states that a false prophet must die, 'because he spoke so as to lead you astray (πλανῆσαι) from the Lord your God.' The allegation that Jesus sought to lead astray the people remained firm in Jewish tradition" (Beasley-Murray, *John*, 107).

crowds' assessment of Jesus, they spoke only amongst themselves "for fear of the Jews" (7:13). Von Wahlde appeals to this verse as indicating the Gospel of John's distinction between the inhabitants of Judea and "the Jews."[100] The reason for this is that the crowds gathered in Jerusalem were certainly Jews and yet they were fearful of a particular segment of their society.[101]

Then, when Jesus arrives in Jerusalem for the Festival of Booths in John 7, he makes a series of statements[102] and interacts with a number of groups: the crowd, Jerusalemites, "the Jews," chief priests, Pharisees, and authorities. Jesus causes division among the crowd (7:12) and he "astonished" "the Jews" (7:15) with his teaching. The Jerusalemites then wondered if "the authorities really know that this is the Messiah?" (7:26). However, the division among the crowd continued with some trying to arrest Jesus (7:30) while many others in the crowd believed in him (7:31). In response to the crowds' believing Jesus is the Messiah, "the chief priests and Pharisees sent temple police to arrest him" (7:32: cf. 1:19, 24; 18:3, 12). After the temple police meet with Jesus and leave, the "division in the crowd" (7:43) continues with some confessing that Jesus is "the prophet" (7:40) or "the Messiah" while others were left questioning because "surely the Messiah does not come from Galilee, does he?" (7:41).

The division in the crowd is then mirrored in the gathering of chief priests and Pharisees in 7:45–52.[103] The Pharisees responded to the returning temple police, "Has any one of the authorities or of the Pharisees believed in him?" (7:48). Nicodemus, who was both a Pharisee and "a leader of the Jews" (3:1), raised an objection concerning their knowledge of the Law (7:51). The Pharisees replied to Nicodemus, "who was one of them" (7:50), not only with the same abuse they heaped upon "this [accursed] crowd" (7:49) but they also labeled Nicodemus (even if sarcastically) and Jesus as "from Galilee" (7:52).[104]

---

100   Von Wahlde, "The Terms for Religious Authorities," 234.

101   According to Brown, John 7:13 "is a clear indication that 'the Jews' are the Jerusalem authorities, for the crowds themselves were certainly Jewish and still they fear the Jews" (Brown, *The Gospel According to John*, 1.307). Similarly, Moloney states: "It is not a reference to the Jewish people, as 'the Jews' and 'the people' in v.13 are all Jews" (Moloney, *The Gospel of John*, 241).

102   Dodd observes that in John 7 "the interchange of debate is unusually rapid, especially in the earlier part. Jesus is not allowed a speech of any length without being interrupted by questions or objections. At some points the opponents are more vocal than Jesus himself. Sometimes they hold the stage and He is silent" (*The Interpretation of the Fourth Gospel*, 346).

103   Bultmann also notes that in John 7:45–52 "a kind of σχίσμα is recorded. The division which Jesus's appearance causes among the people makes itself felt to some extent also in the circle of the authorities" (*Gospel of John*, 309).

104   The statement that "this crowd, which does not know the law" (John 7:49) is often associated with *Am Ha'arets* or "people of the land" (cf. Bultmann, *Gospel of John*, 310). However, as Sean Freyne notes: "the designation *'am ha'arets* is never specifically applied

ETHNIC ASSESSMENTS IN THE GOSPEL OF JOHN

John 7 displays not only various reactions to Jesus but also various reactions across the Judean social stratification so that there is not a unified response to Jesus by any identified group of people.[105] There are some in the crowd, and possibly Nicodemus among the authorities and Pharisees, who believe in Jesus. At the same time, there are some among "the crowd" (7:41b) as well as "the authorities" and "the Pharisees" (7:48) who insist upon what they have always known to be true (i.e. they "judge by appearances" [7:24] and "judge by human standards" [8:15]).

Von Wahlde is correct to observe the distinction between social classes within the inhabitants of Judea and that "the Jews" "seems to refer to a certain class (or classes) of persons within Palestinian society."[106] Yet, as we noted in the previous section, "the Jews" do not *always* refer to the authorities. Nonetheless, since there are distinct social classes, as von Wahlde suggests, then we can also determine if there are distinct class interests. In the Gospel of John, it is an interest of the religious authorities to maintain the status quo, which is legitimated by their position within their social group. In John 11:45–52 the religious authorities, and especially the priests, demonstrate their particular status' interest in avoiding the destruction of the temple by the Romans because without the temple they lose their authority and status within their ethnic group.[107] The distinction, then, is not between "neutral" and "Johannine use" (as a designation for the hostile religious authorities). Instead the distinction is between those who share the particular interest of the authorities (cf. 5:15; 11:46), who insist on maintaining the status quo and the boundaries of their ethnic group

---

to Galileans in the rabbinic sources. As a term of censure, if not opprobrium, its use was not restricted to anyone region or class, and even the high priest could be an *'am ha'arets*" (Seán Freyne, "Jesus and the Galilean 'Am Ha'arets: Fact, Johannine Irony, or Both?," in *John, Jesus, and History, Volume 2: Aspects of Historicity in the Fourth Gospel*, ed. Paul N. Anderson, Felix Just, and Tom Thatcher [Society of Biblical Literature, 2009], 147).

105 Since Bultmann interprets "the Jews" as the symbolic rejection of Jesus (or, put simply, the enemies of Jesus), it is surprising he also acknowledges a distinction is made between "the ὄχλος (which is of course itself Jewish) ... from the Ἰουδαῖοι, who are the authorities (vv. 12, 40, 43, 31f)" (Bultmann, *Gospel of John*, 295). Earlier in his commentary, Bultmann addresses this issue stating: "Only the distinction between the mass of the people and its spokesmen occasionally proves to be necessary for the Evangelist's presentation of his theme; but this, characteristically, is often drawn in such a way that the Ἰουδαῖοι, who are distinguished from the ὄχλος, appear as an authoritative body set over the Jewish people" (Bultmann, *Gospel of John*, 86–87).

106 Von Wahlde, "The Johannine 'Jews'," 37.

107 In this regard, Bultmann rightly notes that "the reply of the authorities (vv. 47f), who think that the opinion of the official representatives of the people is ground enough for convicting Jesus as a seducer of the people [cf. 7:12; 47], shows that blindness precisely of men in positions of responsibility, those whom the world has charged with its government" (Bultmann, *Gospel of John*, 310).

(cf. 11:50, 18:14), and the alternative interests of Jesus to gather "the children of God" amongst the sheepfolds even in spite of "misrecognized" (i.e. the tacitly presumed and self-legitimating) boundaries of the Judean ethnic group.

Consequently, "the Jews" are not limited to the "religious authorities." "The Jews" are representatives of a particular vision of the Judean ethnic group (that is legitimated by the "religious authorities") but is also shared among at least some of the members of the Judean ethnic group beyond their leadership.[108] Examples of those who share the interest of their religious leaders are those who both inform on Jesus to the authorities such as the healed paralytic man and "the Jews" who witnessed the raising of Lazarus (5:15; 11:46).[109] Similarly, shared ethnic group interests are evidenced in the convergence of assessments between some in the crowd and their authorities; namely, that Jesus is leading the people astray (7:12, 47) and is from Galilee (7:41–42, 52).

3.5 "The Jews" as the Enemies of Jesus—Jesus and the Bultmannian Jews

The distinction between the interests of Judean ethnic identity and Jesus's trans-ethnic identity comes into sharper view in light of Bultmann's symbolic reading of "the Jews." Bultmann contends that "the Jews," throughout the Gospel of John, are the opponents of Jesus and the "representatives of unbelief."[110] According to this symbolic reading, "the Jews" have a singular definition as the enemies of Jesus/God. Yet, in order to attribute to "the Jews" their role as enemies of Jesus, Bultmann must disregard any positive statements concerning "the Jews."[111] In Bultmann's commentary, the most notably absent example of positive statements concerning "the Jews" is Jesus's statement in 4:22b: "For salvation is from the Jews." For Bultmann, whose only comment on John 4:22b is in a footnote, it is an editorial gloss. His reasoning is not based upon manuscript evidence but is strictly theological. Bultmann explains the phrase:

> The ὅτι ἡ σωτηρία ἐκ τῶν Ἰουδαίων ἐστίν [for salvation is from the Jews] is impossible in John and that not only because of 8:41ff.; for 1:11 already made it clear that the Evangelist does not regard the Jews as God's chosen and saved people (see p. 56 n. 1), and in spite of 4:9 it is hard to see how

---

108 For example, commenting on John 7:26, Schnackenburg observes that "the people, accustomed as they are to look to their leaders (cf. v. 26)" (Schnackenburg, 2.144).

109 In this regard Michaels states: "Those who were not believers became informants, and their information led to the Sanhedrin's decision that Jesus must die (see 11:47–53)" (Michaels, *The Gospel of John*, 299).

110 Bultmann, *Gospel of John*, 89.

111 Anders Gerdmar, *Roots of Theological Anti-Semitism: German Biblical Interpretation and the Jews, from Herder and Semler to Kittel and Bultmann* (Leiden: Brill, 2010), 392.

ETHNIC ASSESSMENTS IN THE GOSPEL OF JOHN 169

the Johannine Jesus, who constantly disassociates himself from the Jews (8:17; 10:34; 13:33; and p. 86 n. 3) could have made such a statement (see also W. Grundmann, *Jesus der Galilaer und das Judentum*, 1940, 229ff).[112]

In regards to Bultmann's statement, Gerdmar notes that "it is also interesting that he refers to Grundmann's book, with its radical and racist dissociation of Jesus from Judaism."[113] After all, it was Walter Grundmann who concluded that "with the highest probability (we can) assert that *Jesus* was *no Jew*."[114] Furthermore, Gerdmar calls attention to the fact that Grundmann cites Bultmann's comment on John 4:22 in support of his argument. According to Gerdmar,

> although Bultmann's commentary was not yet published, in quoting it, Grundmann dates it to 1938, and so must have been able to read page proofs. Building on Bultmann, Grundmann omits 4:22, which indicates that Bultmann's omission could serve National Socialist interests. This does not imply that Bultmann's interpretation of the Johannine Jews was motivated by National Socialist ideology, but it is clear that in a situation where racial discrimination was established in Germany, Bultmann's choice of words and exegetical practice may have contributed to a negative picture of the Jews.[115]

Consequently, in contrast to at least one of his contemporary scholars working in Nazi Germany, Bultmann's singular symbolic reading of "the Jews" is problematic. Walter Gutbrod, who died as a Nazi lieutenant, noted a number passages where Jesus interacts with "the Jews" (οἱ Ἰουδαῖοι) without any sign of hostility (e.g. 7:11; 8:31; 10:19; 11:19, 31, 33, 36; 12:9, 11) and concluded that "an inimical note is not necessarily contained in the name Ἰουδαῖος as such."[116]

Bultmann's assertion that John 4:22 is a gloss, without argumentation but simply stating that Jesus could not have said this, discloses not only his

---

112 Bultmann, *Gospel of John*, 189–190 n. 6.

113 Gerdmar, *Roots of Theological Anti-Semitism*, 393.

114 Gerdmar, *Roots of Theological Anti-Semitism*, 570; original emphasis. See Grundmann, *Jesus der Galilaer und das Judentum*, 199–200.

115 Gerdmar, *Roots of Theological Anti-Semitism*, 394–395. See Grundmann, *Jesus der Galilaer und das Judentum*, 201–231.

116 Walter Gutbrod, "Ἰουδαῖος, Ἰσραήλ, Ἑβραῖος," *TDNT* 3.378. There is an *In Memoriam* page of *TWNT* volume 4, omitted in *TDNT*, which lists Walter Gutbrod as a fallen (Nazi) Lieutenant on July 28, 1941 in Russia ("Walter Gutbrod gefallen als Leutnant am 28. Juli 1941 in Rußland").

170   CHAPTER 5

portrayal of "the Jews" in John, but of Jesus as well.[117] Most notably, Bultmann
elsewhere states, "In fact, the evangelist feels the church's estrangement from
Judaism to be so great that in his account Jesus already appears as no longer
a member of the Jewish people or its religion but speaks to the Jews of their
Law as 'your Law' as if he were a non-Jew (8:17; 10:34; cf. 7:19, 22)."[118] Bultmann's
references "your Law" as evidence for the Johannine Jesus distancing himself
from "the Jews" ignores the broader context of the Gospel of John in which
there is 1) the Testimony of Abraham, Moses, the Law and the Prophets of
Jesus (cf. 1:45; 5:45–46; 8:56); 2) belief in the Scriptures (cf. 2:22; 20:9); and 3) the
language of "fulfilling Scripture" (cf. 12:38; 13:18; 17:12; 19:36).[119]

Bultmann presents Jesus's conflict with "the Jews" so that "Jesus stands over
against the Jews."[120] Bultmann's scheme, therefore, presents Jesus as a critique
from *without* rather than as a critique from *within*. However, in contrast to this
approach, part two of the edited volume *John and Judaism* is devoted to "John
as a Source for Understanding Judaism." From this perspective, the Gospel of
John participates within the spectrum of Judean texts from the Second Temple
period.[121] In this regard, this perspective is also evident in Richard Horsley's
and Tom Thatcher's *John, Jesus and The Renewal of Israel* where they explicitly
note that

> The reading of John as presenting Jesus versus 'the Jews' generally is a
> carryover from an older theological scheme of Christian origins in which
> Jesus was understood as the great revealer whose teaching and cruci-
> fixion led to the emergence of one religion, Christianity, from another,
> Judaism.[122]

---

117   Gerdmar, *Roots of Theological Anti-Semitism*, 393.
118   Bultmann, *Theology of the New Testament*, 2.5.
119   In regards to John 8:17, 10:34, and 15:25, Whitarcre is certainly correct that Jesus's "refer-
      ence to 'your law' should not be interpreted as disparaging the Law, but rather disparaging
      the Jewish opponents' use of it. Abraham is referred to as 'your father Abraham' (8:56),
      though obviously no disparagement of Abraham is intended (cf. 8:39–40), but rather of
      their appeal to him" (*Polemic*, 65–66). Also see Keener, who notes "John's repeated treat-
      ment of Scripture as authoritative for disciples as well as for Jesus' opponents (e.g., 2:22;
      7:38; 13:18; 17:12; 19:24, 28, 36–37; 20:9)" (*John*, 1.741).
120   Bultmann, *Gospel of John*, 86.
121   Craig R. Koester, "The Gospel of John as a Source for First-Century Judaism," in *John and
      Judaism a Contested Relationship in Context*, ed. R. Alan Culpepper and Paul N Anderson
      (Atlanta: SBL Press, 2017), 59–76; Catrin H. Williams, "John, Judaism, and 'Searching the
      Scriptures,'" in *John and Judaism a Contested Relationship in Context*, ed. R. Alan Culpepper
      and Paul N Anderson (Atlanta: SBL Press, 2017), 77–100.
122   Richard A. Horsley and Tom Thatcher, *John, Jesus, and the Renewal of Israel* (Grand Rapids:
      William B. Eerdmans Publishing Company, 2013), 156.

ETHNIC ASSESSMENTS IN THE GOSPEL OF JOHN

Horsley and Thatcher convincingly demonstrate that "this scheme involves a projection of the later synthetic constructs of 'Judaism' and 'Christianity'" on the Gospel."[123] This shift in perspective, from interpreting the Gospel of John as Jesus/Christianity versus Jews/Judaism to reading the Gospel within Judean traditions, also signals the distinction between the text of the Gospel of John and its anti-Semitic/anti-Judaism interpretation.[124]

For Reinhartz, however, this distinction is not possible because the "anti-Jewish elements are *inherent* in the texts themselves and not attributable solely to the interpretative tradition."[125] However, it is worth noting that in his reception history of the Johannine "Jews," Michael Azar concludes that "the general hostility within John ... was not simply assumed by the patristic readers [i.e. "Compliant Readers"]."[126] Azar rightly notes "the effects of transferring inner-Jewish polemic to a Gentile world undoubtedly resulted in Gentile, anti-Jewish readings. But ... such a point cannot be taken to assume that Gentile readers *always* and *simply* read the Fourth Gospel in such ways."[127] Nevertheless, Reinhartz has more recently reinforced her position that "the seventy-fold repetition of the term ['Ιουδαῖος] does not allow readers to ignore or make light of this hostile portrayal."[128]

Reinhartz's reading is centered on the Gospel of John's "labeling the Jew as Other" and as such "the Jews" "provides the antagonist demanded by the Gospel's narrative form and the negative pole against which the community's identity can be defined."[129] Reinhartz's assertion, however, is not as readily demonstrable from the text of the Gospel of John and, as Judith Lieu rightly observes, "the Jews" in the Gospel of John "have no antithetical counterpart:

---

123 Horsley and Thatcher, *John, Jesus, and the Renewal of Israel*, 138. Instead, Horsley and Thatcher argue that "it should be clear that in the Gospel of John, Jesus is not attacking 'Judaism' and 'the Jews' generally. In fact he is doing virtually the opposite: Jesus is generating a renewal of Israel in fulfillment of the deep longings expressed in Israelite culture, a renewal that includes Judeans as well as Galileans and even Samaritans" (Horsley and Thatcher, *John, Jesus, and the Renewal of Israel*, 157).

124 James D. G. Dunn "The Embarrassment of History: Reflections on the Problem of 'Anti-Judaism' in the Fourth Gospel," in *Anti-Judaism and the Fourth Gospel*, ed. R. Bieringer, Didier Pollefeyt, and F. Vandecasteele-Vanneuville (Louisville, KY: Westminster John Knox Press, 2001), 41–61.

125 Reinhartz, "'Jews' and Jews in the Fourth Gospel," 214; added emphasis.

126 Michael Azar, *Exegeting the Jews: The Early Reception of the Johannine "Jews"* (Leiden: Brill, 2016), 208.

127 Azar, *Exegeting the Jews*, 210; original emphasis.

128 Reinhartz, "The Vanishing Jews of Antiquity," 9.

129 Reinhartz, *Befriending the Beloved Disciple*, 78.

172   CHAPTER 5

they are not obviously a negative pole within a fixed scheme of oppositions."[130]
As we have seen, although "the Jews" are presented as hostile towards Jesus
in certain instances (e.g. 8:59; 10:31), this is not the *only* way that they are presented in the Gospel of John.[131] Instead, we must consider the totality of occurrences, including the neutral or ethnic ones, and not just the so-called hostile
occurrences.

3.6   *Every Jewish Occurrence*

Although the debate concerning the identity of "the Jews" will continue for
years to come, we can conclude that no single meaning of "the Jews" can account for all of the occurrences in the Gospel.[132] Rudolf Bultmann assigned
"the Jews" the singular identity as "the enemies of Jesus."[133] We noted that
Walter Gutbrod, a contemporary in Germany, had already observed that this
is not the case (e.g., John 7:11; 8:31; 10:19; 11:19, 31, 33, 36; 12:9, 11).[134] Von Wahlde's
distinction between two uses for "the Jews," the "neutral" and the "Johannine,"
better accounts for the Gospel of John's story of Jesus. Yet, as Stephen Motyer
comments, "The prior distinction (between neutral and Johannine) is loaded

---

130   Lieu, "Anti-Judaism, the Jews, and the Worlds of the Fourth Gospel," 179. Lieu adds that
       "although it could be argued that Jesus, or even his disciples, are the counterpart of 'the
       Jews' in narrative terms, this is never made explicit, and it may even be undermined."
       For example, Jan van der Watt observes that "we have Jews who accept Jesus and Jews
       who reject him; we have Jews who accept and then reject; we have Jews who wonder
       about him and others who have already made up their minds—all in the same narra-
       tive. The impression created in the narrative is that there is not a single Jewish group
       with a single response to Jesus but a varied picture of some rejecting Jesus but others
       still prepared to listen, still asking, still being interested, and having some contact with
       the Johannine group" (Jan G. van der Watt, "'Is Jesus the King of Israel'?: Reflections on
       the Jewish Nature of the Gospel of John," in *John and Judaism a Contested Relationship in
       Context*, ed. R. Alan Culpepper and Paul N. Anderson [Atlanta: SBL Press, 2017], 56).
131   Robert L. Brawley "argues on the basis of the ethics of interpretation for specifying the
       identity of the Ἰουδαῖοι to the extent that the text allows. This includes refusing to vilify
       characters or the narrator beyond what the text warrants. Therefore, in spite of pejorative
       characterizations of certain Ἰουδαῖοι, the notion that John vilifies Jesus's people is possible
       only when John is read apart from specifications of time, place, and personages" (The
       Ἰουδαῖοι In the Gospel of John," *Bridging Between Sister Religions: Studies of Jewish and
       Christian Scriptures Offered in Honor of Prof. John T. Townsend* ed. Isaac Kalimi [Leiden,
       Brill, 2016], 109).
132   In this regards, Jan van der Watt states: "In light of current research it cannot be denied
       that the description of the Jews in John is varied and complex and cannot be confined
       single aspect or perspective only" ("Is Jesus the King of Israel'?: Reflections on the Jewish
       nature of the Gospel of John," 55).
133   Bauer, "Ἰουδαῖοι," *Griechisch-Deutsches Wörterbuch*, 591.
134   Gutbrod, "Ἰουδαῖος, Ἰσραήλ, Ἑβραῖος," *TDNT* 3.378.

ETHNIC ASSESSMENTS IN THE GOSPEL OF JOHN

with the conclusion he wants to reach ... many of these 'neutral' uses are actually positive."[135]

The shortcoming of von Wahlde's approach, and others that distinguishes between multiple uses of "the Jews" in the Gospel of John, is that they fail to examine the relationship between the two (or more) distinctions of "the Jews." For example, if "the Johannine use" signifies "the religious authorities," then what is their authoritative status in relation to the "neutral" uses such as the festivals (2:13; 5:1; 6:4; etc.), the land of Judea (3:22), and "'Jews' in a context which separates them from non-Jews (e.g. i.e. Jesus himself; cf. 4:9a, 9b, 22; 18:35)."[136] In fact, among the Gospel of John's seventy uses of "Jew(s)," the singular commonality is as an ethnic term,[137] that is derived from a geographical region,[138] and also includes their leadership[139] who represent their ethnic group. To be clear, every occurrence of "Jew(s)" is ethnic in the Gospel of John, just as it is in Greco-Roman literature, but, because ethnic identity is situationally constructed, different aspects of ethnic identity (i.e. H-S#1–6) is "activated in different social contexts."[140] For this reason, then, "Jew(s)" as an ethnic term is an umbrella concept that accounts for the relationship between the two (or more) distinctions of "Jew" and "the Jews."

Accordingly, under the category of ethnic groups we can examine both Jesus's and "the Jews'" common ancestry (H-S#2), festivals (H-S#3), customs (H-S#4), homeland (H-S#5), and communal solidarity (H-S#6) (i.e. items included in von Wahlde's "neutral" use). The distinction—in the Gospel of John—is not between Jesus and "the Jews" but rather between those who believe Jesus is "the Jews'" Messiah (20:31; cf. 4:22, 42) and those who do not believe in him and remain conditioned by "the world of men"[141] who assess Jesus only as the son of Joseph (6:42) from Nazareth (19:19).

---

135   Stephen Motyer, *Your Father the Devil?*, 52. Motyer adds that "most notably the references in ch. 11, and the Jews who had believed in him; of 8:31." The same critique is also true for Reinhartz's brief acknowledgment of neutral and positive occurrences.

136   Von Wahlde, "The Johannine 'Jews'," 46.

137   Mason, "Jews, Judeans, Judaizing, Judaism," 457–512.

138   Lowe, "Who Were the ΙΟΥΔΑΙΟΙ?," 101–130.

139   Von Wahlde, "The Terms for Religious Authorities in the Fourth Gospel," 231–253; von Wahlde, "The Johannine 'Jews'," 33–60.

140   Siân Jones, *The Archaeology of Ethnicity: Constructing Identities in the Past and Present* (London; New York: Routledge, 1997), 91. Also see Hall, *Ethnic Identity in Greek Antiquity*, 1–3.

141   Bultmann, *Gospel of John*, 56.

174 CHAPTER 5

4 Implications of John's Employment of the Ethnic Label "Jew(s)"

Instead of minimizing Jesus as a Jew, as does Bultmann, we should recognize that "it is this very fact that gives his conflict with "the Jews" its particular sharpness."[142] Although it is the case in the Gospel of John that only non-Jews label Jesus a Jew (4:9; 18:35) it is often overlooked that Jesus was labeled a non-Jew by "the Jews" themselves (8:48). In light of Lewis Coser's proposition that "the closer the relationship, the more intense the conflict,"[143] we are in a better position to understand their intense conflict if Jesus was an insider—a Jew—rather than a non-Jew (such as a Samaritan). Perhaps no other conflict between Jesus and "the Jews" is as intense as in John 8:31–59. As we saw in the Chapter Four, it was because Jesus challenged the facticity of their social order that "the Jews" were forced to choose either to accept what Jesus said (e.g. the Samaritan woman) or reinforce the facticity of their challenged social order.[144] Instead of continuing to believe and accept Jesus's word (8:31), "the Jews" identified in John 8:48–59 chose the latter and, as part of their reinforcement effort, they labeled Jesus a "Samaritan" in order to mark off the boundaries between the choice he is offering and their self-legitimated social categories.

Also, as we saw in the Chapter Four, the "children of God" are an ethnic faction *within* the Judean ethnic group for adhering to Jesus's alternative interpretation of Judean ethnic identity that is broadened to include others outside of the Judean ancestral inheritance (and, from the Judean perspective, includes the Samaritans). Consequently, the "children of God' do not replace "the Jews" as an ethnic group, any more than any other Jewish factions would (such as the Pharisees), but rather they are participating *within* the Judean ethnic heritage. As an ethnic factionalist, Jesus acts a social deviant and it was his "deviancy" for challenging the centrality of patriarchal ancestry (8:33) that led "the Jews" to label Jesus a "Samaritan" (8:48). Bultmann noted that "the Jews'" labeling Jesus a "Samaritan" was to call him a heretic and yet, Jesus can *only* be a "heretic" *if* he is actually a member of the ethnic group; that is a Jew.

According to the non-Judean outsiders, Jesus is explicitly categorized as a Jew (4:9; 18:35) but, according to the Judean insiders, Jesus is only implicitly a Jew (6:42; 8:20). The reason for this is that being a Jew is not a static identity,

---

142 Silva, "Σαμαρίτης," *NIDNTTE* 4.247.

143 Coser, *The Functions of Social Conflict*, 67.

144 For example, recall Peter Berger's observation: "The facticity of the social world or of any part of it suffices for self-legitimation as long as there is no challenge. When a challenge appears, in whatever form, the facticity can no longer be taken for granted" (*The Sacred Canopy*, 31).

ETHNIC ASSESSMENTS IN THE GOSPEL OF JOHN

but is constructed in everyday interactions.[145] Furthermore, Jesus cannot confront "the Jews" or "Judaism" as a monolithic entity because they are, in fact, in a constant state of flux that only seems to be static for both the ancient people involved as well as to scholars who study them.

In this regard, labeling Jesus and assessing his ethnic identity discloses the interlocutors' social perceptions about what their ethnic identity means to them and how they have constructed their sense of ethnic identity. For example, the immediate purpose of the interlocutor's questions in John 1:46; 6:42; 7:41, 52 are to express Jesus's ethnic identity in terms of genealogical (H-S#2) and geographical descent (H-S#5). However, in the broader scope of the Gospel of John, their questions signify their abiding in "the world of men" and the primacy it attaches to ethnic distinctions, or to their abiding in "the truth" (of God's reality), in which the Judean ethnic categories are broadened in order "to gather into one the dispersed children of God" (11:52). In other words, the disciples, "the Jews" in Galilee, and the religious authorities in Jerusalem all interact with Jesus from their view of humanity that is divided into ethnic groups. However, their exposure to the presence of Jesus (the "truth") reveals the "misrecognized" state of being a "Jew" according to "the world of men," and, in response, they react either positively (1:46) or negatively (6:42; 7:41, 52).

Also, given that each individual has their own social perceptions of what it means to be a member of their ethnic group, it is no wonder that Jesus caused division among "his own people" (1:11; such as in 7:12 when some said Jesus is a good man and others said that he is leading them astray). As we saw in the Chapter Four, those in positions of authority ultimately determine the boundaries of the ethnic group and, therefore, who is inside and who is outside of the group.[146] The reason for this is that social acts are not deviant until society, and those in authority who represent it, label it as deviant (such as Jesus being labeled a "Samaritan" in 8:48 and then later labeled a criminal in 18:30).[147] Since

---

145 Here we call attention to Chapter Three where it states: "Ethnicity is an umbrella concept consisting of multiple cultural features—such as religion (H-S#4) and geography (H-S#5)—that are attributes of an ethnic group's identity, and are used situationally to differentiate their group from others" (page 69).

146 In Chapter Four section 4.0 we stated that "the definition of deviance serve to reinforce in-group identity by categorizing others into out-groups. The maintenance of these social boundaries preserves the social order and, as a result, the definitions of deviance ultimately serve those in legitimated roles who define Us/Them. An etic term for those in legitimated roles within their social group is the 'elites'" (page 140).

147 In Chapter Four we stated: "In terms of labeling theory, the purpose for 'the Jews' labeling of Jesus as a 'Samaritan' was an act of institutional labeling that categorized Jesus as "not one of us" and placed him outside the boundaries of the Judean ethnic identity" (page 137–138).

176   CHAPTER 5

those in positions of authority determine the boundaries of the group, this means that their interpretation or construction of the Judean ethnic identity is also the only legitimate one; albeit, one that has to be collectively enforced.

5   Conclusion

The Gospel of John does *not* use the ethnic label "the Jews" because the response was negative or that it shows hostility towards Jesus (Bultmann; Reinhartz).[148] The reason for this is, as Walter Gutbrod observed, "A man is not called a Ἰουδαῖος simply because he does not believe and rejects Christ."[149] Instead the Johannine Jesus, as a Jew himself (4:9; 18:35), proclaims a critique from *within* "the Jews" (7:12, 47) in order to bring salvation from "the Jews" (4:22) to the world (4:42). We saw a particular aspect of this in Chapter Four with Jesus's broadening "the Jews'" ethnic categories in order to gather the "children of God" (1:12–13; 11:52) into one flock (10:16). The Gospel of John uses the ethnic label "Jew" in order to contest its tacit (i.e. "misrecognized") identity by contrasting it with Jesus's variant interpretation of what it means to be a "Jew"; namely, "to become children of God, who were born, not of blood or of the will of the flesh or of the will of man, but of God" (John 1:12–13). In Chapter Four we saw that Jesus's variant interpretation entails the Father who seeks true worshipers that will worship in spirit and truth (regardless of ethnic priorities; 4:23–24) which dissolves the arbitrariness of the "We-You" boundaries between the Judeans and Samaritans. Similarly, we also saw Jesus's variant interpretation also involves that people cannot identify themselves as "children of Abraham" or "children of God" if they are not doing the things that Abraham did (8:39–40) because the children of Abraham, Jacob, and indeed of God are those who receive the Father's Son (1:12–13). The Gospel of John presents the coming to (cf. 3:2; 4:30, 40) and being gathered (cf. 10:16; 11:52; 12:32) by Jesus via belief in him (1:12–13) as overcoming the "misrecognition" of "the world of men" that prioritizes categorizing Jesus, and one another, in terms of ethnic identity.

---

148   Bultmann, *The Gospel of John*, 54–56, 86–87; Adele Reinhartz, *Befriending the Beloved Disciple*, 61–70.

149   Gutbrod, "Ἰουδαῖος, Ἰσραήλ, Ἑβραῖος," *TDNT* 3.379.

Conclusion

(Jesus) asked them, 'Whom are you looking for?' They answered, 'Jesus of Nazareth'

JOHN 18:4–5

∵

The conclusion of this book is that Jesus's role as a factionalist Jew altered the significance of Judean cultural traits in order to broaden Judean ethnic identity into the "children of God." One of the most puzzling (and at times disturbing) aspects of John's Gospel is its relationship to Judaism, as particularly evidenced in the exchanges between Jesus and "the Jews" in John 8. Perhaps the best summary statement of this particular Johannine puzzle is C. K. Barrett's statement that "John is both Jewish and anti-Jewish."[1] Wayne Meeks provocatively nuances the problem in John's Gospel in this statement: "To put the matter sharply, with some risk of misunderstanding, the Fourth Gospel is most anti-Jewish just at the points it is most Jewish."[2] One of the more dramatic illustrations of this Johannine puzzle that we have discussed is the contrasting statements in John 4:22 and 8:44, which respectively read "For salvation is from the Jews" and "You are from your father the devil." How can the Johannine Jesus claim that "salvation is from the Jews" while speaking with the Samaritan woman in John 4, but then while speaking with "the Jews" in John 8 say to them "you are from your father the devil"?

The answer is that the Gospel of John portrays Jesus as a "Jew" who has issues with other "Jews." More specifically, Jesus is a factionalist "Jew" who has conflicts with other "Jews" due to their prioritization of being descendants of Abraham (8:33) and disciples of Moses (9:28), over against hearing (8:47), knowing (8:55), and loving (5:42; 8:42) "he of whom you say, "He is our God'" (8:54).

---

1 Barrett, *The Gospel of John and Judaism*, 71.
2 Wayne A. Meeks, "'Am I a Jew?' Johannine Christianity and Judaism," in *Christianity, Judaism and other Greco-Roman Cults: Studies for Morton Smith at Sixty* (ed. J. Neusner; Leiden: Brill, 1975), 172.

Throughout the Gospel of John, Jesus, as a factionalist "Jew," causes schisms among the crowd (7:43), the Pharisees (9:16), and "the Jews" (10:19). That factionalism extends especially to assessments of Jesus himself. Some come to believe in Jesus, such as "many [of the crowd]" (2:23; 7:31; 10:42), "many of the Jews" (11:45), and even "many of the Jews were deserting and were believing in Jesus" (12:11). Some do not come to believe in Jesus, for "fear of the Jews" (7:13; 9:22; [12:42 the Pharisees]; 19:38; 20:19) and particularly for fear of being excommunicated (9:22; 12:42; 16:2). Consequently, Jesus's factionalism comes with the price of being labeled a "Samaritan" (i.e. a non-Jew) by "the Jews" (8:48).

As noted in the Introduction, according to Barrett, the dual ethnic labeling of Jesus as a "Jew" (4:9) and as a "Samaritan" (8:48) indicates that "in this world Jesus is never anything but a stranger."[3] Yet, from the point of view of the people with whom Jesus interacts, Jesus is anything but a stranger. They clearly identify him: "They were saying, 'Is not this Jesus, the son of Joseph, whose father and mother we know?'" (John 6:42). Instead of concluding that Jesus is a stranger in the Gospel of John, we have demonstrated that the ethnic labeling function is to structure socially the interactions between Jesus and his interlocutors. In particular, these interactions are structured in reference to the cultural features (H-S#1–6) of the Samaritan and Judean ethnic groups. Jesus's answer to the Samaritan woman's (4:9) and "the Jews'" (8:48) questions, therefore, would presumably be the same: "I am a 'Jew,' but being a 'Jew' does not (necessarily) mean what you think it means."[4] This is therefore another clear instance in which "John is both Jewish and anti-Jewish."[5] Jesus, as a factionalist Jew, ruptures the "misrecognized" assessments of the ethnic labels "Jew" and "Samaritan" for the purpose of transforming Judean ethnic identity into a trans-ethnic identity—the "children of God."[6]

---

3 Barrett, *Gospel According to St. John*, 232.
4 The reason for this answer is due the nature of ethnic identity that is situationally constructed. See Jones, *The Archaeology of Ethnicity*, 84–105; and Hall, *Ethnic identity in Greek Antiquity*, 1–3.
5 Barrett, *The Gospel of John and Judaism*, 71.
6 The "children of God" are not a universalistic non-people group, which Denise Buell has rightly criticized, but rather the "children of God" are a people group (united by fictive-kinship; cf. John 1:13) embedded *within* the Judean ethnic group's culture and traditions that, according to the Gospel of John, Jesus broadened into a pan-Judean group (cf. Denise K. Buell, *Why This New Race: Ethnic Reasoning in Early Christianity* [Columbia University Press, 2005]; and "Challenges and Strategies for Speaking about Ethnicity in the New Testament and New Testament Studies," *SEÅ* 79 [2014]: 33–51).

CONCLUSION

Areas of Future Research

An immediate research project is to expand the function of labeling to the Johannine Letters which also use the labels "children of God" and "children of the devil" (1 John 3:10). Of particular interest are the possible correlations between "the Jews" in the Gospel of John and the antichrists in 1 and 2 John, in light of the fact that they are both given the same labeling treatment. The driving question for this project would be: Is John addressing the same, or at least a similar, group and situation? In John 8:44 it was "the Jews who had believed in him" and in 1 John the antichrists who have "gone out from us" (2:19) who are labeled "children of the devil" (3:10). In addition, or perhaps as a separate project, could be a study examining the way in which 1 John develops the identity of the "children of God" (1 John 2:29; 3:1, 10; 5:2, 10).

The role of ethnic labels in the Johannine Corpus regarding the "parting-of-the-ways" between Judaism and Christianity is yet another avenue of research that parallels this thesis. Daniel Boyarin has already proposed that rather than two bounded religions separating, members from each group constructed their own identity by categorizing the other group through discourses in order to "eradicate the fuzziness of the borders, semantic and social, between Jews and Christians."[7] Bearing this in mind, a more comprehensive research project on how the Gospel of John constructs the identity of "the Jews" could be conducted. Specific attention would be given to which cultural features were enacted in particular interactions when constructing the identity of the group. The question could then be asked if John's establishment of the self-category "children of God" shows any correlation to the "parting-of-the-ways."

---

7 Daniel Boyarin, *Borderlines: The Partition of Judeo-Christianity* (Philadelphia: University of Pennsylvania, 2004), 2.

Bibliography

Critical Biblical Texts

Aland, Barbara et al., ed. *Novum Testamentum Graece*. 28th ed. Stuttgart: Deutsche Bibelgesellschaft, 2012.

Elliger, K. and W. Rudolf, eds. *Biblia Hebraica Stuttgartensia*. Revised by A. Schenker. 5th ed. Stuttgart: Deutsche Bibelgesellschaft, 1997.

Schenker, Adrian et al., ed. *Biblia Hebraica Quinta*. 5th ed. Stuttgart: Deutsche Bibelgesellschaft, 2004.

Primary Sources

Ancient Near Eastern Texts Relating to the Old Testament. Edited by James Bennett Pritchard, 3d ed. with supplement. Princeton: Princeton University Press, 1969.

The Ante-Nicene Fathers. Edited by Alexander Roberts and James Donaldson. 1885–1887. 10 vols. Repr. Peabody, MA: Hendrickson, 1994.

The Babylonian Talmud. Translated by Isidore Epstein. London: Soncino Press, 1935.

Chronicle Adler. Pages 61–87. John Bowman, *Samaritan Documents: Relating to Their History, Religion, and Life*. Pittsburgh Original Texts and Translation Series 2. Pittsburgh: Pickwick Press, 1977.

Cyril of Alexandria. *Commentary on the Gospel according to Saint John*. Translated by Philip Edward Pusey. 2 vols. London: James Parker & Co., 1874.

Chrysostom, John. *Commentary on Saint John the Apostle and Evangelist*. Translated by Thomas Aquinas Goggin. 2 vols. The Fathers of the Church v. 33 and 41. Washington: Catholic University of American Press, 1969.

Epiphanius, and Frank Williams. *The Panarion of Epiphanius of Salamis, Book I (Sects 1–46)*. Leiden; Boston: Brill, 2009.

Genesis Rabbah: The Judaic Commentary to the Book of Genesis: A New American Translation. Jacob Neusner ed. BJS 104. Atlanta: Scholars Press, 1985.

Herodotus. *Histories*. Translated by A. D. Godley. 4 vols. Loeb Classical Library. London: William Heinemann, 1921.

Josephus. Translated by H. St. J. Thackeray et al. 10 vols. Loeb Classical Library. Cambridge: Harvard University Press, 1926–1965.

Josephus, Flavius. *The Works of Josephus: Complete and Unabridged*. Translated by William Whiston. Peabody, MA: Hendrickson, 2003.

182

Isocrates. Translated by George Norlin. 3 vols. Loeb Classical Library. Cambridge: Harvard University Press, 1986–1992.

The Israelite Samaritan Version of the Torah: First English Translation Compared with the Masoretic Version. Tsedaka, Benyamim, ed. Grand Rapids: Eerdmans, 2012.

The Mishnah. Translated by Jacob Neusner. New Haven: Yale University Press, 1988.

New Testament Apocrypha. Edited by Edgar Hennecke, Wilhelm Schneemelcher, and R. McL Wilson. 2 vols. Philadelphia: Westminster, 1963.

Origen. *Contra Celsum*. Translated by Henry Chadwick. Cambridge: Cambridge University Press, 1953.

Origen. *Commentary on the Gospel according to John: Books 1–10*. Translated by Ronald E. Heine. The Fathers of the Church, a new translation v. 80. Washington, DC: Catholic University of America Press, 1989.

Origen. *Commentary on the Gospel according to John: Books 13–32*. Translated by Ronald E. Heine. The Fathers of the church v. 89. Washington, DC: Catholic University of America Press, 1993.

The Kitāb Al-Tarīkh of Abu 'L-Fath. Translated by Paul Stenhouse. Sidney: University of Sidney, 1985.

The Samaritan Chronicle: Or The Book of Joshua the Son of Nun. Translated by Oliver Turnbull Crane. New York: J. B. Alden, 1890.

Targum Pseudo-Jonathan, Genesis. Michael Maher ed. The Aramaic Bible v. 1B. Collegeville, MN: Liturgical Press, 1992.

Tertullian. *Adversus Marcionem*. Translated by and Ernest Evans. Oxford Early Christian Texts. Oxford: Clarendon, 1972.

Theodore of Mopsuestia. *Commentary on the Gospel of John*. Edited by Joel C. Elowsky. Translated by Marco Conti. Ancient Christian Texts. Downers Grove, IL: InterVarsity Press, 2010.

Secondary Sources

Aharoni, Yohanan. *The Land of the Bible: A Historical Geography*. 2d ed. Philadelphia: Westminster, 1979.

Albertz, Rainer. *A History of Israelite Religion in the Old Testament Period*. 2 vols. OTL. Louisville: Westminster John Knox, 1994.

Anderson, Paul N. "Aspects of Historicity in the Gospel of John: Implications for Investigations of Jesus and Archaeology." Pages 587–618 in *Jesus and Archaeology*. Edited by James H. Charlesworth. Grand Rapids: Eerdmans, 2006.

Anderson, Paul N. "Anti-Semitism and Religious Violence as Flawed Interpretations of the Gospel of John." *John and Judaism a Contested Relationship in Context*. Edited by R. Alan Culpepper and Paul N. Anderson. Atlanta: SBL Press, 2017.

BIBLIOGRAPHY

Anderson, Paul N. "Forward." *The Prophet-King Moses Traditions and the Johannine Christology.* Wipf & Stock Pub, 2017.

Anderson, Robert T., and Terry Giles. *The Keepers: An Introduction to the History and Culture of the Samaritans.* Peabody, MA: Hendrickson, 2002.

Anderson, Robert T., and Terry Giles. *Tradition Kept: The Literature of the Samaritans.* Peabody, MA: Hendrickson, 2005.

Anderson, Robert T., and Terry Giles. *The Samaritan Pentateuch: An Introduction to Its Origin, History, and Significance for Biblical Studies.* Atlanta: Society of Biblical Literature, 2012.

Arditi, George. "Role as a Cultural Concept." *Theory and Society* 16, no. 4 (1987): 565–91.

Ashton, John. "The Identity and Function of The Ἰουδαῖοι in the Fourth Gospel." *NovT* 27, no. 1 (1985): 40–75.

Ashton, John. *Understanding the Fourth Gospel.* Oxford University Press, 1993.

Ashton, John. *Understanding the Fourth Gospel.* 2d ed. Oxford University Press, 2007.

Ashton, John. *The Gospel of John and Christian Origins.* Minneapolis: Fortress Press, 2014.

Augstein, Hannah Franziska. *Race: The Origins of an Idea, 1760–1850.* Bristol: Thoemmes Press, 1996.

Avi-Yonah, Michael. *The Holy Land: A Historical Geography from the Persian to the Arab Conquest (536 BC to AD 640).* Jerusalem: Carta, 2002.

Azar, Michael G. *Exegeting the Jews: The Early Reception of the Johannine Jews.* Leiden; Boston: Brill, 2016.

Bahat, Dan. "Jesus and the Herodian Temple Mount." Pages 300–308 in *Jesus and Archaeology.* Edited by James H. Charlesworth. Grand Rapids: Eerdmans, 2006.

Banton, Michael. "Max Weber on 'Ethnic Communities': A Critique." *Nations and Nationalism* 13, no. 1 (2007): 19–35.

Banton, Michael. "The Sociology of Ethnic Relations." *Ethnic and Racial Studies* 31, no. 7 (2008): 1267–85.

Barclay, John M. G. "Deviance and Apostasy: Some Applications of Deviance Theory to First-Century Judaism and Christianity." Pages 114–127 in *Modeling Early Christianity: Social-Scientific Studies of the New Testament in Its Context.* Edited by Philip Francis Esler. London; New York: Routledge, 1995.

Barclay, John M. G. "Constructing Judean Identity after 70 CE: A Study of Josephus's Against Apion." Pages 99–112 in *Identity and Interaction in the Ancient Mediterranean: Jews, Christians and Others: Essays in Honour of Stephen G. Wilson.* Edited by S. G. Wilson, Zeba A Crook, and Philip A Harland. Sheffield: Sheffield Phoenix, 2007.

Barrett, C. K. *A Critical and Exegetical Commentary on the Acts of the Apostles.* ICC 30–31. Edinburgh: T&T Clark, 1994.

Barrett, C. K. *The Gospel according to St. John: An Introduction with Commentary and Notes on the Greek Text.* 2d ed. Philadelphia: Westminster, 1978.

Barrett, C. K. *The Gospel of John and Judaism*. Translated by D. Moody Smith. Philadelphia: Fortress, 1975.

Barth, Fredrik. *Models of Social Organization*. Glasgow: The University Press, 1966.

Barth, Fredrik. "Introduction." Pages 9–38 in *Ethnic Groups and Boundaries: The Social Organization of Culture Difference*. Edited by Fredrik Barth. Boston: Little, Brown and Company, 1969.

Barth, Fredrik. "Pathan Identity and its Maintenance." Pages 117–34 in *Ethnic Groups and Boundaries: The Social Organization of Culture Difference*. Edited by Fredrik Barth. Boston: Little, Brown and Company, 1969.

Barth, Fredrik. "Overview: Sixty Years in Anthropology." *Annual Review Anthropology* 36 (2007): 1–16.

Bassler, Jouette M. "The Galileans: A Neglected Factor in Johannine Community Research." *CBQ* 43.2 (1981): 243–57.

Bauckham, Richard. "The Scrupulous Priest and the Good Samaritan: Jesus' Parabolic Interpretation of the Law Of Moses." *NTS* 44.4 (1998): 475–89.

Bauer, Walter. *Das Johannesevangelium*. Handbuch zum Neuen Testament 6. Tübingen: Mohr Siebeck, 1933.

Bauer, Walter. *Griechisch-deutsches wörterbuch zu den schriften des NeuenTestaments und der übrigen urchristlichen literatur*. 3. völlig neu bearb. Aufl. Berlin: Töpelmann, 1937.

Baum, Gregory. *The Jews and the Gospel: A Re-Examination of the New Testament*. Westminster, MD: Newman Press, 1961.

Beasley-Murray, George Raymond. *John*. 2d ed. WBC 36. Waco, TX; Dallas; Nashville: Word, 1999.

Becker, Howard S. *Outsiders*. New York: Simon & Schuster, 1963.

Becking, Bob. "Continuity and Discontinuity after the Exile: Some Introductory Remarks." Pages 1–8 in *Crisis of Israelite Religion: Transformation of Religious Tradition in Exilic and Post-Exilic Times*. Leiden: Brill, 1999.

Becking, Bob. *The Fall of Samaria: An Historical and Archaeological Study*. Studies in the History of the Ancient Near East vol. 2. Leiden: Brill, 1992.

Bennema, Cornelis. "The Identity and Composition of Οἱ Ἰουδαῖοι in the Gospel of John." *TynBul* 60.2 (2009): 239–63.

Bennema, Cornelis. "The Ethnic Conflict in Early Christianity: An Appraisal of Bauckham's Proposal on the Antioch Crisis and the Jerusalem Council." *JETS* 56.4 (2013): 753–63.

Bennema, Cornelis. *Encountering Jesus: Character Studies in the Gospel of John*. Minneapolis, MN: Fortress Press, 2014.

Bentley, G. Carter. "Ethnicity and Practice." *Comparative Studies in Society and History* 29.1 (1987): 24–55.

Bentley, G. Carter. "Response to Yelvington." *Comparative Studies in Society and History* 33.1 (1991): 169–75.

BIBLIOGRAPHY

Berger, Peter L. *The Sacred Canopy: Elements of a Sociological Theory of Religion*. New York: Anchor Books, 1969.

Berger, Peter L., and Thomas Luckmann. *The Social Construction of Reality: A Treatise in the Sociology of Knowledge*. New York: Doubleday, 1989.

Berlin, Adele, *Esther: The Traditional Hebrew Text with the New JPS Translation*. The JPS Commentary. Philadelphia: Jewish Publication Society, 2001.

Berlin, Adele, ed. *The Oxford Dictionary of the Jewish Religion*. 2d ed. New York: Oxford University Press, 2011.

Berlinerblau, Jacques. "Toward a Sociology of Heresy, Orthodoxy, and Doxa." *HR* 40.4 (2001): 327–51.

Bernard, J. H. *A Critical and Exegetical Commentary on the Gospel according to St. John*. 2 vols. ICC v. 29. Edinburgh: T&T Clark, 1928.

Beutler, Johannes. "Greeks Come to See Jesus (John 12,2 of)." *Biblica* 71.3 (1990): 333–47.

Beutler, Johannes. "Two Ways of Gathering: The Plot to Kill Jesus in John 11:47–53." *NTS* 40.3 (1994): 399–406.

Beutler, Johannes. "Faith and Confession: The Purpose of John." Pages 19–31 in *Word, Theology, and Community in John*. Edited by John Painter, R. Alan Culpepper, and Fernando F. Segovia. St. Louis: Chalice, 2002.

Beutler, Johannes. *Judaism and the Jews in the Gospel of John*. Roma: Pontificio Istituto Biblico, 2006.

Beutler, Johannes. "Jesus in conflict : history and theology in John 5–12." *New Studies on the Johannine Writings*. Bonner Biblische Beiträge Bd. 167. Göttingen: Vandenhoeck & Ruprecht, 2012.

Beutler, Johannes. *Das Johannesevangelium: Kommentar*. Freiburg: Herder, 2013.

Beutler, Johannes. "Jesus in Judea." *In Die Skriflig* 49.2 (2015): 1–6.

Black, Matthew. *The Scrolls and Christian Origins: Studies in the Jewish Background of the New Testament*. Brown Judaic Studies 48. Chico, CA: Scholars Press, 1983.

Blass, Friedrich, Albert Debrunner, and Robert Walter Funk. *A Greek Grammar of the New Testament and Other Early Christian Literature*. Chicago: University of Chicago Press, 1961.

Blenkinsopp, Joseph. *Ezra-Nehemiah: A Commentary*. Old Testament Library. Philadelphia: Westminster, 1988.

Blenkinsopp, Joseph. "The Judaean Priesthood during the Neo-Babylonian and Achaemenid Periods: A Hypothetical Reconstruction." *CBQ* 60.1 (1998): 25–43.

Blenkinsopp, Joseph. *Judaism, the First Phase: The Place of Ezra and Nehemiah in the Origins of Judaism*. Grand Rapids: Eerdmans, 2009.

Blenkinsopp, Joseph. "Judaeans, Jews, Children of Abraham." Pages 461–82 in *Judah and the Judeans in the Achaemenid Period: Negotiating Identity in an International Context*. Winona Lake, IN: Eisenbrauns, 2011.

Bock, Darrell L. *Luke*. 2 vols. BECNT 3. Grand Rapids: Baker Books, 1994.

Bock, Jerry, Joseph Stein, Sheldon Harnick, and Sholem Aleichem. *Fiddler on the Roof.* New York: Limelight Editions, 2002.

Boers, Hendrikus. *Neither on This Mountain nor in Jerusalem: A Study of John 4.* SBLMS 35. Atlanta: Scholars Press, 1988.

Böhm, Martina. *Samarien und die Samaritai bei Lukas: eine Studie zum religionshistorischen und traditionsgeschichtlichen Hintergrund der lukanischen Samarientexte und zu deren topographischer Verhaftung.* Tübingen: Mohr Siebeck, 1999.

Boismard, M. E. *Moses or Jesus: An Essay in Johannine Christology.* Minneapolis: Fortress Press, 1993.

Bond, Helen Katharine. *Caiaphas: Friend of Rome and Judge of Jesus?.* Westminster John Knox, 2004.

Boomershine, Thomas E. "The Medium and Message of John: Audience Address and Audience Identity in the Fourth Gospel." *The Fourth Gospel in First-Century Media Culture.* Edited by Anthony Le Donne and Tom Thatcher. Library of New Testament studies 426. New York: Bloomsbury T&T Clark, 2013.

Borgen, Peder. "The Gospel of John and Hellenism: Some Observations." Pages 98–123 in *Exploring the Gospel of John: In Honor of D Moody Smith.* Edited by R. Alan Culpepper and C. Clifton Black. Louisville: Westminster John Knox, 1996.

Bornhäuser, Karl. *Das Johannesevangelium: Eine Misionschrift Für Israel.* Gütersloh: Bertelsmann, 1928.

Botha, J. Eugene. *Jesus and the Samaritan Woman: A Speech Act Reading of John 4:1–42.* Leiden; New York: Brill, 1991.

Botterweck, G. Johannes, and Helmer Ringgren. *Theological Dictionary of the Old Testament.* Rev. ed. Grand Rapids: Eerdmans, 1977.

Bourdieu, Pierre. *Outline of a Theory of Practice.* Translated by Richard Nice. Cambridge; New York: Cambridge University Press, 1993.

Bourdieu, Pierre. "The Social Space and the Genesis of Groups." *Theory and Society* 14.6 (1985): 723–744.

Bourdieu, Pierre. "What Makes a Social Class? On the Theoretical and Practical Existence of Groups." *Berkeley Journal of Sociology* 32 (1987): 1–17.

Bourdieu, Pierre. *The Logic of Practice.* Cambridge: Polity Press, 1990.

Bourdieu, Pierre. *Practical Reason: On the Theory of Action.* Stanford, CA: Stanford University Press, 1998.

Bourdieu, Pierre, and Loïc J. D. Wacquant. *An Invitation to Reflexive Sociology.* Chicago: University of Chicago Press, 1992.

Bowman, John. "Samaritan Studies." *BJRL* 40, no. 2 (1958): 298–327.

Bowman, John. *Samaritan Documents: Relating to Their History, Religion, and Life.* Pittsburgh Original Texts and Translation Series 2. Pittsburgh: Pickwick, 1977.

Boyarin, Daniel. "The Ioudaioi in John and the Prehistory of 'Judaism.'" Pages 216–239 in *Pauline Conversations in Context: Essays in Honor of Calvin J. Roetzel.* Edited by

Janice Capel Anderson, Philip Harl Sellew, and Claudia Setzer. JSNTSup 221. London: Sheffield Academic, 2002.

Boyarin, Daniel. *Border Lines: The Partition of Judaeo-Christianity*. Philadelphia: University of Pennsylvania Press, 2004.

Boyer, Paul S., and Melvyn Dubofsky, eds. *The Oxford Companion to United States History*. Oxford; New York: Oxford University Press, 2001.

Brant, Jo-Ann A. *John*. Paideia: Commentaries on the New Testament. Grand Rapids: Baker Academic, 2011.

Bratcher, Robert G. "'The Jews' in the Gospel of John." *BT* 26.4 (1975): 401–409.

Brass, Paul R. *Ethnicity and Nationalism: Theory and Comparison*. Thousand Oaks, CA: Sage Publications, 1991.

Brawley, Robert L. "The Ἰουδαῖοι in the Gospel of John." Edited by Isaac Kalimi. *Bridging between Sister Religions* (2016): 105–27.

Brown, Colin, ed. *The New International Dictionary of New Testament Theology*. 3 vols. Grand Rapids: Zondervan, 1975.

Brown, Raymond Edward. *The Gospel according to John*. 2 vols. The Anchor Bible no. 29–29A. Garden City, NY: Doubleday, 1966.

Brown, Raymond Edward. *The Community of the Beloved Disciple*. New York: Paulist Press, 1979.

Brown, Raymond Edward. *An Introduction to the Gospel of John*. Edited by Francis J. Moloney. The Anchor Bible reference library. New York: Doubleday, 2003.

Browning, W. R. F., ed. *A Dictionary of the Bible*. 2d ed. Oxford; New York: Oxford University Press, 2009.

Brubaker, Rogers. *Ethnicity without Groups*. Cambridge: Harvard University Press, 2006.

Bruce, F. F. *The Gospel of John*. Grand Rapids: Eerdmans, 1983.

Bruce, F. F. *The Acts of the Apostles: The Greek Text with Introduction and Commentary*. 3d rev. ed. Grand Rapids: Eerdmans, 1990.

Brueggemann, Walter. *The Prophetic Imagination*. 2d ed. Minneapolis: Fortress, 2001.

Brueggemann, Walter. *Theology of the Old Testament: Testimony, Dispute, Advocacy*. Minneapolis: Fortress, 2005.

Bruneau, Philippe. "Les Israélites de Délos' et La Juiverie Délienne." *BCH* 106.1 (1982): 465–504.

Bruner, Frederick Dale. *The Gospel of John: A Commentary*. Grand Rapids: Eerdmans, 2012.

Buell, Denise K. "Rethinking the Relevance of Race for Early Christian Self-Definition." *HTR* 94.4 (2001): 449–76.

Buell, Denise K. *Why This New Race: Ethnic Reasoning in Early Christianity*. Columbia University Press, 2005.

Buell, Denise K. "Constructing Early Christian Identities Using Ethnic Reasoning." *ASE* 24.1 (2007): 87–101.

Buell, Denise K. "Challenges and Strategies for Speaking about Ethnicity in the New Testament and New Testament Studies." *SEÅ* 79 (2014): 33–51.

Bultmann, Rudolf Karl. *Theology of the New Testament*. Translated by Kendrick Grobel. 2 vols. New York: Scribner, 1951.

Bultmann, Rudolf Karl. *The Gospel of John; A Commentary*. Translated by George Raymond Beasley-Murray. Philadelphia: Westminster, 1971.

Calhoun, Craig J., ed. *Dictionary of the Social Sciences*. Oxford; New York: Oxford University Press, 2002.

Carson, D. A. *The Gospel According to John*. Grand Rapids: Eerdmans, 1991.

Carter, Warren. *John: Storyteller, Interpreter, Evangelist*. Grand Rapids: Baker Books, 2006.

Casey, Maurice. *Is John's Gospel True?* London; New York: Routledge, 1996.

Casey, Maurice. "Some Anti-Semitic Assumptions in the *Theological Dictionary of the New Testament*." *NovT* 41.3 (1999): 280–91.

Chapoulie, Jean-Michel. "Everett Hughes and the Chicago Tradition." *Sociological Theory* 14.1 (1996): 3–29.

Charlesworth, James H. "What Is a Variant?: Announcing a Dead Sea Scrolls Fragment of Deuteronomy." *Maarav* 16.2 (2009): 201.

Charon, Joel M. *Symbolic Interactionism: An Introduction, an Interpretation, an Integration*. 6th ed. Upper Saddle River, NJ: Prentice Hall, 1998.

Clines, David J. A., ed. *The Dictionary of Classical Hebrew*. Sheffield: Sheffield Academic, 1993.

Coggins, R. J. *Samaritans and Jews: the Origins of Samaritanism Reconsidered*. Atlanta: John Knox, 1975.

Coggins, R. J. "The Samaritans in Josephus." Pages 257–73 in *Josephus, Judaism, and Christianity*. Edited by Louis H. Feldman and Gohei Hata. Leiden; Boston: Brill, 1987.

Cohen, Shaye J. D. "'Those Who Say They Are Jews and Are Not': How Do You Know a Jew in Antiquity When You See One?" Pages 1–45 in *Diasporas in Antiquity*. Atlanta: Scholars Press, 1993.

Conzelmann, Hans. *Acts of the Apostles: A Commentary on the Acts of the Apostles*. Edited by Eldon Jay Epp and Christopher R. Matthews. Hermeneia. Philadelphia: Fortress, 1987.

Coser, Lewis A. *The Functions of Social Conflict*. Glenco, IL; New York: Free Press, 1964.

Cox, Oliver C. *Caste, Class, & Race: a Study in Social Dynamics*. Garden City, NY: Doubleday, 1948.

Crawford, Sidnie White. *Rewriting Scripture in Second Temple Times*. Studies in the Dead Sea Scrolls and Related Literature. Grand Rapids: Eerdmans, 2008.

Cromhout, Markus, and Andries G. Van Aarde. "A Socio-Cultural Model of Judean Ethnicity: A Proposal." *HvTSt* 62.1 (2006): 69–101.

BIBLIOGRAPHY

Cronin, Sonya. *Raymond Brown, "the Jews," and the Gospel of John: From Apologia to Apology.* LNTS 504. London; New York: Bloomsbury T&T Clark, 2015.

Cross, F. L., and Elizabeth A. Livingstone, eds. *The Oxford Dictionary of the Christian Church.* 3d rev. ed. Oxford: Oxford University Press, 2005.

Crossley, James G. *The Date of Mark's Gospel: Insight from the Law in Earliest Christianity.* Edinburgh: T&T Clark, 2004.

Crown, Alan D. "Redating the Schism between the Judeans and the Samaritans." *JQR* 82.1–2 (1991): 17–50.

Crown, Alan D., ed. *The Samaritans.* Tübingen: Mohr Siebeck, 1989.

Crown, Alan D., ed. "Qumran, Samaritan Halakha and Pre-Tannaitic Judaism." Pages 420–441 in *Boundaries of the Ancient Near Eastern World: A Tribute to Cyrus H. Gordon.* Edited by Cyrus H Gordon, Meir Lubetski, Claire Gottlieb, and Sharon R Keller. Sheffield: Sheffield Academic, 1998.

Crown, Alan D., and Reinhard Pummer. *A Bibliography of the Samaritans.* 3d ed., Expanded, and Annotated. ATLA Bibliography Series no. 51. Lanham, MD: Scarecrow Press, 2005.

Crown, Alan D., Reinhard Pummer, and Abraham Tal, eds. *A Companion to Samaritan Studies.* Tübingen: Mohr Siebeck, 1993.

Culpepper, R. Alan. *Anatomy of the Fourth Gospel: A Study in Literary Design.* Philadelphia: Fortress, 1987.

Culpepper, R. Alan, and Paul N. Anderson, eds. *John and Judaism a Contested Relationship in Context.* Atlanta: SBL Press, 2017.

Danker, Frederick W., Walter Bauer, and William F. Arndt. *A Greek—English Lexicon of the New Testament and Other Early Christian Literature.* 3d ed. Chicago: University of Chicago Press, 2000.

Daube, David. "Jesus and the Samaritan Woman: The Meaning of Συγχράομαι." *JBL* 69.2 (1950): 137–47.

Davies, W. D., and Dale C. Allison. *A Critical and Exegetical Commentary on the Gospel according to Saint Matthew.* ICC v. 26A–C. Edinburgh: T&T Clark, 1988.

Dennis, John A. *Jesus' Death and the Gathering of True Israel: The Johannine Appropriation of Restoration Theology in the Light of John 11:47–52.* WUNT 217. Tübingen: Mohr Siebeck, 2006.

deSilva, David Arthur. *Honor, Patronage, Kinship & Purity: Unlocking New Testament Culture.* Downers Grove, IL: InterVarsity Press, 2000.

Dever, William G. *What Did the Biblical Writers Know, and When Did They Know It?: What Archaeology Can Tell Us about the Reality of Ancient Israel.* Grand Rapids: Eerdmans, 2001.

Dever, William G. *The Lives of Ordinary People in Ancient Israel: Where Archaeology and the Bible Intersect.* Grand Rapids, Eerdmans, 2012.

Dexinger, Ferdinand. "Limits of Tolerance in Judaism: The Samaritan Example." Pages 88–114 in *Jewish and Christian Self-Definition: Aspects of Judaism in the Graeco-Roman Period*. Edited by E. P. Sanders, A. I. Baumgarten, and Alan Mendelson. Vol. 2. Philadelphia: Fortress, 1981.

Dexinger, Ferdinand. "Samaritan Eschatology." Pages 266–92 in *Samaritans*. Tübingen: Mohr Siebeck, 1989.

Diaz, José Ramon. "Palestinian Targum and New Testament." *NovT* 6, no. 1 (1963): 75–80.

Dodd, C. H. "Behind a Johannine Dialogue." Pages 41–57 in *More New Testament Studies*. Grand Rapids: Eerdmans, 1968.

Dodd, C. H. *The Interpretation of the Fourth Gospel*. CAM, 517. Cambridge: Cambridge University Press, 1970.

Dorsey, David A. *The Roads and Highways of Ancient Israel*. The ASOR Library of Biblical and Near Eastern Archaeology. Baltimore: Johns Hopkins University Press, 1991.

Du Bois, W. E. B. *The Souls of Black Folk*. Rockville, MD: Arc Manor, 2008.

Duling, Dennis C. *A Marginal Scribe: Studies in the Gospel of Matthew in a Social-Scientific Perspective*. Matrix—The Bible in Mediterranean Context 7. Eugene, OR: Cascade, 2012.

Dunn, James D. G. *The Acts of the Apostles*. Valley Forge, PA: Trinity Press International, 1996.

Dunn, James D. G. "The Embarrassment of History: Reflections on the Problem of 'Anti-Judaism' in the Fourth Gospel." Pages 40–60 in *Anti-Judaism and the Fourth Gospel*. Edited by R. Bieringer, Didier Pollefeyt, and F. Vandecasteele-Vanneuville. Louisville: Westminster John Knox, 2001.

Dunn, James D. G. *Jesus Remembered*. Christianity in the Making v. 1. Grand Rapids: Eerdmans, 2003.

Dunn, James D. G. *Beginning from Jerusalem*. Christianity in the Making v. 2. Grand Rapids: Eerdmans, 2009.

Dunn, James D. G., and J. W. Rogerson, eds. *Eerdmans Commentary on the Bible*. Grand Rapids: Eerdmans, 2003.

Durkheim, Émile. *The Rules of Sociological Method*. Edited by George Edward Gordon Catlin. Translated by Sarah A. Solovay and John Henry Mueller. 8th ed. Glencoe, IL; New York: Free Press, 1950.

Durkheim, Émile. *The Elementary Forms of Religious Life*. Translated by Karen E. Fields. Glenco, IL; New York: Free Press, 1995.

Dušek, Jan. *Aramaic and Hebrew Inscriptions from Mt. Gerizim and Samaria between Antiochus III and Antiochus IV Epiphanes*. Leiden: Brill, 2012.

Edelman, Diana Vikander, ed. *The Triumph of Elohim: From Yahwisms to Judaisms*. Grand Rapids: Eerdmans, 1996.

Edwards, M. J. *John*. Blackwell Bible Commentaries. Malden, MA: Blackwell, 2004.

BIBLIOGRAPHY

Eller, Jack David, and Reed M. Coughlan. "The Poverty of Primordialism: The Demystification of Ethnic Attachments." *Ethnic and Racial Studies* 16.2 (1993): 183–202.

Elliott, John Hall. *What Is Social-Scientific Criticism?* New Testament Series. Minneapolis: Fortress, 1993.

Elliott, John Hall. "Jesus the Israelite was neither a 'Jew' nor a 'Christian': On Correcting Misleading Nomenclature." *Journal for the Study of the Historical Jesus* 5.2 (2007): 119–154.

Ericksen, Robert P., and Susannah Heschel. *Betrayal: German Churches and the Holocaust*. Minneapolis: Fortress, 1999.

Eriksen, Thomas Hylland. *Ethnicity and Nationalism: Anthropological Perspectives*. 3d ed. Anthropology, Culture, and Society. London; New York: Macmillan, 2010.

Esler, Philip Francis. *Community and Gospel in Luke-Acts: The Social and Political Motivations of Lucan Theology*. Monograph Series, Society for New Testament Studies 57. Cambridge: Cambridge University Press, 1989.

Esler, Philip Francis. *The First Christians in Their Social Worlds: Social-Scientific Approaches to New Testament Interpretation*. London ; New York: Routledge, 1994.

Esler, Philip Francis. "Jesus and the Reduction of Intergroup Conflict: The Parable of the Good Samaritan in the Light of Social Identity Theory." *BibInt* 8.4 (2000): 325–57.

Esler, Philip Francis. *Conflict and Identity in Romans: The Social Setting of Paul's Letter*. Minneapolis: Fortress Press, 2003.

Esler, Philip Francis. "From Ioudaioi to Children of God: The Development of a Non-Ethnic Group Identity in the Gospel of John." *In Other Words: Essays on Social Science Methods and the New Testament in Honor of Jerome H. Neyrey*. Edited by Anselm C Hagedorn, Zeba A Crook, and Eric Clark Stewart. Sheffield: Sheffield Phoenix, 2007.

Esler, Philip Francis. "Judean Ethnic Identity in Josephus' Against Apion." Pages 73–91 in *A Wandering Galilean: Essays in Honour of Seán Freyne*. Edited by Zuleika Rodgers, Margaret Daly-Denton, and Anne Fitzpatrick McKinley. Leiden: Brill, 2009.

Esman, Milton J. *An Introduction to Ethnic Conflict*. Oxford: Polity, 2004.

Fee, Gordon D. "Codex Sinaiticus in the Gospel of John: A Contribution to Methodology in Establishing Textual Relationships." *NTS* 15.1 (1968): 23–44.

Feldman, Louis H. *Studies in Hellenistic Judaism*. Leiden: Brill, 1996.

Fenton, Steve. *Ethnicity*. 2d ed. Key concepts. Cambridge: Polity Press, 2010.

Finegan, Jack. *The Archeology of the New Testament: The Life of Jesus and the Beginning of the Early Church*. Rev. ed. Princeton: Princeton University Press, 1992.

Finkelman, Paul, ed. *Encyclopedia of African American History, 1619–1895: From the Colonial Period to the Age of Frederick Douglass*. New York: Oxford University Press, 2006.

Finkelstein, Israel. *The Forgotten Kingdom: The Archaeology and History of Northern Israel*. ANEM 5. Atlanta: Society of Biblical Literature, 2013.

Fitzmeyer, Joseph A. *The Gospel according to Luke: Introduction, Translation, and Notes.* Anchor Bible v. 28. Garden City, NY: Doubleday, 1981.

Fleure, H. J. "The Problems of Race." Edited by Julian S. Huxley and A. C. Haddon. *Geographical Review* 26.4 (1936): 704–704.

Foakes-Jackson, F. J., Kirsopp Lake, James Hardy Ropes, and Henry Joel Cadbury, eds. *The Acts of the Apostles.* The Beginnings of Christianity. Grand Rapids: Baker Book House, 1979.

Förster, Hans. "Die Begegnung am Brunnen (Joh 4.4–42) im Licht der 'Schrift': Überlegungen zu den Samaritanern im Johannesevangelium." *NTS* 61.2 (2015): 201–218.

Fossum, Jarl. "Samaritan Sects and Movements." Pages 293–389 in *Samaritans.* Tübingen: Mohr Siebeck, 1989.

Freyne, Seán. "Behind the Names: Galileans, Samaritans, Ioudaioi." Pages 39–55 in *Galilee through the Centuries: Confluence of Cultures.* Edited by Eric M. Myers. Winona Lake, IN: Eisenbrauns, 1999.

Freyne, Seán. "Jesus and the Galilean 'Am Ha'arets: Fact, Johannine Irony, or Both?" *John, Jesus, and History, Volume 2: Aspects of Historicity in the Fourth Gospel.* Edited by Paul N. Anderson, Felix Just, and Tom Thatcher. Society of Biblical Literature, 2009.

Fuhse, Jan A. "Embedding the Stranger: Ethnic Categories and Cultural Differences in Social Networks." *Journal of Intercultural Studies* 33.6 (2012): 639–55.

Funk, Robert W., and Roy W. Hoover, eds. *The Five Gospels: The Search for the Authentic Words of Jesus: New Translation and Commentary.* San Francisco: Harper SanFrancisco, 1997.

Gagarin, Michael, and Elaine Fantham, eds. *The Oxford Encyclopedia of Ancient Greece and Rome.* New York: Oxford University Press, 2010.

Gaster, Moses. *The Samaritans: Their History, Doctrines and Literature.* The Schweich Lectures 1923. London: Published for the British Academy by H. Milford, Oxford University Press, 1925.

Gates, R. Ruggles. "*We Europeans: A Survey of Racial Problems* by Julian S. Huxley and A. C. Haddon." *Man: Royal Anthropological Institute of Great Britain and Ireland* 36 (1936): 161–62.

Geertz, Clifford. *The Interpretation of Cultures: Selected Essays by Clifford Geertz.* New York: Basic Books, 1973.

Gerdmar, Anders. *Roots of Theological Anti-Semitism: German Biblical Interpretation and the Jews, from Herder and Semler to Kittel and Bultmann.* Leiden: Brill, 2010.

Gil-White, Francisco J. "How Thick Is Blood? The Plot Thickens ...: If Ethnic Actors Are Primordialists, What Remains of the Circumstantialist / Primordialist Controversy?" *Ethnic and Racial Studies* 22.5 (1999): 789–820.

BIBLIOGRAPHY

Glare, P. G. W., and Christopher Stray, eds. *Oxford Latin Dictionary*. 2d ed. Oxford: Oxford University Press, 2012.

Glazer, Nathan and Daniel Moynihan ed. *Ethnicity: Theory and Experience*. Cambridge: Harvard University Press, 1975.

Godet, Frédéric Louis. *Commentary on John's Gospel*. Edited by Timothy Dwight. Translated by Timothy Dwight. Kregel reprint library. Grand Rapids: Kregel, 1978.

Goffman, Erving. *The Presentation of Self in Everyday Life*. New York: Anchor Books, 1959.

Gottwald, Norman K. *The Tribes of Yahweh: A Sociology of the Religion of Liberated Israel, 1250–1050 BCE*. Maryknoll, NY: Orbis Books, 1979.

Gourgues, Michel. "The Priest, the Levite, and the Samaritan Revisited: A Critical Note on Luke 10:31–35." *JBL* 117.4 (1998): 709–13.

Grässer, Erich. "Die Antijüdische Polemik Im Johannesevangelium." *NTS* 11.1 (1964): 74.

Green, Joel B. *The Gospel of Luke*. NICNT. Grand Rapids: Eerdmans, 1997.

Griffith, Terry. "'The Jews Who Had Believed in Him' (John 8:31) and the Motif of Apostasy in the Gospel of John." Pages 183–92 in *Gospel of John and Christian Theology*. Edited by Richard Bauckham and Carl Mosser. Grand Rapids: Eerdmans, 2008.

Grosby, Steven. "Debate: The Verdict of History: The Inexpungeable Tie of Primordiality—a Response to Eller and Coughlan." *Ethnic and Racial Studies* 17.1 (1994): 164–71.

Gruen, Erich. "Did Ancient Identity Depend on Ethnicity? A Preliminary Probe." *Phoenix* 67.1/2 (2013): 1–22.

Grundmann, Walter. *Jesus der Galiläer und das Judentum*. Leipzig: Georg Wigand, 1941.

Haenchen, Ernst. *The Acts of the Apostles: A Commentary*. Oxford: Basil Blackwell, 1971.

Haenchen, Ernst. *John: A Commentary on the Gospel of John*. Edited by Ulrich Busse. Translated by Robert Walter Funk. 2 vols. Hermeneia. Philadelphia: Fortress, 1984.

Hall, David R. "Meaning of Synchraomai in John 4:9." *ExpTim* 83.2 (1971): 56–57.

Hall, Jonathan M. *Ethnic Identity in Greek Antiquity*. Cambridge; New York: Cambridge University Press, 2000.

Hanson, K. C., and Douglas E. Oakman. *Palestine in the Time of Jesus: Social Structures and Social Conflicts*. 2d ed. Minneapolis: Fortress, 2009.

Head, Peter M. "The Nazi Quest for an Aryan Jesus." *Journal for the Study of the Historical Jesus* 2.1 (2004): 55–89.

Henderson, John. "A1–Zythum: Domimina Nustio Illumea, Or Out with the OLD (1931–82)." Pages 139–176 in *Classical Dictionaries Past, Present and Future*. Edited by Christopher Stray. London: Duckworth, 2010.

Heschel, Susannah. *The Aryan Jesus: Christian Theologians and the Bible in Nazi Germany*. Princeton: Princeton University Press, 2008.

Hjelm, Ingrid. *The Samaritans and Early Judaism: A Literary Analysis*. Sheffield: Sheffield Academic, 2000.

Hjelm, Ingrid. "What Do Samaritans and Jews Have in Common?: Recent Trends in Samaritan Studies." *CBR* 3.1 (2004): 9–59.

Hjelm, Ingrid. "Simon Magus in Patristic and Samaritan Sources: The Growth of Traditions." *The Samaritans and the Bible: Historical and Literary Interactions Between Biblical and Samaritan Traditions*. Edited by Jörg Frey, Ursula Schattner-Rieser, and Konrad Schmid. Berlin; Boston: de Gruyter, 2012.

Hobbs, T. R. *2 Kings*. WBC 13. Waco, TX; Dallas; Nashville: Word, 1985.

Horsley, Richard A. *Archaeology, History, and Society in Galilee: The Social Context of Jesus and the Rabbis*. Valley Forge, PA: Trinity Press International, 1996.

Horsley, Richard A. *Sociology and the Jesus Movement*. 2d ed. New York: Continuum, 1994.

Horsley, Richard A., and Tom Thatcher. *John, Jesus, and the Renewal of Israel*. Grand Rapids: Eerdmans, 2013.

Hoskyns, Edwyn Clement. *The Fourth Gospel*. Edited by Francis Noel Davey. 2d ed. London: Faber and Faber, 1947.

Howard-Brook, Wes. *Becoming Children of God: John's Gospel and Radical Discipleship*. Maryknoll, NY: Orbis Books, 1994.

Hughes, Everett C. *On Work, Race, and the Sociological Imagination*. Edited by Lewis A. Coser. The Heritage of Sociology. Chicago: University of Chicago Press, 1994.

Hunter, Robert. *A Box of Rain*. New York: Penguin Books, 1993.

Hurtado, Larry W. *Lord Jesus Christ: Devotion to Jesus in Earliest Christianity*. Grand Rapids: Eerdmans, 2003.

Hutchinson, John, and Anthony D. Smith, eds. *Ethnicity*. Oxford Readers. Oxford; New York: Oxford University Press, 1996.

Huxley, Julian, Alfred C. Haddon, and A. M. Carr-Saunders. *We Europeans; a Survey of "Racial" Problems,*. London: J. Cape, 1935.

Hylen, Susan. *Imperfect Believers: Ambiguous Characters in the Gospel of John*. Louisville: Westminster John Knox, 2009.

Isser, Stanley Jerome. "The Samaritans and Their Sects." Page 569–595 in *CHJ vol. 3*. Cambridge: Cambridge University Press, 1999.

Jenkins, Richard. "Categorization: Identity, Social Process and Epistemology." *Current Sociology* 48.3 (2000): 7–25.

Jenkins, Richard. *Rethinking Ethnicity*. 2d ed. Los Angeles; London: Sage, 2008.

Jenkins, Richard. *Social Identity*. 3d ed. Key ideas. London; New York: Routledge, 2008.

Jeremias, Joachim. *Jerusalem in the Time of Jesus: An Investigation into Economic and Social Conditions during the New Testament Period*. Philadelphia: Fortress, 1975.

BIBLIOGRAPHY

Jocz, Jakob. "Die Juden Im Johannesevangelium." *Judaism* 9 (1953): 129–142.

Johnson, Luke Timothy. "The New Testament's Anti-Jewish Slander and the Conventions of Ancient Polemic." *JBL* 108.3 (1989): 419–41.

Johnson, Luke Timothy. *The Gospel of Luke*. Sacra Pagina 3. Collegeville, MN: Liturgical Press, 1991.

Johnson, Luke Timothy. *The Acts of the Apostles*. Sacra Pagina 5. Collegeville, MN: Liturgical Press, 1992.

Jones, C. P. "Ἔθνος and Γένος in Herodotus." *CQ* 46.2 (1996): 315–20.

Jones, Siân. *The Archaeology of Ethnicity: Constructing Identities In the Past and Present*. London; New York: Routledge, 1997.

Kalimi, Isaac. *Early Jewish Exegesis and Theological Controversy: Studies in Scriptures in the Shadow of Internal and External Controversies*. Jewish and Christian Heritage Series v. 2. Assen: Van Gorcum, 2002.

Kalimi, Isaac, and James D. Purvis. "The Hiding of the Temple Vessels in Jewish and Samaritan Literature." *CBQ* 56.4 (1994): 679–85.

Kartveit, Magnar. *The Origin of the Samaritans*. VTSup 128. Leiden; Boston: Brill, 2009.

Kasher, Aryeh. "'The Enclave of Cuthaeans'—Factor in Jewish-Samaritan Relations in Antiquity." Pages 205–221 in *Proceedings of the Fifth International Congress of the Société d'Études Samaritaines: Helsinki, August 1–4, 2000: Studies in Memory of Ferdinand Dexinger*. Paris: Geuthner, 2005.

Kazen, Thomas. "The Good Samaritan and a Presumptive Corpse." *SEÅ* 71 (2006): 131–44.

Keener, Craig S. *The Gospel of John: A Commentary*. 2 vols. Peabody, MA: Hendrickson, 2003.

Keener, Craig S. *Acts: An Exegetical Commentary*. Grand Rapids: Baker Academic, 2012.

Kelley, Shawn. *Racializing Jesus: Race, Ideology, and the Formation of Modern Biblical Scholarship*. Biblical limits. London; New York: Routledge, 2002.

Kessler, Rainer. *The Social History of Ancient Israel: An Introduction*. Minneapolis: Fortress Press, 2008.

Kierspel, Lars. *The Jews and the World in the Fourth Gospel: Parallelism, Function, and Context*. Tübingen: Mohr Siebeck, 2006.

Kittel, Gerhard, and Otto Bauernfeind. *Theologisches Wörterbuch Zum Neuen Testament*. Stuttgart: Kohlhammer, 1949.

Kittel, Gerhard, Geoffrey William Bromiley, Gerhard Friedrich, and Ronald E. Pitkin, eds. *Theological Dictionary of the New Testament*. 10 vols. Grand Rapids: Eerdmans, 1964.

Kivisto, Peter, and Paul R. Croll. *Race and Ethnicity: The Basics*. London; New York: Routledge, 2012.

Klink, Edward W. *The Sheep of the Fold: The Audience and Origin of the Gospel of John*. SNTSMS 141. Cambridge: Cambridge University Press, 2007.

Knoppers, Gary N. "Mt. Gerizim and Mt. Zion: A Study in the Early History of the Samaritans and Jews." *SR* 34.3–4 (2005): 309–38.

Knoppers, Gary N. "Ethnicity, Genealogy, Geography, and Change: The Judean Communities of Babylon and Jerusalem in the Story of Ezra." Pages 147–71 in *Community Identity in Judean Historiography: Biblical and Comparative Perspectives.* Winona Lake, IN: Eisenbrauns, 2009.

Knoppers, Gary N. *Jews and Samaritans: The Origins and History of Their Early Relations.* New York, NY: Oxford University Press, 2013.

Koester, Craig R. "Aspects of Historicity in John 1–4: A Response." Pages 93–106 in *John, Jesus, and History.* Edited by Paul N. Anderson, Felix Just, and Tom Thatcher. Society of Biblical Literature symposium series 44. Atlanta: Society of Biblical Literature, 2007.

Koester, Craig R. "'The Savior of the World' (John 4:42)." *JBL* 109.4 (1990): 665–80.

Koester, Craig R. *The Word of Life: A Theology of John's Gospel.* Grand Rapids: Eerdmans, 2008.

Koester, Craig R. "The Gospel of John as a Source for First-Century Judaism." Pages 59–76 in *John and Judaism a Contested Relationship in Context.* Edited by R. Alan Culpepper and Paul N Anderson. Atlanta: SBL Press, 2017.

Köhler, Ludwig, Walter Baumgartner, M. E. J. Richardson, and Johann Jakob Stamm. *The Hebrew and Aramaic Lexicon of the Old Testament.* Leiden; New York: Brill, 1994.

Konstan, David. "Defining Ancient Greek Ethnicity." *Diaspora: A Journal of Transnational Studies* 6.1 (1997): 97–110.

Kopp, Clemens. *The Holy Places of the Gospels.* New York: Herder and Herder, 1963.

Köstenberger, Andreas J. *John.* BECNT. Grand Rapids: Baker Academic, 2004.

Kraabel, A. T. "New Evidence of the Samaritan Diaspora Has Been Found on Delos." *BA* 47.1 (1984): 44–46.

Kuecker, Aaron. *Spirit and the "Other": Social Identity, Ethnicity and Intergroup Reconciliation in Luke-Acts.* LNTS 444. London; New York: T&T Clark, 2011.

Kysar, Robert. *Voyages with John: Charting the Fourth Gospel.* Waco, TX: Baylor University Press, 2005.

Kysar, Robert. *John, the Maverick Gospel.* Louisville: Westminster John Knox, 2007.

Lagrange, Marie-Joseph. *The Gospel of Jesus Christ.* Westminster, MD: Newman Press, 1958.

Leidig, Edeltraud. *Jesu Gespräch Mit Der Samaritanerin: Und Weitere Gespräche Im Johannesevangelium.* 2. Aufl. Theologischen Dissertationen Bd. 15. Basel, Switzerland: F. Reinhardt, 1981.

Lewis, Charlton Thomas, Charles Short, E. A. Andrews, and William Freund. *A Latin Dictionary.* Oxford: Clarendon Press, 1879.

Liddell, Henry George, Robert Scott, Henry Stuart Jones, and Roderick McKenzie. *A Greek—English Lexicon.* 9th ed. Oxford: Oxford University Press, 1996.

Lieu, Judith. *Christian Identity in the Jewish and Greco-Roman World*. Oxford ; New York: Oxford University Press, 2004.

Lieu, Judith. "Anti-Judaism, the Jews, and the Worlds of the Fourth Gospel." Pages 168–82 in *Gospel of John and Christian Theology*. Edited by Richard Bauckham and Carl Mosser. Grand Rapids: Eerdmans, 2008.

Linafelt, Tod, David W. Cotter, Jerome T. Walsh, Chris Franke, and Timothy K. Beal. *Ruth*. Berit Olam. Collegeville, MN: Liturgical Press, 1999.

Lincoln, Andrew T. *Truth on Trial: The Lawsuit Motif in the Fourth Gospel*. Peabody, MA: Hendrickson, 2000.

Lincoln, Andrew T. *The Gospel according to Saint John*. BNTC 4. Peabody, MA: Hendrickson, 2005.

Lindars, Barnabas. *The Gospel of John*. NCB. London: Oliphants, 1972.

Louw, J. P., and Eugene Albert Nida, eds. *Greek—English Lexicon of the New Testament: Based on Semantic Domains*. New York, NY: United Bible Societies, 1989.

Lowe, Malcolm. "Who Were the IOYΔAIOI?" *NovT* 18.2 (1976): 101–30.

Lowe, Malcolm. "Ιουδαῖοι of the Apocrypha: A Fresh Approach to the Gospels of James, Pseudo-Thomas, Peter and Nicodemus." *NovT* 23.1 (1981): 56–90.

Lowe, Malcolm. "Concepts and Words." Jew and Judean: A MARGINALIA Forum on Politics and Historiography in the Translation of Ancient Texts. Edited by Timothy Michael Law and Charles Halton. *The Marginalia Review of Books*, 33–37.

Lust, J., Erik Eynikel, and K. Hauspie. *Greek—English Lexicon of the Septuagint*. Rev. ed. Stuttgart: Deutsche Bibelgesellschaft, 2003.

Lütgert, Wilhelm. "Die Juden Im Johannesevangelium." *Neutestamentliche Studeien Für Georg Henrici*. Edited by Paul Krüger and C. F. Georg Heinrici. Leipzig: Hinrichs, 1914.

Luz, Ulrich, and Helmut Koester. *Matthew: A Commentary*. Hermeneia. Minneapolis: Fortress, 2001.

Maccini, Robert Gordon. "A Reassessment of the Woman at the Well in John 4 in Light of the Samaritan Context." *JSNT* 53 (1994): 35–46.

Maccini, Robert Gordon. *Her Testimony Is True: Women as Witnesses according to John*. JSNTSup 125. Sheffield: Sheffield Academic, 1996.

Macdonald, John. *The Theology of the Samaritans*. NTL. Philadelphia, Westminster Press, 1964.

Magen, Yitzhak. "The Dating of the First Phase of the Samaritan Temple on Mount Gerizim in Light of the Archaeological Evidence." Pages 157–211 in *Judah and the Judeans in the Fourth Century BCE*. Winona Lake, IN: Eisenbrauns, 2007.

Malina, Bruce J. *The New Testament World: Insights from Cultural Anthropology*. 3d ed., and expanded. Louisville: Westminster John Knox, 2001.

Malina, Bruce J., and Jerome H. Neyrey. *Calling Jesus Names: The Social Value of Labels in Matthew*. Sonoma, CA: Polebridge, 1988.

Malina, Bruce J., and John J. Pilch. *Social-Science Commentary on the Book of Acts*. Minneapolis: Fortress, 2008.

Malina, Bruce J., and Richard L. Rohrbaugh. *Social-Science Commentary on the Gospel of John*. Minneapolis: Fortress, 1998.

Marshall, Gordon, and John Scott. *A Dictionary of Sociology*. Oxford: Oxford University Press, 2005.

Martyn, J. Louis. "A Gentile Mission That Replaced an Earlier Jewish Mission?" Pages 124–46 in *Exploring the Gospel of John: In Honor of D. Moody Smith*. Edited by D. Moody Smith, R. Alan Culpepper, and C. Clifton Black. Louisville: Westminster John Knox, 1996.

Martyn, J. Louis. *History and Theology in the Fourth Gospel*. 3d ed. NTL. Louisville: Westminster John Knox, 2003.

Mason, Steve. *Flavius Josephus Translation and Commentary*. 10 vols. Boston: Brill Academic Publishers, 2001.

Mason, Steve. "Jews, Judaeans, Judaizing, Judaism: Problems of Categorization in Ancient History." *JSJ* 38.4–5 (2007): 457–512.

Master, Daniel M., ed. *The Oxford Encyclopedia of the Bible and Archaeology*. 2 vols. Oxford: Oxford University Press, 2013.

Matthews, Victor Harold. *Manners and Customs in the Bible: An Illustrated Guide to Daily Life in Bible Times*. 3d ed. Peabody, MA: Hendrickson, 2006.

Mayhew, Susan. *A Dictionary of Geography*. Fourth edition. Oxford: Oxford University Press, 2009.

McHugh, John, *A Critical and Exegetical Commentary on John 1–4*. ICC. Edinburgh: T&T Clark, 2009.

McNamara, Martin. *Targum and Testament Revisited: Aramaic Paraphrases of the Hebrew Bible: A Light on the New Testament*. 2d ed. Grand Rapids: Eerdmans, 2010.

Meeks, Wayne A. *The Prophet—King: Moses Traditions and the Johannine Christology*. Leiden: Brill, 1967.

Meeks, Wayne A. "Galilee and Judea in the Fourth Gospel." *JBL* 85.2 (1966): 159–69.

Meeks, Wayne A. "'Am I a Jew?' Johannine Christianity and Judaism." Pages 163–86 in *Christianity, Judaism and Other Greco-Roman Cults: Studies for Morton Smith at Sixty*. Edited by Morton Smith and Jacob Neusner. Eugene, Oregon: Wipf & Stock, 2004.

Meier, John P. *A Marginal Jew: Rethinking the Historical Jesus*. Vol. 1. New York: Doubleday, 1991.

Meier, John P. "The Historical Jesus and the Historical Samaritans: What Can Be Said?" *Bib* 81.2 (2000): 202–32.

Metzger, Bruce Manning. *A Textual Commentary on the Greek New Testament*. 2d ed. Stuttgart: Deutsche Bibelgesellschaft, 2002.

Metzger, Bruce Manning, and Michael David Coogan, eds. *The Oxford Companion to the Bible*. Oxford: Oxford University Press, 1993.

Michaels, J. Ramsey. *The Gospel of John*. NICNT. Grand Rapids: Eerdmans, 2010.

Miller, David Marvin. "The Meaning of Ioudaios and Its Relationship to Other Group Labels in Ancient 'Judaism.'" *CBR* 9.1 (2010): 98–126.

Miller, David Marvin. "Ethnicity Comes of Age: An Overview of Twentieth-Century Terms for Ioudaios." *CBR* 10.2 (2012): 293–311.

Miller, David Marvin. "Ethnicity, Religion and the Meaning of Ioudaios in Ancient 'Judaism.'" *CBR* 12.2 (2014): 216–65.

Moloney, Francis J. *Signs and Shadows: Reading John 5–12*. Minneapolis: Fortress, 1996.

Moloney, Francis J. *The Gospel of John*. SP 4. Collegeville, MN: Liturgical Press, 1998.

Moloney, Francis J. "Israel, the People and the Jews in the Fourth Gospel." *Israel Und Seine Heilstraditionen Im Johannessevangelium: Festgabe Für Johannes Beutler SJ Zum 70. Geburtstag*. Paderbron: Schöningh, 2004.

Moloney, Francis J. *Love in the Gospel of John: An Exegetical, Theological, and Literary Study*. Grand Rapids: Baker Academic, 2013.

Mommsen, Wolfgang J. "Max Weber's 'Grand Sociology': The Origins and Composition of Wirtschaft Und Gesellschaft: Soziologie." *HistTh* 39.3 (2000): 364–83.

Montagu, Ashley. *Man's Most Dangerous Myth: The Fallacy of Race*. Walnut Creek, CA: Alta Mira Press, 1997.

Montgomery, James A. *The Samaritans, the Earliest Jewish Sect; Their History, Theology and Literature*. Philadelphia: The J.C. Winston Company, 1907.

Moore, Carey A. *Esther*. The Anchor Bible 7B. Garden City, N.Y: Doubleday, 1971.

Morris, Leon. *The Gospel according to John*. Rev. ed. NICNT. Grand Rapids: Eerdmans, 1995.

Morwood, James. *The Pocket Oxford Latin Dictionary*. Oxford: Oxford University Press, 2000.

Motyer, Stephen. *Your Father the Devil?: A New Approach to John and "the Jews."* Carlisle: Paternoster, 1997.

Motyer, Stephen. "Bridging the Gap: How Might the Fourth Gospel Help Us Cope with the Legacy of Christianity's Exclusive Claim over against Judaism?" Pages 143–67 in *Gospel of John and Christian Theology*. Edited by Richard Bauckham and Carl Mosser. Grand Rapids: Eerdmans, 2008.

Neusner, Jacob, *The Mishnah: A New Translation*. New Haven: Yale University Press, 1988.

Neyrey, Jerome H. *The Gospel of John*. New Cambridge Bible Commentary. New York: Cambridge University Press, 2007.

Neyrey, Jerome H. "Are You Greater than Our Father Jacob?" Pages 87–122 in *The Gospel of John in Cultural and Rhetorical Perspective*. Edited by Jerome H Neyrey. Grand Rapids: Eerdmans, 2009.

Neyrey, Jerome H. "Secrecy, Deception, and Revelation: Information Control in the Fourth Gospel." Pages 252–281 in *The Gospel of John in Cultural and Rhetorical Perspective*. Grand Rapids: Eerdmans, 2009.

Neyrey, Jerome H., and Bruce J. Malina. "Conflict in Luke-Acts: Labeling and Deviance Theory." Pages 97–124 in *The Social World of Luke-Acts: Models for Interpretation.* Edited by Jerome H. Neyrey. Peabody, MA: Hendrickson, 1991.

Nodet, Etienne. *A Search for the Origins of Judaism: From Joshua to the Mishnah.* Translated by Ed Crowley. JSOTSup 248. Sheffield: Sheffield Academic, 1997.

North, Wendy E. S. "'The Jews' in John's Gospel." Pages 148–68 in *A Journey Round John: Tradition, Interpretation and Context in the Fourth Gospel.* London ; New York: Bloomsbury T&T Clark, an imprint of Bloomsbury Publishing, 2015.

O'Day, Gail R. *Revelation in the Fourth Gospel: Narrative Mode and Theological Claim.* Philadelphia: Fortress, 1986.

O'Day, Gail R., and Susan Hylen. *John.* Westminster Bible Companion. Louisville: Westminster John Knox, 2006.

Okure, Teresa. *The Johannine Approach to Mission: A Contextual Study of John 4:1–42.* Tübingen: Mohr Siebeck, 1988.

Olsson, Birger. *Structure and Meaning in the Fourth Gospel; a Text-Linguistic Analysis of John 2:1–11 and 4:1–42.* Lund: Gleerup, 1974.

Oxford English Dictionary Online. Oxford: Oxford University Press. 2016.

Painter, John. *The Quest for the Messiah: The History, Literature, and Theology of the Johannine Community.* 2d ed. Nashville: Abingdon, 1993.

Painter, John. "Bultmann, Archaeology, and the Historical Jesus." Pages 619–38 in *Jesus and Archaeology.* Grand Rapids: Eerdmans, 2006.

Painter, Nell Irvin. *The History of White People.* New York: Norton, 2010.

Park, Robert Ezra. *Race and Culture.* Edited by Everett C. Hughes. Glencoe, IL; New York: Free Press, 1950.

Pietersen, Lloyd K. "Despicable Deviants: Labelling Theory and the Polemic of the Pastorals." *Sociology of Religion* 58.4 (1997): 343–52.

Porter, Stanley E. "Jesus, 'the Jews,' and John's Gospel." Pages 149–73 in *John, His Gospel, and Jesus: In Pursuit of the Johannine Voice.* Grand Rapids: Eerdmans, 2015.

Pryor, John W. *John, Evangelist of the Covenant People: The Narrative & Themes of the Fourth Gospel.* Downers Grove, IL: InterVarsity Press, 1992.

Pummer, Reinhard. "Argarizin: A Criterion for Samaritan Provenance?" *JSJ* 18.1 (1987): 18–25.

Pummer, Reinhard. *Early Christian Authors on Samaritans and Samaritanism: Texts, Translations and Commentary.* Texts and Studies in Ancient Judaism. Tübingen: Mohr Siebeck, 2002.

Pummer, Reinhard. "The Samaritans and Their Pentateuch." Pages 237–69 in *Pentateuch as Torah: New Models for Understanding Its Promulgation and Acceptance.* Winona Lake, IN: Eisenbrauns, 2007.

Pummer, Reinhard. *The Samaritans in Flavius Josephus.* Texts and Studies in Ancient Judaism. Tübingen: Mohr Siebeck, 2009.

BIBLIOGRAPHY

Pummer, Reinhard. "Samaritanism" Pages 1181–1184 in John J. Collins and Daniel C. Harlow, eds. *The Eerdmans Dictionary of Early Judaism*. Grand Rapids: Eerdmans, 2010.

Pummer, Reinhard. *The Samaritans: A Profile*. Grand Rapids: Eerdmans, 2015.

Purvis, James D. "Ben SIRA' and the Foolish People of Shechem." *JNES* 24.1/2 (1965): 88–94.

Purvis, James D. *The Samaritan Pentateuch and the Origin of the Samaritan Sect*. Harvard Semitic monographs v. 2. Cambridge: Harvard University Press, 1968.

Purvis, James D. "The Fourth Gospel and the Samaritans." *Novum Testamentum* 17.3 (1975): 161–98.

Puvogel, Hans. *Die leitenden Grundgedanken bei der Entmannung gefährlicher Sittlichkeitsverbrecher*. Düsseldorf: Göttingen, 1937.

Radkau, Joachim. *Max Weber: A Biography*. Cambridge: Polity, 2009.

Rainbow, Paul A. *Johannine Theology: The Gospel, the Epistles and the Apocalypse*. Downers Grove, IL: InterVarsity Press, 2014.

Rainey, Anson F., and R. Steven Notley. *The Sacred Bridge: Carta's Atlas of the Biblical World*. Second Emended & Enhanced Edition. Jerusalem: Carta Jerusalem, 2014.

Rasmussen, Carl, and Carl Rasmussen. *Zondervan Atlas of the Bible*. Rev. ed. Grand Rapids: Zondervan, 2010.

Reinhartz, Adele. *Befriending the Beloved Disciple: A Jewish Reading of the Gospel of John*. New York: Continuum, 2001.

Reinhartz, Adele. "John 8:31–59 from a Jewish Perspective." Pages 787–97 in *Remembering for the Future: The Holocaust in an Age of Genocide*. Hampshire: Palgrave, 2001.

Reinhartz, Adele. "'Jews' and Jews in the Fourth Gospel." Pages 213–231 in *Anti-Judaism and the Fourth Gospel*, ed. R. Bieringer, Didier Pollefeyt, and F. Vandecasteele-Vanneuville. Louisville, KY: Westminster John Knox Press, 2001.

Reinhartz, Adele. "How 'the Jews' Became Part of the Plot." Pages 99–116 in *Jesus, Judaism, and Christian Anti-Judaism: Reading the New Testament after the Holocaust*. Edited by Paula Fredriksen and Adele Reinhartz. Louisville: Westminster John Knox, 2002.

Reinhartz, Adele. "Judaism in the Gospel of John." *Int* 63.4 (2009): 382–93.

Reinhartz, Adele. "The Vanishing Jews of Antiquity." Jew and Judean: A MARGINALIA Forum on Politics and Historiography in the Translation of Ancient Texts. Edited by Timothy Michael Law and Charles Halton. *The Marginalia Review of Books*: 5–10.

Richardson, Peter. *Herod: King of the Jews and Friend of the Romans*. Fortress Press. Minneapolis: Fortress Press, 1999.

Ridderbos, Herman N. *The Gospel According to John: A Theological Commentary*. Grand Rapids: Eerdmans, 1997.

Samkutty, V. J. *The Samaritan Mission in Acts*. LNTS 328. London; New York: T&T Clark, 2006.

Sanders, E. P. *Judaism: Practice and Belief, 63 BCE–66 CE*. London: SCM Press, 1992.

Schiffman, L. H. "The Samaritans in Tannaitic Halakhah." *JQR* 75.4 (1985): 323–50.

Schnabel, Eckhard J. *Early Christian Mission.* 2 vols. Downers Grove, IL: InterVarsity Press, 2004.

Schnackenburg, Rudolf. *The Gospel According to St. John.* 3 vols. New York: Crossroad, 1982.

Schnelle, Udo. *Theology of the New Testament.* Translated by M. Eugene Boring. Grand Rapids: Baker Academic, 2009.

Schorch, Stefan. "The Samaritan Version of Deuteronomy and the Origin of Deuteronomy," Pages 23–38 in *Samaria, Samarians, Samaritans: Studies on Bible, History and Linguistics.* József Zsengellér and Société d'études samaritaines, eds. Studia Judaica Forschungen zur Wissenschaft des Judentums Bd. 66. Berlin; Boston: de Gruyter, 2011.

Schreiber, Monika. *The Comfort of Kin: Samaritan Community, Kinship, and Marriage.* Leiden: Brill, 2014.

Schur, Nathan. *History of the Samaritans.* New York; Bern: Lang, 1989.

Schürer, Emil. *A History of the Jewish People in the Time of Jesus Christ.* Being a 2nd and rev. ed. of a "Manual of the history of New Testament times." Peabody, MA: Hendrickson, 1994.

Schwartz, Seth. "John Hyrcanus I's Destruction of the Gerizim Temple and Judaean—Samaritan Relations." *Jewish History* 7.1 (1993): 9–25.

Schwartz, Seth. "The 'Judaism' of Samaria and Galilee in Josephus's Version of the Letter of Demetrius I to Jonathan ('Antiquities' 13.48–57)." *HTR* 82.4 (1989): 377–91.

Sheridan, Ruth. *Retelling Scripture: "the Jews" and the Scriptural Citations in John 1:19–12:15.* BibInt 110. Leiden; Boston: Brill, 2012.

Sheridan, Ruth. "Issues in the Translation of Οἱ Ἰουδαῖοι in the Fourth Gospel." *JBL* 132.3 (2013): 671–95.

Sherwin-White, A. N. *Roman Society and Roman Law in the New Testament.* The Sarum lectures 1960–1961. Oxford: Clarendon, 1963.

Shils, Edward. "Primordial, Personal, Sacred and Civil Ties: Some Particular Observations on the Relationships of Sociological Research and Theory." *The British Journal of Sociology* 8.2 (1957): 130–45.

Silva, Moisés, ed. *New International Dictionary of New Testament Theology and Exegesis.* 5 vols. Second edition. Grand Rapids: Zondervan, 2014.

Simmel, Georg. *The Sociology of Georg Simmel.* Edited by Wolff. Translated by Kurt H. Wolff. Glencoe, IL; New York: Free Press, 1964.

Sloyan, Gerard S. "The Samaritans in the New Testament." *Horizons* 10.1 (1983): 7–21.

Sloyan, Gerard S. *John.* Interpretation. Atlanta: John Knox, 1988.

Smedley, Audrey. "'Race' and the Construction of Human Identity." *American Anthropologist* 100.3 (1998): 690–702.

Smedley, Audrey, and Brian D. Smedley. "Race as Biology Is Fiction, Racism as a Social Problem Is Real: Anthropological and Historical Perspectives on the Social Construction of Race." *American Psychologist* 60.1 (2005): 16–26.

BIBLIOGRAPHY 203

Smiga, George M. *Pain and Polemic: Anti-Judaism in the Gospels*. New York: Paulist, 1992.

Smith, Anthony D. *The Ethnic Origins of Nations*. Oxford: Blackwell, 1986.

Smith, D. Moody. *John*. ANTC. Nashville: Abingdon, 1999.

Smith, D. Moody. *The Theology of the Gospel of John*. Cambridge: Cambridge University Press, 1995.

Smith, Daniel L. *The Religion of the Landless: The Social Context of the Babylonian Exile*. Bloomington, IN: Meyer-Stone Books, 1989.

Snodgrass, Klyne. *Stories with Intent: A Comprehensive Guide to the Parables of Jesus*. Grand Rapids: Eerdmans, 2008.

Southwood, Katherine. *Ethnicity and the Mixed Marriage Crisis in Ezra 9–10: An Anthropological Approach*. Oxford: Oxford University Press, 2012.

Spencer, F. Scott. *Journeying through Acts: A Literary-Cultural Reading*. Peabody, MA: Hendrickson, 2004.

Stenhouse, Paul. "The Kitab Al-Tarikh of Abu 'L-Fath." Dept. of Semitic Studies, University of Sydney, 1980.

Stenhouse, Paul. "Who Was the Man Who Fell Among Robbers on the Jericho Road?" Pages 195–203 in *Proceedings of the Fifth International Congress of the Société d'Études Samaritaines: Helsinki, August 1–4, 2000: Studies in Memory of Ferdinand Dexinger*. Paris: Librairie orientaliste Paul Geuthner, 2005.

Stibbe, Mark W. G. *John's Gospel*. London: Routledge, 1994.

Stray, Christopher. *Classical Dictionaries: Past, Present and Future*. London: Duckworth, 2010.

Swartz, David. *Culture & Power: The Sociology of Pierre Bourdieu*. Chicago: University of Chicago Press, 1997.

Talmon, Shemaryahu. "Ezra and Nehemiah." Pages 357–64 in *Literary Guide to the Bible*. Cambridge: Harvard University Press, 1987.

Talmon, Shemaryahu. "The Emergence of Jewish Sectarianism in the Early Second Temple Period." Pages 587–616 in *Ancient Israelite Religion: Essays in Honor of Frank Moore Cross*. Edited by Patrick D. Miller, Paul D. Hanson, and S. Dean McBride. Philadelphia: Fortress, 1987.

Taylor, Bernard A., J. Lust, Erik Eynikel, and K. Hauspie. *Analytical Lexicon to the Septuagint*. Expanded ed. Stuttgart: Deutsche Bibelgesellschaft, 2009.

Thatcher, Tom, ed. *What We Have Heard from the Beginning: The Past, Present, and Future of Johannine Studies*. Waco, TX: Baylor University Press, 2007.

Theobald, Michael. *Studien Zum Corpus Iohanneum*. WUNT 267. Tubingen: Mohr Siebeck, 2010.

Thompson, Marianne Meye. *The Incarnate Word: Perspectives on Jesus in the Fourth Gospel*. Peabody, MA: Hendrickson, 1993.

Thompson, Marianne Meye. *John: A Commentary*. Louisville: Westminster John Knox, 2015.

Thornton, Timothy Charles Gordon. "Anti-Samaritan Exegesis Reflected in Josephus' Retelling of Deuteronomy, Joshua, and Judges." *JTS* 47.1 (1996): 125–30.

Thyen, Hartwig. *Das Johannesevangelium*. Tübingen: Mohr Siebeck, 2015.

Tonkin, Elizabeth, Malcolm Chapman, and Maryon McDonald, eds. *History and Ethnicity*. London; New York: Routledge, 1989.

Tov, Emanuel. "Proto-Samaritan Texts and the Samaritan Pentateuch." Pages 397–407 in *Samaritans*. Tübingen: Mohr Siebeck, 1989.

Tov, Emanuel. *Textual Criticism of the Hebrew Bible*. 3d rev. and expanded ed. Minneapolis: Fortress, 2012.

Tsedaka, Benyamim. "The Keepers: Israelite Samaritan Identity." *Israelite-Samaritans .com*, August 27, 2014. https://www.israelite-samaritans.com/history/keepers-israelite -samaritan-identity/.

Twelftree, Graham. "In the Name of Jesus: A Conversation with Critics." *Journal of Pentecostal Theology* 17.2 (2008): 157–69.

van der Watt, Jan G. "'Is Jesus the King of Israel'?: Reflections on the Jewish Nature of the Gospel of John." *John and Judaism a Contested Relationship in Context*. Edited by R. Alan Culpepper and Paul N Anderson. Atlanta: SBL Press, 2017.

Van Gemeren, Willem, ed. *New International Dictionary of Old Testament Theology & Exegesis*. 5 vols. Grand Rapids: Zondervan, 1997.

Verkuyten, M. *The Social Psychology of Ethnic Identity*. New York: Psychology, 2012.

Von Wahlde, Urban C. "The Terms for Religious Authorities in the Fourth Gospel: A Key to Literary-Strata." *JBL* 98.2 (1979): 231–53.

Von Wahlde, Urban C. "The Johannine 'Jews': A Critical Survey." *NTS* 28.1 (1982): 33.

Von Wahlde, Urban C. "Community in Conflict: The History and Social Context of the Johannine Community." *Int* 49.3 (1995): 379–389.

Von Wahlde, Urban C. "The Relationships between Pharisees and Chief Priests: Some Observations on the Texts in Matthew, John and Josephus." *NTS* 42.4 (1996): 506–522.

Von Wahlde, Urban C. "'The Jews' in the Gospel of John: Fifteen Years of Research (1983–1998)." *ETL* 76.1 (2000): 30–55.

Von Wahlde, Urban C. "Archaeology and John's Gospel." Pages 523–86 in *Jesus and Archaeology*. Edited by James H. Charlesworth. Grand Rapids: Eerdmans, 2006.

Von Wahlde, Urban C. *The Gospel and Letters of John*. 3 vols. Eerdmans critical commentary. Grand Rapids: Eerdmans, 2010.

Webb, Jen, Tony Schirato, and Geoff Danaher. *Understanding Bourdieu*. London: Sage, 2002.

Weber, Max. *Gesammelte Aufsätze Zur Soziologie Und Sozialpolitik*. Tübingen: Mohr Siebeck, 1924.

Weber, Max. *Ancient Judaism*. Translated by Hans H. Gerth and Martindale. Glencoe, IL; New York: Free Press, 1952.

Weber, Max. *Economy and Society: An Outline of Interpretive Sociology*. Edited by Guenther Roth and Claus Wittich. Translated by Ephraim Fischoff. 2 vols. Berkeley: University of California Press, 1978.

Weber, Max. *The Sociology of Religion*. Translated by Ephraim Fischoff. Beacon series in the sociology of politics and religion. Boston: Beacon Press, 1969.

Weber, Robert. "Preface to the First Edition." Page xxix in *Biblia Sacra: Iuxta Vulgatam Versionem*. Stuttgart: Deutsche Bibelgesellschaft, 1994.

Wesley, John, ed. *Explanatory Notes upon the New Testament*. 12th ed. New York: Carlton & Porter, 1857.

Westcott, Brooke Foss, ed. *The Gospel according to St. John: The Authorized Version with Introduction and Notes*. Grand Rapids: Eerdmans, 1971.

Wetter, Anne-Mareike. "How Jewish Is Esther?: Or: How Is Esther Jewish? Tracing Ethnic and Religious Identity in a Diaspora Narrative." *ZAW* 123.4 (2011): 596–603.

Wheaton, Gerry. *The Role of Jewish Feasts in John's Gospel*. Cambridge: Cambridge University Press, 2015.

Whitacre, Rodney A. *Johannine Polemic: The Role of Tradition and Theology*. SBLDS 67. Chico, CA: Scholars Press, 1982.

White, L. Michael. The Social Origins of Christian Architecture. Harvard theological studies 42-. Valley Forge, PA: Trinity Press, 1996.

Williams, Catrin H. "John, Judaism, and 'Searching the Scriptures.'" Pages 77–100 in *John and Judaism a Contested Relationship in Context*. Edited by R. Alan Culpepper and Paul N Anderson. Atlanta: SBL Press, 2017.

Wilson, S. G. *Related Strangers: Jews and Christians, 70–170 CE*. Minneapolis: Fortress, 1995.

Wimmer, Andreas. "Elementary Strategies of Ethnic Boundary Making." *Ethnic and Racial Studies* 31.6 (2008): 1025–55.

Wimmer, Andreas. "The Making and Unmaking of Ethnic Boundaries: A Multilevel Process Theory." *American Journal of Sociology* 113.4 (2008): 970–1022.

Wimmer, Andreas. *Ethnic Boundary Making: Institutions, Power, Networks*. New York: Oxford University Press, 2013.

Witherington, Ben. *John's Wisdom: A Commentary on the Fourth Gospel*. Louisville: Westminster John Knox, 1995.

Witherington, Ben. *The Acts of the Apostles: A Socio-Rhetorical Commentary*. Grand Rapids: Eerdmans, 1998.

Witherington, Ben. *Matthew*. The Smyth & Helwys Bible commentary 19. Macon, GA: Smyth & Helwys, 2006.

Wright, G. Ernest. "The Samaritans at Shechem." *HTR* 55.4 (1962): 357–66

Yelvington, Kevin A. "Ethnicity as Practice? A Comment on Bentley." *Comparative Studies in Society and History* 33.1 (1991): 158–68.

Zangenberg, Jürgen. *Frühes Christentum in Samarien: topographische und traditionsgeschichtliche Studien zu den Samarientexten im Johannesevangelium.* Tübingen: Francke, 1998.

Zangenberg, Jürgen. "Between Jerusalem and the Galilee: Samaria in the Time of Jesus." Pages 393–432 in *Jesus and Archaeology.* Edited by James H. Charlesworth. Grand Rapids: Eerdmans, 2006.

Index of Modern Authors

Albertz, Rainer   57, 57n43, 182
Alexandre, Yardenna   122n131
Anderson, Robert T. and Terry Giles   58n44, 60n55, 183
Anderson, Paul N.   153, 153n43, 182–183
ANET   54n33, 57n43
Ashton, John   13, 13n25, 13n26, 53n30, 125n141, 148, 148n7, 158n65, 162n84, 183
Augstein, Hanah Franziska   25n28, 25n29, 183
Azar, Michael   171, 171n126, 171n127

Banton, Michael   30n45, 183
Barclay, John M. G.   3n7, 44, 44n97, 47n6, 120, 139, 139n208, 140n213, 142, 142n220, 183
Barrett, C. K.   2, 2n2, 6n13, 9n4, 9n7, 15, 15n39, 17, 17n47, 17n49, 89n197, 90n205, 101n30, 102, 103n38, 103n39, 119n113, 136, 136n195, 145, 145n232, 157, 157n59, 157n61, 177, 177n1, 178, 178n3, 178n5, 183–184
Barth, Fredrick   32–33, 32n53, 32n54, 32n55, 39, 39n78, 83n173, 121n125, 155n50, 184
Bauckham, Richard   84n178, 86n184, 184
Bauer, Walter   9n6, 13n27, 17n46, 90n202, 136n197, 172n133, 184
Beasley-Murray, George Raymond   15, 15n35, 15n37, 90n201, 97n12, 102n32, 106n50, 113n84, 119n114, 124n137, 127n148, 128n158, 130n168, 133n178, 133n179, 137, 137n203, 144n229, 157n63, 158n64, 165n99, 184
Becker, Howard S.   4n9, 42, 42n88, 42n89, 139n209, 184
Becking, Bob   52, 52n25, 56n40, 184
BDAG   9, 9n6, 13n27, 21n7, 22n14, 23n16, 65n69, 76n126, 87n192, 90n201, 91n214, 92n217, 105n48, 107n57, 108n61, 111n77, 117n107, 119, 119n114, 119n116, 124n136, 127n151, 139n207
BDF   9n4, 111n77
Bennema, Cornelis   12n23, 132n174, 147n3, 184
Berger, Peter   3n8, 28, 28n38, 29n41, 29n43, 36, 36n67, 38n77, 121n123, 160n77, 174n144, 185

Berlin, Adele   49n14, 50, 50n18, 185
Berlinerblau, Jacques   121n124, 185
Bernard, J. H.   11n17, 14, 14n30, 97, 97n11, 120n119, 122n129, 132, 132n176, 137n204, 185
Beutler, Johannes   101, 102, 102n31, 102n32, 102n35, 103n40, 104, 104n44, 127, 127n152, 129n160, 143n227, 156n57, 159n67, 159n70, 185
BHQ   50, 50n17, 181
Bietenhard, Hans   21n7
Black, Matthew   17n46, 185
Blenkinsopp, Joseph   49, 49n12, 49n13, 51n22, 52n23, 52n24, 53n29, 55n7, 72n106, 148n13, 185
Bock, Jerry   43n91, 186
Bock, Daryl   85, 85n181, 185
Boers, Hendrikus   107n55, 119n118, 186
Böhm, Martina   111n76, 119nn116, 136n200, 186
Bóid, Rory M.   86n186, 86n187
Borgen, Peder   100, 100n23, 100n24, 186
Botha, J. Eugene   106, 107n54, 120n121, 121n125, 121n126, 123n133, 186
Bourdieu, Pierre and Loïc J. D. Wacquant   36n68, 154n48, 154n49, 155n52, 156n56, 161n78, 161n79, 186
Bourdieu, Pierre   37n69, 141n217, 154, 186
Bowman, John   16n43, 113n87, 116n102, 133n180, 186
Boyarin, Daniel   13, 13n26, 53, 53n27, 53n30, 54n31, 97n10, 179, 179n7, 186–187
Brant, Jo-Ann A.   11n15, 187
Brawley, Robert L.   172n131, 187
Brinkman, John A.   54n34
Brown, Raymond E.   9n7, 14, 14n31, 96n3, 97n12, 99, 99n15, 101n29, 103n42, 106–107, 106n50, 106n52, 107n57, 112n80, 116n102, 117n108, 119n113, 120n119, 123n134, 128, 128n155, 128n156, 128n157, 130n165, 130n166, 134n184, 147n5, 158n64, 160n74, 161–62, 161n82, 162n84, 166n101, 187
Browning, W. R. F.   107n56, 187
Bruce, F. F.   88n195, 187
Brueggemann, Walter   39, 39n79, 187

208   INDEX OF MODERN AUTHORS

Bruneau, Philippe   58–59, 58n45, 58n46, 187
Bruner, Frederick Dale   4, 5n10, 112n81, 128n156, 187
Buell, Denise   178n6, 187–188
Bultmann, Rudolf   3n6, 12–14, 12n20, 12n21, 12n23, 13n24, 13n25, 13n26, 14n32, 16, 16n42, 17n47, 90n206, 96–97, 96n2, 97n7, 97n8, 97n9, 97n10, 117n104, 120n120, 125n141, 126, 126n145, 127n149, 131n170, 136n197, 137, 137n201, 148, 148n10, 150, 150n25, 151–152, 151n26, 151n27, 151n28, 151n29, 154n47, 157n58, 158, 158n65, 160n72, 160n74, 163, 163n90, 166n103, 166n104, 167n107, 168–170, 168n110, 169n112, 170n118, 170n120, 172, 173n141, 174, 176, 176n148, 188

Calhoun, Craig   20n2, 188
Calvin, John   15n40
Carson, D. A.   9n7, 15n41, 17n49, 109n68, 119n113, 188
Charlesworth, James H.   63–64, 63n65, 64n65, 64n66, 64n67, 188
Charon, Joel M.   41n87, 188
Chrysostom, John   10–11, 11n13, 11n17, 111n78, 112n79, 117n106, 117n109, 117n110, 118n112, 120n121, 122n129, 132n175, 181
Coggins, R. J.   56n41, 71n97, 72n107, 79n146, 188
Conzelmann, Hans   88n193, 90, 90n209, 91n211, 188
Coser, Lewis   38, 38n74, 38n75, 38n76, 38n77, 39n80, 43n92, 47, 67, 73n108, 74n120, 99, 99n19, 104n43, 110, 120, 137, 144, 174, 174n143, 188
Crawford, Sidnie White   50n16, 60, 60n53, 61n56, 188
Cronin, Sonya Shetty   147nn5, 189
Crossley, James G.   85n179, 189
Crown, Alan D.   46n2, 82n167, 86n187, 189

Danker, Frederick   9, 13n27, 22, 189
Darwin, Charles   25
Daube, David   9–10, 9n7, 9n8, 10n10, 119, 119n113, 189
Davies, W. D. and Dale Allison   82, 82n165, 82n166, 189

Dennis, John A.   102n37, 189
deSilva, David   100n21, 110n73, 111n75, 115n96, 115n98, 129, 129n159, 164, 164n94, 189
Dexinger, Ferdinand   89n199, 190
Díaz, José Ramón   109n64, 112n78, 190
Dodd, C. H,   116n99, 125n141, 166n102, 190
Dorsey, David   106n52, 190
DuBois, W. E. B.   37n72, 190
Dunn, James   16, 16n45, 89n198, 90n203, 92n218, 132n174, 136, 136n196, 171n124, 190
Durkheim, Emile   28–29, 28n39, 28n40, 30n44, 31–32, 35, 190
Dušek, Jan   62n60, 87n192, 190

Edelman, Diana V.   51n21, 190
Eller, Jack and Reed Coughlan   31n48, 191
Elliott, John H.   20, 20n3, 47n8, 69n88, 99n16, 99n17, 191
Epstein, Isidore   91n213, 181
Esler, Philip F.   3n7, 27, 27n36, 34n61, 47n5, 77n136, 84n177, 98n14, 99n16, 191
Esman, Milton   43, 43n93, 43n94, 43n95, 143n226, 143n228, 159n68, 159n69, 191

Feldman, Louis H.   68, 68n86, 69, 69n87, 81n162, 191
Finegan, Jack   124n139, 191
Finkelman, Paul and Matthew Wilhelm Kapell   25n30, 191
Finkelstein, Israel   63n63, 191
Fitzmeyer, Joseph A.   84n174
Fleure, H. J.   26n33, 192
Förster, Hans   110, 110n71, 139n206, 192
Fossum, Jarl   90, 90n209, 91, 91n210, 91n211, 91n212, 192
Freyne, Sean   122n130, 166n104, 167n104, 192
Fuhse, Jan A.   38n73, 72n103, 192

Gaster, Moses   65n71, 192
Geertz, Clifford   31–32, 31n48, 31n49, 31n50, 31n51, 32n52, 41n86, 41n87, 121n124, 192
Gerdmar, Anders   168n111, 169, 169n113, 169n114, 169n115, 170n117, 192
Godet, Frédéric Louis   11, 12n18, 15n41, 122n129, 193
Goffman, Erving   35n64, 193
Gourgues, Michel   84n175, 87n188, 193

INDEX OF MODERN AUTHORS

Grosby, Steven   31n48, 193
Grundmann, Walter   12n21, 97n9, 169, 169n114, 169n115, 193
Gutbrod, Walter   12n22, 27n37, 153n41, 169, 169n116, 172, 172n134, 176, 176n149

Haacker, Klaus   14n33, 81, 82, 82n164, 82n168, 113n86, 136n194
Haenchen, Ernst   10n9, 88n195, 89n200, 90, 91n211, 119n114, 193
Hall, David R.   10n10
Hall, Jonathan M.   22n12, 34n60, 100n25, 173n140, 178n4, 193
HALOT   49n10, 51n20, 65n70
Hanson, K. C. and Douglas Oakman   43n95, 110n73, 193
Henderson, John   23n18, 193
Heschel, Susannah   12n21, 191, 193
Hjelm, Ingrid   69, 69n89, 71n97, 75–78, 75n124, 77n130, 78n139, 78n140, 79n145, 86n183, 86n187, 91n216, 194
Hobbs, T. Raymond   57, 57n42, 194
Horsley, Richard A.   170n122, 171, 171n23
Hoskyns, Edwyn Clement   16n44, 17n49, 112, 113n83, 197, 194
Howard-Brook, Wes   131n173, 194
Hughes, Everett C.   32n53, 33–35, 33n57, 33n58, 35n62, 35n63, 35n64, 41n85, 46n3, 78n141, 78n142, 140n210, 194
Hunter, Robert   146n1, 194
Hurtado, Larry   155, 155n54, 156n55, 194
Hutchinson, John and Anthony Smith   33–34, 35n59, 46–47, 46n4, 47n5, 64, 96, 104, 194
Huxley, Julian and A. C. Hadon   26–27, 26n33, 26n34, 194
Hylen, Susan   125n142, 130n163, 194

Isser, Stanley   91n215, 91n216, 194

Jackson, F. J., Foakes Kirsopp Lake, and Henry Joel Cadbury   88n196, 192
Jenkins, Richard   19n1, 29, 30n44, 33n56, 41, 41n83, 41n84, 41n87, 42n90, 42n91, 47n7, 140n214, 194
Jeremias, Joachim   9n5, 68, 68n82, 68n83, 68n84, 79–80, 79n149, 80n153, 108n61, 194

Johnson, Luke Timothy   90n201, 120n120, 135, 135n193, 195
Jones, C. P.   21n8, 23n17, 195
Jones, Siân   173n140, 178n4, 195

Kalimi, Isaac   9n8, 15n37, 172n131, 195
Kartveit, Magnar   58n46, 67n80, 71n96, 74n118, 74n119, 76n125, 79n145, 79n147, 195
Kasher, Aryeh   81n157, 195
Kazen, Thomas   85n180, 195
Keener, Craig   5n11, 17, 18n50, 89n198, 92n220, 106n50, 109n67, 114n88, 121n128, 122n132, 134n187, 157n60, 170n119, 195
Kelley, Shawn   27n37, 195
Kivisto, Peter and Paul R. Croll   24n24, 27n35, 195
Knoppers, Gary N.   55n36, 63n64, 66, 66n76, 78n138, 79n147, 79n148, 82n169, 107n59, 114n59, 119n117, 196
Koester, Craig   2n3, 8n1, 112n81, 153, 153n42, 159n71, 160, 160n73, 170n121, 196
Kopp, Clemens   107n58, 196
Köstenberger, Andreas J.   16n44, 16n45, 17n49, 97n12, 109n68, 119n115, 137n202, 157n58, 158n64, 163n92, 164, 164n95, 196
Kuecker, Aaron   89n197, 196
Kuhn, K.G.   27n37

L&N   10n10, 96n6, 109n68, 124n136, 126n146, 127n151, 139n207, 147n6
Lagrange, Marie-Joseph   11n15, 196
LEH   87n191
Lewis, Charlton T. and Charles Short   23n18, 196
Lieu, Judith   146n2, 164n93, 171, 172n130, 197
Lincoln, Andrew T.   3n6, 11n16, 16, 16n44, 100n22, 106n50, 127n152, 133n183, 134n183, 137n202, 158n64, 197
Lindars, Barnabas   10, 10n10, 14n29, 15n38, 16n42, 119n114, 197
Lowe, Malcolm   148–150, 148n8, 148n12, 148n13, 149n14, 149n15, 149n16, 149n17, 149n18, 150n23, 150n24, 158, 158n66, 161–162, 162n83, 173n138, 197
LSJ   9n6, 21, 21n5, 21n6, 21n7, 21nn8, 22n12, 22n13, 22n15, 71n100, 92n221

INDEX OF MODERN AUTHORS

Lütgert, Wilhelm   12n19, 122n130, 197
Luz, Ulrich   82n168, 197

Madvig, D. H.   124n137
Magen, Yitzhak   73n111, 197
Malina, Bruce and Jerome Neyrey   42n89,
  43n96, 88n193, 100n21, 101n26, 135n192,
  142n221, 144n231, 155n54, 197–198
Malina, Bruce and John J. Pilch   88n193, 198
Malina, Bruce and Richard L.
  Rohrbaugh   100n21, 101n26, 135n192,
  155n54, 198
Mason, Steve   20n3, 21, 22n11, 80n151,
  148–150, 148n9, 149n19, 150n20, 150n21,
  150n22, 162, 162n83, 173n137, 198
Mayhew, Susan   140n216
McHugh, John F.   96n5, 107n59, 111n76,
  160n74, 198
McNamara, Martin   109n64, 198
Meeks, Wayne   177, 177n2, 198
Meier, John P.   83n170, 105n46, 116, 116n103,
  130n165, 130n166, 130n168, 133n181, 198
Metzger, Bruce   2n4, 8n3, 9, 9n5, 88n194,
  128n155, 135n188, 198
Michaels, J. Ramsey   10, 10n11, 11n17, 12n17,
  14, 15n34, 17n49, 90n201, 90n204,
  101n27, 105n47, 110n74, 114n89, 115n93,
  117n110, 122n129, 125n142, 128n155,
  129n161, 131n169, 132n175, 136n199,
  157n60, 158n64, 168n109, 199
Miller, David   20n4, 27n37, 68n81, 199
Moloney, Francis J.   9n7, 15, 15n39, 102n34,
  103n40, 103n41, 104, 104n44, 104n45,
  109n69, 111n77, 112n82, 117n108, 118n111,
  119n113, 126n148, 131n172, 132n175,
  135n191, 157n62, 158n64, 160n72, 160n75,
  165n98, 166n101, 199
Montagu, Ashley   24, 25n25, 25n26, 26n31,
  199
Moore, Carey M.   50n17
Mopsuestia, Theodore of   13, 14n29, 117n109,
  135, 135n189, 182
Morris, Leon   9n7, 109n68, 119n113, 199
Motyer, Stephen   132n174, 172, 173n135, 199

Neusner, Jacob   114n90, 181, 182, 199, 83n169
Neyrey, Jerome   8n2, 42n89, 43n96, 100n20,
  107n58, 108–109, 109n64, 109n66,

  125–126, 125n143, 126n144, 129n159,
  142n220, 144n231, 157n61, 197, 199–200
Nodet, Etienne   75n122, 200
North, Wendy E. S.   153n44, 200

O'Day, Gail R.   108n62, 108n63, 110n72,
  111n77, 125n142, 130n163, 200
Olsson, Birger   112n79, 200

Painter, John   161n80, 200
Park, Robert Ezra   32n53, 35–36, 35n64,
  36n65, 36n66, 40, 41n82, 121n122,
  154n49, 200
Porter, Stanley   161n80, 163n88, 200
Pummer, Reinhard   9n8, 10, 10n12, 17n48,
  54n35, 59n49, 60n50, 60n54, 66, 66n75,
  66n77, 79n147, 80n150, 80n154, 80n156,
  84n176, 87, 87n190, 116, 116n101, 136–137,
  136n197, 136n198, 137n204, 200–201
Puvogel, Hans   26, 26n31, 201

Radkau, Joachim   26n32, 201
Rainbow, Paul   101n28, 201
Rainey, Anson F. R. Steven Notley   106n51,
  106n52, 106n53, 201
Rasmussen, Carl   106n49, 201
Reinhartz, Adele   123, 123n134, 123n135, 135,
  135n190, 142n222, 143n223, 143n224, 148,
  148n10, 151–152, 151n30, 151n31, 151n32,
  152n40, 155n53, 171, 171n125, 171n128,
  171n129, 173n135, 176, 176n148, 201
Richardson, Peter   106n51
Ridderbos, Herman N.   99n18, 102n36,
  119n115, 121n122, 121n127, 129n162,
  133n183, 158n64, 161, 161n81, 162, 201
Ruggles, R. Gates   26–27, 26n34, 192

Samkutty, V. J.   88n194, 92n218, 201
Sanders, E. P.   125n140, 201
Schiffman, Lawrence   85n182, 201
Schmidt, Karl Ludwig   21, 21n7, 21n9,
  21n10
Schnabel, Eckhard   92, 93n222, 202
Schnackenburg, Rudolf   5n11, 9, 9n4, 10n9,
  16n42, 17n47, 97n8, 115, 115n97, 115n98,
  117n108, 119n114, 126, 126n146, 127n149,
  127n150, 128n153, 130n168, 137n201,
  158n64, 160n74, 160n76, 168n108, 202

Schorch, Stefan   62–64, 62n60, 62n61,
    63n62, 63n63, 63n64, 202
Schreiber, Monika   67n79, 202
Schur, Nathan   46n1, 53n28, 85n182, 202
Schürer, Emil   86n185, 202
Scott, John   30n46, 140n216, 198
Sheridan, Ruth   163n92, 164n93, 202
Silva, Moisés   115, 116n99, 126n147, 130n167,
    136n198, 154n47, 163n91, 165n96,
    174n142, 202
Simmel, Georg   37, 37n70, 37n71, 37n72, 47,
    202
Sloyan, Gerard S.   15n41, 202
Smedley, Audrey   24n24, 25n27, 27n35, 202
Smedley, Audrey and Brian D.
    Smedley   27n35, 202
Smith, D. Moody   17n49, 155n51, 203
Smith, Anthony D.   30n47, 34n59, 46–47,
    46n4, 47n5, 64, 96, 104, 194, 203
Smith, Daniel L.   49n15, 203
Snodgrass, Klyne   85n183, 203
Southwood, Katherine   55n37, 55n38, 55n39,
    203
Spencer, F. Scott   92n219, 203
Stenhouse, Paul   57n43, 65–67, 65n72,
    65n73, 66n74, 67n78, 87n189, 182, 203
Swartz, David   36n68, 37n69, 140n211, 203

Talmon, Shemaryahu   53n27, 53n29, 53n30,
    54n31, 54n32, 203
Taylor, Bernard A.   22n14, 203
TDNT   9n5, 12n22, 21n7, 21n9, 21n10, 27n37,
    68, 68n82, 68n83, 68n84, 79n149,
    108n61, 126, 126n145, 153n41, 169n116,
    172n134, 176n149
Thatcher, Tom   170n122, 171, 171n23
Thompson, Marianne Meye   147n4, 203

Thornton, Timothy   74n118, 204
Tonkin, Elizabeth, Maryon McDonald, and
    Malcolm Chapman   23n19, 23n22, 204
Tov, Emanuel   60–62, 60n52, 60n53, 61n56,
    61n57, 62n59, 64, 204
Tsedaka, Benyamim   62n58, 65n71, 182, 204
Twelftree, Graham H.   14n33, 204

Van der Watt, Jan   172n130, 172n132, 204
Von Wahlde, Urban C.   13n28, 17n47, 106n53,
    148, 148n11, 151–153, 151n33, 151n34,
    152n35, 152n36, 152n37, 152n38, 152n39,
    153n45, 158, 158n64, 158n66, 161–163,
    162n85, 162n86, 163n87, 163n89,
    165–167, 166n100, 167n106, 172–173,
    173n136, 173n139, 204

Webb, Jen, Tony Schirato, and
    Geoff Danaher   40n81, 204
Weber, Max   6, 6n14, 26, 26n32, 28–30,
    29n42, 30n45, 33, 42n91, 44n98, 53n27,
    204–205
Weber, Robert   23n18
Wesley, John   117n110, 205
Westcott, Brooke Foss   135n192, 205
Wetter, Anne-Mareike   50, 50n19, 205
Whitacre, Rodney A.   134n185, 170n119, 205
White, L. Michael   58n46, 59n47, 59n48,
    59n49, 205
Witherington, Benjamin   82n168, 89n197,
    89n198, 205

Yamauchi, Edwin   47n9, 49, 49n11
Yohanan, Aharoni   65n70, 182

Zangenberg, Jürgen   110n70, 206
Zobel, H.-J.   52–53, 53n26

Index of Ancient Sources

Old Testament

Gen 10:31	34
Gen 12:6	62
Gen 12:7	115n95
Gen 17:1	91
Gen 18:1–18	143, 144n230
Gen 29:10	109, 109n65, 112n78
Gen 33:18–20	62, 107
Gen 33:20	115n95
Gen 48:22	111
Exod 12:38	55
Exod 12:48–49	55
Exod 19:5	97
Exod 20:14	61
Exod 20:2–3	61
Exod 20:4–6	61
Lev 19:18	87
Lev 21:1	84
Deut 11	62, 83
Deut 11:29	61, 115n95
Deut 11:30	62
Deut 12	79, 82, 121
Deut 13:10	143
Deut 13:1–5	143
Deut 18:15	89, 113n86
Deut 18:18	113, 113n86
Deut 27	62, 83
Deut 27:12	115n95
Deut 27:2–7	61
Deut 27:4	63, 64
Deut 27:4–8	62, 63
Deut 27:4b–6	63
Deut 28:7	63
Deut 5:18	61
Deut 5:5–6	61
Deut 5:7–10	61
Josh 18:1	48
Josh 24:32	76, 107, 111
Josh 6:22–23	55
Judg 9	74
Judg 12:6	12, 33

Ruth 4:10–11	55
2 Sam 6:12–16	48
1 Kgs 11:33	75
1 Kgs 11:5	75
1 Kgs 16:24	64–65, 88
2 Kgs 16:6	6, 49, 148
2 Kgs 17	54, 56, 57, 69–70, 93, 95
2 Kgs 17:23	57
2 Kgs 17:24	113
2 Kgs 17:24–34	54
2 Kgs 17:24–41	57, 65
2 Kgs 17:26	56, 113
2 Kgs 17:27	56
2 Kgs 17:28	56
2 Kgs 17:29	56, 57
2 Kgs 17:29	56, 57
2 Kgs 17:3	56
2 Kgs 17:30–31	113
2 Kgs 17:33	56, 70
2 Kgs 17:34	57
2 Kgs 17:5–6	56
2 Kgs 17:5–6	56
2 Kgs 17:6	57
2 Kgs 17:7–23	56
2 Kgs 23:13	75
2 Kgs 25:25	6, 49
2 Kgs 27:24	56
1 Chr 4:18	49
2 Chr 13:11	66n76
2 Chr 30:1	54
2 Chr 31:1	54
2 Chr 34:33	54
2 Chr 34:6	54
Ezra 1:11	51
Ezra 1:3	52
Ezra 10:11	55
Ezra 10:12	55
Ezra 2:1	51
Ezra 2:2 51	55
Ezra 2:21–35	51
Ezra 2:3–20	51

INDEX OF ANCIENT SOURCES

Ezra 2:36–58	51	Neh 7:7	51, 55
Ezra 2:59	52	Neh 7:73	52
Ezra 2:59–63	51	Neh 7:8–25	51
Ezra 3:2	52	Neh 9:26	123
Ezra 4	54, 73	Neh 9:30	123
Ezra 4:1	52, 54, 72		
Ezra 4:12	52	Esth 2:5	49
Ezra 4:1–5	54, 55	Esth 3:10	50
Ezra 4:2	54, 55, 72	Esth 3:13	50
Ezra 4:23	52	Esth 3:6	50
Ezra 4:2–3	95	Esth 4:7	50
Ezra 4:3	52, 54	Esth 7:10	50
Ezra 4:4	54	Esth 7:3–6	50
Ezra 4:8–6:18	52	Esth 8:1	50
Ezra 4:9–10	55	Esth 8:17	50
Ezra 5:1	52, 67	Esth 8:5	50
Ezra 5:14	52	Esth 9:10	50
Ezra 5:5	52	Esth 9:24	50
Ezra 6:14	52		
Ezra 6:17	52	Isa 11:12–13	54
Ezra 6:21	51, 52	Isa 29:13	141n219
Ezra 6:22	52	Isa 30:10	40, 115
Ezra 6:7	52		
Ezra 6:8	52	Jer 14:14–16	39
Ezra 7:10	52	Jer 23:5–6	54
Ezra 7:15	52	Jer 24:3–6	101
Ezra 8:35	52	Jer 26:11	39
Ezra 9	55	Jer 26:8	39, 123, 131n171
Ezra 9:1	55	Jer 26:8–11	115
Ezra 9:15	52	Jer 26:8–11	115
Ezra 9:4	52	Jer 28:3	40
Ezra 9–10	54, 55	Jer 28:3–4	115
		Jer 28:4	40
Neh 10:34[33]	52	Jer 3:15	101
Neh 11:3	52	Jer 31:17–20	54
Neh 12:47	52	Jer 38:2	40
Neh 13:23	52	Jer 38:2–6	115
Neh 13:3	52, 53	Jer 38:3	40
Neh 2:16	52	Jer 38:4–6	40
Neh 3:33–34		Jer 40:11–12	49
[4:1–2]	52	Jer 41:5	54, 91
Neh 4:6 [12]	52	Jer 42:19–21	141n219
Neh 5:17	52	Jer 43:9	49
Neh 5:8	52	Jer 43:9	49
Neh 7:26–38	51	Jer 44:1	49
Neh 7:39–60	51	Jer 3:28	49
Neh 7:6	51, 52	Jer 52:30	49
Neh 7:61	52	Jer 6:13–14	40
Neh 7:61–65	51	Jer 8:9–11	40

Old Testament (cont.)

Ezek 16:15	130n167
Ezek 16:33–34	130n167
Ezek 34:23–24	101
Ezek 37:15–28	54
Dan 9:10	123
Dan 9:6	123
Hos 1:2	130n167
Hos 2:4	130
Hos 4:1	143n225
Hos 4:12	143n225
Hos 4:15	130n167
Hos 4:46	130n167
Hos 4:6	143n225
Hos 5:4	130n167
Amos 7:10–13	123
Amos 7:12	40
Amos 7:13	40
Amos 7:9	40
Amos 7:9–13	115
Zech 10:6–12	54
Zech 8:13	54
Zech 8:23	49
Zech 9:13	54

Ancient Near Eastern Texts

Esarhadon, Syrian campaign (*ANET*)	54n33

Deuterocanonical Books

Jdt 9:2	87n191
Sir 45:13	87n191
Sir 50:25–26	68n85
1 Macc 1:54	76
1 Macc 1:57–64	76
1 Macc 10:12	87n191
1 Macc 3:36	87n191
1 Macc 3:45	87n191
2 Macc 5:22–23	78
2 Macc 5:23	78
2 Macc 5–6	78
2 Macc 6:2	78
2 Macc 6:2	78
1 Esd 8:66–67	87n191
1 Esd 8:80	87n191
1 Esd 8:89–90	87n191
1 Esd 9:12	87n191
1 Esd 9:17–18	87n191
1 Esd 9:36	87n191
1 Esd 9:7	87n191
1 Esd 9:9	87n191
4 Macc 15:4	129n159

Dead Sea Scrolls

4QpaleoExodm 4Q22	60n55

Ancient Jewish Writers

Josephus, Ant.	
5.240–1	74
Josephus, Ant. 5.243	74
Josephus, Ant. 5.247	74
Josephus, Ant. 5.248	74
Josephus, Ant.	
5.250–1	74
Josephus, Ant.	
9.277–291	69–70
Josephus, Ant.	
9.278–9	88n90
Josephus, Ant. 9.288	70n91, 70n92, 70n93
Josephus, Ant. 9.290	70n91, 70n94, 70n95, 71n101
Josephus, Ant. 9.291	71n97, 71n98, 71n99, 71n102, 73, 76n128, 76n129, 77n132
Josephus, Ant. 10.184	68, 81n163
Josephus, Ant. 11	72–73
Josephus, Ant. 11.1–119	72n103
Josephus, Ant. 11.19	72n104
Josephus, Ant.	
11.19–30	54
Josephus, Ant. 11.84	72, 72n105
Josephus, Ant.	
11.84–8	54
Josephus, Ant. 11.85	72

INDEX OF ANCIENT SOURCES

Josephus, Ant. 11.87	73n109, 73n110	Josephus, Ag.	
Josephus, Ant. 11.88	73	Ap. 2.103–104	124n138
Josephus, Ant. 11.302	81n158	Philo, Embassy 212	124n139
Josephus, Ant. 11.310	73n113	Philo, Spec.	
Josephus, Ant. 11.340	15n36, 16, 59n47,	Laws 1.156	125n140
	74n114, 74n116,	Philo, Spec.	
	76	Laws 1.332	130n167
Josephus, Ant. 11.341	73n112, 74n115, 76,	Philo, Virt. 195	128n158
	76n127, 76n128,		
	76n129, 77n132,		
	107, 110	**New Testament**	
Josephus, Ant. 11.342	81n160	Matt 3:9	5n12
Josephus, Ant.		Matt 5:47	22
11.343–344	75n123	Matt 10:5	48, 82, 93
Josephus, Ant. 11.344	16, 75n121, 81n159,	Matt 10:5–6	81, 83, 93
	81n160	Matt 15:22	75n124
Josephus, Ant.		Matt 26:73	33
11.346–347	74n117	Mark 6:3	164
Josephus, Ant. 11.347	81n160	Mark 7:26	75n124
Josephus, Ant. 12.257	71n97, 76, 76n129,	Luke 3:8	5n12
	77n133	Luke 9:51	83
Josephus, Ant. 12.258	81n159	Luke 9:51–19:48	83
Josephus, Ant.		Luke 9:51–56	48
12.258–259	77n134	Luke 9:52	83
Josephus, Ant. 12.261	77n135, 77n136,	Luke 9:53	83
	77n137	Luke 9:54	83
Josephus, Ant. 12.262	81n159	Luke 9:54–56	83
Josephus, Ant. 13.171	68	Luke 10:25–37	48, 84
Josephus, Ant. 13.255	79n143, 79n144	Luke 10:29	84, 86
Josephus, Ant.		Luke 10:30	84
13.74–79	114n90	Luke 10:31–32	84
Josephus, Ant. 15.7.7	65	Luke 10:33	83
Josephus, Ant. 17.20	68, 81n163	Luke 10:36	86
Josephus, Ant. 18.30	79, 82, 83n171	Luke 10:37	87
Josephus, Ant. 18.85	68, 81n163, 114n91	Luke 17:11	87
Josephus, Ant. 20.97	92n221	Luke 17:11–19	48, 87
Josephus, Ant. 20.118	80n152, 80n155, 82,	Luke 17:16	83, 87
	83n172, 83n171, 105,	Luke 17:18	48, 84, 87, 92
	122	John 1:1	150
Josephus, Ant.		John 1:6	159
20.118–136	80	John 1:9	97
Josephus, J.W. 1.63	79n143, 79n144,	John 1:10	97, 154
	81n161	John 1:11	11n14, 18, 96–97,
Josephus, J.W. 1.403	65		99, 103, 123–124,
Josephus, J.W. 2.232	82, 83n171, 122n131		139, 144, 154, 156,
Josephus, J.W.			168, 175
2.232–44	80	John 1:11–12	96, 96n3
Josephus, J.W. 2.261	92n221	John 1:12	5, 7, 96, 99,
Josephus, Life 260	106n49		100–102, 104, 115,

New Testament (cont.)

	118, 123, 126–127, 138, 143–144, 146
John 1:12–13	6–7, 96, 101, 103, 122–123, 138, 141, 144, 156, 163, 176
John 1:13	5, 96, 99, 100, 104, 115, 146
John 1:14	8, 126, 164
John 1:18	147, 156, 164
John 1:19	150, 156, 158, 158n66, 159, 166
John 1:19–24	152
John 1:19–28	147, 158, 160, 165
John 1:20–21	157
John 1:21	164
John 1:22	157, 159
John 1:23	157, 159
John 1:24	105, 140, 140n215, 158n64, 166
John 1:24–25	157
John 1:25	157n61, 159
John 1:26–27	157
John 1:26–27	157
John 1:31	157, 159
John 1:32–33	157
John 1:33	157
John 1:34	158, 159
John 1:35–51	104, 147, 159
John 1:38	117n105, 159
John 1:40	159
John 1:40–51	117
John 1:41	104, 117, 155, 159–160
John 1:43	159
John 1:45	17, 104, 122, 148, 155, 159–160, 170
John 1:46	117, 155–156, 160, 175
John 1:47	160
John 1:48	113, 160
John 1:49	104, 113, 133n85, 133n86, 122, 160
John 1:50	104, 160
John 2:12	98
John 2:13	173
John 2:22	170
John 2:23	98, 105, 154n46, 178
John 3:1	98, 166
John 3:2	176
John 3:16	103
John 3:22	105, 105n48, 173
John 3:22–23	106
John 3:23	106
John 3:25	154n46
John 4:1–6	105
John 4:1–42	108, 122
John 4:1	105
John 4:4	64, 105–106
John 4:5	64, 107, 109–110
John 4:6	107, 107n68
John 4:7	64, 108, 112, 123, 139
John 4:7–26	105, 108, 121–122
John 4:8	9, 83n171, 119
John 4:9	1–6, 8–13, 16–17, 65, 97–98, 105, 108, 110, 115–116, 118–122, 124, 132n177, 135, 137, 139–142, 146, 150, 151n30, 154–155, 163, 168, 173–174, 176, 178
John 4:10	108, 111–112
John 4:10–15	112
John 4:11	109
John 4:11–12	109, 111
John 4:12	100, 107–112, 107n58, 114–115, 133, 139, 141, 143, 147
John 4:12–14	111n78
John 4:13	111, 111n77
John 4:14	111
John 4:15	112, 139
John 4:16–18	112–113
John 4:16–26	112
John 4:17–18	113, 160
John 4:18	112–113
John 4:19	113, 115
John 4:20	59, 62, 114–115, 122–123, 133, 141, 147
John 4:20–22	12
John 4:20–24	147
John 4:20–24	147
John 4:21	5, 115, 121, 132
John 4:22	6, 97, 98, 98n13, 122, 146–148, 151,

INDEX OF ANCIENT SOURCES

217

	168–169, 173, 176–177
John 4:23	115–117, 138
John 4:23–24	176
John 4:23–24	176
John 4:24	115
John 4:25	116
John 4:26	116
John 4:27	116–117
John 4:28	116
John 4:29	113, 117, 122
John 4:30	176
John 4:32	106
John 4:34	106
John 4:35–38	116
John 4:39	83, 118
John 4:39–42	101, 105, 122
John 4:40	118, 176
John 4:41	118
John 4:42	5–6, 118, 139, 144, 147, 176
John 4:45	98, 105, 154n46
John 5:1	98, 154n46, 173
John 5:9	98, 154n46
John 5:10	98, 154n46, 155
John 5:15	167, 168
John 5:16	98, 154n46, 155
John 5:17	123
John 5:18	98, 127, 154n46, 155, 160
John 5:39	151
John 5:42	177
John 5:45–46	170
John 5:46	147
John 6:2	152, 162
John 6:4	98, 154n46, 173
John 6:5	152, 162
John 6:14	155
John 6:22	152, 162
John 6:22–59	161
John 6:24	152, 162
John 6:29	156
John 6:41	98, 152, 161–164, 162n84, 162n85, 162n86
John 6:41–42	133n182, 163
John 6:41–42	163
John 6:41–43	162

John 6:41–43	162
John 6:42	154–156, 160–162, 164–165, 173–175, 178
John 6:43	161
John 6:52	98, 152, 161–162, 162n85, 162n86
John 6:59	98, 162n82
John 6:60	153
John 6:66	153
John 6:70	153
John 6:71	153
John 7:1	127, 165, 165n97
John 7:2	98, 124, 154n46
John 7:5	163
John 7:10	98, 105, 124, 154n46
John 7:11	12, 153, 165, 169, 172
John 7:12	143, 155, 165, 166, 168, 175–176
John 7:13	152, 166, 166n101, 178
John 7:15	166
John 7:19	170
John 7:22	98, 154n46, 170
John 7:22–23	155
John 7:23	98, 154n46
John 7:24	155, 164, 167
John 7:26	98, 166, 168n108
John 7:30	166
John 7:31	156, 166, 178
John 7:32	140, 140n215, 158, 158n64, 165, 166
John 7:32–36	152, 165
John 7:32–36	152, 165
John 7:40	155, 160 166
John 7:40–42	159
John 7:41	122, 155–156, 166–167, 175
John 7:41–42	160, 168
John 7:42	155
John 7:43	101, 123, 144, 166, 178
John 7:45	98, 140, 158
John 7:45–52	166, 166n103
John 7:47	143, 155, 165, 168, 176
John 7:48	98, 166–167
John 7:48–49	165

218 INDEX OF ANCIENT SOURCES

New Testament (cont.)

John 7:49	166
John 7:50	166
John 7:51	166
John 7:52	122, 155–166, 168, 175
John 8:15	155, 164, 167
John 8:17	170, 170n119
John 8:20	124
John 8:21–58	126
John 8:30	126
John 8:30–31	99
John 8:31	12, 98, 125–128, 131, 133–135, 133n178, 139, 142, 142n222, 153, 169, 172, 174
John 8:31–40	129
John 8:31–47	142
John 8:31–59	99, 124–126, 125n141, 135–139, 142–144, 143n223, 174
John 8:32	126, 139
John 8:33	5–6, 98, 100, 126, 129, 139, 142–144, 147, 154, 174, 177
John 8:34	126
John 8:35–38	126
John 8:37	127–130, 127n151, 130n164, 134, 138n205, 142–143
John 8:38	128
John 8:39	5–6, 16, 126, 100, 128–129, 134, 137, 142–144, 144n230
John 8:39–40	170n119, 176
John 8:39–40	176
John 8:41	129–130, 142–143
John 8:41–44	128
John 8:41–59	129
John 8:42	6, 99, 101, 177
John 8:42–47	132
John 8:44	137–138, 177, 179
John 8:47	123, 126–127, 143–144, 147, 177
John 8:48	1–6, 8, 11, 14–15, 15n40, 17, 17n46, 65–66, 90, 110, 124, 132, 132n177, 133,

	135–138, 136, 136n198, 136n199, 142, 146, 155, 174–178
John 8:48–59	132, 133, 138, 142, 174
John 8:48–59	138, 142
John 8:49	14, 132, 133
John 8:51	139
John 8:52	133, 139, 142
John 8:52–53	133
John 8:53	100, 110, 133, 139, 143
John 8:54	143, 177
John 8:55	143, 177
John 8:56	142–143, 147, 170
John 8:57	135, 142
John 8:59	125, 127, 172
John 9:13–41	152
John 9:14	98, 154n46
John 9:16	98, 123, 129, 144, 154n46, 155, 178
John 9:17	113
John 9:22	140n215, 152, 178
John 9:28	147, 177
John 10:3–4	101
John 10:14	160
John 10:15	103
John 10:15–16	103
John 10:16	101, 103, 103n41, 105, 118, 120, 144, 165, 176
John 10:19	12, 123, 144, 153, 169, 172, 178
John 10:26–27	101
John 10:27	160
John 10:31	172
John 10:33	155, 160
John 10:34	161, 170, 170n119
John 10:42	178
John 11:8	98n13
John 11:19	12, 153, 169, 172
John 11:31	12, 153, 169, 172
John 11:33	12, 153, 169, 172
John 11:36	12, 153, 169, 172
John 11:45	99, 156, 178
John 11:45–52	158, 160, 167
John 11:45–53	101, 140n215
John 11:46	167–168

INDEX OF ANCIENT SOURCES

John 11:46–52	152	John 18:31	154n46
John 11:47	101	John 18:35	11n14, 18, 97, 98,
John 11:47–53	101		98n13, 137, 146, 150,
John 11:48	98, 102, 114		154, 163, 165n97,
John 11:49–51	140		173–174, 176
John 11:50	102, 168	John 18:37	160
John 11:51	99	John 18:39	98
John 11:51–52	102, 103	John 19:6	140
John 11:52	5, 96, 99, 103, 116,	John 19:7	154n46, 155, 160
	118, 123, 141, 144,	John 19:14	98
	163, 165, 175–176	John 19:19	173
John 11:53	120	John 19:31	98, 154n46
John 11:55	98	John 19:36	170
John 12:1	98	John 19:38	178
John 12:4	153	John 20:9	170
John 12:9	12, 153, 169, 172	John 20:19	98, 178
John 12:11	12, 153, 169, 172, 178	John 20:31	156, 164, 173
John 12:12	98, 154n46		
John 12:19	103	Acts 1:8	88
John 12:20	154n46	Acts 5:36	89
John 12:20–21	103	Acts 8:1	88
John 12:23	103	Acts 8:4–25	88
John 12:32	103, 176	Acts 8:5	88–89, 88n194,
John 12:38	170		91
John 12:42	156, 178	Acts 8:5–25	48, 93
John 13:1	98, 154n46	Acts 8:5–7	89
John 13:2	153	Acts 8:6	89–90, 90n201
John 13:3	98n13	Acts 8:7	89
John 13:18	170	Acts 8:8	88–89
John 13:26	153	Acts 8:9	48, 89–91
John 13:33	169	Acts 8:9–11	89
John 14:6	126	Acts 13:6–11	92
John 15:25	170n119	Acts 19:13–14	92
John 16:2	178		
John 17:12	170	Gal 2:14	22
John 17:16	165		
John 18:2–5	153	1 John 2:19	179
John 18:3	140, 166	1 John 2:29	179
John 18:3–14	152	1 John 3:1	179
John 18:4–5	177	1 John 3:10	179
John 18:12	140, 166	1 John 5:2	179
John 18:12–14	152	1 John 5:10	179
John 18:12–14	152		
John 18:14	99, 102, 102n33, 160,		
	168	**Rabbinic Works**	
John 18:18	140	Mishnah	
John 18:20	98n13	m. Nazir 7.1	85
John 18:22	140	m. Nidd. 4.2	86
John 18:28	98	m. Qidd 4:3 F–G	82n169, 91n213

Rabbinic Works (cont.)

Mishnah (cont.)

m. Seb. 8.10	85, 85n183
m. Seb 8.11	86n183

Tosefta

t. Ter. 4:12	91n213

Babylonian Talmud

b. Beṣa 32b	128n159
b. Qidd. 75a	57
b. Qidd. 75b	86
b. San 107b	135
b. San 43a	135
b. Sanh. 57a	85
b. Sotah 22a	15n37, 16n42, 91

Targums

Tg. Ps.-J. Gen 28:10	109, 109n65, 112n78

Midrash and Related Literature

Gen Rab. 81.3	114n90
Exod. Rab. 19.81c	127n148

Early Christian Writings

Acts of Pilate 2.3	130n165
Augustine, Homilies on Gospel of John 43.2	15n40, 66n77
Chrysostom, Hom. Jo. 31.107	11n13, 11n17, 120n121, 122n129
Chrysostom, Hom. Jo. 32	111n78, 112n79
Chrysostom, Hom. Jo. 34	117n106, 117n109, 117n110
Chrysostom, Hom. Jo. 55	132n175
Chrysostom, Hom. Jo. 55.1	132n175
Cyril of Alexandria	108, 108n60, 134, 134n184, 134n186

Epiphanius, Panarion 16.1.16	86n185
Eusebius, Hist. eccl. iv. 22	2n5, 15n38
Justin Martyr, 1 Apol. 26	2n5, 15n38, 88, 90, 90n207
Justin Martyr, 1 Apol. 53	82n169
Justin Martyr, 1 Apol. 56	2n5, 15n38
Justin Martyr, 2 Apol 15	2n5, 15n38
Justin Martyr, Dial. 20	2n5, 15n38
Justin Martyr, Dial. 69	90
Justin Martyr, Dial. 120	90
Origen, Cels. 1.28	130n165
Origen, Cels. 1.57	2n5, 15n38
Origen, Cels. 6.11	90
Origen, Cels. 7.9	90
Origen, Cels. 8.8	90
Origen, Comm. Jo. 13.80	114n90
Origen, Comm. Jo. 13.169	117n106
Tertullian, Adversus Marcionem 4.35	110n74
Theodore of Mopsuestia, Commentary on John, 43	14n29, 117n109, 135n189

Greco-Roman Literature

Cicero, Pro Flacco, 69	149n16
Dio Cassius, Roman History 37.16.5–17.7	149n15

INDEX OF ANCIENT SOURCES

Diodorus Siculus
   18.13   22

Isocrates,
   Panegyricus 50   100, 100n25

Polybius 30.13.6   22
Strabo,
   Geography 2.3.1   22

Samaritan Literature
   The Kitāb al-Tarīkh of
      Abu 'l-Fatḥ
     (The Samaritan
     Chronicle of,)   65

AF, 46   77n132
AF, 48   110
AF, 57   77n132
AF, 169–171   91n215, 117n215

Index of Subjects

Abimelech 74
Abraham 5, 115n95, 129, 133, 134, 135, 136, 143, 147, 170
Abraham, descendants of 5, 5n12, 6, 10, 16, 98, 100, 126–131, 133–135, 137–139, 142–144, 147, 154, 176–177
Aenon near Salim 106
αἵρεσις 68, 81, 92
Alexander the Great 22
Alexandria 114n90, 162
ἀλλογενής 84, 87
Am Ha'arets/People of the Land 16, 53–55, 54n32, 95, 166n104
Ammon 49, 75, 148n13
Ammonites 55
Amorites 55
Amos 40
Andrew, disciple 117, 117n105, 159
Antioch 162
Antiochus Epiphanes 77–78
Apollonius 77
Argarizein/Ἀργαριζεῖν 59, 64. *See also* Mount Gerizim
Assyria 54, 56–57, 63, 66, 68–69, 94–95
Augustus 65
Avva 56

Babylon 40, 49, 56, 67, 148n13
Babylonians 40
Benjamin, tribe of 54, 72
Bethel 40, 56, 72n106
"bread of life discourse" 161
broaden, social boundaries 1, 5, 93–95, 99–100, 100n23, 101, 103–105, 115, 118, 120, 122, 138–139, 144, 160, 174–177. *See also* social boundaries

Caiaphas 99, 102, 102n33
Canaanites 55, 68, 75, 81
Capernaum synagogue 156, 161
chief priests/high priests 98, 101–102, 140, 152, 163, 165–166
"children of God" 1, 5–7, 95–96, 99–105, 111, 115–116, 118, 122–123, 126–127, 130–131,

130n164, 138–139, 141–147, 163, 165, 168, 174–179
children of the devil 175
Coserian "heretics" 47–48, 69, 72, 74, 83, 93, 95
Court of the Israelites 124
Court of Women 98, 124–125, 129, 138n205, 145
"the crowd" in John's Gospel 152, 155–156, 155n53, 161–163, 165–168, 178
Cuthah 56
Cutheans 4, 69–72, 72n103, 74, 76, 79–81, 86, 94, 114n90, 136

Dead Sea Scrolls 60
Delos Inscriptions 16, 47, 58–59, 64, 77, 83, 93, 110, 132n177
Delos Inscription, "the Menippos Honorific" 58–59
Delos Inscription, "the Sarapion Honorific" 58–59
Deuteronomist 56–57, 62–63, 93, 95
Dositheus 2n5, 15, 15n38, 91

Edom 49, 148n13
Edomites 49, 148n13
Egypt 49, 55, 148n13
Egyptians 55
Eli 67, 89
Elijah 157, 161, 164
emic 20, 23, 30, 31n48, 44, 47, 69, 144, 149, 150, 150n20. *See also* etic
Ephraim, tribe of 66, 74, 76
Esarhaddon 54
Esther 47, 49–51
ethnic group 1, 3, 6–7, 19–22, 24, 26–27, 29–35, 33n56, 39, 41, 43–44, 46–47, 51–53, 52n25, 67–69, 81, 95–99, 101, 103–104, 108, 113, 118, 120–123, 136, 138, 140, 142, 142n220, 144–150, 154–156, 158, 160–162, 162n83, 165n97, 167–168, 168, 173–175, 175n145, 178
ethnicity 3–4, 11n14, 19–23, 27, 29–31, 33n56, 44, 50, 69, 110, 117, 120, 143, 175n145

INDEX OF SUBJECTS

ἔθνος   19–23, 68, 70, 78, 81, 89, 92, 98–99, 102, 138, 149

etic   20, 27, 30, 44, 47, 69, 137, 140, 175n146. *See also* emic

false prophet   135, 143, 155, 165
Festival of Booths   124, 165–166
fictive kinship   6, 96, 101–101, 100n21, 103–104, 115n98, 118, 141, 146, 165
First Temple (National) Yahwism   51–52, 55

Galileans   6, 12, 33, 79–80, 80n151n, 82–83, 95n1, 98, 105, 122, 161–162, 171n123
Galilee   87, 98, 105–106, 122, 152, 155, 161–163, 165, 175
Genealogy "segmented genealogy"   164
γένος   21n8, 77n136, 78–79
gentiles/goyim   4, 10, 21–23, 53, 68, 81–84, 86, 88, 91n213, 93, 124, 146, 171
Gitta, village of   80, 88, 90
Golah Judeans   51–56, 72–73, 72n103, 78, 94–95
"good shepherd discourse"   101, 103
Gozan, the river of   56
"the Greeks" in John's Gospel   103, 148
group identification   19, 22, 32, 35–37, 39, 41, 44, 46–48, 50–52, 55, 58–59, 64, 66, 76–77, 93, 108, 123, 129, 140–142, 175n146, 175n147. *See also* social categorization

habitus, Bourdieu   36–37, 41, 140–141
Halah, on the Habor   56
Hamath   56
Herod the Great   65, 108n61
Hezekiah   54
high priests. *See* chief priests
Hittites   55
H-S#1–6 (Hutchinson and Smith Diagnostic Criteria of Ethnicity)   97–98, 101, 108, 122, 144, 154, 159, 173, 178
H-S#1 (A common proper name to identify the group)   50, 64, 70, 98, 105
H-S#2 (A myth of common ancestry)   49, 51, 64, 76, 98, 100–103, 103, 110–11, 115, 118, 122, 127–128, 139, 143, 173, 175
H-S#3 (A shared history or shared memories of a common past, events, and their

commemoration)   64, 71, 98, 100, 104–105, 163, 173
H-S#4 (A common culture, embracing such things as customs, language and religion)   49–50, 64, 69–70, 91, 98, 100, 104, 111, 115, 118, 122, 137, 173, 175n145
H-S#5 (A link with a homeland, either through actual occupation or by symbolic attachment to the ancestral land, as with diaspora peoples)   49, 51, 64, 69, 98, 104–105, 111, 115, 173, 175, 175n145
H-S#6 (A sense of communal solidarity)   51, 71, 98, 111n75, 113, 119, 137, 173
Hyrcanus   64, 79, 81n161, 114n92

institutional labeling   19–20, 40, 42–43, 45, 138, 146, 175n147
interactive labeling   19, 40–41, 45, 120–121, 146
Isaiah   131n171, 141n219
Israelite   16, 39, 51–52, 54n34, 55–59, 64, 66–72, 67b81, 74, 77, 81, 84, 86, 93, 95, 110, 114, 116n100, 131, 132n177, 141, 159, 163

Jacob   11, 77, 100, 107–112, 115, 115n95, 122, 129, 139, 176
Jacob's Well   105, 107, 109, 112, 116, 118, 121
James, disciple   83–84
Jebusites   55
Jeremiah   39–40, 49
Jerusalem   5, 12, 39, 48, 51, 53–54, 59, 62–63, 72, 74, 76, 78–80, 83–84, 87–88, 98, 103, 105, 110–11, 114–115, 122, 124, 127, 137–138, 141, 155–156, 165–166, 175
Jerusalem Temple   5, 51, 78–79, 87, 124, 138
Jerusalemites   166
Jesus, as a false prophet   134, 143, 155, 165
Jesus, a Jew   104, 173
Jesus, as factionalist Jew   99, 123, 142–144, 155, 174, 177–178
Jesus, from Galilee   156, 166, 168
Jesus, leading people astray   135, 139, 143, 165, 168, 175
Jesus, of Nazareth   2, 155–156, 159–160, 173, 177
Jesus, Rabbi   104, 113, 122, 159
Jesus, son of Joseph   154–156, 159, 161, 164, 173, 178

"the Jews" in John's Gospel 1–6, 10, 12, 16, 18, 95, 97–101, 105, 110, 114, 120, 123–129, 132–139, 142–153, 155–156, 158–159, 161–179
John the Baptist 105, 106, 147, 155–159, 161, 165
John, disciple 83–84
Jordan Rift/Valley Road 106
Jordan River Valley 106
Josiah 54
Judah, region of 40, 48–49, 51–53, 55–56, 148
Judah, tribe of 49, 54, 67–68, 72, 77, 93, 110, 141
Judea, region of 4, 47, 64, 68, 71, 88, 105, 141, 148, 151, 153, 158, 161–162, 165–166, 167, 173
Judeans, an ethnic group 47–56

"the Keepers," Samaritans as 15n40, 65–67, 93

Law of Moses 84–87, 133, 154n46
Lazarus 168
Levite 84–87, 140, 156–158

Manasseh, tribe of 74, 76
Masoretic Text 60
Medaba 79
Medes 56, 68, 77
Messiah 5, 88–89, 92–93, 104, 108, 113, 116–117, 122, 156–157, 159–160, 166, 173
Mishnah 85
misrecognition, Bourdieu 40–41, 93–94, 109, 111–112, 115, 121–122, 126–127, 129, 131, 135, 139–143, 154, 160, 168, 175–176, 178
Moab 49, 75, 148n13
Moabites 55, 68
Mordecai 49–50
Moses 10, 64, 84–85, 87, 104, 113, 133, 147, 159, 163, 170, 177
Mount Ebal 63, 64
Mount Gerizim 48, 58–64, 59n47, 72–74, 73n111, 76, 78–79, 83, 88–89, 93, 95, 111, 114–115, 114n90, 114n91, 114n92, 115n95, 147. *See also* Argarizein/'Αργαριζεὶν

Nablus 88, 90n208
Nathanael, disciple 104, 113, 117, 122, 156, 159–160
Nazareth 124, 164
Nazirite 85
Neapolis 88, 90n208, 107n56
Nicanor 77
Nicodemus 165n97, 166–167
Northern Kingdom of Israel 4, 54, 56–57, 62, 64, 69, 94–95

Omri 64

Passover, Festival of 79, 98
People of the Land. *See under* Am Ha'arets
Perizzites 55
Peshitta 63
Pharisees 98, 101–103, 105, 140, 140n215, 152, 158n64, 159, 165–167, 174, 178
Philip, disciple 117, 159–160
Philip, Evangelist 48, 88–90, 93
Philo of Alexandria 91
Phoenician 75, 81
Pilate 11n14, 17, 98, 98n13
"the Prophet," in John's Gospel 89, 113, 116, 155, 160, 164, 166
Pseudo-Jonathan Targum 108–109

Qumran 60, 64

Rabbi Akiba 85
Rabbi Eliezer 85
Rabbi Simeon b. Gamaliel 86
race, social category 21n8, 23–27
Rahab 55
Romans, the 98, 102
Routes "National Highway," "Ridge Route," or "Watershed Route" 106
Ruth 55

Sabbath 98–99, 154n46, 155
Sadducees 86
Samaria 48, 54, 56–57, 64–65, 70, 72, 80, 83, 87–90, 105–108, 106n52, 113, 116, 122, 141
Samaritan Chronicles 65–67
Samaritan Pentateuch 58, 60–65, 60n51, 60n55, 78

INDEX OF SUBJECTS   225

Samaritan Pentateuch: "the Samaritan
    ideology"   60
Samaritan Pentateuch: "the site which the
    LORD will choose/has chosen"   61, 63
Samaritan Targum   91, 109
Samaritan woman   1, 3–6, 10–14, 17, 40, 59,
    93, 95–96, 98, 98n13, 105, 107–118,
    120–125, 129, 133, 138, 138, 140–146,
    140n212, 154, 160, 174, 177–178
Samaritans, an ethnic group   68, 81, 91
Samaritans, as Hebrews   76–77
Samaritans, as Yahwists   73, 76–78, 92, 111,
    115
Samaritans, as Demonic   2, 6, 14–15, 17,
    90–92, 92n221, 135–136
Samaritans, as Descendants of Joseph   66,
    71–72, 74, 76–78, 107, 109–111
Samaritans, as lion converts   57, 114n90
Samoga   79
Sanaballetes   73
Sargon II   54, 57n43
Sebaste   65, 88, 108n61
Seleucids   76–77
Sepharvaim   56
Septuagint   22, 50, 59n47, 60, 87n192
Shalmaneser   54, 56
Shechem   15n36, 62, 72, 74–76, 79, 88, 107,
    114n90
Shechemites   4, 70, 74–75, 81, 88
Shemer   64–65
Shiloh   48, 67, 72
Sidonians   4, 70, 75–77, 81
Simmelian "strangers"   47–48, 71–72, 74, 80,
    83, 93–94, 137

Simon Magus   2n5, 15, 15n38, 48, 88–92,
    91n215, 91n216, 92n221, 136
Simon Peter, disciple   33, 88–89, 159, 159
social boundaries   4–5, 41, 55, 120–122, 138,
    140, 145, 174, 176
social categorization   19, 35–37, 39, 41,
    47–48, 55, 67, 98, 105, 110, 114, 121–122,
    138, 140–141, 174–176, 175n146, 175n147,
    179. See also group identification
social deviance   3, 16, 18, 39, 42, 44, 120, 139,
    140, 142, 174, 175n146
συγχράομαι   2, 9–10, 119
Sychar   5, 83n171, 101, 107, 117, 122, 144,
    144n230, 147, 156, 165
Sycharian Samaritans   101, 117, 122, 141, 144,
    147, 156, 165
Syrians   49, 68, 148n13

Taheb   89, 92, 113, 116, 116n102
Targum Onkelos   63
Targumim Neofiti   108
temple police   140, 158, 165–166
Temple treasury   124
Ten Commandments/Decalogue   61, 64, 114
Theudas   89, 92n221
trans-ethnic   1, 5–6, 94–96, 118, 131, 139, 144,
    163, 168, 178

Yavneh   85
Yehud   51–52, 54–56

Zerubbabel   54, 72, 95
Zeus Hellenios   77

Printed in the United States
By Bookmasters